Placing Psyche

Spring Journal Books

Analytical Psychology & Contemporary Culture Series
Series Editor
Thomas Singer, M.D.

Other Titles in the Series

Ancient Greece, Modeern Psyche: Archetypes in the Making
Rutter and Singer, eds.

Psyche and the City: A Soul's Guide to the Modern Metropolis
Thomas Singer, ed.

Violence in History, Culture and the Psyche: Essays
Luigi Zoja

Placing Psyche
Exploring Cultural Complexes in Australia

Craig San Roque, Amanda Dowd,
and David Tacey
Editors

Spring Journal Books
New Orleans, Louisiana

© 2011 by Spring Journal, Inc.
All rights reserved.

Spring Journal™, Spring: A Journal of Archetype and Culture™, Spring Books™, Spring Journal Books,™ Spring Journal and Books™, and Spring Journal Publications™ are all trademarks of Spring Journal Incorporated.
All Rights Reserved.

Published by:
Spring Journal, Inc.
627 Ursulines Street #7
New Orleans, Louisiana 70116
Website: www.springjournalandbooks.com

Cover Image:
Ephemeral Creek. © 2011 Jenny McFarland.
This image was graciously provided in honor of Paul Quinlivan.

Cover design and typography by
Northern Graphic Design & Publishing
info@ncarto.com

Text printed on acidfree paper

Library of Congress Cataloging-in-Publication Data Pending

Contents

Acknowledgements vii

Maps x

Preface xii

Introduction 1

Chapter 1: The Nullarbor: Contact Zone as Imaginal Space
Peter Bishop 21

Chapter 2: The Lemon Tree: A Conversation on Civilisation
Craig San Roque 45

Chapter 3: The Rapture of "Girlshine": Land, Sacrifice, and Disavowal in Australian Cinema
Terrie Waddell 75

Chapter 4: The Feeling of Salt, Water, and Land
Patricia Please 95

Chapter 5: Finding the Fish: Memory, Displacement Anxiety, Legitimacy, and Identity
Amanda Dowd 123

Chapter 6: Lost for Words: Embryonic Australia and a Psychic Narrative
David B. Russell 159

Chapter 7: Language is My Second Skin: Speaking and Dreaming between Germany and Central Australia
Ute Eickelkamp 173

Chapter 8: Taking It With Me: A South African's Cultural Complex in Aotearoa New Zealand
Chris Milton 197

Chapter 9: A Question of Fear
Alexis Wright 231

Chapter 10: Sorry, It's Complex: Reflecting on the Apology to
Indigenous Australians
Melinda Turner 259

Chapter 11: The Australian Resistance to Individuation:
Patrick White's Knotted Mandala
David Tacey 283

Chapter 12: Sydney—"a city of truant disposition": *East West 101* (the 2008-2011 Knapman Wyld Australian TV Series)
Craig San Roque with *Kristine Wyld* 307

Index 331

Acknowledgements

The regional editors would like to take this opportunity to thank Series Editor Thomas Singer and Publisher Nancy Cater of Spring Journal Books for their invitation to contribute to the Analytical Psychology and Contemporary Culture series, and for their support of our efforts in creating *Placing Psyche*. We would also like to thank our contributors who have each taken this project so much to heart.

Special thanks also to cartographer Richard Tuckwell, Alice Springs, for his generosity and painstaking work on the following maps: Australia, Oceania, Murray-Darling Basin, and the Nullarbor; to Jenny McFarland and Rod Moss for their generosity in allowing us to reproduce their fine work; and to Northern Graphic Design and Publishing for its work with the remaining maps and images.

We wish to acknowledge that the map on page *x* depicting Aboriginal Australia prior to 1788 can be found at http://www.janesoceania.com/australia_home/index.htm. The two areas named as Pitjandjara and Djangu are examples only and spellings appear here as on the source map. The map represents an adaptation of the Aboriginal Australia map produced by the Australian Institute of Aboriginal and Torres Strait Islander Studies (AIATSIS). Readers are directed to the AIATSIS website http://www.aiatsis.gov.au/asp/map.html for further information.

A Note about Cover Photographer Jenny McFarland

Jenny McFarland provided the photograph, "Ephemeral Creek", for the front cover of this book. In addition several other of her photographs are included in Amanda Dowd's chapter in this volume. Jenny has lived in Central Australia for 24 years. Her professional background ranges across visual arts, anthropology, community development, and cross-cultural law and justice. She has worked for local Aboriginal peoples on the protection of sacred sites and the remote Aboriginal community Night Patrols—a contemporary application of Aboriginal cultural law. Jenny says that, "The fascination of places and people found here has never worn thin; working with the Aboriginal people of the region has forever changed the way I see country. It is a profound experience to walk or drive through these amazing landscapes and see the stories and secrets embedded in the tracks and landforms. I hope there is some sense of this in the photographs you see in this book". Contact: jennymcfarland650@gmail.com.

A Note about Rod Moss

Rod Moss provided the photograph of his painting, *The Interpretation of Dreams*, which appears on page 8 of the Introduction to this volume. Rod is a renowned Central Australian artist, deeply imbued with the cultural history of Western painting. His work is collected and exhibited throughout Australia and internationally. Many of those works are frank and intimate depictions from within Aboriginal family situations. His book, *Hard Light of Day: An Artist's Story of Friendships in Arrernte Country*, is an account of those relationships and how the many paintings came about. The book was published by UQP, St. Lucia, Queensland, Australia, 2010, and won the Northern Territory Writer's Award, 2011 and the Prime Minister's Literary Award for non-fiction, 2011. See www.uqp.com.au.

ACKNOWLEDGEMENTS

The Editors and Publisher wish to acknowledge and thank the following:

Allen & Unwin, Sydney, Australia, Alexis Wright, and Sydney PEN Voices – the three Writers Project for permission to reproduce Alice Wright's essay "A Question of Fear". This essay was originally published by Allen and Unwin in 2008 in the book *Tolerance, Prejudice and Fear*. This book, with an Introduction by Nobel Laureate, J. M. Coetzee, was based upon lectures by Alexis Wright, Christos Tsiolkas, and Gideon Haigh, who were commissioned by the Sydney branch of PEN International, which is dedicated to the support of writers anywhere who work under persecution, exile, imprisonment or "silencing".

Hannah Rachel Bell and Magabala Books, Broome, Western Australia for their permission to reproduce the drawing *Bandaiyan* by Bungal (David) Mowaljarlai from the book *Yorro Yorro Everything Standing Up Alive*, Magabala Books, Mowaljarlai and Jutta Malnic, Broome, WA, 1993.

National Gallery of Victoria, Australia, for permission to reproduce *Lost*, 1886, by Frederick McCubbin.

Museum Victoria for their permission to reproduce "Nullarbor Plain, 1935" and "Ooldea Soak, Nullarbor Plain, 1919".

Jenny McFarland for her permission to reproduce her photographs from central Australia: "Simpson Desert Salt Lake", "Ephemeral Watercourse Lake Nash (Alpururrurlam) Way", and "Ephemeral Creek Floodout, North Simpson Desert".

Rod Moss for his permission to reproduce his painting, *The Interpretation of Dreams*, 2009.

Miguel Angel Biazzi for his permission to reproduce *Personaje en el valle*, 70 x 40 cm., Tec. Mixta, 1970.

Knapman Wyld Television for permission to reproduce still photographs by Jimmy Pozarik from the SBS television programme *East West 101*.

Figure 1: Ortelius World Map, Terra Australis Nondum Cognita (The South Land–Not Yet Known), 1570. http://en.wikipedia.org/wiki/File:OrteliusWorldMap1570.jpg.

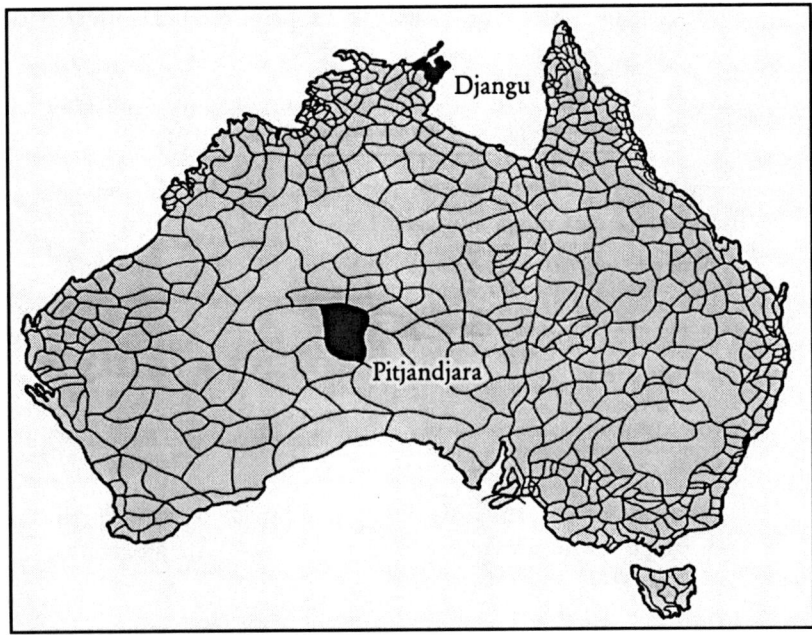

Figure 2: Aboriginal Australia prior to 1788. This map is intended as a general indication only of the complexity and totality of the pattern of indigenous enculturation prior to European occupation in 1788. Each "area" broadly represents the location of larger groupings of language groups, tribes, nations.

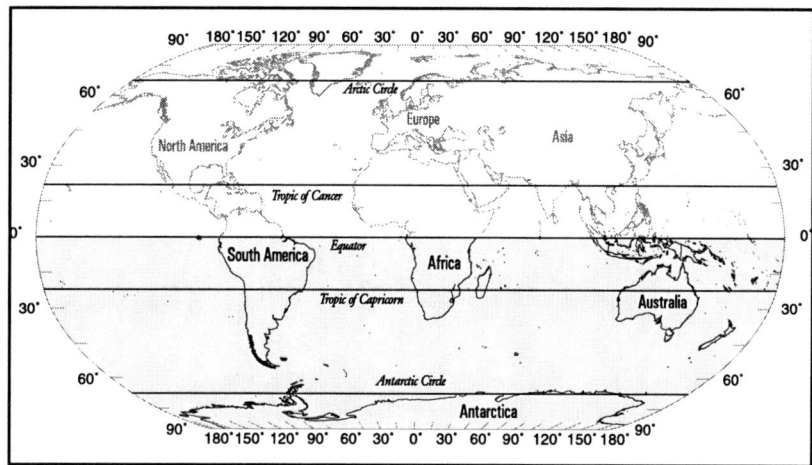

Figure 3: Australia's relationship to the world. (Source: Northern Graphic Design and Publishing).

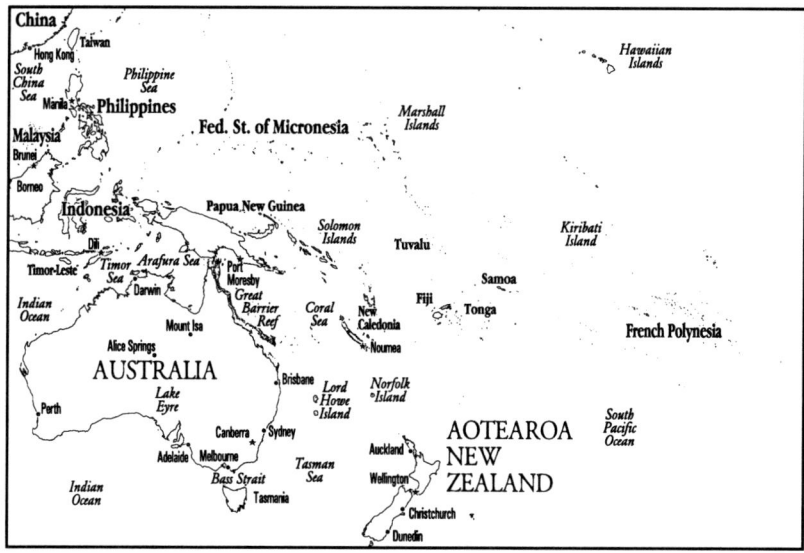

Figure 4: The Australasian region and western Pacific. (Source: Northern Graphic Design and Publishing).

Preface

Thomas Singer, Series Editor

Placing Psyche: Exploring Cultural Complexes in Australia is the first volume in a series of books which will explore the theory of cultural complexes in different parts of the world. These books will be published by Spring Journal Books as part of its Analytical Psychology and Contemporary Culture Series, of which I serve as the Series Editor. The purpose of this volume, and the ones which will follow, is to investigate how the theory of cultural complexes may stimulate fruitful discussions about the nature of psychological reality within and between groups and how these realities live in the psyches of both groups and individuals. This series of books builds on *The Cultural Complex: Contemporary Jungian Perspectives on Psyche and Society*[1] that I co-edited with Samuel Kimbles which extended Jung's notion of the personal complex into the cultural domain by introducing and describing the notion of the cultural complex.

Jung's earliest theoretical contribution to the emerging field of psychiatry in the beginning of the twentieth century was his theory of complexes. The complex theory originated in the word-association test in which timed responses to a list of words revealed blocks or delays in response time to certain words that triggered emotional reactions. Jung called the cluster of ideas, images, and affects that caused these blocks "complexes". These complexes turned out to be highly reactive, and Jung came to think of them as sub-personalities, functioning separately from ego consciousness and often having memories, beliefs, behaviours, and even body postures that comprised a very definite and separately identifiable content. It is these early studies in complex theory that led to Jung's short-lived relationship to Freud.

Jung's application of complex theory was confined largely to the study of the individual, and it is only recently that the theory of complexes has been extended to the life of groups. A cultural complex is defined as an autonomous, largely unconscious, emotionally charged aggregate of memories, affects, ideas, and behaviours that tend to cluster around an archetypal core and are shared by individuals within a group.² (See the Introduction for more details as to the content, structure, and characteristics of cultural complexes.) Cultural complexes are active both in the psyche of the group as a whole and in the individual at what we can think of as the group level of the individual's psyche.

The study of the history of science teaches us that a working hypothesis is only as valuable as the research that it spawns. In fact, that is the purpose of good theory—to stimulate further study, not to stop the speculative mind from wondering about man, nature, and the cosmos. Good theory does not explain away the object of its inquiry, but opens doors to the curious mind to ask more questions, including challenging the validity of the theory itself. In time, the research that is generated by a theory either gives it more solid legs to stand on or proves the theory inadequate or wrong.

The fact is that there are many useful theories through which one may gain some understanding of the conflicts that plague people around the world—sociological, economic, political, religious. The theory of cultural complexes is a psychological theory that offers a perspective on social conflict by focusing on the psychology of individuals and groups. It places emphasis on psyche, which is a most elusive reality that, unlike other objects of study in the social sciences, defies precise measurement or accounting. Yet it is no less real or powerful simply because of its inherently subjective nature. In fact, over time, its very subjectivity can take on an objective reality. This series seeks to discover if and how the theory of cultural complexes, which considers especially the tremendously powerful influence of unconscious psychological factors in group behaviour, may serve as a useful tool in analysing the psyche as it expresses itself in group psychology and how it may serve to facilitate the imagining of healing change.

It is quite possible that in the not-too-distant future, the scientific tool of neuroimaging may soon show that what we are calling cultural complexes can be triggered in the neurobiologist's laboratory by something akin to the word-association test but geared towards words or phrases that trigger cultural complexes rather than personal complexes. Such studies may well reveal interconnected pathways in the brain that link affect, memory, image, thought, and behaviour—an actual patterned locus for "cultural complexes" in the brain's circuitry.

This unique Australian volume explores the theory of cultural complexes through the eyes of a group of varied observers, all of whom have a remarkable sensitivity to the cultural level of the psyche. For many of the book's authors the fate of Australia's indigenous people has become a crucible for pained reflections about inequity and injustice. The focus on the plight of the Aboriginal Australians reveals primal fault lines in the Australian collective psyche, much as has occurred with Blacks and Native Americans in the United States. These fault lines concern not just the relationships between indigenous and non-indigenous people but between all racial and cultural/social groups as they grapple with sorting out their relationships with one another.

Many cultures have such fault lines around which cultural complexes form which can become carriers of other tensions in the society. Exclusive focus on a particular group such as the Aborigines in Australia or the Native Americans in the United States can become a symbolic lightning rod for other related issues in the psyche of the continent. At the same time, a culture's complexes can become the cutting edge for its psychological growth. From this more positive perspective, cultural complexes can serve as a stimulus for a society's individuation, if it is up to the task to bring consciousness to its collective psychological and social conflicts rather than continuously act them out from one generation to the next, repeating the same old behaviors with the same old emotions and ideas about other groups.

Living in an "in-between space" between groups is a primary focus of the authors' concerns in this volume. This "in-between space" can be experienced between ethnic groups, racial groups, religious groups, gender groups, and linguistic groups. Living in a space between groups or in a borderland space implies the capacity and flexibility to tolerate differences between groups without getting stuck in a fixed identity with one group or another. It means that an individual is able to tolerate ambiguity rather than depend on the fixed certainty of knowing who one is by virtue of belonging to a particular group. In a global environment of increasing anxiety about security, it makes sense that many would retreat to fundamentalist assertions about the nature of one's existence and about the group with which one identifies. In a way, identifying with one's own "native" group may be a more natural position than living in-between group identities, which can be thought of as an "opus contra naturum" or work against the natural psychological and social state of affairs. The tension between holding on to a fixed identity in one group versus living in uncertainty between groups is a central issue or cultural complex of almost every place in the world. It is not unique to Australia, although this volume brings that world-wide complex into sharp and unique focus as it lives in the Australian psyche.

I have come to think that what Jung said of personal complexes is equally true of cultural complexes. Cultural complexes are "the hand that fate had dealt us". The fact that they exist is no rarity or special circumstance of one particular group or place. Cultural complexes seem to be a naturally occurring part of the human condition. What makes them interesting is not that they exist but what human beings choose to do or not to do about them. The easiest, perhaps most natural, thing to do about them is nothing and allow them to pass unchallenged and unconscious from generation to generation. They do give a deep sense of belonging to a particular group, clan, or tribe, even as they occasionally wreak destructive havoc in the social order. Another possible course of action with a cultural complex is to try to bring it into group consciousness so that something new may happen. I view this way as having the potential for soul-making at the group level of the psyche. I believe that soul-making occurs in a culture when the painful tensions between different groups or within one group are endured and struggled with long enough to open up the possibility for transformation in the sense of leading to new feelings, new behaviors, new attitudes, and new possibilities. This may be rare, but it is possible. The tensions generated by cultural complexes that pit groups against one another often end in prolonged stalemates or dangerous regressions, but sometimes these tensions can result in innovative soul-making in a culture.

As you will discover in this book, several cultural complexes have been identified by the authors. They tend to cluster around issues of land, indigenous people, immigration, migration, displacement, language, and individuation. If I am correct, that soul-making can occur when the conflicts generated by colliding cultural complexes are suffered authentically and brought to consciousness, then one might imagine the following for the cultural complexes of Australia: that the land might be related to with more heart, that language might deepen in its capacity for reflection, that indigenous people might be treated with respect in their own terms, that those who have immigrated, migrated, or been otherwise displaced might be embraced with understanding of their being both different and part of the whole, and that cultural blocks to individuation might loosen their grip and permit individuation in both individuals and groups.

Soul-making can occur when the conflicts generated by unconscious cultural complexes are actively engaged in dialogue rather than acted out or identified with. Such engagement can lead to change in the psyches of the community and its individuals. Furthermore, such soul-making can be thought of as taking place in the psychic and physical "borderlands" or "contact zones" that exist in the streets of the city or in the outback—and perhaps most intimately that take place in the "borderland" or "contact zone" of the soul of every citizen.

The regional editors, Amanda Dowd, Craig San Roque, and David Tacey embraced this project with a passion and seriousness of purpose that was unfailing and sustained over three years of gestation. This project was truly a collaborative effort at the heart of which has been the work and dedication of the regional editors and the book's authors.

Nancy Cater, the Publisher of Spring Journal Books, has been instrumental in every aspect of the creation of this book—from the most abstract vision underlying the series to the most detailed realization of this particular volume. Nancy envisioned the series; she supported the idea for the first volume on Australia; she helped edit the content of every chapter; she oversaw the book's organization; she wrestled with the map making process; and she copy-edited the final proofs of the book. No part of the creation of this book was too large or too small for her rare blend of intuitive imagination and hawk-eyed attention to detail. All of the book's editors owe her a tremendous debt of gratitude.

Notes

[1] Thomas Singer and Samuel Kimbles, editors, *The Cultural Complex: Contemporary Jungian Perspectives in Psyche and Society* (New York: Brunner-Routledge, 2004).

[2] Thomas Singer with Catherine Kaplinsky, "Cultural Complexes in Analysis", in *Jungian Psychoanalysis: Working in the Spirit of C.G. Jung*, ed. Murray Stein (Chicago: Open Court, 2010), pp. 22-37.

Introduction

Craig San Roque, Amanda Dowd, David Tacey, and Thomas Singer

"Will Phantom glimpsed the town's psychosis twinkling in the sunshine."
Alexis Wright, *Carpentaria*[1]

"erinnerungsreste" or "remains of memory"—a term Freud took to mean "associations that occur in the unconscious where they unfold their potency". It is only through a translation into language that they can be made conscious.

Part One: Placing Psyche

Placing Psyche: Exploring Cultural Complexes in Australia is a collection of twelve essays by authors drawn from the fields of Jungian psychoanalysis, anthropology, environmental science, cultural studies, creative writing, literature, and film. The purpose of this collection is to use the theory of cultural complexes, as described in the Preface, as a stimulus for these thoughtful observers to frame their own ideas and experiences of their encounters with Australian cultures and "places" in the hope of revealing something about the group level of psyche as it operates in Australia today.

The "placing of psyche", as the title suggests, speaks both to the powerful outer, sensate realities of the actual landscapes of Australia and to the equally powerful metaphoric, inner landscapes of the multiple psyches of Australian culture. Many new to the continent can experience a reversal of perspective that brings the mind's eye and the pull of the soul out and across horizontally but not, as in the countries of Europe, up or down vertically. There is a "different sensibility" that is required of living in Australia, but getting the feel of it can be unsettling. We hope to add to this ongoing conversation about "placing psyche" in Australia by offering readers a wide range of perspectives from which to view their experiences personally and culturally.

Part Two: Many Peoples, Many Languages, Many Histories

Although the history of Australia is well known to most Australians, we would like to offer a brief sketch for those readers from other parts of the world who are much less familiar with the peoples and lands of this huge continent and the ways in which it came to take its current cultural shape. Prior to colonisation the continent of Australia was home to diverse Aboriginal peoples of approximately 600 language groups. The non-indigenous migration to Australia and the subsequent colonial expansion and settlement into every part of the continent eventually created a landscape of many histories, often layering one on top of the other.

Australia was first claimed for Great Britain as a site for colonial expansion by Lieutenant James Cook on 22 August 1770. Eighteen years later, the first English convict ships bearing a total of 1,030 souls arrived in Sydney Cove carrying with them a Northern and Western European cultural heritage completely alien to the local indigenous patterns of thinking and imagining. This was to be an "experiment": the continent would become a penal colony built by convict labour. Records show that around 160,000 men, women, and children were transported in bondage to Australia by the Georgian Crown in the ninety years before the system came to an end in 1868. Of the 788 convicts (including 192 women) who were transported in the first fleet in 1788, many were selected because their skills were deemed useful for the establishment of a colonial outpost, and this trend of selection continued. Thus, under the direction of the British parliament, those first convicts and settlers established a foothold on what had, until then, been *terra incognita*—land unknown—or, to play upon the word "*incognito*", a place whose identity was concealed or disavowed. The pattern of concealment also continued as an ongoing tendency toward unconsciousness or remaining blind to the realities and nature of the environment and peoples of the pre-existing southwest Pacific.

And so, one century before Freud began to write *The Interpretation of Dreams* unearthing facts about human unconsciousness, the "case" of Australia was beginning.[2] The European imaginative projection onto what was for those first settlers an unknown, "empty" land was (arguably) that of a human waste dump, an eighteenth-century detention centre for the petty thieves, pimps, and prostitutes spilling out of British gaols. In effect, these convicts established the infrastructure—the roads and buildings—of the southern British colonies.

Waves of Immigration

Modern Australia has been built by successive waves of immigration. At first, approximately one third were Irish convicts, and many were Irish political dissidents exiled by English forces then taking over Ireland's arable land. It is this that accounts for the strong Irish stream in Australia's bloodline. The first English "free settlers" arrived in January 1793, taking up land grants, and from around 1815 (under Governor Lachlan Macquarie) non-convict British immigrants seeking land, a future, and imagined prosperity began moving first along the Australian coastline and then inland across the Great Dividing Range—a formidable mountain barrier that extends along the eastern edge of the country for almost its entire length. Arduous exploration expeditions were mounted in much the same way as they were in the Americas and Africa, mapping rivers and locating pastures which later enabled settlers to take up land for sheep, wheat, and cattle. Some of these expeditions went in search of the "mythical" inland sea which was hypothesized to account for the flow of the rivers.

Gold was discovered in Victoria in the 1850s which brought an influx of Chinese and European prospectors, many of whom moved there from the California goldfields. Chinese trade, market gardens, and gold processing were essential, though disavowed elements in Australia's development and the Chinese presence was strong, especially in the Victorian gold fields and the northern Carpentaria region. In the 1860s, following the explorers, vast cattle rangelands began to develop on the western and northeastern inland plains, and thence through the central deserts from Adelaide in the south to Darwin and the Gulf of Carpentaria in the tropical north. It was during this expansion that Christian missionaries established (sometimes protective) sanctuaries in indigenous areas.

Although Dutch, German, and French colonial ambitions extended into the region, it has been the English, Irish, and Scots who, during the 19th century as part of the British Empire, progressively established Australian culture, governance, and commerce. This perhaps more familiar "public face" of settler Australia began to change after the Second World War with the arrival of European and Jewish displaced peoples. Developing industries and the need for re-population in the post World War Two era of the 1940s, 50s, and 60s saw massive subsidised immigration programmes undertaken under the auspices of the "White Australia" policy, a controversial policy which precluded non-white—meaning black, Islander, or Asian immigrants. This second wave was mostly invited from Italy,

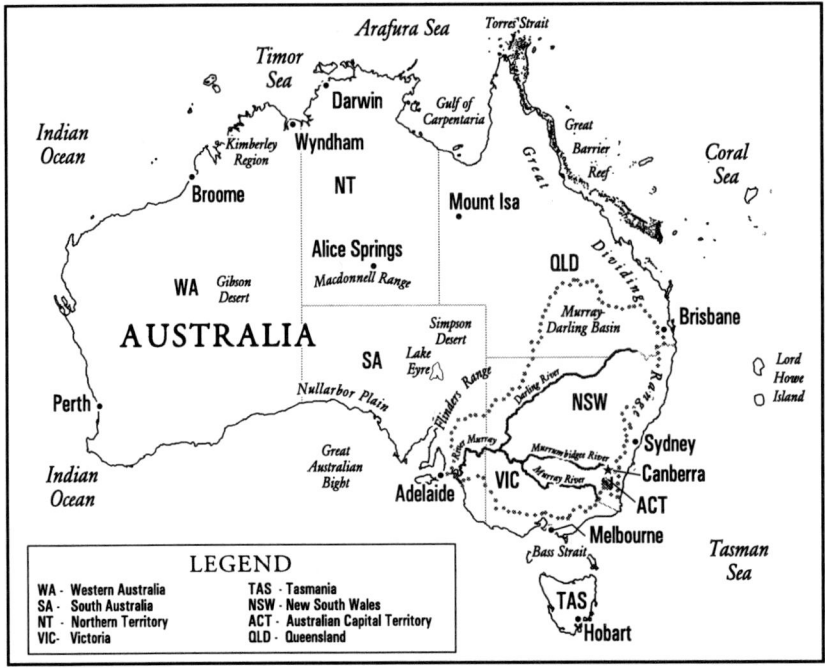

Figure 1: Australia: a guide to state boundaries, cities and key locations, referred to in this book. (Source: Richard Tuckwell and Northern Graphic Design).

Greece, eastern Europe, south-west Russia (White Russia), and Great Britain. Later, successive waves of conflict and economic hardship in southeast Asia, South America, eastern Europe, the Middle East, and northern and southern Africa have brought people of many races and religions, and many a run-down working class Australian suburb has been revitalised by their presence. The Australian population now includes strong Islamic, Jewish, Vietnamese, Korean, Chinese/Hong Kong, Indian, and Islander communities as well as a large New Zealand community. Continuing diversity is a keynote. It can be fairly said, without minimising tensions, that the planned integration policy has been constructive.

From the 1960s to the present what might be called "aspirational development immigration" rather than "refugee immigration" continues to change the face (and the building codes) of Australia.

The Geography of Expansion

It was not, however, "aspirational development immigration" that led to the early exploration and settlement of Australia. British ships needed safe harbours to offload their human cargo of convicts and would-be migrant settlers. Sydney Harbour, Port of Melbourne, Port of Adelaide, and Perth's Fremantle Harbour provided the main gateways for arrival and eventual dissemination inland by following the river systems through the ranges into the rolling western plains. Further coastal settlements gradually established themselves around the southern coastal fringe for whaling. The move north for timber incorporated the Brisbane River region and then pushed along the north-eastern, subtropical coast, in what is now known as Queensland. In the far north-west, the Kimberley region and the port of Darwin served cattle nurturing ventures. These northern tracts developed into "cattlemen's kingdoms" operated by pastoral consortiums. The iconic Victoria River Downs, owned first by the Kidman family and now by the Holmes à Court family, is one of the best known of these Australian cattle kingdoms.[3]

Throughout the mid-1800s, vigorous expansion and commercial settlement took place in the New South Wales and Victoria regions, stimulated by the discovery of gold in 1851. The eastern coastal region, favored by temperate climate and rich soils, supported intensive agriculture. The western savannah river plains of the Murray Darling Basin attracted exceptionally hardy settlers.

The developmental history of Anglo Australia is, to a significant extent, the history of the movement of cattle, sheep, and horses. During this expansion the indigenous tribal modes of self sustainment and culture were decimated, vulnerable to infectious disease, sugar foods, alcohol, and covert warfare. There was no "native war", as such, recognised politically by the British Government, but resistance by Aboriginal warriors was a feature in the continual dissonance between Black and White interests.

Expansion into the arid centre from Adelaide in South Australia began around 1840. (See Peter Bishop article in this volume.) An extraordinary accomplishment—characteristic of the dogged determination of the early settlers—is the 3,200 kilometre Overland Telegraph communications line laid and completed in 1872. This line bisected the dry centre—running from Adelaide through Alice Springs to Darwin—and it eventually connected Australia to London. Along this route, exploration and transport depended on camels and Afghan cameleers imported in the 1860s from Pakistani regions. This Afghan presence is part of the richly toned story of a widening country. Eventually the railroad and trucks replaced resilient camels.

Such an expansive colonising dream over a course of a hundred years gave little credence to the human realities already present. The lands of

Australia and the neighbouring region had in fact been very well known to generations of other, non-European cultures carrying thousands of years of human memory and civilisation. The complex intricacy of human history in this region, when studied with care, reveals a layered and breathtaking enterprise of dissemination and safeguarding of culture.

One of the things that distinguishes a "New World" country from the "Old World" is that a specific time can be located as origin; the time when original or occupying peoples met with the incoming or invading peoples. Originating stories of the "European makeover" period of the region hover round the idea of "the first": the first fleet, the first sightings, the first settlement, the first arrivals, the first encounters with "natives", the first farm, the first hanging, the first journey across the mountains, the first births, the first deaths. Among these first realisations and adaptations, some almost within living generational memory, are experiences stoically and existentially absorbed by people on both sides of the frontier. The first Aboriginal deaths from small pox, influenza, venereal disease, the first reprisals, the first massacres, and the first cohabitations perhaps also represent signs of the laying down of inter-racial patterns which may have become trauma systems. A chronicle is there to be told of the first "us"—the first "them".

For some people, Australia, in all its farflung parts, is seen as a paradise of natural beauty—a playground. For others, the region appears to be a frenzied site of seminal prosperity, with international mining giants gouging gold, iron, coal, uranium, oil, and gas from newly opened sources both under ground and under sea. But for others, dingy rubbish-strewn yards in suburbs and Aboriginal settlements are sites of shameful, bewildering impoverishment. The lines are not split with indigenous on one side and non-indigenous on the other: it is an illusion to mark Australia with simplistic apartheid thinking, to impose on it a conceptual Berlin wall between Black and White. The truth is complex and this complexity and diversity may be its hidden asset—it's potential.

Australia is the site of multiple beginnings for various sets of incoming peoples; and, for another set, it is the site of the end of long practised ways of life. In essence, this region is a contact zone between many different groups of people where pragmatic, poetic, spiritual, and moral realities reveal competing symbolic frames of reference that generate both potential and anxiety in strange and often paradoxical ways. It remains at the same time a zone in fear of that contact. In a peculiarly devious manner, the blank and avaricious stare of colonial entitlement continues as a fact. Many people in many different ways seek to "place their psyche" here, some resolute in being at home—some displaced and still seeking a place where self, soul, and psyche might feel at home.

Part Three: The History of Studying the Australian Psyche

Any history of inquiry into the mental landscape of Australia must acknowledge the Strehlow family, who were part of the early Lutheran missionary immigration from Germany and who were among the first Europeans to enter the indigenous desert regions of central Australia in the 1880s. The Lutherans established a mission re-named Hermannsburg at N'taria, an Arrernte tribal location 130 kilometre west of Alice Springs, which became a refuge for Aboriginal people beset by famine, disease, and pastoralist incursion. This extraordinary undertaking is partly recounted in Barry Hill's *Broken Song*[4] which focuses on the achievements (and despairs) of T.G.H. Strehlow, son of the Lutheran missionary Carl Strehlow, whose own German language ethnographies and contacts may have contributed to the early psychoanalytic efforts in the German language to come to terms with the mentalities of the Australian Aborigines. T.G.H. Strehlow became an anthropologist and author of the monumental work, *Songs of Central Australia*[5], a masterful bi-lingual English/Arrernte text which brings Aboriginal traditions of sung mythology into companionable line with the European, as exemplified in Icelandic sagas and Greek myths. T.G.H. Strehlow's work can be read as a companion to Jung's *Symbols of Transformation*[6] because they both acknowledged the cultural depth and value of original peoples and the value of the mythopoetic heritage of mankind.

The Strehlows and their indigenous companions (such as the renowned Arrernte cultural custodian known as "Moses"[7]), are exemplars of determined, intelligent, and often eccentric individualists of both indigenous and settler origins who opened up the psychological relationship between cultures. It is meetings such as this between remarkable minds which have set the tone of Australasian cultural diversity, though such pioneers of intelligence were usually either grudgingly respected or even reviled at the time. Some of these folk have become iconic after their deaths (for instance Daisy Bates, described in this volume by Peter Bishop); some died tragically, perhaps, of heartbreak or a cultural depression. Such individuals attracted, like magnets, bits of a prevailing cultural complex. In fact, such eccentric liaisons still continue. The effort at co-residency continues, battered though it is.

The first twentieth century "explorer" of Australian subterranean psychic territory was, arguably, Ronald Conway in his book *The Great*

Figure 2: Rod Moss painting, *The Interpretation of Dreams*.**

Australian Stupor: An Interpretation of the Australian Way of Life.[8] Many owe a personal and professional debt to Ronald Conway who blazed a trail for others to follow. In the 1960s and early 70s, Conway saw that psychoanalysis could shed light not only on the individual or personal dilemma but that it could also put Australia itself on the couch and explore its psychological patterns and complexes. Numerous other works followed such as Xavier Pons' *Out of Eden*[9], and a series of works by the psycho-social analyst Graham Little, including *The Public Emotions, Politics and Personal Style*, and *Political Ensembles*.[10]

From the 1960s to 1980s, the exploration of collective psyche in Australia was strictly governed by Freudian and post-Freudian points of

---

**This painting by well known Australian artist, Rod Moss, offers a gently ironic view of black/white relations; a poetic reversal of the customary position. A Freud character, modelled by Dr. Howard Goldenberg, is on the couch in a setting like Freud's Vienna room, transposed to Alice Springs. The doctor is recounting his dreams to Hayes, a local Arrernte man, a friend of the artist's who willingly posed for this painting. Hayes, a custodian of Arrernte cultural dreaming, listens with wily attention, enjoying perhaps, the sharing of perspectives—an arrangement into which the doctor, like Rod Moss, has willingly entered. For more information on Rod Moss and his work, see the Acknowledgements at the beginning of this volume.

view, and Jungian and post-Jungian perspectives had yet to be explored in this context. But by the late 1980s and early 90s, writings began to emerge from David Tacey and Jungian analysts Craig San Roque and Leon Petchkovsky. Australian artists and writers already had incorporated Jungian insights into their works as early as the 1940s and 50s, with writings by Judith Wright, Patrick White, and Morris West showing clear influence, particularly of Jungian archetypal theory. But it has taken longer for Jungian perspectives to find their way into theoretical and social analyses of the Australian experience.

Most studies of Australian cultural experience adopt the standard social science model of knowledge. Influential writings such as *The Australian Legend*[11], *The Australian Tradition*[12], or *Inventing Australia*[13] assume that national character and "Australianness" are a product of social and historical conditioning. Such studies tend to ignore or overlook the insights of psychology and biology, much less those of depth psychology or psychoanalysis. Freud and Jung are still felt to be "foreign", European, and esoteric, having no real purchase on the practical reality of national character. The social science model sees human beings as shaped by external and historical forces only and tends to view Jung and those who follow his tradition as "biological determinists" who have little or nothing to say to those who seek to study the patterns of cultural experience. And so it is perhaps not surprising that it is in the arts and later in the humanities, persuaded by the "suggestive power" of archetypal theory, that we find Jungian thinking outside of the consulting room in Australia.

However, since the late 1970s Jungian analysis as a professional discipline has continued to grow in Australia and New Zealand, and there is now a flourishing Jungian analytic training in this part of the world. In 2001 Jungian analysts from Australia and New Zealand published *Landmarks*[14], a collection of papers in which archetypal and psychodynamic perspectives were applied to a range of cultural, political, social, and clinical issues. It is also important to note at least two other local events that serve as markers in the development of the linkage between psychoanalytic thinking and cultural discourse. In 2000 a significant event took place at Uluru (central Australia). This was the Australian Psychoanalytical Association conference, "This Whispering in our Hearts—Intuition in the Service of Psychoanalytical Work in the Australian Milieu" (at which Craig San Roque presented "Coming to Terms with the Country"[15]). This conference brought local psychoanalysts into the heart of the Australian "condition". In 2007, an Australian and New Zealand Society of Jungian Analysts (ANZSJA) conference in Melbourne, "The Uses of Subjective

Experience", as a Jungian initiative brought analysts, anthropologists, and academics together for the first time to reflect mutually on Jungian and socio-cultural subjective experiences in our region.[16]

Part Four: Methodology for Creating *Placing Psyche*

A Parable of a Method: Dreams and their Interpretation

In *The Dictionary of the Khazars: A Lexicon Novel* by Milorad Pavic[17], a poetic/prophetic tale is told based on the legend of the Khazars, an autonomous and powerful tribe of warlike and nomadic people who settled the land between the Caspian and Black Seas some thirteen hundred years ago. Facing fateful incursion from the encroaching powers of Christianity, Islam, and Judaism, the Khazar leader, known as the Khagan, aware of the unique quality of his culture, language, and subtle metaphysics of his people, nevertheless accepted that behind the three faiths was a material power which could not be resisted. He concluded that the safest course for his people would be to submit to one of the dominating ideologies, and in this way attempt a balanced tension between them rather than obliteration. He declared that he would convert to the faith of the sage who gave the most satisfactory interpretation of a troubling and persistent dream; and so a dervish, a rabbi, and a monk were summoned. In the dream, the Khagan is wading waist high through a river and reading a book. Whenever a big wave comes, he lifts his book high and continues to read. He is approaching deep waters and must finish reading before he reaches the deep. Suddenly an angel with a bird on his wrist appears saying, "the Lord is pleased by your intentions but not by your deeds". The Khagan awakes and opens his eyes. Even awake, he is waist high in water, wading in the river, with the book in his hand and before him stands the angel. The Khagan shuts his eyes, but the river, the angel, the bird, and the book are still there. There is no escape from the dream/vision whether the Khagan is asleep or awake. He looks again (in his dream) into his book and has a realisation. He says: "I realised there was no more shutting of your eyes to the truth, no salvation in being blindfolded, no dream and reality, no being awake or asleep. Everything is one and the same continuing eternal day and world, coiling around you like a snake".

The point of telling this story in a book concerning itself with cultural complexes is to dramatize the idea that in any given country there are many possible "dreams" or categories of dreams and multiple

INTRODUCTION

"interpretations". It is never clear if we are awake or asleep; and sometimes at crucial moments, it is necessary to surrender to another person's point of view.

We can, somewhat simply, list the following possible "dreams states" in Australia:

1. the dreams of pre-contact indigenous peoples
2. the dreams of post-contact indigenous peoples
3. the dreams of seventeenth and eighteenth century colonial minds
4. the dreams of the first settler families and their descendents
5. the dreams of later immigrants
6. the dreams of those of mixed descent
7. the dreams of the native born
8. the dreams of those in close contact with indigenous persons
9. the dreams of those who have no relation with the indigenous mentality

Depending on where one comes from and out of which historical matrix one arises, cultural complexes are experienced differently, even though they may constellate around similar emotional cores. And so we envisage each contributor to this book as a bit like the Khagan, each with territory to protect or develop and a troubling "dream" to interpret. Some dream of water, some of language, some of fear, some of disappearing children, some of angels, some of cultures drowning, some of opportunity. The temporarily lost or disoriented state, illustrated in the Khagan legend by the collapse of the distinction between the awake and asleep state, is akin to a borderline/psychotic confusion between phantasy and reality. This is a state where one is never quite sure if one is grasping what is real or not. Cultural complexes often place one in a borderland territory akin to being between dream and reality, not unlike the state in which the Khagan finds himself. The complex itself can be so disorienting that one becomes unsure of where and who one is.

Characteristics of Cultural Complexes

Singer offers the following checklist as an aid to distinguish whether one might be in the grips of a cultural complex.[18]

1. Is there an unconscious affective force that underlies the "problem"? Does it present with a big dose of collective emotion?

2. Does the problem seem to have a life of its own—is it autonomous?

3. Does it recur over time in such a way that it gains a history and selective memory of its own that becomes self-fulfilling? Is it repetitious?

4. Does it have a set of relatively simplistic beliefs and ideas which are also repetitive and tend to reduce problems to simplistic and formulaic or stereotypical ideas?

5. Does the problem seem to be highly resistant to consciousness, rendering impotent conscious efforts at managing or controlling the problem?

6. Is it difficult to think clearly about or challenge the overly simplified set of ideas and powerful emotions that accompany the appearance of the "problem"?

7. Is it triggered (as in Jung's original word association test) by words or phrases that immediately lead to powerful affect—somewhat like stepping on a land mine?

If there are enough "yes" answers, then we might be in cultural complex territory.

Premises of *Placing Psyche*

If the notion of the cultural complex accurately describes the powerful emotional forces that bind people into groups and function in ways that are highly resistant to consciousness, it quickly becomes clear that enormous tensions about identity and belonging will be generated in these states, especially in times of economic and other social distress. These tensions may arise around boundaries and loss, inclusion and exclusion; and they occur within the individual, between the individual and others, both of one's own group and groups of others. Nowhere are these tensions greater than when matters of land, territory, and ownership are involved. By defining the compass of this book regionally, that is specifically by "place", we encounter a major theme threading through this collection, namely that "place" matters, for there is no person without their place.

And so if there are disturbances "twinkling in the sunshine" of our collective (southern) psyche, how might we overcome resistances and recognise these disturbances and our individual relationship to them? How might we enquire into them psychologically? Who might we ask to speak and write to them? These questions underlie the method, for as regional editors we began our engagement by accepting that, by definition, cultural complexes have us, that is, whatever the collective trauma systems and enculturated patterns that are shared amongst many, we swim in unclear waters, pulled by currents and rips in which we ourselves are also caught.

We envisaged the book as reflecting an experimental process and making a modest attempt to draw upon experiences emerging out of the mental and emotional landscapes of Australia. Authors were invited to find their own way—to play with the notion of the cultural complex, to give descriptions—subjective, personal, individualized, and exploratory. They are not speaking for the country but out of their own experience and through the lens of their own personal and professional milieu. We hope that the effort to describe experience and to clarify language helps to better understand the psychic pain of the place where we live and to glimpse some of the cultural complex "states" inhabiting the Australian psyche.

Part Five: Major Themes

Peter Bishop in "Singing the Land: Australia in Search of its Soul" references Jung who wrote:

> Almost every great country has its collective attitude. Sometimes you can catch it in a formula, sometimes it is more elusive, yet nonetheless it is indescribably present as a sort of atmosphere that pervades everything.[19]

Bishop continues:

> Jung suggested that the more well defined a culture, with a solid historical background, the easier it generally was to express its genius in a single phrase. Paradoxically, a relatively young country—such as the United States that Jung visited in the 1920s and which he referred to as "childlike, impetuous and naïve"—could well have "the most complicated psychology of all...". The apparent "simplicity and straightforwardness" of people in such cultures hides a "complex fragmentation, a lack both of coherence and of connectedness with the land itself, the ancestral soil".[20]

What Jung said about the United States is also an apt description of Australia today. This "complex fragmentation, a lack both of coherence and of connectedness with the land itself, the ancestral soil" is apparent in several major themes that surface in various chapters of the book. Some of these themes converge around the following issues:

1. LANGUAGE AND THE LOSS OF WORDS

Many of the authors of *Placing Psyche* note the challenge of finding words to adequately convey the experience of being caught in a cultural complex or to even describe what a cultural complex might be. This is exemplified in David Russell's "Lost for Words" and also explored in Ute Eikelkamp's "Language is My Second Skin". This is not surprising given that a complex, by definition, is unconscious. Emphasising the connection between words and the complex derives from the work of both Jung and Freud in which word associations and slips of the tongue are noted to betray subconscious ideas and feelings. Not only do words reveal and conceal complexes at the same time, they can become complexes themselves, functioning defensively where language is used to talk around or hide difficult things or where silence, not speaking, is used to avoid painful experiences. On the other hand, well chosen words may clarify enigmas of unconsciousness, and that is the goal of this book. Language used in this way means something akin to comprehension. In Australia there is a resonance between the use of language as comprehension and the way in which Aboriginal people use the word "language"—where it means "everything", that is, culture, relationships, meaning, and place. To lose language is to lose the link to meaning; words without this link simply fill up space.

2. Relationship with Environment and Climate

The ancestral soil is everywhere in this book in terms of both people and the law, both Aboriginal and settler. Peter Bishop's "The Nullabor: Contact Zone as Imaginal Space" and Patty Please's "The Feeling of Salt, Water, and Land" directly address the relationships between people and land, both indigenous and non-indigenous.

3. Migration/Displacement

Many authors in this volume touch on the complex fragmentation and lack of coherence between peoples of diverse race, language, and ancestry. Since the founding story of modern Australia is one of displacement, this emerges as a major theme of the book. All non-indigenous people have come from somewhere else, bringing cultures alien to the people, country, and climate already here. The fact is that just about every group in Australia, indigenous and non-indigenous, carries the complex ancestral baggage of histories of migration, displacement, and discrimination. Amanda Dowd's "Finding the Fish", for example, explores the treacherous waters and painful consequences of migration and displacement among both indigenous and non-indigenous peoples.

4. Indigenous Perspectives

All authors acknowledge the history of the indigenous peoples of Australia and point to relations between the indigenous first peoples and the waves of incoming settlers, a meeting or non-meeting over time which is described as a "contact zone" and which has become fertile ground for generating cultural complex tensions. Most of the chapters in this book bring focus to the hazardous borderland between indigenous and non-indigenous peoples. Alexis Wright's "A Question of Fear" and Melinda Turner's "Sorry, It's Complex" bring heart-breaking focus to this borderland.

5. THE IMAGE – FILM/LITERATURE/TELEVISION

An image points to something, capturing what can be intimated but cannot yet be said, perhaps not even thought. Our image-makers, our dreamers, visionaries, poets, artists, writers, and film makers intuitively pick up what is emergent in the personal and cultural psyche. Several chapters use images and/or discuss film, literature, and television as a source of understanding something of the psychological development of both individuals and groups in Australia. Such images are deeply revealing of the people of Australia in their quest for survival, coherence, connection, meaning, and even occasionally individuation in a challenging physical and cultural landscape. Terrie Waddell's "The Rapture of 'Girlshine'", David Tacey's "The Australian Resistance to Individuation", and Craig San Roque and Kris Wyld's "Sydney—'a city of truant disposition': *East/West 101*" explore the image of the Australian cultural and psychological landscape in film, literature, and television.

6. THE "CLINIC"

The theme of "the clinic" is broadly defined here to include all efforts at deliberate therapy, repair, and reparation which are progressively taking place in diverse forms throughout Australia. This need for repair implies some sort of pre-existing damage, around which cultural complexes often accrue. It can be fairly said that the therapeutic intention of many professionals (of any and all races and of many professions, including education, law, policing, and health) is to work to heal the damage that has occurred to many different groups of people in the course of the country's unfolding development. This effort is not confined to the consulting and counselling rooms of the rapidly expanding psychological professions. Two chapters in particular focus on "the clinic": Craig San Roque's "The Lemon Tree" and Chris Milton's "Taking It With Me."

Taken as a whole, *Placing Psyche* presents the work of an interconnected body of psychotherapists, scientists, educators, authors, film makers, and scholars who are imagining and developing a language to explore multifaceted perspectives on psyche in Australia. They have learned from history, from cultural narrative, and from personal experience. Each and all together can be seen as working towards a more individuated and possibly maturing culture in which the complexes of entrenched feeling, memory, and behaviour of older cultural patterns are being challenged and made more conscious.

Notes

[1] Alexis Wright, *Carpentaria* (Artamon, NSW, Australia: Giramondo, 2006), p. 461. Will Phantom is an heroic Aboriginal activist "on a mission" approaching the town of Desperance.

[2] Sigmund Freud, *The Interpretation of Dreams* (New York: The Modern Library, 1994).

[3] http://www.heytesburycattle.com.au/Stations/StationsVictorianRiverDowns.aspx.

[4] Barry Hill, *Broken Song: T.G.H. Strehlow and Aboriginal Possession* (New York: Alfred A. Knopf, 2002).

[5] T. G. H. Strehlow, *Songs of Central Australia* (Sydney: Angus and Robertson, 1971).

[6] C. G. Jung, *Symbols of Transformation, Collected Works of C. G. Jung*, Vol. 5 (London: Routledge Kegan Paul, 1956).

[7] The Arrernte cultural custodian known as Tjalkabota was born near N'taria/ Hermannsburg in 1872 and was rechristened "Moses" by the Lutheran missionary, Carl Strehlow. Moses became a significant advocate for his own people to convert to Christianity.

[8] Ronald Conway, *The Great Australian Stupor: An Interpretation of the Australian Way of Life* (Melbourne: Sun Books, 1971).

[9] Xavier Pons, *Out of Eden: Henry Lawson's Life and Works—A Psychoanalytic View* (Sydney: Sirius Books, 1984).

[10] See Graham Little, *The Public Emotions: From Mourning to Hope* (ABC Books, 1999); *Politics and Personal Style* (Nelson Australia Paperbacks, 1973); and *Political Ensembles: A Psychosocial Approach to Politics and Leadership* (Oxford University Press, 1985).

[11] Russel Braddock Ward, *The Australian Legend* (Oxford University Press, 1966).

[12] A. A. Phillips, *The Australian Tradition: Studies in a Colonial Culture* (Melbourne: Cheshire, 1958).

[13] Richard White, *Inventing Australia* (Sydney: Allen & Unwin, 1991).

[14] *Landmarks: Papers from Jungian Analysts from Australia and New Zealand*, compiled by Heather Formani, published by Australian and New Zealand Society of Jungian Analysts, ACT, Australia, 2001.

[15] "Coming to Terms with the Country" is published in *Landmarks* and in *The Geography of Meanings: Psychoanalytic Perspectives on Place, Space, Land, and Dislocation* (IPA: The International Psychoanalysis Library), Maria Teresa Hooke and Salman Akhtar (Editors) (London: Karnac Books, 2007).

[16] Several of the contributors to this volume also contributed to the 2007 conference in Melbourne: Peter Bishop, David Tacey, Craig San Roque, David Russell, Amanda Dowd, and Terrie Waddell. An epublication of papers from this conference can be found on the Australia and New Zealand Society of Jungian Analysts website: www.anzsja.org.au.

[17] Milorad Pavic, *The Dictionary of the Khazars, A Lexicon Novel*, trans. Christina Pribicevic-Zoric (New York: Knopf, 1988).

[18] Personal communication from Thomas Singer to Craig San Roque.

[19] C. G. Jung, "The Complications of American Psychology", Civilisations in Transition, *Collected Works* 10, para. 972, quoted in Peter Bishop, "Singing the Land: Australia in Search of its Soul", *Spring: A Journal of Archetype and Culture*, 1989.

[20] C. G. Jung, *Collected Works* 10, paras. 980 and 946, quoted in Bishop, "Singing the Land."

Peter Bishop, Ph.D., was born in London from a working-class background, and came to Australia in 1971. He has an M.A. in Sociology and a Ph.D. in Religious Studies, and he is Associate Professor in Communications and Cultural Studies at the University of South Australia. His books include: *Dreams of Power: Tibetan Buddhism & the Western Imagination* (1993); *The Greening of Psychology: The Vegetable World in Myth, Dream & Healing* (1991); *The Myth of Shangri-la: Tibet, Travel Writing and the Western Creation of Sacred Landscape* (1989); *An Archetypal Constable: National Identity & the Geography of Nostalgia* (1995); *Bridge* (2008); and as a co-author, *Hope: The Everyday and Imaginary life of Young People on the Margins* (2010).

●●●●●●●●●●●●●●

In this chapter, Peter Bishop focuses on the Nullabor Plain, for many years a disregarded region of Australia that runs along the southern edge of the continent for a thousand kilometres. At the heart of this vast region lies a 200,000 square kilometre plateau of limestone, virtually devoid of trees; consequently, this area has been seen as a landscape grossly deficient in significant features and means to support life. Edward Eyre's desperate sea voyage of 1840-1841 along the coast of the Great Australian Bight, the large open bay located off the central and western portions of the southern coastline of Australia, was the first non-indigenous report of what seemed to be a wasteland: he described the part of the Nullarbor Plain that borders the coastal waters through which he sailed as "a hideous anomaly, a blot on the face of Nature, the sort of place one gets into in bad dreams". By land, the Nullarbor was crossed first by the overland telegraph, crude tracks and then, in the early 20th century by a railway; it is now traversed by a sealed highway. Its use during the 1950s as a site for testing Britain's atomic bomb was dramatic confirmation of its lowly status in non-indigenous imagination, virtually a non-place.

Over the past half century, however, new paradigms have emerged throughout Australia that facilitate a re-imagining of this region—including environmentalism, tourism, recognition of indigenous rights, and the need for reconciliation. Peter's chapter discusses the psychological process of the imaginal re-population and re-envisioning of this unique Australian landscape.

1

The Contact Zone as Imaginal Space: The Nullarbor in the Non-indigenous Australian Imagination

Peter Bishop

Since the early days of white settlement non-indigenous Australians have attempted, albeit often in inappropriate and unconscious ways, to assign imaginative significance, at an archetypal or imaginal level, to the continent's indigenous peoples, fauna, and flora, plus to the varied landscapes, particularly those for which no close precedence existed back in Britain and Europe.

For example, most non-indigenous Australians, when they have given it any consideration at all, have viewed the thousand kilometres along the southern edge of the continent that separate the last reasonably fertile zone of South Australia with that in Western Australia as a landscape grossly deficient in significant features and means to support life. For much of Australia's white settlement the Nullarbor Plain (from the Latin words *null* and *arbor,* meaning "no tree" or "treeless") presented an almost impassable barrier between an isolated and sparsely-populated Western Australia and the bulk of the population to the east. Crossed only by the overland telegraph completed in 1877 (and abandoned in 1929) by a crude track, and then in 1917 by a railway, it is now traversed by a sealed highway, although most people cross it by aeroplane.

Edward Eyre's desperate trek of 1840-1841 along the edge of the Great Australian Bight produced the first non-indigenous report of the region.

Figure 1: Nullarbor Plain, 1935 (Reproduced courtesy of Museum Victoria).

Everything seemed scarce to him except flat horizons. Water, plants, animals, birds, and indigenous inhabitants were few and far between. At the heart of this vast region lies a 200,000 square kilometre plateau of limestone virtually devoid of trees hence known as the Nullarbor. Its use during the 1950s as a site for testing Britain's atomic bomb was a dramatic confirmation of its apparently lowly status in non-indigenous imagination. However, over the past half century, new paradigms have emerged that both insist on and facilitate a re-imagining of this region—including environmentalism and conservation, tourism, recognition of indigenous rights, and the need for reconciliation.

I have chosen to begin with Eyre's journey, and the cultural complex it signals, not just because it was the first non-indigenous encounter with the Nullarbor but because of its apparent simplicity. Even at the start it was a very small group, but after two of the indigenous men killed Eyre's European companion and then fled, only a solitary white man, Eyre, and a solitary indigenous man, Wylie, were left to complete the journey. These two struggled across an unknown, seemingly featureless, arid landscape that simply appeared to repeat itself day after day. However, this simplicity is deceptive. In fact, a drama of great complexity was being enacted.

Although not directly referring to the Nullarbor, in an extraordinary passage the anthropologist Strehlow attempted to evoke a profound difference between an indigenous and non-indigenous perception of such landscape:

THE CONTACT ZONE AS IMAGINAL SPACE

Locator Map

AUSTRALIA

NORTHERN TERRITORY | QUEENSLAND

Lower Southern Arrernte Tribal Area

Simpson Desert

SOUTH AUSTRALIA

WESTERN AUSTRALIA

Nullarbor Plain

Great Australian Bight Marine Park

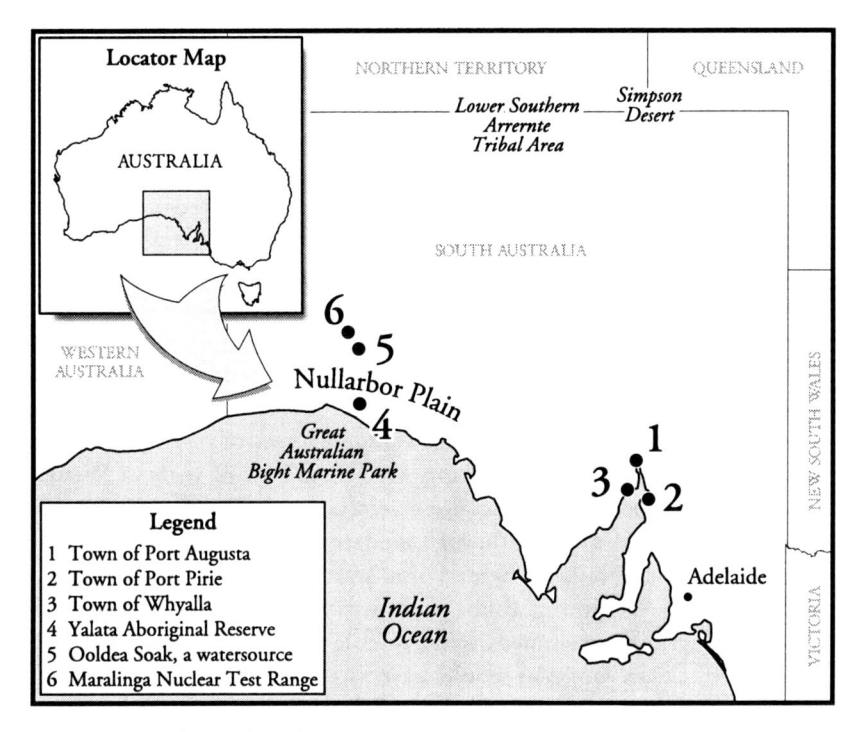

Adelaide

Indian Ocean

NEW SOUTH WALES

VICTORIA

Legend
1. Town of Port Augusta
2. Town of Port Pirie
3. Town of Whyalla
4. Yalata Aboriginal Reserve
5. Ooldea Soak, a watersource
6. Maralinga Nuclear Test Range

Figure 2: Southern Australia.

> Even the most desolate portions of the most arid lands in the Centre were lit up by myths and songs with the light of the eternal landscape ... A European standing ... in the Simpson desert would have seen only the vastness of desolation in the treeless plain, the red tops of the long dune ridges and the mean and broken rubbly hills, in the circular-horizoned landscape around him. A Lower Southern Aranta [Arrernte]man's vision would have been filled with different and far more magnificent sights. In his mind's eye he would have caught sight of the great Amewara Tnatana totem pole brought from Port Augusta, towering against the western horizon, the flames of its plumed crest-top shooting skyward at night toward the desert-bright stars. Close at hand he would have seen the broad trunk of a great casurina tree rising up and touching the sky above him with its branches, forming a firm bridge between sky and earth. He would have seen the native cat travelling from Port Augusta winding their trail across the vast plain ....[1]

While Strehlow's account goes some way to acknowledging the richness and depth of an indigenous Australian imagining of land and country, it simultaneously reinforces the belief that non-indigenous perception, experience, and relationship is somehow non-imaginal, that Edward Eyre's perspective, which saw only desolation and focused on the prospects for colonisation, was straightforward and non-mythic, was non-imaginal. The persistence of this judgement is a significant hindrance to the deepening of non-indigenous soulfulness and to the processes of reconciliation, of eco-sustainability, of soul work in general. It is an easy binary in which to fall and I, too, have not avoided participating in it in the past. It also simultaneously effaces the "rational" dimensions of indigenous knowledge and perception.[2]

Let us return to Eyre's encounter with the vast arid plain, with what came to be known as the Nullarbor. It would be easy to claim the whole of Eyre's journey for the Hero but this would be a case of mythic-reduction. Informing his sensibility/imagining were thousands of years of Western mythologising about nature (e.g. Germanic/Greco-Roman/Christian), plus more recent shifts instigated through modernity such as Romanticism, the picturesque, etc. Similarly, Eyre's vision was informed by an ancient but ever-changing imagining about mobility, whether for travel, science, tourism, pilgrimage, conquest, trade, or colonisation. Along with this, a wealth of ancient fantasies would have saturated his world view about exile, home, the "Other" or otherness, and the unknown. In his make-up would have been ancient traces and modern shifts in fantasies about identity—gender, age, nation, race—even the very notion of identity. He carried an imagining of science, reason, religion, and spirituality that was current for his pre-Darwinian, post-Newtonian time.[3] Of course Eyre had his own take on these perspectives, but the key point is that they are imaginal and soulful. "The psyche is situated in an historical present that trails behind it the roots of a thousand ancestral trees", argues Hillman, who continues: "The historical 'facts' may be but fantasies attached to and springing from central archetypal cores...".[4]

Hillman points out that: "We can extend depth psychology from

Figure 3: Edward Eyre.

persons to things, places and ideas as manifestations of imagination. The same imagination, the same soul, that presented itself in fifteenth and sixteenth century alchemy showed itself in the extraverted psychology of the explorers....The world as metaphor".[5] Desolation, even emptiness, are mythopoetic statements. From Homer to the Icelandic Sagas, Dante to the Romantic poets, desolation has often been an important imaginal character. The move into a fearsome unknown, with an apprehension of desolation, is akin to a descent into the psyche and to an accompanying psychopathology. Over 30 years ago, on one of the first of my many encounters with the Nullarbor, I stopped to refuel before the long haul to the next service station. The man at the next pump half-closed his eyes and gazed out across an imaginary plain and slowly said: "There's nothing for the next 1000 miles". He wasn't talking about petrol. Nor was it a "nothing" that suggested boredom. This was a richly resonant but daunting "nothing". It was a "nothing" that was "something" to experience.

So, one could rewrite Strehlow's piece:

> Eyre standing on the edge of the cliffs would have seen stretching out before him the vast southern ocean with its tentative links to complex albeit invisible sea-borne trade and communication routes. These "song lines" linked sites where rituals of empire and national identity were regularly and rigorously performed in order to activate the myths. At the centre of these song lines/trade routes was the sacred, mythic homeland from which all imaginal identity, purpose, and meaning radiated. Overhead the stars formed immense constellations, which were viewed in complex ways by an educated, much travelled Briton well-versed in navigation, geometry, poetry, Christianity, and Empire in 1840. Behind him lay a vast uncharted, yet long mythologised land crossed by tentative tracks to ....

Just as the Lower Southern Arrernte (old spelling: Aranta) man would not have considered his complex vision as imaginary or "mythic", but "real" and "true", so too Eyre would not have considered his complex vision (of national and individual identity, colonising purpose, "England", the emerging sense of globalism, of empire, trade, ownership, religion, law, justice, science, geology, species, history, etc., etc.) as imaginary or mythic but very real and very true.

The imagination is not an option, not a creative embellishment to be added. An archetypal imagination is found everywhere and is ever present. An essential task is to somehow recognise the imaginal at work. As a way of uncovering imaginal patterns and poetic images, this kind of re-turning of images and fantasies to some more fundamental ground of symbolisation, of mythic resonance, is common to many theorist/philosophers of the imaginal. Vico, for example, stressed poetic thinking, which he called *ricorsi*. This is both an attitude and a method for seeing the history of fantasies and the fantasies of history.[6] Corbin, who originally coined the term "imaginal", similarly discusses Ibn 'Arabi's notion of *ta'wil*, as "symbolic understanding, the transmutation of everything visible into symbols".[7] The *ta'wil* leads fantasies back to their archetypal ground.

A Contact Zone as an Imaginal Space

In order to draw out some of the postcolonial implications of this imaginal complexity I want to turn to the notion of "contact zone" first proposed by Mary Louise Pratt.[8] Contact zones describe social spaces "where cultures meet, clash and grapple with each other, often in contexts of highly asymmetrical relations of power, such as colonialism, slavery, or their aftermaths as they are lived out in many parts of the world today".[9] Contact zones also define encounters with the land—including its flora, fauna.[10]

Contact zones also offer spaces where a decolonialising of cross-cultural communication and action can occur, where there can be alternative possibilities. However, in the many re-workings and applications of this notion of a contact zone one rarely encounters mention of the imagination let alone of the imaginal.

Over the past decade much of my work has been with reconciliation, not just in Australia, but as a radical, transforming notion and practice. I am convinced that a turning to the imaginal is critical.[11] For example, when discussing the important issue of land ownership in Australia, Helen Verran insists on a radical re-imagining of the whole idea about "ownership". She suggests that intercultural disputes between indigenous and non-indigenous Australians need to be resolved within an imaginal context, one in which there is a shared commitment to the reality of the depth imagination and a mutual empathy with symbolic or mythic commonalities, what could be called a shared imaginary. In her discussion of the encounter between indigenous Australians and pastoralists over the meanings of land ownership, Verran argues that "by restoring imaginaries to modern theories of knowledge, we rediscover the capacity to re-imagine ourselves and devise ways ... [of working] with other communities".[12] In other words, it is the task of mythopoetics to re-mythologise Western systems of knowledge and practice (such as Real Estate, accountancy, and trespass), whose imaginal roots are too often effaced and denied.

In addition to land ownership, the sense of national identity that Eyre carried onto the plain was also inevitably imaginal. Benedict Anderson, in his seminal study *Imagined Communities*, claims that "human communities exist as *imagined* entities". In these communities most people will never know or meet most of the other members. Despite this lack of direct interaction "in the minds of each lives the image of their communion". What is important is how communities are imagined and the power that this imagining has in a contact zone. The European bourgeoisie, the kind of human community that Eyre came from, gained much of its strength and power according to Anderson, from their capacity to "achieve solidarity on an essentially imagined basis" to an extent that was unprecedented in history.[13] It has been argued that cultural complexes "provide a simplistic certainty about a group's place in the world in the face of otherwise conflicting and ambiguous uncertainties".[14] The idea of contact zones moves in the opposite direction by complicating "notions of static, fixed, bounded socio-cultural wholes" and in so doing undermines simplistic certainties while providing a richer sensibility.[15]

Contact zones are spaces where identities are made and remade, where holistic, tightly bound notions of culture are no longer viable. "What matters increasingly is how culture and cultural identity are evoked, by whom, for what purposes, and with what potential consequences in specific locations".[16] In a sense, the Nullarbor only emerges and owes its very existence as a place, because it is a contact zone. "Cultural centers, discrete regions and territories, do not exist prior to contacts, but are sustained through them, appropriating and disciplining the restless movements of people and things".[17]

Through a consideration of what Edward Casey called an "archetypal topography"[18] I want to bring an imaginal perspective into this notion of a contact zone. Archetypes belong to complex fields. A cultural complex is one such field or array. One only has to think of the extraordinary family drama that orders, structures, and gives meaning to the classic Greek pantheon. Casey asked: "What regulates the regulators? How do archetypes which impart patterns to particular imagined contents, *themselves* form an ordered pattern?".[19] Archetypal topography is the mapping of topoi (places and sites): "it is a matter of determining where archetypes are to be located in relation to each other and thus what groupings they form".[20] While there can be deliberate attempts to tightly orchestrate the topography, all too often the ordering is more diffuse, a loose amalgamation of hegemonic assumptions.[21] Images generally have a complex and contradictory multiplicity even within an occasional, overall, imaginal coherence.

In any contact zone archetypal forms are changing, new forms are emerging. New formations and relationships between archetypes are always coming into being, as are new hierarchies of fantasy. A contact zone is a site where multiple imaginal typographies encounter each other and within which cultural complexes are transformed, perhaps even emerge. The orchestration by a dominant archetypal theme affects the relationships and imaginal significations of all other archetypal themes.

In a cultural complex, "cultural identities may be forged and transformed as the tensions between past history, collective memory, and present social discourses are encountered".[22] In addition, these complexes are also themselves transformed through a multiplicity of engagements within a contact zone. Previous imaginings are frequently challenged, superseded, reorganised, or their importance re-evaluated. The archetypal orchestrator dominant at any specific moment ensures that there is a very particular reading and understanding of the multiplicity of imaginal activity that is taking place in and around a contact zone.

When Edward Eyre brought such an archetypal field into a space which later emerges as the Nullarbor, it became a contact zone of multiple encounters: with other archetypal typographies expressed through indigenous peoples, plus with an imaginally animated land.

A contact zone is many-sided. My aim is not to map the full complexity and dynamics of a contact zone but to begin to work along one interface, that of non-indigenous encounters, plus to do this in a specific way, that of invoking the imaginal. In this paper I'm not looking at the myriad everyday encounters that take place in, and create, a contact zone. Instead I simply want to draw on a few examples to develop the notion of the contact zone as an imaginal space, a space where fields or clusters of archetypes engage, perform, and transform. In particular I want to emphasise the place of the dominant orchestrating fantasy within the complex, the "regulator" as Casey puts it.[23] A crucial part of this work is the sometimes difficult task of beginning to re-turn images and notions to some more fundamental ground of symbolisation, of possible mythic resonance.

Elegy and Celebration

Almost one hundred years after Eyre's crossing, Ernestine Hill crossed the plain on her famous journey in the 1930s around Australia.[24] The sense of desolation experienced by Eyre still persisted, although his fearsome scenario had tempered into something less fierce, becoming instead a "mighty circle of monotony".[25] This is understandable given that the Plain was no longer a complete blank on the non-indigenous map. Indeed by the 1930s the route was well trod and lined with widely spaced settlements. However, the extensive network of caves that lie beneath the Plain and had just been recently discovered allowed her to invoke a vision that echoed Eyre's. The blow holes are her entrance to a watery underworld: "the dank smell, the unhealthy foetid breath of earth, and the screeching of the winds at night".[26]

Four issues continue on from Eyre, albeit transformed in Hill's imagining: the vastness and barrenness of the Plain, water, indigenous peoples, and settlement. There is also a new issue: technology.

It is not possible, nor desirable, to assign a particular archetype to each of these issues as each is in itself a mini- complex, is its own archetypal field. Water, for example, in Eyre's account was firstly about his own survival, secondly about the possibilities for settlement, and thirdly about relationships with indigenous peoples. Clearly the last two issues are related. In Hill's account the focus on water covers similar imperatives albeit without that of individual, heroic survival. She states that the plain has been discovered to be "not a sand desert, but the roof of a mighty honeycomb of mysterious caves of crystalline limestone and subterranean rivers that wing 50 miles southward to the sea".[27] She continues: "water could be obtained anywhere... Bores are being put down with success, and as soon as they can provide sufficient drinking water for increased stock, the frightening Nullarbor will become a fine sheep country".[28] In almost a Demeter-Persephone scenario, to this underground water, brought to the surface through technology for agricultural and farming purposes, there is also sky water. Hill contrasts the "stark horror" of the plains "in the drought years, and its remarkable beauty after a downfall of rain" when carpets of wild flowers burst into bloom.[29] When she goes to find the eccentric missionary-teacher-scholar Daisy Bates, who had been living alone in a tent among the local Aborigines for many years at Ooldea Soak on the edge of the Nullarbor, still dressing with British Edwardian formality with boots, gloves, and a veil, Hill encounters another type of imaginal water. The clear, fresh water of the Soak had been at the heart of

Figure 4: Daisy Bates.

local indigenous physical and cultural survival for thousands of years but had been virtually destroyed by the railway construction and operation, with around 70,000 gallons a day being pumped out according to Hill.[30] By the time Daisy Bates set up her mission camp there, the Soak was all but ruined. The local indigenous people, the Anangu, of course have their own stories, including historical accounts, about this water.[31]

Figure 5: Ooldea Soak, Nullarbor Plain, 1919 (Reproduced courtesy of Museum Victoria).

Drawing on Bachelard's notion of a "material imagination", Illich argues that the "form and matter of our imagining cannot be understood separately because one cannot be understood without the other".[32] In his study of an imagination of water, Bachelard points to a "system of poetic fidelity".[33] By turning his gaze onto "clear waters", "springtime waters", "running waters", "deep waters", "dormant waters", "dead waters", "heavy waters", "maternal and feminine waters", Bachelard invokes a "poetic chemistry, which would study images by measuring the density of their inner reverie".[34] For example, Bachelard suggests that Edgar Allan Poe's repeated invocation of deep, dormant, sad, and dead waters led to the creation of an "inspired monotony", that they had a place on "the map of melancholy" and "the map of human misery".[35] There is a Poe-like imaginal aspect to many of both Eyre's and Hill's encounters with a watery imagination.

Hill does not criticise the railway. The railway is considered to be a technological triumph, an inevitable aspect of civilisation, of Enlightenment reason, and of modernity. Through such technology natural obstacles must and will be overcome.[36] The necessity and inevitability of this transformation lies at the heart of Hill's complex vision. Yet, she doesn't welcome it. Despite this apparent optimism and hope for the future, a mood of loss and melancholy pervades Hill's entire account. This is the imaginal tone, or character, which orchestrates all others: "the Nullarbor Plain is one of the most melancholy patches in Australia".[37] This was not an "inspired melancholy" but one of bitter-sweet loss and sadness. Technological advances are a prime cause of the passing of an older, idiosyncratic, rugged Australia, a passing which Hill mourns.

Certainly, new colourful imaginal figures appear in her account: the farms and the settlements, especially those associated with the recently built transcontinental railway, plus tourists passing through on the trains. From the 1920s onward there had been a shift in non-indigenous engagement with the desert. Arid zone research and an appreciation of arid land ecology led to a critique of grazing and other established farming practices. *The Red Centre*, by the zoologist H. H. Finlayson, was a key text from this period. There was a new appreciation of the desert's intense colours, its energy, and beauty.[38] How those so-called "empty spaces" were filled suddenly became important.[39] In an upsurge of "Desert Nationalism" many artists were drawn to Australia's arid regions. In such an imaginative climate even for Hill, the plain's "immensity and its vast age" start to be viewed "as positive qualities".[40]

While they obviously had a significant place in Eyre's journey and in his subsequent reflections, indigenous people are mainly presented in his account in terms of his capacity to survive and to complete his journey, either as part of his expedition or as guides to water.[41] They are certainly not just figures in the landscape for Eyre but are active individual agents, continually interacting and often guiding and assisting him. In return, Eyre expresses deep concern about their welfare under the inevitable impact of colonisation. Colonisation, its correctness and inevitability, forms the "regulator" of Eyre's archetypal field. In Hill's account, colonisation is not even mentioned as such. It is a given. The Indigenous people who live on the Nullarbor are not individuals but are addressed as a group, a social category. She details, though in a misleading, tangled, and condescending way, Aboriginal stories that criss-cross the country. But, for Hill the indigenous people living on the Nullarbor are another signifier of a sad but inevitable passing of an older Australia. She sees them as a dying, lost people. They are a people without hope. Like the vanishing water at Ooldea

Soak their passing has to be accepted, albeit as with Daisy Bates' life-long labour, the passing can be shown compassion and given care.[42]

Once again, it is crucial to remember that this is only one interface of the contact zone. From another side of the contact zone, the local Anangu have their own stories of this time, their own imaginal complexity and archetypal typography.[43] Also, as Singer and Kimbles point out, cultural complexes cannot be generalised into some kind of national character or complex.[44] For example, the contrasting fantasies occurring at that time within the Nullarbor contact zone can be readily appreciated by comparing Hill's vision with that of Charles Holmes, who gives a brief account of his journey by rail across the Nullarbor in the 1930s. Holmes describes the rail's construction: "Came the white man with long bars of metal and laid them side by side across the heart of the Nullarbor. Soon a great snake glided over them. In the far distance the Pitjintaras [local indigenous people] stood aghast".[45] Other accounts differ both from Holmes' patronising primitivism and Hill's elegiac contemplation. For example, in 1920 the India-Pacific train carrying the Prince of Wales was due to make a scheduled stop at Cook, a tiny and remote railway siding on the Nullarbor, in order for him to meet the "natives". It has been reported that Daisy Bates attempted to organise the indigenous people to greet him with a traditional ceremonial performance involving dance, music, and costume, generally known as a *corroboree*. Apparently the locals were adamant that they did not want a "white-fellow King" and insisted that the country was theirs and had been stolen. They eventually went ahead with the *corroboree* but only after some hard talking by Daisy Bates.[46] This initial refusal and eventual reluctance was probably the only form that Anangu resistance could take and can be seen in terms of what Scott calls "weapons of the weak".[47]

There is a continually shifting field of archetypal fantasies. Sometimes themes are foregrounded, while sometimes they disappear and then reappear. New ones emerge. Old ones are transformed. New relationships develop or dissolve. A key question is how all of these are organised at any time. What dominant fantasy orchestrates and over-determines the rest?

Technological Nationalism: A New Beginning for the Atomic Age

Many of Hill's themes persist, albeit transformed, in Frank Clune's account of his 1950s journey by car, in one of the first iconic Holdens, Australia's first mass-produced car which had appeared in 1948 and which still holds a special place in the Australian popular imagination, across the Nullarbor. But a crucial new issue also emerges: the atomic threat of the Cold War.[48] The archetypal typography summoned by Clune when he enters the Nullarbor contact zone is orchestrated around the fantasies of an Atomic Age. Post-WWII there is a heightened sense of security/insecurity instigated by the new global confrontation between the West and the Soviet Union.

This archetypal complexity begins to emerge when Clune arrives in the region of Port Augusta. In Clune's vision the "Iron Triangle" of Port Augusta, Port Pirie, and Whyalla around Spencer Gulf becomes "a region of intense industrial activity of many kinds – probably the most vital strategic area now in all Australia, and by far the most difficult area for any potential enemy to attack".[49] To the north of Port Augusta is uranium mining and also Woomera with its weapon testing and promise of space rockets.[50] To the immediate west lies the Nullarbor with its "strategic road" built in 1941 just in case the Japanese invaded Western Australia.[51] The whole region was "far from the prying eyes of Communist agents".[52]

Water again becomes a key issue: "Nullarbor Station carries 2200 sheep, watered from wells – but the water is salty, and the troughs have to be cleaned out daily or the salt sediment would make the next day's water undrinkable".[53] He points to the huge, "beautiful" caves and the potential of pumping water from them: "What a paradise this Nullarbor Country would become, if scientists could only discover some cheap method of de-salting water! Perhaps some day 'Atomic' fuel will be used to distil salt water, even sea-water in immense quantities".[54] This is a profoundly mythic scenario, one that resonates with alchemical overtones: subterranean and oceanic water saturated with salt, the primal arcane substance, purified by atomic power, used to fertilise and enrich the land.[55] Perhaps even Clune would not have predicted that his atomic-powered "magnificent sheep country" would shortly become blasted and contaminated by atomic bomb testing. Even less did he suspect that the shadow of this atomic utopia would bring misery, sickness, and death to the indigenous inhabitants. Indeed, unlike Hill, Clune was hopeful about Aboriginal culture and people prospering under the atomic regime. Already there were plans for Yalata station—an Aboriginal Reserve—to be run as a sheep station. Although demands of the space age did intrude and he suspected that indigenous people were moved from Ooldea to Yalata, less because the water had run out than "so they'll be kept well away from the Rocket Range area".[56] The Aboriginal culture and people are also pushed out to the margins of Clune's account. The Rocket range is far more central to his archetypal field.

Even Clune's technologically-driven optimism could make little headway in an appreciation of the aesthetics of the Nullarbor. While he admired the stars and vast night-silence, he also complained of "another fifty miles of monotony".[57] "In retrospect", he continues, "the most interesting sights of the Nullarbor Plain, along the roadside, are 'dead marines' and 'dead tyres'".

A rhetoric of a robust "nation building" dominates and orchestrates Clune's account of this region, particularly through an ideology of mega-engineering. It is a new Australia for the Atomic Age and the Cold War that finds its heartland around the edge of the Nullarbor. Livingston, in his discussion of the role of communication and transportation during the build up to Federation, coins the phrase "techno-triumphalism" to describe the total faith in large-scale engineering projects to unite and to develop Australia.[58]

Unsettling of Australia

In the 1980s Howard Jacobson crossed the Nullarbor by train as part of his journey around Australia. British, but previously living in Australia, he returns determined to utilise his caustic wit in order to reveal and perhaps ridicule much about contemporary middle-Australian culture. The Nullarbor provides him with the perfect setting. From the carriage window the Nullarbor appears not only boring and tedious, but also surreal and absurd: "Meticulous rock piles. Sudden stone circles. Disused mine shafts. Inexplicable towers and pylons, apparently attached to nothing, feeding nothing, receiving nothing, offering a panoramic command of nothing".[59] Like others before him, he comments on "the vast monotony of the plain", but the fierceness of the land has been replaced by blandness.[60] He struggles to find a perspective that adds interest: "I lay on my side and stared interest back into the plain. I discerned strange shapes. I caught the reflection of queer lights. I saw things move".[61] The memory of Daisy Bates is summoned but purely for the purpose of ridiculing her and British Royalty, alongside tourists and the elderly, in a reoccurring trope of Jacobson's that questions the assumptions of white settlement.

A few years after Jacobson's journey, another British visitor, Brian Johnston, also crossed the Nullarbor, albeit in a campervan. Like Jacobson, part of Johnston's mission is to critically reflect and deconstruct many of the myths about Australia, and he remarks at length on Edward Eyre's journey but as a kind of post-imperial reverie on courage and futility. Like Jacobson, it is the vast monotony of the Plain which dominates: "The region's legends were greater than its scenic interest… [and] there was little enough to see on this vast and featureless stretch".[62] In both accounts the indigenous population have almost vanished except as a distant and vague accusatory cipher by which to ridicule white pretensions.

Despite its apparent lack of interesting features, by the beginning of the third Millennium the Nullarbor has achieved a significant place on the tourist map of Australia. Indeed, the tourist has emerged as a major archetypal character in the Nullarbor contact zone, and at times desperate attempts have been made to entice them, such as the construction of the world's longest golf course stretching some 1365 kilometres from Kalgoorlie to Ceduna. However, two other features have considerably more significance, and while both have tourist connections, this is not the source of their imaginal substantiality. The establishment of the Great Australian Bight Marine National Park and the continuing legacy of A-bomb testing at Maralinga point to a major shift in the imagining of the Nullarbor, one that signals both uncertainty and healing.

The last two decades of the twentieth century ushered in an unease about the foundations of European settlement particularly in the wake of the Mabo (1992) and Wik (1996) decisions in Australia's High Court confirming the existence of Native Title for traditional lands. These landmark rulings overturned the oppressive doctrine of *terra nullius* which proclaimed that the land was devoid of any indigenous ownership prior to its settlement by Europeans. Indigenous peoples were now free to pursue claims to their traditional lands even if non-indigenous people had settled on them. This (un)settling of Australian culture resulted in an uneasy, often ambivalent and contradictory relationship to itself and to the land, one in which intense confidence and independence vies with uncertainty and anxiety.[63] The Nullarbor has not escaped this disturbing yet also celebratory scenario. It has its place within a deep, long-term, and complex process of healing soul and reconciliation in terms of both social and eco-justice.

Whales

The Great Australian Bight Marine National Park has become a key location in the recent upsurge of eco-tourism. In particular, the cliffs that line the southern edge of the Nullarbor have become significant sites for whale watching. These now protected waters are the breeding ground of the once threatened Southern Right Whale. Tourist activities and access to prime viewing places are monitored by indigenous people from Yalata as much of this coast forms part of their country. Environmental concern, tourism, and respect for indigenous culture form an important imaginal conjuncture in the process of reconciliation and healing.

In many ways whales have become the prime sentient symbol of the new eco-spirituality. Encapsulating high intelligence and dire threat, the whale joins the rainforest as a key marker of deep ecology, or ecopsychology. Whales haunt the Nullarbor as a contact zone. Whalers plied this coast long before official white settlement. Eyre and Wylie were saved by the chance encounter with the French Whaler, "Mississippi" whose captain not only helped them recover their health but also provided them with adequate provisions to complete their journey. Australia's last whaling station was at Albany just beyond the far western end of the plain. From Jonah to Moby Dick, Jungian psychology has long acknowledged the archetypal power of the whale and its latest manifestation is expressed through the popular phenomenon of whale watching.

The coast, so critical for Eyre's survival, now makes a long overdue reappearance. However, this reappearance is not from the rather simplistic view that the Australian coast is a long beach to which most of the population cling, but from this newly emergent ecological sensibility.[64] The Marine National Park makes the Nullarbor more of a place to visit than just a land to cross. As Paul Carter points out about the Great Ocean Road further to the East, the road "makes the coast a highway, its engineering triumph is to sculpt the cliffs into a bypass for the eye, to smooth them into a single, continuous view".[65] It reminds us that a road (and a long outback road trip) is always a fantasy (often heavily gendered and deeply insinuated into Australian culture and psyche), one which profoundly orchestrates both the land and archetypal complexes, which deflects other ways of encountering and imagining the country.

Maralinga

In terms of re-turning events, images, and notions to some more fundamental ground of symbolisation, of possible mythic resonance, Maralinga presents a most difficult challenge. It presents another face, far removed from whale-watching. Through the 1950s and into the 60s atom bombs were tested in the atmosphere at Maralinga and its vicinities. The indigenous population was moved from its traditional lands, many to Yalata nearer to the coast. Attempts were made to clear people from the desert, but many hid and were still there when the first bombs exploded. Sickness and death followed reports of a black cloud covering the land.[66] The contact zone here is complex and multi-sided, distressing and shameful. Turning Maralinga and these events to their imaginal ground presents a major challenge. Treating history, personal memory, and experience as *metaphorical* rather than *literal* realities, especially in situations where there has been gross suffering, injustice, and oppression, is a profound test of psychological faith, of the acceptance of imaginal reality, of the imagination as a reality.

The events at Maralinga comprise many imaginal traces not the least those of imperialism, colonialism, racism, war, space, energy, and power. Even the working class soldiers and civilians from Britain and Australia carelessly co-opted or employed during the tests were long denied compensation or just acknowledgement of associated sickness and death. The land was only returned to its traditional Anangu owners in December 2009. There are plans to open the town itself to tourists (nuclear industry, bomb testing, Anangu culture), but on tourist maps there is no mention yet of the bomb tests.

Memory as an imaginal place, a theatre, an entire cosmos, is not apolitical. Studies such as Perlman's *Imaginal Memory and the Place of Hiroshima*, complement a wealth of witness or testimony literature and ficto-autobiographical writing which sustain an imaginal perspective without in any way whatsoever compromising the actuality of the events.[67]

Returning just "the bomb" (let alone the tests and their terrible impact on local people, the land, and on the legacy of complex racist and colonialist issues) to an imaginal ground is not easy nor is it simple. At the height of the Cold War David Holt warned: "Jung's psychology puts us at risk between the holy and the mad. It is its strength and its weakness. If it is to speak to our fearful fascination with nuclear holocaust we must be willing to accept that risk".[68] Holt is not only suggesting here that Jung's perspective allows both the sacredness and the horror of the nuclear bomb to be appreciated, but that the very ability to encompass both within the same frame, plus to enter into the fascination with such extremes, could entail a kind of madness. He continued: "The telling requires that we listen, listen as we may never have listened before. A mute witness waits to be heard, bound in our machines and in what we have chosen to call the inorganic".[69]

Around the same time, Wolfgang Giegerich also applied himself to the same question of listening to the nuclear bomb: "We really do not hear. We do not even know what hearing could possibly mean in this context. It is absolutely out of the question for us that such a thing as the bomb might have a message for us, could be a source of insight or even of wisdom".[70] Giegerich, paradoxically, makes a plea to save the nuclear bomb, not literally but imaginally. He writes: "saving the nuclear bomb has nothing to do with defending it against the peace movement, but it means a third way beyond the entire alternative of pro or con, war or peace. It means listening to its voice, seeing its face, acknowledging its reality, and releasing it into its own essence …The question is …where to find its legitimate place".[71] For Giegerich the loss of fierce, all-encompassing nature, the mysterious open expanse which used to surround humanity, and the nuclear bomb are inextricably linked. As if directly addressing the changes in the way that the Nullarbor has been experienced since Eyre's time, he asks how the same view has gone from awesomeness to merely thrilling and warns: "The more that irrational terror [of nature] is captured in a safe container ... the more concentrated and literal...the terror will become".[72] For Giegerich the bomb is vital: "It is our last *genuine* and *real* connection to something bigger and more powerful than we. And what is the face staring at us from within the bomb? Ultimately, it is the face of the dark God, *deus absconditus, mysterium tremendum*...".[73]

Maralinga raises key issues facing mytho-poetics, or imaginal psychology, in the context of a reconciliation process. It forces an acknowledgement of the extreme demands that a reconciliation agenda places upon the imagination and on any mytho-poetic engagement.

Conclusions: Cultural Complex and Display Cabinet

A 2000 brochure from the Eyre Peninsula Tourism Association draws attention to the Balladonia Sheep Station as the site of the old telegraph station. We are told that the 1882 homestead, at the far western end of the Nullarbor region, houses an art collection and local memorabilia. Thirty-five kilometres away is the modern Hotel/Motel which has a "Cultural Heritage Museum using the latest in computer controlled interactive audio/visual technology to recreate the areas history—Aboriginal, sheep stations, Afghan cameleers to the crashlanding of NASA's Skylab in 1979". The memorabilia and "histories" are synecdoches pointing to archetypal clusters which contribute to the Nullarbor contact zone, and to various cultural complexes that circulate through this contested space. Small, highly local, and idiosyncratic museums such as this are concrete examples of archetypal topographies within a contact zone. Carter describes one at Apollo Bay, over 2,000 kilometres to the east along the same coast. Cable Station Museum houses many disparate objects—some Aboriginal (an axe head and grinding stone), some from early settlers, both domestic and farming. Some of the objects are quite recent – "a fire-stained cup and egg cup found at Lorne Golf Club after the 1983 fires".[74] As Carter puts it: "There was no need to apologise for the confusion. Science might not classify these objects together, but they belonged in the same cabinet".[75] The same comment can be made of the Balladonia Cultural Heritage Museum. I suggest that these apparently bizarre, or at least random, collections are closer to the phenomenology of a cultural complex than are the well-catalogued displays of State and National museums, yet they are also different from the private display cabinets of curios kept in one's home.

Balladonia is just one attempt to gather up the wildly disparate and fragmented imaginal field of the Nullarbor contact zone, to generate some coherence and at the same time to create an identity that is, at one and the same time, private and public.

Notes

[1] T. Strehlow, "Geography and the Totemic Landscape in Central Australia: A Functional Study," in *Australian Aboriginal Anthropology*, ed. R. Berndt (Perth: University of Western Australia Press, 1970), p. 134.

[2] J. Jacobs, "Earth Honouring: Western Desires and Indigenous Knowledges," in *Feminist Postcolonial Theory: A Reader*, ed. R. Lewis and S. Mills (Edinburgh: Edinburgh University Press, 2003).

[3] E. Eyre, *Journals of Expeditions of Discovery into Central Australia and Overland From Adelaide to King George's Sound in the Years 1840-1* (2 Vols.) (London: T. and W. Boone, 1845).

[4] J. Hillman, "Senex and Puer: An Aspect of the Historical and Psychological Present", in *Puer Papers*, eds. J. Hillman *et al.* (Irving, Texas: Spring Publications, 1979), p. 6.

[5] J. Hillman, "The Imagination of Air and the Collapse of Alchemy," in *Eranos Jahrbuch 50-1981* (Frankfurt: Insel Verlag, 1982), pp. 283-4.

[6] G. Vico, *The New Science of Giambattista Vico*, trans. T. Bergin and M. Fisch (Ithaca: Cornell University Press, 1975).

[7] H. Corbin, *Creative Imagination in the Sufism of Ibn 'Arabi* (Princeton, NJ: Princeton University Press, 1969), p. 13; H. Corbin, "Mundus Imaginalis or the Imaginary and the Imaginal", *Spring 1972* (1972).

[8] M. Pratt, "Arts of the Contact Zone", in *Mass Culture and Everyday Life*, ed. P. Gibian (New York: Routledge, 1997).

[9] *Ibid.*, p. 62.

[10] For example, see L. Robin, *How a Continent Created a Nation* (Sydney: UNSW Press, 2007).

[11] P. Bishop, "The Shadow of Hope: Reconciliation and Imaginal Pedagogies," in *Pedagogies of the Imagination: Mythopoetic Curriculum in Educational Practice*, eds. T. Leonard & P. Willis (New York: Springer, 2008); M. Watkins, & J. Lorenz, *Toward Psychologies of Liberation* (London & New York: Palgrave Macmillan, 2009).

[12] H. Verran, "Re-imagining Land Ownership in Australia," *Postcolonial Studies* Vol. 1, No. 2 (1998): 237-254, p. 249. See also, Jacobs, "Earth Homcoming".

[13] Anderson, cited in Pratt, "Arts of the Contact Zones," p. 68.

[14] T. Singer, "The Cultural Complex and Archetypal Defenses of the Group Spirit", in *The Cultural Complex: Contemporary Jungian Perspectives on Psyche and Society*, eds. T. Singer and S. Kimbles (London and New York: Routledge, 2004), p. 21.

[15] P. Singh and C. Doherty, "Global Cultural Flows and Pedagogic Dilemmas: Teaching in the Global University Contact Zone," *TESOL Quarterly* Vol. 38, No. 1 (2004): 9-42, p. 12.

[16] *Ibid.*, p. 10.

[17] *Ibid.*, p. 12.

[18] E. Casey, "Toward an Archetypal Imagination," *Spring 1974* (1974): 1-32.

[19] *Ibid.*, p. 6.

[20] *Ibid.*

[21] P. Bishop, "The Karma-Kargyudpa Lineage Tree: A Contribution to Archetypal Topographies," *Spring 1981* (1981): 67-76.

[22] B. Feldman, "Towards a Theory of Organizational Culture: Integrating the 'Other' from a Post-Jungian Perspective", in Singer and Kimbles, eds., *The Cultural Complex*, p. 257.

[23] Casey, "Toward an Archetypal Imagination," p. 6.

[24] E. Hill, *The Great Australian Loneliness* (Melbourne: Robertson and Mullens, 1942).

[25] *Ibid.*, p. 248.

[26] *Ibid.*, p.249.

[27] *Ibid.*, p. 250.

[28] *Ibid.*

[29] *Ibid.*

[30] *Ibid.*, p. 251.

[31] Yalata and Oak Valley Communities, with Christobel Mattingley, *Maraling: The Anangu Story* (Adelaide: Allen & Unwin, 2008).

[32] G. Bachelard, *Water & Dreams* (Dallas: Pegasus Press, 1983), p. 5; I. Illich, *H2O and the Waters of Forgetfulness* (Dallas: Dallas Institute of Humanities & Culture, 1985), p. 6.

[33] Bachelard, *Water & Dreams*, p. 5.

[34] *Ibid.*, p. 46.

[35] *Ibid.*, pp. 45, 63.

[36] R. Haynes, *Seeking the Centre: The Australian Desert in Literature, Art & Film* (Cambridge: CUP, 1998), p. 150.

[37] Hill, *Great Australian Loneliness*, p. 248.

[38] Haynes, *Seeking the Centre*, pp. 148-9.

[39] Robin, *How a Continent Created a Nation*, pp. 99ff.
[40] Haynes, *Seeking the Centre*, p. 149.
[41] Eyre, *Journals of Expedition*.
[42] Hill, *Great Australian Loneliness*, pp. 254-5.
[43] Yalata and Oak Valley Communities, *Maraling: The Anangu Story*.
[44] Singer and Kimbles, *The Cultural Complex*, p. 5.
[45] C. Holmes, *We Find Australia* (London: Hutchinson, 1933), p. 21.
[46] H. Jacobson, *In the Land of Oz* (London: Penguin), pp. 199-200. On Daisy Bates from an Indigenous perspective, see Yalata and Oak Valley Communities, *Maraling: The Anangu Story*.
[47] J. Scott, *Weapons of the Weak: Everyday Forms of Peasant Resistance* (New Haven: Yale University Press, 1985).
[48] F. Clune, *Land of Australia: 'Roaming in a Holden'* (Melbourne: The Hawthorn Press, 1953).
[49] *Ibid.*, p. 197.
[50] *Ibid.*, pp. 196-7.
[51] *Ibid.*, p. 222.
[52] *Ibid.*, p. 197.
[53] *Ibid.*, p. 219.
[54] *Ibid.*, p. 220.
[55] S. Marlan, ed., *Salt and the Alchemical Soul* (Woodstock, Connecticut: Spring Publications, 1995).
[56] Clune, *Land of Australia*, p. 219.
[57] *Ibid.*, p. 223.
[58] K. Livingstone, *The Wired Nation Continent: The Communication Revolution and Federating Australia* (Melbourne: Oxford University Press, 1996), p. 16.
[59] Jacobson, *In the Land of Oz*, p. 199.
[60] *Ibid.*, p. 199.
[61] *Ibid.*, p. 201.
[62] B. Johnston, *Into the Never-never: Travels in Australia* (Melbourne: Melbourne University Press, 1997), p. 188.
[63] K. Gelder and J. Jacobs, "Uncanny Australia," *The UTS Review*, Vol. 1, No. 2, (1995): 150-169.
[64] P. Drew, *The Coast Dwellers: Australians Living on the Edge* (London: Penguin, 1994).
[65] P. Carter, "Travelling Blind: A Sound Geography," *Meanjin*, Vol. 5, No. 2, (1992): 423-445. p. 429.
[66] Yalata and Oak Valley Communities, *Maraling: The Anangu Story*.

[67] M. Perlman, *Imaginal Memory and the Place of Hiroshima* (New York: State University of New York Press, 1988).

[68] D. Holt, "Riddley Walker and Greenham Common: Further Thoughts on Alchemy, Christianity and the Work against Nature," *Harvest* Vol. 29, (1983): 29-54. p. 30.

[69] *Ibid.*, p. 53.

[70] W. Giegerich, "Saving the Nuclear Bomb," in *Facing Apocalypse*, eds. V. Andrews, R. Bosnak & K. Goodwin (Dallas: Spring Publications, 1986), pp. 98-9.

[71] *Ibid.*, p. 99.

[72] *Ibid.*, pp. 103-6.

[73] *Ibid.*, p. 107.

[74] Carter, "Travelling Blind," p. 426.

[75] *Ibid.*, p. 427.

Craig San Roque, Ph.D., is a member of the Australian and New Zealand Society of Jungian Analysts (ANZSJA). He lives in Central Australia, engaged as a consulting psychologist in mental health, substance abuse, and complex cultural trauma. As a relationally attuned practitioner he tries to illumine interactions between cultural forces and the individual and has a special appreciation of Australian Aboriginal thought, perspectives, and the racial dilemma. He contributed to *The Cultural Complex*, with "A Long Weekend in Alice Springs", and to *Psyche and the City* with "Sydney/Purgatorio." Additional publications include *The Sugarman/Dionysos Project*; "Coming To Terms with the Country," in *The Geography of Meanings*; and "On Tjukurrpa and Building Thought" in *Explorations in Psychoanalysis and Ethnography*.

●●●●●●●●●●●●●

This chapter describes how one might begin to detect the presence of cultural complex systems in which one may be caught. Craig San Roque approaches the matter through a conversational exchange with a man who spent most of his working life within indigenous Australian cultures. This man is typical of people who experience intensities of unconscious confusion and communication in ethnic border regions. Craig suggests that a localised cultural complex can be keenly felt by sensitive individuals who, in turn, act out the complex in their own life patterns. As individuals we may be "swimming" in a localised complex without fully understanding what we are immersed in. Some articulate what is going on and, in doing so, they risk being denigrated. Speaking one's mind, while being swept up in the current of enculturated complex systems, requires considerable presence of mind and discipline. Craig describes being sustained by Malinowski's approach to participant observation. The primary field work of Bronislaw Malinowski was situated, circa 1915-1920, among islands north of Australia; of his approach he says this: "It is good for the ethnographer to put aside camera, notebook and pencil, and join in himself in what is going on... I am not certain if this is equally easy for everyone...".[i]

---

[i] B. Malinowski, from the introduction of his *Argonauts of the Western Pacific*, Routledge, 1922 (reprinted Waveland Press, Illinois, 1984), as quoted by Clifford Geertz, *Works and Lives, The Anthropologist as Author*, in the chapter, "*I-Witnessing: Malinowski's Children*" (Palo Alto, CA: Stanford University Press, 1988), p. 76.

2

The Lemon Tree: A Conversation on Civilisation

Craig San Roque

> The town grew up dancing and still the dancing is there under the town. Subdivisions spread, but we still keep going. We still have the culture, still sing the song… It's the same story we have from the old people, from the beginning here in the Centre.
>
> Wenten Rubuntja, indigenous custodian,
> Mbantua/Alice Springs, central Australia[1]

Part One. Location

Winter in the South. Australia; the light in these dry lands, bright, clean. Cold southeast wind. Brilliant night. A radiant Milky Way. Reliable Southern Cross; the constellations of the Southern hemisphere. The central desert region. Latitude, South 23° 40' 12". Longitude, East 133° 53' 07". Alice Springs/ Mbantua. A location.

There are places that haunt the mind, strange sites of human settlement, sites of dire conjunction. This place where I live, this house of concrete blocks and concrete floor, this house in Alice Springs, in winter; a refrigerator. In summer, the surrounding sand, the yard, the concrete, all bake in obliterating sun. Out the back, across the fence of corrugated metal you would see clay-pans and resilient trees, *Eucalyptus Coolibah Arida,* set amid camouflage grey-blue old man saltbush. It's long been known as a place where visitors meet. Hidden in the saltbush,

Aboriginal men camp at nights, or come for a quiet drink in the hot days. Women come. The Coolibah trees, in the local cultural story, are said to be people dancing, waving in ceremony, welcoming an incoming group of

Figure 1: Subdivision fence overlooking Coolibah Swamp, also known as Ankerre Ankerre, a significant heritage site within the township of Alice Springs.

ancestral *Yeperenye* caterpillar beings. The area is a sacred site, perhaps a *Yeperenye* fertility site.

Today, women arrayed in loose black skirts and multi-coloured tops, swaying, waving, are calling out to family members; "Jungarai, Jungarai over here". Men come to meet them; some shouting hoarsely, some remorseless in their intent, some with beer cans in party mood, all escaping from the vigilant eyes of police and liquor restrictions. Hidden in the saltbush.

In my yard, on this side of the fence, seven citrus trees like seven sisters bearing fruit. One tree, a lemon, suffers from an ailment that has eluded diagnosis and treatment. Between the lemon and the mandarin, a round table; on the table, expecting a guest, I have placed two small coffee cups. I will give the visitor Greek coffee—or Turkish—if this morning, like those who live in dissociated places, he prefers one side over the other. We seem to live, these days, in divided selves. My visitor is one of those who work both sides of divided local ethnic associations. The town of Alice Springs is a "contact zone" where many people, in genetic code or in temperament, occupy a kind of "in between" position. In this part of Australia the Aboriginal presence is alive and resilient, incorporating and exploiting the resources that come with the white people. The relationship is sometimes symbiotic, inter-dependent, maybe predatory, and at the same time illuminating, delightful, surprising. There are individuals placed in this region of overlap who can speak the truth of contradictory things; to do so requires a mind capable of holding contradiction. It is the experience of the "in-between" people, the people of the "contact zone", who I am seeking for this book because I believe it is in difficult places, where racial, cultural groupings grind into each other, that the insidious influence of unconscious pressures are felt.

If this were the city, I might seek such impact edges in places frequented by recent immigrants.[2] The restless northern world has poured into Australia countless memories of loss—and countless hopes for a prosperous future. The cities have conquered and are now developing a mind of their own, but here, in the remote places of indigenous Australia, ambition and a sense of immigrant entitlement continue edging into Aboriginal lands, inducing original peoples to conform to the ambitions of a Westernised civilisation—or so it is said. I place my story in a region where the raw edges of Aboriginal mentality and Western mind dominate the scene. If a cultural complex were to surface, it would surface here, in a place of ambivalent contact.

My visitor is a part of that hybrid work force which plays the chess game of white and black interests. I think "chess" because of intricacy, but you could as readily think "poker game"—big money is on the table in government programs, projects, services. All get their cut in this mosaic of Aboriginal territories—in this mosaic of greed.

I am turning your attention to certain people, those whose lives are spent driving thousands of miles (or kilometres, depending upon which measure you prefer) on remote red-sanded roads, passing through the musical landscapes, entering and leaving the business of remote Aboriginal communities. These are the "border linking" people, some indigenous, some not, whose task it is to work between cultures, in schools, clinics, stores, in Aboriginal art centres, police stations, churches, roadhouses. They translate, mediate, and negotiate; they work to support, teach, tend, facilitate; and, they handle drunks, suicides, and fights. Some play for personal gain, some labour under the discipline of altruism, some are dedicated to preserving cultural integrity. For some few (both black and white) the reciprocal engagement becomes a vocation, an enterprise of illumination and hardening, a tempering pressed always between the heat and cold of paradoxical states. Here in this region of contact there are signs and symptoms of borderline cultural complexities.

Land Matters

A cultural complex takes root in primal things. Possession and defence of "territory" is a primal thing.

You may need to appreciate something of how ownership of territory is organised in Australia, for this may be a clue to discerning foundational anxieties and help interpret the history of Australian relations since 1778 and the British arrival.

In its original condition the entire continent was occupied, inlaid with a matrix pattern of indigenous groupings, linguistically and culturally diverse. (See the Aboriginal Australia prior to 1788 map on page *x* of this volume.) The borders of those regions are, even now, invisible to the inexperienced eye. Protocols of behaviour and obligation, when inside indigenous areas are intricate. The country is suffused with interwoven "songlines". The "songlines" or the law, termed in some languages as *Tjukurrpa*, is the coding of indigenous Law, as Jampijimpa Zimran, a Pintubi senior man and Christian pastor in double role provocatively said: "The Yanangu (indigenous people's) Law is like a human being, it works with Aboriginal people—Yanangu. Yanangu and the Law is together. If that Law is weakened, people get weakened and they feel they are weak because they have taken away power in the community. That is the whole issue about community control under Aboriginal Law."[3] I say "provocative" because his statement is simultaneously an accepted and a denied fact in our Australian civilisation. Australia is a country in love with denial. Why this is so can be explained only from a psychological baseline analysing dynamics within unconscious complex behaviours. The habit of psychological denial has done perverse things to our Eurocentric engagement with country. "Ah, that we had achieved a mind that could speak the shape of our country"—as perhaps Rainer Maria Rilke might have said.[4]

The indigenous "Law" is encoded as a neural web of sung narratives and sites which detail activities emanating from the ever-present Creation period. Indigenous lore as law was and is a pragmatic poetic matrix binding memory, ceremonial enactments, cultural authority, cultural narrative involving landforms, fauna, flora, and mythical beings, all woven into a seamless structure engaging sensuality, sexuality, relationship, and humour. Most non-indigenous Australians only roughly understand how Aboriginal mentality is interwoven with territory. The perception of "country" and the intimate matters of indigenous existence are brought to the wider Australian audience in restricted perspectives through contemporary Aboriginal visual art, some music, and occasional films. Deeper layers are conveyed in some anthropological works[5] and through direct, often costly engagement with indigenous men and women.

In 1829 the British Crown audaciously incorporated *Terra Australis* as a part of Great Britain. It became "Crown Land" to be disposed of as the "Crown" thought fit. This action, though understandable in the spirit of colonial empire, was and still is contested by indigenous people who, naturally enough, assume that they have pre-existing authority, responsibility, and accountability for the country. Aboriginal Australians are not centrally organised as a "nation"; which colonial style management practitioners still have trouble configuring. There are no recognisable supreme elders or ratified spokespeople with whom to negotiate, though governments, then and now, try to invent and groom selected candidates. In New Zealand the indigenous resistance was credited with the status of "War"—and thus treaties were enacted. Here, resistance was encountered in guerrilla style, but never formally recognised by Britain as a full-on war over possession.

The absence of a negotiated treaty in Australia has had ramifications. Emotional and psychological resistance by Aboriginal people continues in its unique manner. Because the character of Aboriginal resistance is not recognised by the majority of Australians, strange things happen to apparently benevolent and rational programs designed to relieve disadvantage and social depression. These "strange things" may be signs of a complex.[6] All these territorial factors are contentious. The contentiousness itself is a symptom.

During settlement the original patterning of indigenous land-use, methods of survival, and the functions of ceremony and relationship systems were not understood, not observed, or not explicitly communicated. The primacy of indigenous country was ridden over and over-ridden. Then, in 1976, the Aboriginal Land Rights (Northern Territory) Act[7] established the legality of the original inhabitants to possess lands where continuous occupation or essential cultural connection could be proved. Designated Aboriginal Lands now make up about 22% of the total Australian landmass and about 50% of the Northern Territory (NT), where my story is set. Here, in the Central Australian region of the NT about half the population of 60,000 souls are of indigenous descent, living spread out across small communities and lapping at the edges of the few, mainly Anglo towns. Alice Springs is the largest with 28,000 people. It is a town of government administration, law enforcement, tourism, and, simultaneously. a region of intense eclectic, gracious creativity. The place may have the feel of Native American territories, perhaps; the abandoned rusted car bodies might be familiar. The stories of hope and abandoned hope are similar.[8]

This is the setting for things that go on in a zone of contact, a region of original connectivity overlaid now with subdivisions and systems of governance emanating from a crudely self-interested, British mental heritage. My statement about "original connectivity" is not idealisation of a paradise lost—it is simply a caution to recognise pre-existing territorial identifications and note that there are Aboriginal people who have not given up identification with land—that is to say—with Self. Land matters psychologically, spiritually, practically. Territorial dissonance continues.[9] A frustrated impulse for recognition and independence, on Aboriginal terms, reveals a restive destabilisation beneath the skin of the nation. It is here, perhaps, that there festers a virus of cultural discontent.

A Lie of the Land[10]

There is a governing illusion that Australia is "one nation". This is both true and not true. It is a *selected fact*, in the sense used in psychoanalysis,[11] where a person (almost unconsciously or intuitively) selects a "fact" around which to gather sense, bringing coherence to an otherwise chaotic experience. The "selected fact" may not even be a truth, but it works as a convenient truth, a selected bit of truth. Its purpose, perhaps, is to lead to new thoughts or to pacify anxieties by introducing some notion that might lead to a feeling of composure. The Aboriginal reality breaks up the composure. This is starkly apparent in the Northern Territory. Organised service infrastructure in extreme conditions of remoteness and climate is hard to sustain. Languages are indigenous and do not obey English thought patterns, therefore much indigenous activity is, shall we say, hidden from comprehension. Health statistics reveal a perplexing story; and social health "outposts" labour under difficulties. One can be guilty of simplicity of view, organising Aboriginal behaviour according to the dictate of a "selected fact". The comfort zone of a "selected fact" appeals, but is a lie. The "selected fact" as a habit, used defensively, is (as I see it)something that happens when a distressed brain tries to settle on the "nipple" of a convenient truth. This "selected fact", this simplification, protects against complexity. However, in the borderland region between contradictory cultural groupings, such as we have in Australia, there is no "single nipple" solution, no comforting breast.

Borderlines

From NT coast to the NT border you would drive south about 1,250 miles through tropical savannah woodlands, then through stretches of flat shimmering plains, dramatic serrated ranges, and the rolling beauties of red sand hills, native flowers—iridescent in good season, gently taking your breath away. Glittering white salt lakes spread into rock formations, and the famous Uluru-Kata Tjuta rises with translucent gravitas. (Uluru is an immense monolith, and Kata Tjuta are the rock domes located west of Uluru. They form part of the traditional belief system of one of the oldest human societies in the world, the Anangu Aboriginal people.) Here and there bare mesa forms might remind you of the Indian Deccan or Arizona/ New Mexico. Central Australia, geologically ancient, once a primordial seabed, retains the vast horizons of a lost ocean.

Halfway down the north-south highway you might come over a ridge and pass into Alice Springs. You might feel, perhaps, that it's a cowboy kind of town, Stetsons and boots, the favoured image of weathered Aboriginal men. You might note gleaming utility trucks, the joy of young white tradesmen. In the streets, battered vehicles cruise, stoic Aboriginal families gazing ahead, avoiding eye contact, wide-brimmed cattlemen, dogs, bedrolls, and equipment lashed into mud-spattered four-wheel drive Toyota tray backs. By nightfall you might mutter about violence and drunkenness.

In regions such as this, where seriously different cultural groups meet, some people acquire skill of a special kind which native Australians refer to as "two-way thinking," meaning the bi-partisan skill of making and managing connections across and along cultural borders. The brain systems of such people probably become marvellously fluid, adept at crossing mentalities, negotiating borders in areas of human crossings which Peter Bishop in Chapter One of this volume refers to as "contact zones". Rene Devisch, whose anthropological work spans decades in African Congo regions, uses the term "border linking" to point to this special two-way skill. Jerome Bernstein, in Santa Fe, New Mexico, writes of "borderland personalities"—persons whose toughened character is forged while negotiating survival between divided cultures.[12] Given that most of the world is going the way of breakdown between accustomed racial/ linguistic groups and that many traditional cultures now intersect and are in transition, it might be worth our while to develop such connective capacities.

It is, I believe, embroilment in this double world or double vision that T.E. Lawrence (Lawrence of Arabia) refers to in passages that glow with heat in his *Seven Pillars of Wisdom*, the 1926 memoir of Middle Eastern affairs during WWI. Lawrence, as a British military officer and intelligence agent, identified himself with Arab guerrillas to serve the British cause. He became embedded. He went "native" and gave himself over so completely that he became possessed by the Arab way of life.

Lawrence:

> A man who gives himself to be a possession of aliens leads a yahoo life ["yahoo" meaning "rough, course, uncouth"], having bartered his soul to a brute master. He is not of them. He may stand against them, persuade himself of a mission, batter and twist them into something that they, of their own accord, would not have been. Then he is exploiting his old environment to press them out of theirs. Or, after my model, he may imitate them so well that they spuriously imitate him back again. Then he is giving away his own environment; pretending to theirs; and pretences are hollow, worthless things.
>
> In my case, the efforts for these years to live in the dress of Arabs, and to imitate their mental foundations quitted me of my English self, and let me look at the west and its conventions with new eyes; they destroyed it all for me. At the same time I could not sincerely take on the Arab skin... I had dropped one form and not taken on the other... with a resultant feeling of intense loneliness in life, and a contempt, not for other men but for all they do...Sometimes these selves would converse in the void; and then madness was very near, as I believe it would be near the man who could see things through the veils at once of two customs, two educations, two environments.[13]

Part Two. Three Conversations
June

The visitor who I am expecting is one of these "border-linking" people. A diminutive, sparkling man of Irish descent, Paul Quinlivan has a distinctively independent mind and manner. His independence aggravates some, charms others, and bewilders those who prefer selected facts and one-dimensional solutions. It is because Paul aggravates in an intelligent and informed way that I invite him to take coffee under the lemon tree to propose that he write an article for this book. He may be someone who can speak the double mind of the difficult country—that hybrid, multi-cultured place that we are becoming.

Figure 2: "... to take coffee".

Paul Quinlivan incarnates paradoxical tensions and intensities. I think of him and the Aboriginal men drinking out there over the back fence. I think of us all as if caught in a kind of psychic plague, yet I experience Paul as one who has the potential to help articulate this condition. The men over the fence shout and sing and drink and fight, and I know sometimes they utter phrases with insight and humour, but I also know that this psychic virus does peculiar things to thinking, to comprehension, to speech. I want to think with honesty, yet cannot. I admit to disturbances in thinking, confusions in feeling.

From 1986 Paul and his family worked in remote area Aboriginal services. I came to know him in many such situations through my own engagement in remote area mental health and Aboriginal affairs.[14] In June 2009 I ran into him again, by chance, in Alice Springs. We sat by the dry, sandy Todd River and he recounted with a kind of stoic disappointment, recent events that had interrupted his work as manager of a remote bush health clinic at a place further north (which I refer to as Sandover). I listened to the layers of events within the Aboriginal health services wherein he had become embroiled and within which he had been, perhaps, professionally assaulted. People such as Paul Quinlivan become acculturated to disappointing conditions in Aboriginal communities. They get to know the place from the inside, are inured to the contradictions, and develop a battle- scarred equilibrium; but, sometimes some things are a bit too much.

In indigenous terrain, it is hard to find individuals who are courageous and thoughtful enough to speak the mind of that secluded part of the country. Some can and do speak, perhaps, but few of the general population take it in; they are not the voices which are attended to—and in fact such voices may be deliberately ignored. Excised from the record. For this reason, after the riverside confessions, I invited Paul to visit, and over the delicate Greek coffee cup, amid the reassuring lemon and mandarin trees, I explained the intent of this book and the idea of the cultural complex developed from Freud and Jung's notions of the personal unconscious complex. Paul was instantly and enthusiastically caught by the idea of enculturated illusions, culture specific trauma systems, and the notion of unconscious complexes multiplied or transposed to collective and inter-racial situations. He had a "first causes" question: "Suppose there is something going on around here which you can call a 'cultural complex'— tell me how a complex is made? How is it put together? What is the first cause of a cultural complex?".

"It might take a while to come around to answering that", I said. I picked up a pencil and drew a few things. "OK, try this. Something bad happens to a mob of people. It might be eruption, flood, freeze, or repeated famine. More likely, however, the bad thing is an invasion, some ravage of humanity, or when a country erupts inside out destroying some of its own peoples. The main thing is a lot of people, bound together, unexpectedly suffer together. First cause—maybe—a shared catastrophe, collective trauma?".[15]

"This group, a tribe, a nation, perhaps, find some explanation for what has happened. The explanatory story may be factual or magical, shot with illusion or delusionary explanations. Maybe something never makes sense about what happened. It may be too hard to comprehend and becomes, let's say, stuck in the craw of the group. Maybe tribal revenge cycles begin or an idea of sacrificing someone to a god creature; but a collective feeling goes on repeating as though the real detailed cause cannot be found or explained adequately. Maybe slowly a collective response, a collective story gets built around the experience of the primal traumatic events. "The primary event," I said, drawing it on the table, "could be represented as the core and first cause of the collective group complex". And I drew a serpentine knotted, nuclear kernel of repetitive energies, wrapped into a kind of hard shell, a tumour of grief turning in upon itself yet also spreading like a contamination. Paul added, "Grievous events might be recalled in ceremonies of mourning, in lamentations".[16] I pick up the point, "It may be that the traumatic experience is built into culture in the way the Jewish people have done. This way the story and an explanation are repeated. It might become a cultural myth... anyway, people suffer and that feeling becomes woven into a group memory system. It may be a jagged, broken memory system. I think ceremonies, mourning songs, and folk laments might link to a cultural complex, or express some of it, but the cultural complex thing is too hard to see—to say—it keeps being acted out, repeating...".

I probably stopped here, I forget what we said. I remember looking out over the back fence, into the rubbish of plastic and beer cartons around the Aboriginal camps in the saltbush; it is always so close, this jagged broken fact. And I might have said, "Paul, do these men sing laments about our condition?". And I might have said, "Paul, you might call this place where we live an enculturated trauma system. Is it a complex yet? I don't know. The whole picture is not seen properly." And I scribbled a kind of cloud of obscurity or maybe a silence around the knot.

In the bright sun, his eyes flickering left and right, Paul spoke rapidly, "The dangerous thing is when individual illusions build up a critical mass and become shared by so many people that the illusions become understood as true. To paraphrase the old man Jung himself, 'the astonishing assumptions and fantasies that white or non indigenous people make about black people produce an inexhaustible supply of illogical arguments and false explanations'.[17] Such unquestioned illusions would keep a complex going". And it was here that he took up the contentious ideas in *The Politics of Suffering*.[18] This book, a modern lamentation of sorts by Peter Sutton, was then being reviewed in the national press. Paul had the review with him.

Sutton, a seasoned linguist and anthropologist based in Adelaide, was then under fire, hazarding career and reputation by challenging notions of Aboriginal rights, justice, dysfunction, and "solutionising", vociferously maintained, on one side, by "progressive romantics" and, on the other side, by "carping neo-conservatives"—to use phrases from indigenous Professor Marcia Langton, in her Foreword to *The Politics of Suffering*.

Sutton's personalised "confessions" of a life spent in indigenous affairs laid bare enculturated illusions which, in Quinlivan's view, demonstrated a complex in the way strong ideas grip mind and action, intensely, unconsciously. Paul showed that he had grasped the guts of the idea of a cultural complex by bringing Sutton into the conversation. Sutton had found words to say what people in the contact zone saw, but could not see. Felt, but could not speak. To cut a long story short—from around 1967 those white people who sided with the Aboriginal cause were mostly branded as leftist/ human rights activists while those reluctant to do so were considered "rightist" conservatives. This is simplistic political party dualism. Social activist professionals, like Sutton, immersed themselves in the turbulence of Aboriginal affairs supporting the policy of "self determination". Over three decades a clash of ideas and desires shaped interest groups, agencies, private projects, and the economy of remote areas of Australia. Generous individuals spent years working through Western civilisational notions of compassion, cultural self-determination, economic development, and fellowship with indigenous Australians. Sutton is one of those—but when in his book, he "crossed the floor" (politically speaking), he begged for a clear look at what had become of the well intentioned policies. "Let's look", he said, "at what is actually going on in Aboriginal Australia." As a consequence, "leftist idealist" supporters, in dismay, vilified Sutton as a "traitor" and the "right" welcomed him as a convert. In fact, he did not have his tail between his legs, but was displaying a courageous self-assessment equivalent to the boy in the story of the Emperor's New Clothes.

Sutton's self critique, however, found favour with people like Quinlivan and indigenous lawyer, Noel Pearson, who, as veterans, knew the many sides of the problem of race relations, indigenous behaviours, and saw with a depth of field.[19] Sutton pricked the bubble of an enculturated illusion or maybe a politicised complex, and Quinlivan deferred to him because Sutton had the courage to call those involved to account. Sutton offered an audit of pervasive contemporary governing illusions and at the same time made a simple human plea for restoring feeling, ordinary relationships between persons of whatever racial identification. He writes,

> The worst aspects of "community dysfunction", as it is styled, occur in the emotional, psychological and bodily relationships between people and between people and their damaged selves. That is why this approach for which I am arguing here has to be an individual's story about 'feeling'—to borrow Big Bill Neidjie's words—before it is a story about the political morals of governance.... I also believe that considerations of care should be put before considerations of strict justice, as a matter of principle... The political glamour attracted but those who struggle for rights and justice have long outshone the small glow emitted by those who are in the coalface caring business, the ones who dress the wounds of battered women in remote area clinics at three o'clock on Sunday mornings, or who work to get

petrol sniffers back on track out in the Tanami Desert in the ferocious heat of February...[20]

At our table, spreading out the newspaper review, Quinlivan went on developing the idea that no cultural group is immune from self-interest and self-made illusions. The Aboriginal "mob" carry illusions, some which now ignore the reality of present life in the bush, as do we, the white people. Somewhere here we must have had another coffee and I brought him baklava. Good Greek coffee is hard to come by in Alice Springs; and, if you want fresh baklava, some one has to bring it from the Greek café in Coober Pedy, an opal-mining town six hours south.

Refreshed, Paul tried something complicated on me. This is the gist of it: Humans need to "make understanding", this is what we do. They call us *Homo sapiens* (knowing man) because we manufacture tools, but we also manufacture "understanding". Paul suggested that it mightn't matter to some of us what the "truth" is, so long as we have the comfort of an understanding. A satisfactory understanding is like a child's security blanket or the comfort of having a tool kit in the truck if you break down. He was suggesting that the *Homo sapiens* band that originally inhabited Australia had invented an understanding, a knowledge system that got everyone along fine for thousands of years or so. Meanwhile, we, the white people, were also inventing systems of understanding, and the tools and guns that got us where we are today. These two groups of *homo sapiens* meet from different directions of evolution or civilisation, and it dawns that our systems of understanding are very different. We are living now in a kind of long, uncomfortable silence. "The incoming understandings ... how do they meet?". He paused, smiling a little sadly, "This year in the clinic, I didn't fit the incoming understanding". At Paul's bush clinic something happened to him and someone gave up working at civilisation. Civilisation broke down and Paul ended up leaving the clinic. Things like that happen to many people, black and white, who work under the intense stress of such places. It is a specific local condition, almost unrecognised, almost undiagnosed. Attending to Paul's story, I was beginning to think that such events are truly symptoms of a cultural complex, though, for the life of me, I could not yet describe or justify that idea.

Quinlivan began to speak sensitively about Jung's *Marriage as a Psychological Relationship*, focussing especially on Jung's idea of male and female elements in oneself and the psychosexual struggle between men and women. I mentioned Jung's contemplations on alchemy and the management of transference in relations as a venture in spiritually civilising oneself. Paul outlined how he'd been struggling with perplexing tensions in specific relationships and wondered if Jung's ideas on the politics of transference were a way of explaining the sufferings, not only between men and women but also between black and white people. He picked up Robert Wright's idea, "if self-interested entities are to realise mutual profit two problems typically must be solved: communication and trust." This idea begged for development, and I asked him to write on it, wondering how he might describe a situation if an unconscious complex were instantly activated in the heat between himself and another person—male or female, black or white. I referred to a specific person we both knew well. "What would it look like?" I said, "if you described a situation—a scenario where both she and you were simultaneously in the grip of a cultural complex—as you have been for years in Aboriginal affairs?". The challenge to do a micro-analysis of a living situation caught Paul's interest. We played with the idea that the cultural complex isn't something happening up there at big picture levels of the government desk. The tensions and the transferences here in this town or in remote communities are between individuals where trust and communication is intimate. However, tension at the government level also brings about breakdown among all of us—in our families and personal relationships. This is the theme we agreed had to be developed. Interventions of departmental policy, often hastily thought through, and the penetration of professionals into the daily details of Aboriginal life is intervention into the intimacies of the personal lives of all of us. Overweening entitlement in the politics of black/white relations seems to indicate incompetence in communication and trust—or clumsy management of the alchemic art of relationship.

Quinlivan later sent this email, containing the Robert Wright quote, contexted.

> ... Further to our *orange grove* discussion vis-a-vis the blackfella/whitefella culture complex I have been reading a book titled *Nonzero* by Robert Wright. The book includes in its preface a quote by Charles Darwin, i.e., "as man advances in civilisation, and small tribes are united into larger communities, the simplest reason would tell each individual that he ought to extend his social instincts and sympathies to all the members of the same nation, though personally unknown to him. This point being once reached, there is only an artificial barrier to prevent his sympathies extending to the men of all nations and races." Wright later refers to the philosopher Emile Durkheim: *"In the last analysis men have never worshipped anything other than their own society."* [Paul's emphasis] And to this comment Robert Wright adds: "Still if worshipping your own society finally, in a

global age, involves not denigrating other peoples but, rather, recognising the moral worth of human beings everywhere, then there is something to be said for worshipping your own society." Wright later concludes, "If self-interested entities are to realise mutual profit two problems typically must be solved: communication and trust."[21]

In that first conversation Quinlivan was revealing his deep concern with the question of "what makes a human being civilised". Most especially, he meant *the civilisation of relationships*. He was interested in "Civilisation" as grand humanising enterprises—yes—but most particularly, he was interested in the civilisation of the conduct of relationship between persons. The idea now suggests itself to me that civilisation is the way we train ourselves to take in more and more complicated events, to take in understandings other than our own. Those two pragmatic virtues—the effort at communication and the effort at trust—are key to something essential in how "border linking" people conduct business. They take things in from both sides of "the border"—they link, communicate, and negotiate trusts. At Paul's bush clinic something happened to him and someone gave up working at civilisation. Civilisation in a small place broke down.

The Road

Twenty years ago, before he took on the clinic, Paul and his wife helped establish a small desert Aboriginal community, a settlement of several sheds, houses, a store, and not much else, except beautiful country and red flowing sand hills. Lyrripi (as I will name it for this account) was to be a service base for some of the previously nomadic family groups whose way of life had only recently (in the 1970s) met with the active presence of the white people coming in trucks and helicopters. In so far as this community effort was a success, Paul said, it was because he insisted on developing the art of communication between himself and the Pintubi/Warlpiri-speaking characters with whom he became involved. Communication and trust as a developing fact—not merely as an aspirational idealisation. On occasions it seems Paul succeeded, and there is evidence for this.

The Lyrripi settlement is set in the midst of intricate traditional memories and cultural narrative sites. I first heard of the place in March 1991 through "bad news". An Aboriginal family group of perhaps eleven people were travelling on a back road in an ordinary motorcar, overloaded and without sufficient water. They broke down. There is a fellowship of wayfarers in those desert regions, and sometimes one can rely on it, but on this occasion no other vehicles came by and most of the family perished. The party included several children and a pregnant mother. Her infant, born at the breakdown, survived. The driver, well known and respected as an Aboriginal community policeman, died. His young son survived by being buried in sand to prevent dehydration. Now a young man, the son's occupation today is to help prevent youth suicide. His story, if told, might reveal the system of cultural complexities in which he, as an Aboriginal young man, nowadays, is held. It is not easy. There were enculturated factors (illusions?) which led to his father being unable to refuse the overload of the vehicle. And there are human factors regarding why they travelled with insufficient water on that remote desert road. Paul Quinlivan was involved in the aftermath of this iconic tragedy. It is a familiar story of break-down and the geometric progression of consequences. The boy, who survived by being buried in sand, is now endowed with the bi-cultural systems; as a young man, he must link and survive in both. This dissonance he has to manage in his own way, just as his father, a policeman managed, in his way, both indigenous law procedures and Western judiciary methods.

I worry about mentioning these sad events—but also worry that unmentioned events, the silence about the truth of indigenous conditions, is part of the complex itself, adding to the repetitions of misunderstanding. On occasions Paul has, with discretion, recounted similar events, events engrained with the peculiar errors and tempting of fate that occur consistently on the roads of this region. Strange liminal states exist here; haunted always by a kind of mourning which is hard to bear. The Aboriginal desert is a region of beauty and a region of lament.

Some days after that first meeting, Quinlivan sent another of his email letters. An extract reads:

> Gandhi is attributed with having made two rather famous comments about civilisation. "A question from a newspaper correspondent in the 1930s drew from Mahatma Gandhi one of his pithiest responses. Asked, during his visit to Britain, what he thought of Western civilisation, he replied: "'It would be a very good idea.'"
>
> This quote feeds into the more profound insight into the notion of civilization, namely that, "Civilisation is the encouragement of differences. Civilisation thus becomes a synonym of democracy. Force, violence, pressure, or compulsion with a view to conformity, is both uncivilised and undemocratic."

Paul added: "By comparison one could fairly argue that hunter-gatherer societies are based on the notion of active discouragement of difference or at least *an encouragement of reciprocity.*"

As I re-read that sentence I think that it might simply come down to this: failings in reciprocity disturb and bewilder any civilised human. The Aboriginal contact zone is a place where mutual reciprocity as a value of civilisation is upheld mutually or destroyed mutually. By such acts both our civilisations are held to account.

July
The Clinic

Through July to September, Quinlivan came to talk two more times. On his second visit, because I know it will please him, I have placed again the two Greek coffee cups on the table beneath the lemon tree. There are ripening mandarins beside us. Offering him one, I joke about the baleful influence of government mandarins on his career.

The yard, glittering in reflection on his black-rimmed, rounded spectacles, his mind effervescent, coffee taken slowly; on the table, old diagrams describing the cultural complex. Today I will ask him to definitively agree to write for this book, but I probe a little to see where his thoughts are going.

"What are you reading, Paul? What's on your mind?"

"*The Birth of the Clinic....*" He paused, almost sheepishly, "The philosopher, Michel Foucault; he helps me see what I was dealing with in the clinic. I am trying to look at what happened there without forcing conclusions. I like Foucault's titles—*Madness and Civilisation, Discipline and Punish*... I'm thinking about the death of the clinic".

Because Paul was managing a Western medicine clinic in Aboriginal lands, the history of medicine, or rather the history of how doctors perceive patients, disease, and cure, would be on his mind; this is Foucault's theme, an historical exploration of the invention of "The Hospital", "The Clinic", "The Asylum", and the development of clinical perception in Western medicine.[22] We built clinics in Aboriginal regions, serving the small communities of people who were collected together in settlements. We brought with us a way of perceiving illness, its treatment, and the conduct of cure. We brought with us a way of managing the conduct of doctors and nurses. We brought this naturally enough, as a part of our Western way of life, to deal with the diseases which came with us.

"Paul", I say, "this is the deal: I want to ask you to write an article on madness in local civilisation. The case of the clinic where you worked is a history that might reveal something of the workings of a complex. If Foucault can write the big story of European medicine and the invention of the clinic, you can write the small story of the meeting of that clinic with the Aboriginal world".

Sandover clinic (as I call it here), under Paul's management, consistently attracted good staff and (it seems) attained satisfying outcomes for the patients. In this sense, as some medical staff confirm, it was exemplary. Why then, I ask, was Paul removed from his position there? How was the case for his dismissal built? By whom? And with what intention? What did Quinlivan represent to whomever had the power to "discipline and punish"? This is the story to write, for this story, like so many obscured or forgotten events in our region, carries within it the virus of the complex. The cultural complex is not a grand narrative thing. It is there, erupting in the small details of intimacies between a nurse and patient, between Boards of Management and Aboriginal Health workers, between men and women on the job—black, white, and hybrid. "I do not want to blame anyone", said Paul. "I don't want to drag in people who I have known and loved for years". And this response is correct. The fabric of inter-dependence is delicate. If Paul publically declared what he observed, the consequences for him would be more ostracism. This is how the complex continues—by the code of the scapegoat.

"Then write about civilisation", I said. "Write about what it takes to run a health service on remote Aboriginal lands in a civilised manner. Do what Foucault says. Gaze at the matter. Observe it. Don't give me idealisations. Break the cocoon around the perceptions". Saying this to Paul was a risk; he is good at being elusive, a moving target. "And you", he responded, "what are you reading?". I told him I was reading *The Handbook of Diagnosis and Treatment of Personality Disorders*. "There are ten listed disorders of the singular personality", I said, "but I believe that disorder in the singular personality, in our part of the world, is a reflection of the cultural disordering, as John Donne whispered: 'No man is an island—separate from the whole'; the individual is a feedback system. I think we can detect or diagnose by investigating completely what has happened to the body of one man or one woman injured in our local town. It is a forensic investigation. I do not know how to do this. But I think we begin in a simple way with oneself by observing one single embodied feeling or event almost as though it were a bit of a dream awaiting interpretation or amplification".[23] After a while, settling to the task, I say, "Begin with a scene from a time at the clinic. It can be an incident, a memory, a dream fragment. We can begin with any event. Look at it carefully, calmly; find an emotion, a primal feeling, an image. Something when you are with one of the patients maybe—will give you raw material". In response to my suggestion, Paul related the incident below and we talked about it. I share it as remembered in retrospect, condensed a bit to indicate the approach.

The Airfield

The memory I have of Paul's account and my response is this: Paul said, "On the airfield. I am restless. I go out on the airfield with the doctor, late at night. An emergency evacuation. We wait on the bare strip with beacon lights set for the flying doctor plane; the line of lights on the field, a landing. I know I'm between things. Sometimes at the clinic I get the feeling of what we are caught in. Awaiting something…I could find the words, but which language could best describe this waiting?". [He meant what language, English or the indigenous language.] "I don't know Alyawarre well enough, and I think (in Pintupi language) of *Kulya kanyinu*". [This term means[24]—watching, waiting for something, waiting for a change in the situation, waiting for something to cook; a hunter waiting until an animal is unaware of the danger; holding the moving animal in his rifle sights. Pintupi is a hunter's language and *Kanyinu* is also a euphemism for sexual intercourse, for physical connection.] Paul continued, following the embodied imagination. "In my body I feel the tension—the aim, the rifle, the touch, waiting for something between us to cook".

The Pintubi language is primal in its imagery and subtle in its meaning. Paul's voice continues, "The plane comes, the waiting is over. Everyone plays their part. Western civilisation at its best. The patient is lifted into the plane. She is a woman who is a lynch pin of traditional knowledge in this part of the country; three hundred extended family members are connected with her and her place. Her life is precious. She looks tonight like a bundle of rags. I do not know if she will ever return. I should go back to the clinic and write a report, but I cannot put down the words: paralysis. I do not know what I am waiting for. To be a mother is such a natural thing, you would wait on the airfield all night if a child were to go on that plane. We are forgetting how to be mothers to each other…".

In my mind, I hear Paul say such things. Beginning at a point like that on the airfield as though it were a moment on the royal road to a small unconscious truth.

September
Medusa's gaze

At the end of winter, under the tree, empty now of lemons, Paul returns, and I tell a parable of a man who sits alone in a room of mirrors believing his own thoughts run the business of the world, eternally. Paul unpeels his interpretation of this story as though it were a fruit. He relates an incident from his own life. He comes to a seed moment, describing an event over which he had no power (though God knows he tried). He recalled a death where he could not turn aside the inevitable, where he learned the humility of mortality.

I feel now that, as a clinic manager with some delegated power, Paul was determined to intercept unnecessary listless death, such a constant companion to indigenous life. It was perhaps for this reason that he insisted good doctors come to the bush clinic and made it possible, giving them courage to stay in such isolated under-resourced locations. It was for this reason, I believe, that he sat up at night on the airfield with a patient who might have died of despair and loneliness, and why he insisted himself on driving patients 200 miles into the hospital on rough roads, rather than leave them to neglect and apathy, missing essential appointments.

Paul Quinlivan was not a man sitting in a room alone imagining he was governing the world. He became engaged in humility; but something adversarial, or stubborn—not strategic—about the positions he took got him into trouble on occasion. A gap in his logic somewhere? Vulnerability? I want to ask him, or the clinic doctors, about the gap. I can see that Paul was thinking carefully about what was eating the heart of indigenous patients. I am imagining him there, on the airstrip, or on the road to the hospital, reflecting upon such things; the patient perhaps, a mother who knew significant songs of her country and all the family network relations and who, Paul knew, by dying prematurely would take with her links and the fabric of threads that hold vital Aboriginal relationships in place. These—the unseen—the unrecognised gravity of the country.

It is an inconsolable loss to see the fabric of a society coming apart. The British, my people, are inured to the ruthlessness of invasion, having practised it well. We know not what we do. This is an inconvenient truth that I do not know how to handle.

Our third meeting was a bit frayed. Paul had significant family matters on his mind; he was, maybe, restless; though he consistently kept sending emails, extracts. This had been a quick trip to Alice and he was going back to be with his daughter in the east. However, I felt encouraged that an intricate filigree of situations was building, that the Quinlivan chapter was on the way, and that Paul was beginning to get his aim. In my own essay, I was preoccupied with the idea of how to detect a cultural complex when embedded in it, when asleep in it myself. Intrigued by the peculiar confusion of perception which grips the mind when under the influence of a complex, I kept thinking about the mythological Medusa gaze—where eyes cross and the brain turns to stone. The paralysed sensation is, I feel, a symptom or sign of an active complex. Medusa is the "patron saint" of the complex. Peter Sutton's book, *The Politics of Suffering*, looked the black/white Medusa in the eye. I expected Paul Quinlivan to do the same.

Part Three
A Turbulent Sea

A few weeks after our third meeting, in early October 2009, a rumour passed through town that "a Paul Quinlivan" had died. This was impossible to believe. We learned that the rumour was true. It fell to me to contribute to his obituary in the *Alice Springs News, Nov. 12, 2009*:

> *Paul Quinlivan was lost in exceptional circumstances in turbulent seas on Saturday October 10, 2009 at Bateman's Bay on the coast of south eastern Australia. In a manner characteristic of Quinlivan, his final act was a calculated effort to rescue a human being in difficult conditions. Police reports indicate that while making the rescue, Quinlivan, a fit and astute man, was nevertheless swept from the rocks at a place where the current divides, one rip sweeping eventually to the beach, another dropping down deep through submerged rock shelves. It is assumed that Paul was intending to let the current carry the two men through the 4-5 metre swell. His last gesture was to wave reassuringly to his daughter, standing on the rocks. He suddenly disappeared. Quinlivan's body was not recovered until a month later, on the fifth of November. The search crews have been commended. Quinlivan is recommended by Police for a bravery award. The Minister for Central Australia, Karl Hampton, honored him in Parliamentary proceedings. Paul's pragmatic, intuitive, un-illusioned management of indigenous community operations made him into an experienced, unique observer and pro-active participant in local affairs. His singular position also earned him criticism, excision. The character of central Australia is marked as a region of turbulent currents; human folly, strong opinions; straining sometimes for reconciliation. He made 'Reconciliation' an interpersonal task, grounded in relationships, not political ideals—Paul was not a politician. He is best thought of as a wild (natural) philosopher. Those familiar with the figure of Socrates may appreciate*

that Quinlivan's method was similar. Socrates' ability to irritate those who would not think a thing through may have earned him his trial—Socrates was put to death on the basis of allegations that he was undermining the governance of Athens. He did not defend himself in the expected way, using his own death, in such a manner, as an opportunity to highlight ethical dilemmas facing his accusers. Central Australia has lost an exceptional man, taken in the midst of an ethical action—saving a life...[25]

Figure 3: Paul Quinlivan with small boy. Photo courtesy of Fiona Walsh, 2007.

"Let no man's heart fail..."
David to Saul, Samuel 17.32

There are places that haunt the mind; strange towns blinded like an Oedipus after catastrophe; strange sites of human settlement, city-states, valley plains, rivers of dire conjunction. There are towns where quiet things happen that somehow sew together evidence of enculturated crime, crimes which, though seen, remain unheard. Such places are settings for dramas, which reveal human complexities. Such uniquely placed settlements personalise the psychic pain of a people enmeshed in psychic virus. In this arid, isolated, multi-racial town of Alice Springs, inhabitants mutter into the night around the BBQ or the bottle-strewn campfire. Themes perennial, repetitive; people ask, as though dreaming, how to survive in this town, fertile and productive as it is, where truth takes deformed shape: a town of peculiar couplings, excessive passion, incest, perverse violence, intensities of grief, failure.

There are special forms of music that speak to the borderline, voices which evoke the weight and intensity of that location. In central Australia, "Country Music" carries the affirmation and the lament. As the opener for the eulogy session on the local radio station, they played for Quinlivan the Willie Nelson/Dylan song, "He Was a Friend of Mine". It spoke for the emptiness after Paul was carried away.

> He was a friend of mine/ Every time I think of him/ I just can't keep from cryin'/'Cause he was a friend of mine. He died on the road/ He died on the road/ He just kept on moving/ Never reaped what he could sow/ and he was a friend of mine.

It was the line, "never reaped what he could sow" which gave me instructions for this chapter and explains why, in the story of Paul, I set about trying to reap some of the seed ideas he had sown.

Even an obscure and small place like the Sandover Clinic is a living site of the Australian cultural complex. It bespeaks the whole. Paul Quinlivan placed racial relationships within a context of hope for civilisation—that is to say—the civilisation of relationships. He was able to identify, as an insider, consistent failures in communication and trust between individuals and within institutional systems employing people to manage Aboriginal affairs. In his view, repetitive breakdowns in reciprocal trust and communication revealed the existence of an embedded, institutionalised, unconsciously operating complex. Like a turbulent sea current, this inner force is too big for any of us to navigate, even if we know it is there.

In our three conversations Paul made a start at honesty and he helped to clear my own mind. He reflected on his own and Aboriginal family constellations and his own behaviour. He was especially attentive to reciprocal relational environments within settlements and in the clinic. Paul recognised that his relational style as a manager had significant influence on what happened or failed to happen, day by day in an Aboriginal community. Very little acknowledgement has been made of the value of relational competencies. The relational competency of managers (whether black or white) directly affects the functional wellbeing of all persons in community and in all services. Reciprocity is the clue; reciprocity without idealisation, reciprocity stripped of magical thinking. Indigenous people are attuned to reciprocity in a very culturally defined way and we, the white people, are attuned to a different form of reciprocity. Paul, like some others, probably learned the skill of how to use the repertoire of reciprocity as a quality of civilised behaviour.

The foci of Paul Quinlivan's work was the care of settlements, livelihood, and health in a region of unemployment, depleted food stores, physical ill health, and fading cultural vitality. He, like some others, had a grasp of the history of Aboriginal lands and so had few grandiose messianic expectations, this being a cultural delusion especially favoured within Christian-based governments. It is my understanding that Paul Quinlivan's own view was that a process of mutual civilisation had, for a few generations, been an underlying intent in many Aboriginal/non-Aboriginal

Figure 4: Mandarin and lemon on a table.

interchanges. There is wry humour in this idea, since many good white people might still consider it their God-given task to civilise the "other"; and, many Aboriginal people might be perplexed over how hard it is to civilise white people into the values of an indigenous way of life. If civilisation of relationships is a goal, then the management of communication and trust becomes a personal matter at a micro level. Attaining civilisation is a matter of gravity and balance between persons at a micro level.

I believe now that Paul Quinlivan carried in himself a weight of tensions which are characteristic of the Australian inter-racial cultural complex. In this sense his story is representative. He is a representative of the tensions. He was more conscious than many of us as to what those tensions were, but he did not live long enough to elucidate what he knew or felt to be taking place. His story could resonate with that of any one of a thousand valiant men and women who, in the quietness of our country, face impossible situations. I do not refer to the impossible situations of drought, flood, and fire—these we can meet—but rather the impossible situation of creating a human civilisation encompassing the virtues and vices of the oldest continuously existing peoples on earth and at the same time encompassing the vices and virtues of we, the peoples from the north.

It is true that the lemon tree in the back yard did not survive, but the remaining mandarin and citrus flourish in the recent rains. We have planted two figs. The native mulga thrives and the coolibah trees on the clay pans continue to wave their branchlike arms. This is a fertility site—perhaps it will outlive the present confusion.

Notes

[1] See Wenten Rubuntja, Jenny Green, Tim Rowse, *et al.*, *The Town Grew Up Dancing: The Life and Art of Wenten Rubuntja* (Alice Springs, NT, Australia: IAD Press, 2001), p. 1.

[2] See the works of Melbourne-based immigrant storyteller, Arnold Zable; for example, *Café Scheherazade.*

[3] Jampijimpa Smithy Zimran, quoted at p. 11 of the 2006 report, Western Desert Nganampa Walytja Palyantjaku Tjutaku Aboriginal Corporation, www.wdnwpt.org.au. Smithy Zimran is also referred to by Alexis Wright in her chapter in this volume.

[4] My phrase is suggested by "I feel it now; there is a power in me to grasp and give shape to...my world... all becoming has needed me. My looking ripens things and they come toward me, to meet and be met." Rainer Maria Rilke, *Book of Hours* (New York: Riverhead Penguin, 2005), p. 43.

[5] See the works of W.E.H. Stanner, T.E. Strehlow, Daisy Bates, and Olive Pink, who are among the foundational Australian anthropologists.

[6] The dynamic matter of place/psyche, place/land, possession/dispossession as objective fact and in subjective experience is developed by Bishop, Wright, Milton, Dowd, Please, Russell, Tacey, *et al.* in this volume. See also the respective Notes section at the end of each of these chapters.

[7] For updated information about the Land Rights Act, the Central Land Council, and indigenous land issues, see www.clc.org.au and links.

[8] See Jonathon Lear, *Radical Hope: Ethics in the Face of Cultural Devastation* (Cambridge, MA: Harvard University Press, 2006).

[9] Exemplified in the Combined Aboriginal Nations Congress, (CANCA) Kalkaringi 1996-1998, www.artplan.com.au/BNP/BNP07text/04.htm, also referred to by Alexis Wright in this volume. Wright's novel, *Carpentaria* (2007), evokes many sides of indigenous despair, passion, and the country poetic.

[10] See the illuminatory text by Paul Carter, *The Lie of the Land* (London: Faber and Faber, 1996).

[11] Wilfred Bion. See J and N. Symington, *The Clinical Thinking of Wilfred Bion* (London: Routledge, 1996), chap. 2. There are constructive qualities in the use of the selected fact, as intuitive gathering point of impressions into bundles of sense. I have selected the "selective fact" as the idea of destructive selective attention.

[12] On border-linking, see Rene Devisch, Chapt. 5, "A Psychoanalytic Revisiting of Fieldwork and Inter Cultural Borderlinking", in *Explorations in Psychoanalytic Ethnography*, ed. Jadran Mimica (New York: Berghan Books, 2007) (On the matter of cultural complexes I draw particular attention to note 3 in the notes section following Devisch' chapter at p. 145). The pertinent term, "contact zone", is developed with exactitude by Peter Bishop in Chapter One of this volume from a concept of Mary Louise Pratt. An example of local border-linking and a full-blooded contact dynamic is Rod Moss' award-winning autobiography, *The Hard Light of Day by Rod Moss: An Artist's Story of Friendships in Arrernte Country* (Australia: University of Queensland Press, 2010). See also Jerome Bernstein, *Living In The Borderland: The Evolution of Consciousness and the Challenge of Healing Trauma* (London & New York: Routledge, 2005). He develops the stimulating idea of "borderland personalities".

[13] T. E Lawrence (Lawrence of Arabia), *Seven Pillars of Wisdom* (Harmondsworth, UK, 1962), Ch. 1, p. 29.

[14] Craig San Roque, "A Long Weekend in Alice Springs", in *The Cultural Complex: Contemporary Jungian Perspectives on Psyche and Society* Thomas Singer and Samuel Kimbles, eds. (London & New York, 2004).

[15] In conversation with Tom Singer while thinking about causes of cultural complexes, he suggested that all complexes may not originate in trauma. He said, "America has a cultural complex around the idea of perpetual 'progress'—this notion did not originate in trauma, rather it originated in just the opposite—but it has become fixed in the American psyche as a complex of who we are and what we are entitled to".

[16] *The Lamentations of Jeremiah* in the Old Testament, Chapter 1, begins: "How doth the city sit solitary, that was full of people. How is she become as a widow, she that was great among the nations...She weepeth sore in the night and her tears are on her cheeks..." Glenda Cloughley, an analyst and cultural activist based in Canberra, is developing "the lament" in communal therapeutic function through a range of music performance pieces developed from the template of Aeschylus' *Orestia*. See www.chorusofwomen.org.webloc.

[17] A paraphrase of lines in Jung's 1925 paper, *Marriage as a Psychological Relationship*, accessed by Paul Quinlivan through www.haverford.edu/

.webloc. Paul's creative reading of Jung here substitutes "black and white" for "man and woman" and so elides gender opposition with racial tensions, led by Jung's notion of unconscious archetypal dynamics behind the scenes. Paul was substituting *anima/animus* categories with the potential black/white inner image which persons of differing ethnicity might hold about each other, especially when there is a mutual fascination, as "in love" or "in hate," the duality bound in a kind of *anima/animus*—approach/avoidance coitus.

[18] Peter Sutton, *The Politics of Suffering* (Melbourne, Australia: Melbourne University Press, 2009), is also a chronicle of the "contact zone", referencing many who have contributed to the indigenous Australian story as "border linkers". See Sutton's Chapter 7, "Unusual Couples" on Black/White collaborations.

[19] Individual or intensified groupings can become representatives of, or embodiments of cultural complex phenomena: for instance, Charles Perkins, Eddie Mabo, Vincent Lingiari—all Aboriginal men—and W. Stanner, "Nuggett" Coombs, and B. Dexter, as an Anglo cohort working with them. Their conjoint activity contained the groundwork for the Land Rights Act of 1976 and further (incremental) shifts in national narcissism. They also attracted intense denigration. See *An Appreciation of Difference— W.E.H. Stanner and Aboriginal Australia,* Melinda Hinkson and Jeremy Beckett, eds. (Australia: Aboriginal Studies Press, 2008), esp. Chapter 4 by Barrie Dexter, at p. 86. An observation about himself, Coombs, and Stanner at the end of their intense affair lifting the Australian racial game, Dexter describes Stanner staggering, almost fainting with psychic fatigue, on an airfield. Dexter's reflection on their careers reveals that deep immersion in "native affairs" takes a toll, a kind of messianic sacrifice. This may be exemplified also in the career of Henry Reynolds on Black/White history in his books *With The White People* (Australia: Penguin Books, 1990) and *This Whispering in Our Hearts* (Australia: Allen & Unwin, 1998).

[20] Sutton, *Politics of Suffering,* pp. 11-12.

[21] Robert Wright, see information about his book, *NonZero,* via Bloggingheads.tv (Paul Quinlivan's source).

[22] Michel Foucault, *The Birth of the Clinic* (London: Routledge, 2003). See especially chapter 7, "Seeing and Knowing."

[23] For this approach I am indebted to Robert Bosnak's work with Embodied Imagination.

[24] Definition originally from "Kulya Kanyinyu" in Hansen, *Pintubi/Luritja Dictionary*, 3rd Edition (Alice Spring, NT, Australia: IAD Publications, 1992).

[25] A memorial event held at Emily Gap Alice Springs, November 7, coincided with the news that Paul's body was finally recovered from the sea (on November 5th). Eulogies from Pintubi families, the Federal Member of Parliament for the NT, and seasoned bush and medical workers confirmed the esteem in which this unique individual was held. It was at that point that I recognised that a Quinlivan contribution to this book had to be written, even if by myself. Hence the Lemon Tree conversations I had with Paul became a way of doing so; for help in this delicate task I am particularly indebted to David Moore, Sarita Quinlivan, and family, Fiona Walsh, Glynnis Johns, Christine Godden, and Papunya Tula Artists, Alice Springs, www.papunyatula.com.au/.webloc, and Professor Gill Straker's address on South African apartheid experience, "Thinking Under Fire: Psychoanalytic Reflection on Cognition in the War Zone" (Free Association Conference, 1994).

The conversations between Paul Quinlivan and me are not verbatim but are true to content, email exchanges, and spirit. Some names, places, and incidents have been obscured to protect privacy. The author apologises in advance for any unintentional offense against courtesy and relationship.

Terrie Waddell, Ph.D., is Australian born and a senior lecturer in Media and Cinema Studies at La Trobe University (Victoria, Australia). She has taught and written widely on contemporary media, gender, and mythical approaches to screen texts. Previous publications include: *Wild/lives–Trickster, Place and Liminality on Screen*; *Mis/takes–Archetype, Myth and Identity in Screen Fiction*; *Lounge Critic–The Couch Theorist's Companion*; and *Cultural Expressions of Evil and Wickedness–Wrath, Sex, Crime*.

●●●●●●●●●●●●

Cinema amplifies our most haunting collective complexes, and in this paper Terrie Waddell argues that the concept of "girlshine", one of the frequently recurring obsessions in contemporary Australian film, is one of them. Waddell sees this archetypal eruption, largely imagined as girl-women in their liminal years (16-21), to be a development of the lost child complex that feeds on our collective trauma of post-colonial alienation, separation anxiety (from the European womb), and geographical vulnerability. In contrast to the lost child, the girlshine complex implies a sense of everlasting potential: of being held in a suspended state of "becoming"—unable to "become". The figure embodying this stage of development emerges as a suggestion of adulthood. She seldom grows up. In the bigger, more symbolic picture, though, the girlshine figure addresses Australia's attempt to guide itself from one stage of development to another—from lost, to an awareness of future promise.

Films concentrating on girlshine are often set against the Australian bush/outback, among the most ancient and untouched of environments, and are popularly thought of as "she". The landscape seems to protectively watch over this figure/complex, as if she might one day emerge from the liminal and come to assume maturity. Terrie Waddell explores these ideas through three representative examples from contemporary Australian cinema: Picnic at Hanging Rock (Peter Weir, 1975), The Year My Voice Broke (John Duigan, 1987), and Beautiful Kate (Rachel Ward, 2009). The textual analysis of each film foregrounds the gender divisiveness, obsessive fixation with, and cultural resistance to transcend the girlshine complex.

3

The Rapture of "Girlshine": Land, Sacrifice, and Disavowal in Australian Cinema

Terrie Waddell

> Can anyone deny that we are haunted? What is it that crouches under the myths we have made? Always the physical presence of something split off.
>
> Jeanette Winterson, *Gut Symmetries*[1]

On our school excursion to Hanging Rock in Victoria's Mount Macedon, my friends and I tried to emulate Miranda, the missing Edwardian virgin in Peter Weir's (then) just released *Picnic at Hanging Rock* (1975). In our thigh-high 1970s summer uniforms, a far cry from the film's ankle length linen dresses and tight-laced corsetry, we wandered around the volcanic monoliths where she disappeared, calling out lines from the film—"Miranda! Miranda! Miranda is a Botticelli angel". At 14 years old, we wanted to be plumped up with a just-hatched-Venusesque sexuality. We were besotted with the projections she carried, the desire she embodied, and of course that hair. Angel hair. Long, blond, pre-Raphaelite, and impossibly well-lit so that the glowing wisps caught the wind in slow motion to set-off a halo effect. Perhaps it was all in anticipation of our own inevitable passage through a hormonally flushed adolescence. Looking back at the film, Miranda seems less ethereal and more like a pretty, valium-sedated schoolgirl desperately trying to look otherworldly. A mixture of lost child and bourgeoning womanhood cut short,

Figure 1: *Lost* by Frederick McCubbin (1886).

the character, played by Anne-Louise Lambert, has become the iconic symbol of a particular Australian anxiety that I will call the *girlshine* complex.

Girlshine

Art, literature, film, and the wider media have reinforced the Australian tendency to grieve missing innocents. Not only can we can see this in the famous painting *Lost* by Australian artist Frederick McCubbin (Figure 1), but also through the reportage/cinema/mini-series based on the infant Azaria Chamberlain's disappearance at Uluru (Ayres Rock) and the subsequent incarceration of her mother (later pardoned) for infanticide, the deportation of children (often orphans) from the United Kingdom to Australia with the false promise of a better life, and Aboriginal children taken from their families by government agencies and religious organizations as late as the 1970s (known as the Stolen Generations). Post-colonization, the lost child and all it embodies has become one of our most potent archetypal eruptions; reinforced through Aboriginal history since this period and the mythologizing of abandonment and/or abduction in the outback by non-indigenous Australians. Colonizer and colonized share a hunger for reconciliation with those lost to them. While this need has preoccupied artists and academics, another related and seemingly irreconcilable cultural phenomenon periodically surfaces. For a brief flush, it is as if the child has returned grown and full of possibility. Almost inevitably, though, this energy of *becoming* is driven back to the margins/unconscious by an urge or reflex to subjugate. This sense of frustrated promise is most dominantly imagined in popular culture as mesmerizing, fated young women in the liminal recess between adolescence and adulthood. This libidinal pulse, this glimpse of a future too confrontational to embrace, is best described as *girlshine*.

First phrased by Lisa French in her analysis of film-maker Jane Campion's articulation and aestheticizing of female experience, the girlshine period (around 16-21 years of age) "denotes a time when young women experience a particular physical flowering, and have a sense of power without the caution that age and experience impose. It is a brief, transient, and liminal phase."[2] Taking French's lead, I also understand girlshine as a tangible period in a woman's life: a brief window, difficult to define, not often recognised by those who embody it, but clearly on show and magnetic. Australian popular culture, as a transmitter of myth and amplifier of collectively driven complexes, is preoccupied with this arrested stage of development. Although not confined to this particular country, I would argue that the obsession with youth and the insistence that women on screen (large and small) appear permanently nubile is more noticeable in Australia than in either Europe or the United States. Countless cinema narratives disproportionately worship girlshine, inhibiting any movement beyond this phase by depicting the actual, attempted, or spiritual death of female characters carrying the projection. Womanhood—its wisdom, sexuality, and fecundity—is far less celebrated. Ironically many of these films are set against sweeping Australian landscapes that encapsulate the mythic, atemporal notion of mother/or the mythic *Gaia*. One can almost sense *her* acting as a silent, hopeful witness to a kind of cultural transcendence that is able to take us beyond the bliss/abyss of girlshine.

In this chapter I will explore the manipulation of girlshine in Australian cinema through three potent examples: *Picnic at Hanging Rock* (Peter Weir, 1975), *The Year My Voice Broke* (John Duigan, 1987), and *Beautiful Kate* (Rachel Ward, 2009). The subsequent analysis of these films grapples with the problematic gender issues the girlshine complex stirs up, its ongoing function as one of Australia's most conspicuous obsessions, and its ability to exemplify the desire to remain in a state of *becoming*.

Cultural Complex in Action

Thomas Singer and Samuel Kimbles have grappled with the meaning of cultural complexes since 2004.[3] They repeatedly stress the way in which analytical psychology positions the *complex* on a personal level, tending to lock what might be seen as its collective aspect into archetypal shadow territory.[4] For Jung this pathology exists in a liminal space between "conscious and unconscious, in the half-shadow, in part belonging or akin to the conscious subject, in part an autonomous being, and meeting consciousness as such."[5] Singer and Kimbles see this phenomenon on a larger scale, at play in the conflicts between various global and national collectives, communities, and the individuals within them who have internalized the twisting of disturbing cultural and archetypal material characteristic of Jung's original concept.[6] They further characterize group complexes as cyclic regurgitations (or reimaginings) of past traumas, capable of irrationally erupting on a personal and collective level.[7] As Singer writes:

> Our cultural complexes get all mixed up not only with our personal history and complexes but with other cultural complexes as well. These intermingling complexes take strange twists and turns over a lifetime and generations, creating exotic permutations and combinations within ourselves and between

us and others, creating what I have come to think of as 'recombinant visionary mythologies'.[8]

In line with traditional analytical psychology, he argues that grappling with a cultural complex requires those in its grip to become conscious of the archetypal patterns and outer fixations that combine to drive its associated emotional behaviours/obsessions.

Although it is possible to theorize a number of Australian complexes operating with recurring and uncomfortable intensity, the trauma of "lost-ness" has been a particular driver of anxiety since the 1788 arrival of Captain Arthur Phillip's first fleet and the consequent establishment of multiple penal colonies. This grim beginning of white migration suggests that the sense of lost-ness embedded in the Australian cultural imagination can be linked to early birth trauma—a willing (for settlers) and unwilling (for convicts) wrenching from the British womb. In *The Country of Lost Children: An Australian Anxiety*, Peter Pierce attributes Australia's early and more recent obsessions with reported and fictional lost child narratives to an uneasiness associated with the colonization/seizure of a disturbingly unfamiliar environment. For Pierce, the lost child itself has become a symbol of guilt, separation anxiety, vulnerability, and the physical disorientation of newly arrived emigrants from the United Kingdom.[9]

Pierce argues that lost narratives in the mid-twentieth century tend to substitute the Australian outback (or "the bush") as the backdrop for childhood displacement with more urban settings. The topic of children missing because of their unfamiliarity with a foreign landscape is replaced with notions of abandonment and deliberate cruelty (orphanage abuses, the stolen indigenous generations, abduction, religious cult maltreatment, sexual exploitation, and murder): "It will rather be a human desire to abandon or to prevent the coming of 'the next generation' which will be central to these [later] cheerless versions of an old story."[10]

Culturally treasured tales about children are likely to signify a sense of national future/promise. Those who slip away into the unknown, into the hands of predators or the guardianship of ruthless parents, however, imply that these symbols of futurity might be insecure and undeveloped. Citing Donald Kalsched's influential work on archetypal defences, Singer and Kimbles focus on trauma as the key to cultural complexes.[11] This defining feature takes us to the core of Australia's most pervasive anxiety:

> This struggle for a new, group identity can get all mixed up with the underlying potent cultural complexes which have accrued historical experience and memory over centuries of

trauma and lie slumbering in the cultural unconscious, waiting to be awakened by the trigger of new trauma.[12]

In a sentiment unrelated to analytical psychology, Pierce backs up this idea that complexes develop through repeated trauma and can only be potentially alleviated if the source of the problem is consciously dealt with:

> if the analysis of current anxieties concerning an Australian future, as revealed by factual and imaginative witnesses, show this anxiety to be so deeply wretched and scarcely examined that the next generation is set at hazard, then these stories must be addressed as a matter of moral and cultural urgency.[13]

In various art forms where the image of lost-ness has shifted from the child (as representative of national futurity and trauma) to the bourgeoning adult, there is a suggestion of maturity or forward psychological movement (a function Jung calls *individuation*). These notionally progressed symbols of dislocation and girlshine, though, also demonstrate a thwarted sense of growth. That they are, more often than not, female, helps us to understand the tensions running through the developmentally inhibiting complex they personify.

Girlshine as a Liminal Sense of *Becoming*

While pop culture still produces art informed by the lost child, these stories exist in parallel with girlshine narratives. We might think about the idea of development as "frustrated" in relation to lost-ness as it shifts from children to female adolescents, rarely moving far beyond this point. This girlshine period might then be understood as a time of becoming. The figure embodying this developmental stage can consequently be read as a symbol of potential and plenty. Through *her* the future is ripe with opportunity, but like the nixies and nymphs of classical European myth, she is also only a precursor—an image of budding adulthood. She rarely grows up. The problematic nature of pinning down a tangible definition of girlshine seems to confirm its liminality, trickster-like qualities, and transience. This more or less accords with the early Australian lost child stories, where a sense of limbo is conjured: a holding place in which the child becomes suspended as if awaiting another mythical incarnation.

Like the trickster figures of myth who facilitated passage to and from the underworld (or manifestations of archetypal energies able to draw out unconscious material and so increase self-awareness), the girlshine character might also be thought of as a psychopomp. Similarly, in an allusion to Styx, the Greek river of the netherworld where souls were ferried after death, Pierce talks of thematic waterway crossings in early lost stories as "'liminal moments'" that led children further into the unknown.[14] The metaphor of "crossing" might be furthered to include notions of migration. This narrative feature is repeated in *Picnic at Hanging Rock*. One of the key episodes in the film is a scene where Miranda and her British pedigreed companions cross a small river on their way to the monoliths. Shot in slow motion, this sun-filtered sequence suggests entry into another dimension: a slow transition from one phase of development to another, or a stumbling toward another expression of self. But like the characters in the film who mourn their lost friends-cum-romantic fantasies, there is little beyond the liminality of the girlshine period and its focus on the *promise* rather than the *actuality* of becoming.

A number of Australian films could have been selected for this chapter because of their concentration on the death, or stifled development, of young women who symbolize potential. Some representative Post New Wave (1990 onward) examples of this include: *Angel Baby* (Michael Rymer, 1995), *Lilian's Story* (Jerzy Domaradzki, 1996), *Blackrock* (Steven Vidler, 1997), *Paradise Road* (Bruce Beresford, 1997), *The Boys* (Rowan Woods, 1997), *Wolf Creek* (Greg McLean, 2005), *Jindabyne* (Ray Lawrence, 2006), and *Romulus My Father* (Richard Roxburgh, 2007). Just as potent are texts where young women manage to escape a spiraling girlshine decline, or impending deterioration: *Romper Stomper* (Geoffrey Wright, 1992), *Radiance* (Rachel Perkins, 1998), *Rabbit-Proof Fence* (Phillip Noyce, 2002), *Somersault* (Cate Shortland, 2004), *Little Fish* (Rowan Woods, 2005), *Candy* (Neil Armfield, 2006), and *Sleeping Beauty* (Julia Leigh, 2011). The list could go on, but suffice to say that girlshine in our national cinema is still an enduring theme. Even if these characters manage to escape a potentially turbulent fate, the threat of slippage, or perhaps the wound of trauma (predominantly via drugs or sexual abuse), is still present. The films selected for closer analysis of these themes, *Picnic at Hanging Rock, The Year My Voice Broke,* and *Beautiful Kate,* carry what I consider to be the most significant echoes of the girlshine-come-lost child genre of Australian cinema.

Set in 1900 (February 14) and based on Joan Lindsay's 1967 novel, *Picnic at Hanging Rock* charts the mysterious disappearance of three senior schoolgirls, Miranda, Irma (Karen Robson), Marion (Jane Vallis), and their mathematics teacher Miss McCraw (Vivean Gray). All separate from their Appleyard College excursion at Hanging Rock (see Figure 2) to explore the monoliths and caverns surrounding them. Only Irma is recovered—found lying unconscious in a rock crevice. On waking from her coma she is unable to recollect the fateful last movements of her friends. Weir's wistful vision of Lindsay's story, itself a highly romanticized reworking of reported schoolgirl disappearances at the Rock, creates a sense of intrigue, time-zone liminality, and awakening sexuality—girlshine at its most potent. He explores these themes through Miranda's relationship with those who doted on her beauty *and* the environment into which she vanished.

Nostalgically imagined as a glimpse into how sexist and sexually regressive Australian rural life could be in 1962, *The Year My Voice Broke* is a rite of passage story for the adolescent Danny (Noah Taylor) and his 16-year-old school friend Freya (Loene Carmen). Danny is incurably attracted to the sexually active and vibrant Freya who develops a "reputation" after becoming involved with, and later pregnant by football hero/wild-child, Trevor (Ben Mendelsohn). As the story unfolds, we learn that Freya was the illegitimate daughter of Sarah Amery, a young free spirit remembered fondly and cruelly by the fathers in her small New South Wales town, as compassionate, attractive, and a readily available source of sexual pleasure. She died alone in an isolated farmhouse giving birth to Freya when she was 17. While Freya carries her mother's girlshine legacy, unlike Sarah, she aborts the child and leaves the hypocrisy and isolation of the town for a new beginning. Danny never sees her again after she escapes her emotionally crippled, unsupportive, and sexually fearful community. Still caught by past memories, though, he continues to think of Freya as the embodiment of desire and independence.

The most recent release, *Beautiful Kate*, was adapted from Newton Thornburg's American novel of the same name (1982). Like *The Year My Voice Broke*, and also featuring Ben Mendelsohn (now forty), the film is another *rite of passage* narrative. Mendelsohn's character Ned, a successful fiction writer, is haunted by an incestuous relationship with his twin sister

Figure 2: Hanging Rock, Victoria, Australia.

Kate (Sophie Lowe) and the suicide of his elder brother Cliff (Josh McFarlane). The film opens with Ned's grudging return to "'Wallumbi", the rural family property in South Australia's Flinders Ranges, where his younger sister Sally (Rachel Griffiths) nurses their dying father (Bryan Brown). As he reflects on his childhood and adolescence, we learn of the father's emotional callousness and Ned's sexual and ultimately consummated relationship with Kate. When he refuses her further advances, she turns to Cliff, seducing him on the night of a much anticipated town dance. As the two drive home together, Cliff swerves to miss a kangaroo and Kate dies as the car hits a tree. Unable to reconcile his part in her death and his willingness to be sexually drawn into her pathology, Cliff hangs himself at Wallumbi. Kate's problematic desire is never debased in the film. She remains a troubled, but "shiny" girl in Ned's flashbacks—the singular image of beauty in an emotionally starved adolescence.

Each film is set against the background of a wild marginal country into which the characters embodying girlshine energy become lost/consumed. This link takes us to earlier narratives of colonial anxiety, where the characters exemplifying girlshine are often enchanted by the unfamiliar nature of their environment, embracing it as a refuge against the traumatic invasiveness and restrictions of family and/or community life. For Pierce, the lost children of the nineteenth century also share this element of fascination. But for the storytellers, search parties, and parents, the uncharted topography and the lost child within it became a metaphor for their own alienation.[15] By anthropomorphically endowing the land with the ability to take children, these tales create a sense of fear around the power and unknowability of the landscape, often mythologized as female or a force of the elusive feminine. Ironically each of the girlshine characters in the three films have lost their own mother to varying degrees and seem to find themselves unconsciously embracing the land (mother earth) as a possible maternal substitute.

Although the Australian outback has often been gendered, for Ronald and Catherine Berndt, Aboriginal mythologies have no such overarching sexual bias. They argue that the creation stories of northern and southern Australia were imagined quite differently with only the northern versions carrying concepts of a female creator, variously named, but more generically understood as "Mother" or "Old Woman."[16]

> In recent years, in the struggle for recognition of Aboriginal rights to land, a popular slogan is, "the land is our Mother." That relationship is not usually made explicitly in the traditional mythology which serves as the basis of religious belief and action.

> All "Fertility Mothers" [...] were locally-based deities who were concerned with specific areas of country and/or sites, and not with the whole of the earth per se [...] The concept of the "land our Mother" is a highly symbolic abstraction, having little direct correspondence in local Aboriginal mythologies.[17]

There are however, numerous references to the illusive, essential feminine aspects of Australia in non-indigenous art and literature. Dorothea McKellar's (1911) classic Australian poem "My country", for instance, eulogizes a love of "her far horizons [...] her jewel-sea, her beauty and her terror".[18] Charles Chauvel's film *Sons of Matthew* (1949) is another early example of this proclivity for feminizing the awe-inspiring allure of the Australian landscape. His character, the settler Shane O'Riordan (Michael Pate), likens the bush he's hacking into, or taming, "to a beautiful woman, beautiful to look at, but tough to handle". "Women and the earth" he adds later, "I've always felt they're much the same, only the earth's more exciting". Poet A. D. Hope, on the other hand, finds *her* neither physically striking nor arousing. His gendered Australia is an uninviting wasteland—a bleak and almost sexist allusion to the post-menopausal woman:

> They call her a young country, but they lie:
> She is the last of lands, the emptiest,
> A woman beyond her change of life, a breast
> Still tender but within the womb is dry.[19]

Breasts also feature (without any of Hope's derisive overtones) in the majestic images of the colossal volcanic formation (or *mamelon - nipple* Fr.) of Hanging Rock that swallowed Miranda and her followers. Shots of the girls' sensual relationship with the rocks they cling to on their climb hint at a cleaving to the bosom of the earth and an entry into an inviting inner sanctum/womb.[20] Within these and other descriptions/images there is the tendency to pluralise, so that the land is, for example: beautiful and terrifying, fecund and barren, alluring and dangerous, old and young, tender and dry ... but unambiguously *she*.

Woman as *other* and the stereotypical bearer of femininity makes it all too easy to essentialize her as inextricably linked to the landscape and its mistreatment. In *Edge of the Sacred*, however, David Tacey associates the land with a spiritual *otherness* comparable to the unconscious that "we" (non-indigenous Australians) need to resource and appreciate, rather than handle for profit or settlement. He argues that: "if we paid more specific care and attention to our relationship with nature, to the maternal earth and the archetypal feminine, we would be in much better shape culturally and spiritually than we are today."[21] Tacey posits that the relationship between the earth and settlers has not been one of reciprocal honour. We ignore the landscape to our detriment: through rape and pillage, we have justifiably reaped the consequences of this disavowal. He encourages us to look past Western patriarchal readings of "the feminine", to the core archetypal concept itself. With this new mythopoetic appreciation, it is possible to develop a more legitimately mature relationship with the Australian interior.

Australian cinema goes some way toward this goal via its image-centred fascination with the environment. In its reverence for the beauty of this country it has been able to expose the kind of abuse Tacey writes about. Playwright Louis Nowa talks of 2009's Australian film releases as further verification that "our cinematographers have superb eyes for figures in a landscape" and sit within "our great tradition of landscape artists".[22] He is less flattering in relation to their skill, or even interest, in capturing the physical beauty of characters inhabiting these vistas. This kind of flattery, he argues, is more central to Hollywood's tradition of immortalizing the human face as "a dreaming site for the audience."[23] When looking at the films selected for this study, I would have to take exception to Nowra's critique. *Picnic at Hanging Rock*, *The Year My Voice Broke*, and *Beautiful Kate* uniformly cast each lead against a sun-drenched landscape, light streaming through their long blond hair to evoke a halo-like, golden glow and Botticelli angel-ness. This technique, though, consequently collapses women and the earth into an illusive otherness or "promised land"—sites for dreaming.

Each of the female characters embodying girlshine energy is without exception shot to capture a sense of ethereal beauty. They are mesmerizing in close-ups designed to accentuate their youth and sexual appeal. The striking landscapes against which they are often shot serves to enhance their "shine" and symbiotic relationship with nature. As Danny in *The Year My Voice Broke* says of Freya and "Willy Hills", her secret hiding place where we often see her body illuminated by the sun;

> she'd still go there, even when she was 16. It was her special place. When night was falling it was like you were on a ship and the hills sailed on through the night with the land in the sky lapping past. Every tree and rock to her was almost like they were living things.[24]

Dreamtime Parallels

There's a sense (conscious or unconscious, on the part of the filmmakers) of trespass into another dimension where these girl-women, immortalized in their "lost" stasis, become ghosts haunting the atemporal, all-seeing landscape into which they have vanished. This is comparable to the slippage of memory and dreams into a seamless past/present framework. It also evokes a sense of the indigenous spirituality, or perhaps philosophy, called "The Dreaming" or "Dreamtime". This concept, in part, revolves around a union of time and nature. It is a metaphysical awareness that as W. E. H. Stanner argues in *White Man Got No Dreaming: Essays 1938-1973*, is problematic for European colonizers educated into linear and hierarchical ways of thinking about the world:

> The truth of it [The Dreaming] seems to be that man, society and nature, and past, present and future, are at one together within a unitary system of such a kind that its ontology cannot illuminate minds too much under the influence of humanism, rationalism and science.[25]

The Dreamtime, though, is more popularly understood as the creation period in Aboriginal myth where the earth and spirits came into being, followed by various deities, or Dreaming Ancestors, who shaped the features of the land, endowing them with physical and spiritual characteristics. During this process of creation, as Lynne Hume writes, they "left an essential part of themselves, an essence, in certain places and in ritual objects."[26] The Ancestors gave birth to humans, whose coming, argue Berndt and Berndt, "was not a question of replacing the mythic beings [...] Both mythic and human beings were and are co-existent, but conceptually within different dimension of time-span and action-frame."[27] Stanner, who sees the Dreamtime as a cosmological theory of order and morality, divides its mythic creation stories into three essential categories: the formation of "the great *marvels*"—fire, sun, water, land features, solar system; the *institution* or development of various human, animal features and behaviours; and the social traditions still operating today that "were *already ruling* in The Dreaming".[28]

When viewing (and of course simplifying) each of the films under analysis, this notion of the Dreaming as a past/present philosophy built around union with the environment can be linked to the central girlshine characters who emerge as trickster-like psychopomps oscillating between linear and non-linear frames: life and death, past and present, spirit and soul, human and archetypal energy. Kate, Freya, Sarah, and Miranda are also simultaneously constructed as romantic fantasies able to engender a sense of self, identity, and reconciliation to certain emotional "truths". They do this by facilitating a spiritual awakening to the reflecting male characters who hold them up as the single impetus for formative change.

In *Picnic at Hanging Rock*, though, Miranda and her ethereal friends are erotically resurrected in the memories of teachers and students, and in the imagination of two young men (who catch glimpses of them crossing the transitional stream). There is more than a hint of desire on the part of both sexes as they become caught in the magnetic pull of Miranda's girlshine, her sacrifice to mysterious other-worldly forces, and her consequent passage into the abyss. She becomes a Persephone of sorts, leading her devotees to the underworld or its brink.[29] We also see this kind of attraction in *Beautiful Kate* and *The Year My Voice Broke*, with the death of those who are inextricably bound by the energy of their shiny girl-lovers: Kate's brother Cliff and Freya's boyfriend Trevor.

The examples of female sacrifice, a prevailing theme in Western fiction, is more often telling of those who benefit from the suffering *other*. While the keepers of girlshine energy might act as soul-guides to the unconscious, the fundamental question revolves around the negation of their maturity. Why do the (largely) male characters need to succeed them rather than exist in parallel with the women these girls could become? It is as if the *transcendent function* (which guides unconscious material to consciousness) is blocked or frustrated. One might argue that the kind of awareness driving individuation is only stimulated so that all we see is the *potential* for growth.

Still Caught in the Rapture

The girlshine phenomenon of thwarted potential suggests a resistance to transformation, or transcendence from unconscious to conscious awareness. Notions of becoming embody the exhilaration of fantasizing about change and consequent growth; being caught in a kind of rapture where the real and imagined failures that will inevitably arise during this period of change are kept on hold by the fantasy of what *might* eventuate. It is entirely possible that movement beyond this stage will be symbolized in screen culture's more genuine embrace of female maturity. On the face of it, though, there is a seemingly concerted effort (conscious or unconscious) to keep women (rarely men) locked in perpetual pre- or early adulthood. If Australian myth, the marker of cultural currents and developments, has extended its stories of lost children to stories of extinguished girl-women, it is then logical to question how we will move to the next stage.

Theoretically, it might have something to do with the way Jung talked about easing the personal complexes of archetype-shadow fusion. That is, disentangling girlshine energy from a sense of cultural identity: being freed from this arrested stage of becoming. Looking at the principal films mentioned above, it seems as if the atemporal land/mother, who pushes girlshine forward before re-enfolding her/it somehow bears witness to the cultural complex. As a backdrop to these stories it can represent a number of influences that play into girlshine: a sense of the unconscious, the elusive "feminine", timelessness, otherness, death, and renewal. Rachel Ward goes some way to combining these elements in *Beautiful Kate*, and in doing so opens up the possibility of new stories beyond *potential* and about *becoming*.

She closes the film with an intimate exchange between the morally conflicted Ned and his sister Sally, who remained at the family property to care for their father and work with the neighbouring Aboriginal community. She tells him of Kate's ongoing sexual involvement with their elder brother Cliff. With this revelation, the anxiety and guilt that Ned has built around his and Kate's complicated desire eases and he is able to develop more of an insight into this troubled child-woman, or as Sally puts it, "messed up little girl."

Sally embodies a new story, a new phase of awareness beyond girlshine. She eclipses Miranda, Sarah, Freya, and Kate. She draws on the environment as a source of renewal and, one senses, transformation by endowing the outback that Ned has shunned with the capacity to give rather than take life. But more than this, Sally allows us to reflect on the ephemeral nature of girlshine and its associated complex. She is not a transient, disembodied, or lost character who slips back into the landscape or protective womb of the lost mother. Sally has found her place on the land and an inner sense of mothering. Her largely unexplored and peripheral presence in *Beautiful Kate* challenges the cultural anxiety at the heart of this chapter, for Ward lets us know that girlshine is not the end of the Australian story, but a rite of passage to which we must submit and transcend.

With a sense of release from his past, Ned tells Sally that she, not Kate, should have had the greater claim on the heart of her all-male family: of his father and by extension himself, he says, "a man can live his whole life and never cop to his greatest achievement—you." Instead, they remained intoxicated by the glow of a siren, a trauma, a complex.

Concluding Remarks

One could argue that the Australian entertainment industry in general is caught by a similar intoxication. From calling out to Miranda at Hanging Rock with my friends, I worked my way into a full-time career as an actor until I was about 28 years old. There were many reasons for leaving that reality for academia—the other end of the emotional spectrum. But the main push came from older female actors. They convincingly argued that you were only ever as employable as your last gig and that these opportunities would rapidly decline in your mid-to-late 40s. Basically, I had few middle-aged female role models whose clout (or even visibility) in the industry might have made it worth pushing through the barriers of such a competitive market.

That was the 1980s, but even now in the twenty-first century Australia is flooded with girlshine to the detriment of womanshine. If film is one of the contemporary mediums for myth, and myth is a means of collectively understanding ourselves, then Australia needs to address the complexes that govern its cinema and therefore its audiences. We need to see girlshine for what it is—an opportunity for growth rather than a never-ending "opportunity". This empty, euphoric sense of promise takes us to the core of girlshine in an Australian context, for *we* are always talking about our country as "a land of opportunity", "a promised land", "a luck country", and it's at this point that the excited allusions to *a* future fossilize. There is a reluctance to extend our self-image to outcomes, as if this is somehow just beyond our grasp. We still want to play with the possible because here we are invulnerable, safe from the risks inherent in moving forward, and protected from our own mortality. It is the girlshine complex that carries this heightened emotion of "basking", most probably a response to the trauma of colonial beginnings where venturing into the unknown and the grim consequences of this imperative were interlaced.

I have no daughters, but each year a stream of shiny girl-women filter in and out of my university life on their way into the world. I like to imagine that their shine will evolve, that each will *become* a vibrant and luminous presence on the Australian cultural landscape, and that our screen myths will begin to reflect their authority. Maybe then the girlshine complex will ease its grip.

Notes

[1] Jeanette Winterson, *Gut Symmetries* (London: Granta Books, 1997), p. 4.

[2] Lisa French, *Centering the Female: The Articulation of Female Experience in the Films of Jane Campion*, Ph.D. Thesis (Melbourne: La Trobe University, 2007), p. 183.

[3] Thomas Singer and Samuel L. Kimbles, *The Cultural Complex: Contemporary Jungian Perspectives on Psyche and Society* (London and New York: Routledge, 2004); Thomas Singer, "Unconscious Forces Shaping International Conflicts: Archetypal Defenses of the Group Spirit from Revolutionary America to Confrontation in the Middle East", *Psychotherapy and Politics International*, 5:1 (2007: 45-61); Betty De Shong Meador, Andrew Samuels, Thomas Singer, "Panel: The Transcendent Function in Society", *San Francisco Journal of Analytical Psychology*, 55 (2010: 228–253).

[4] *CW* 9i, para. 88.

[5] *CW* 7, para. 295.

[6] Singer and Kimbles, *The Cultural Complex*, p. 20.

[7] *Ibid.*, p. 7.

[8] Thomas Singer, "The Cultural Complex and Archetypal Defenses of the Group Spirit: Baby Zeus, Elian Gonzales, Constantine's Sword, and Other Holy Wars (with special attention to 'the axis of evil')," in Singer and Kimbles, *The Cultural Complex*, p. 32.

[9] Peter Pierce, *The Country of Lost Children: An Australian Anxiety* (Cambridge, UK: Cambridge University Press, 1999), p. 6.

[10] *Ibid.*, p. 92.

[11] Donald Kalsched, *The Inner World of Trauma: Archetypal Defences of the Personal Spirit* (London and New York: Routledge, 1996).

[12] Singer and Kimbles, *The Cultural Complex*, p. 5.

[13] Pierce, *Country of Lost Children*, p. xviii.

[14] *Ibid.*, p. 50.

[15] *Ibid.*, pp. xii-xiii.

[16] Ronald M. Berndt and Catherine H. Berndt, *The Speaking Land: Myth and Story in Aboriginal Australia* (Ringwood, Victoria: Penguin, 1989), p. 17.

[17] *Ibid.*

[18] Dorothea McKellar, *My Country and Other Poems* (Victoria: Currey O'Neil, 1982), p. 11.

[19] A. D. Hope, *Collected Poems* (New South Wales: Angus and Robertson, 1966), p. 13, cited in David Tacey, *Edge of the Sacred: Transformation in Australia* (Victoria: HarperCollins, 1995), p. 17.

[20] Hanging Rock Development Advisory Committee and the Macedon Ranges Shire Council, "Hanging Rock General Information and Geology", http://www.hangingrock.info/reserve/general.html.

[21] Tacey, *Edge of the Sacred*, p. 107.

[22] Louis Nowra, "Nowhere Near Hollywood", *The Monthly* (Dec 2009–Jan 2010: 44-52), p. 47.

[23] *Ibid.*

[24] John Duigan, [writer and director], *The Year My Voice Broke* (New South Wales: Kennedy Miller, 1987).

[25] W. E. H. Stanner, *White Man Got No Dreaming: Essays 1938-1973* (Canberra: Australian National University Press, 1979), p. 27.

[26] Lynne Hume, *Ancestral Power: The Dreaming, Consciousness, and Aboriginal Australians* (Melbourne: Melbourne University Press, 2002), p. 25.

[27] Berndt and Berndt, *Speaking Land*, pp. 17-18.

[28] Stanner, *White Man Got No Dreaming*, p. 28.

[29] Not only do Marion and Miss McCraw disappear on the rock as they follow Miranda, but the two characters most effected by her death also mysteriously die (the young orphan Sara and the college's headmistress Mrs. Appleyard—the former via a fall from the lofty college and the latter, wandering the rock). There are also those who return from the brink of consciousness: Urma, one of the original lost girls, and the love-struck Michael who tries to trace Miranda's last steps on the rock.

Patricia Please, Ph.D., was born in England, lived in America as a child, and returned to England for studies. In 1988 she migrated to Australia looking for a big, youthful, sunny land to settle in. Patricia has worked as a psychotherapist, hydrogeologist, petroleum geologist, environmental social psychologist researcher on land-based issues, and a senior policy analyst for water issues. Combining her professional interests in environmental water science and the psyche, she earned a Ph.D. exploring "Aspects of Self in Dryland Salinity Science" at Charles Sturt University, New South Wales. She is currently working as a social science researcher for the Australian Bureau of Agricultural and Resource Economics and Sciences (ABARES) in Canberra where she explores the psycho-social aspects of a range of agriculture, forest, and fisheries issues, including the social impacts of wild dog attacks on landholders and the effects of the establishment of marine parks on fishermen and coastal communities.

●●●●●●●●●●●●●

Patricia Please writes about a psycho-social research project in which she explored the emotional/affective dimension of the experience of individuals and groups working on the pressing environmental issue of dryland salinity in Australia. Land clearing has been an environmental disaster worldwide. For example, in Australia European settlement led to the clearing of millions of hectares of native vegetation and its replacement with shallow-rooted crops and pastures. This change in land use has contributed to dryland salinity. Over the past few decades, significant resources and effort has gone into research to better understand this issue and into implementing remediation strategies. What makes Patricia's contribution unique is that she describes her personal responses to the process of research itself and to her relationship to her country through dreams and other experiences while working on this project. What emerges is a deeper understanding of the affective component of land use research and attitudes to the Australian environment in a culture in transition.

4

The Feeling of Salt, Land, and Water

Patricia Please

Introduction

Thomas Singer and Samuel Kimbles write that: "Intense collective emotion is the hallmark of an activated cultural complex at the core of which is an archetypal pattern".[1] They go on to say that cultural complexes tend to be based on repetitive, historical group experiences which have taken root in what Joseph Henderson has called the cultural unconscious.[2]

My intention in this chapter is to explore the psycho-social research I undertook during 2004-2008 in light of the concept of the cultural complex. This research utilised a clinical psychotherapeutic method known as the Conversational Model to explore the emotional/affective dimension of the experiences of various individuals working on the environmental issue of dryland salinity in Australia. My findings are discussed to see how they might contribute to an understanding of a possible cultural complex that is reflected in those working on this particular environmental issue in Australia, or more generally, at a broader, cultural level.

I have spent over twenty years working in Australia on rural water/land issues, initially as a scientist from a technical-object focussed perspective, and more recently as a psycho-social scientist from a human-subject focussed perspective. So I bring two very different views to my work. It was during my training and working as a psychotherapist, while also working as a hydrogeologist on salinity issues, that I began to recognise the lack of attention being paid to the psychological dimension of our efforts to deal with salinity. In addition, since I spent the first 30 years of my life between the USA and England, I also bring something of those two cultural perspectives to bear on this exploration of the psychological aspects of Australia's cultural complexes that may be observed in dealing with the environmental issue of dryland salinity.

Background to the Australian Environmental Issue of Dryland Salinity

Australia is very different geologically from either the USA or Britain (and Europe). It is an ancient, stable landscape that has undergone long-term weathering *in situ*—in contrast to what is more common in the USA and Europe where weathered material is often transported by rivers and other means and deposited in different physical environments. As a result, Australia's physical environment, landscape processes, and the associated environmental issues it has to deal with, as well as the impact of the environment on the psyche of those living in Australia, is quite distinct and often not well understood or appreciated by people in other parts of the world. Even non-indigenous Australians themselves have had to work hard to try to understand the physical environment here because it is so different from what they and their ancestors were familiar with from their countries of origin. This evolution in understanding of their Australian "new home" landscape has been relatively slow in coming and has often been spurred on by environmental disasters and associated agricultural production/settlement infrastructure failures. There is even less understanding of the impact of the Australian landscape on the collective psyche.

The environmental issue of dryland salinity is a case in point. In Australia, dryland salinity is very much linked to the island nation being an ancient, stable landmass where salts have accumulated and built up in the soil and water over long time periods. Dryland salinity takes on two broadly different forms—primary and secondary salinity. Primary salinity occurs naturally in the landscape while secondary salinity results from land use impacts by people, either as a result of dryland farming management systems or from irrigation. Technically speaking, both dryland and irrigation salinity are created by an accelerated rising watertable which mobilises salt in the soil and brings it to the surface. Increasing salt concentration has a significant impact on agricultural production, river and stream salinity, man-made infrastructure, and soil erosion, and contributes to an acceleration of the loss of biodiversity.[3]

In Australia, land use changes since European settlement have significantly contributed to the problem of dryland salinity. Thousands of hectares of native vegetation have been cleared and replaced with shallow-rooted crops and pastures which have significantly different seasonal growth patterns. As a result, more water seeps into the groundwater system and causes the subsurface water levels to rise and bring salts, where they exist, to the surface. While the causes are now well documented, dryland salinity degradation and its remediation have proven to be very complex issues to think about when policy makers, environmentalists, land holders, and traditional owners try to relate the science to specific biophysical locations and to different socio-economic environments.

Figure 1: Salinised landscape – Trees Killed by Rising Saline Groundwater.

The past few decades have seen an enormous effort being made to better understand the issue.[4] Throughout the 1990s, land and water salinisation took centre stage among Australians' concerns about their environment both in terms of government funding and in terms of a concerted effort by a range of scientists, policy-makers, and people on the ground. Since the start of the new millennium, the impact of a long drought period and changing climate patterns has shifted the focus of concern away from dryland salinity to a significant extent—particularly in terms of government policy and funding. However, this environmental problem is still a very significant issue in many parts of Australia, especially in Western Australia, and both scientists and those concerned with care of the land are aware that returning wetter periods could cause the salinity problem to re-emerge. Many regions are still engaged in remediation activities to deal with the issue as they implement their salinity plans.

It is worth noting that the many people, including myself, who work on environmental natural resource management, agricultural and water issues, have become collectively referred to as "the salinity industry". This is because, in addition to employing many people over the years and providing significant funds for the science, management, and remediation of the problem, "the salinity industry" has appeared to take on a life of its own.[5] We can see that the salinity industry therefore seems to fulfil two of the criteria described previously in the Introduction to this book as being the hallmarks of an activated cultural complex: it has a "life of its own" and has also become self-fulfilling.

My Dreamings about this Work

While thinking about writing this chapter, I had the following dream:

I have been in Australia for a while, originally coming from the UK (with many years spent in America still evident in my accent and manner at times). I am asked to go through Australian passport control again. This particular passport control office was located in a bush setting; it was a beige-coloured temporary shack type of building; it was set out with very basic wooden furniture and a minimal amount of office equipment; the general atmosphere was hot and dry. The passport official opens my passport and it is clearly written: "You are not permitted to enter Australia". At that point I was turned around and escorted to a door that would lead me out of the country.

This dream of course has many possible layers of meaning, but I understood it to reveal some of my hesitation in writing about water/land-based issues in Australia. My feeling response to the dream was anger because I have devoted many years of work to Australian land and water problems, efforts that almost cost me my life, as I describe below; and so to be told in my dream that I could not enter the country now seemed to negate these efforts. In spite of my experience, my hesitation in writing about my experiences concerned my "legitimacy" to do so. I was not born in Australia, I am an Americanised English-born woman who has spent the bulk of my life living in suburbia and inner cities, with only a few short spells living in rural environments; any close family links to the land that

I may have had died away at least two generations ago. Although I do like to imagine that sometimes the "outsider" perspective can have some value (I will leave the reader to decide if this is the case).

A few years ago, while in a coma as a result of a severe vehicle accident when undertaking some hydrogeological/salinity field work in outback southern Queensland, I had another experience which relates to my work in this area. I have been told that while in my hospital bed and completely unconscious, I talked about and described my body as the Murray-Darling Basin. I was talking about drilling in various parts of my body/the Basin. Apparently there was a metal structure over my badly injured leg and I was interpreting this as a drill rig.

The Murray-Darling Basin is located in south-east Australia and covers 14 per cent of the country's total area with a river system that extends 1365 kilometres (848 miles) from its source to the mouth. The river system is flat, low-lying, far inland, and receives little rainfall. The many rivers it contains tend to be long and slow-flowing, and carry a volume of water that is large only by Australian standards. It incorporates part of four states —Queensland, New South Wales, Victoria, and South Australia. The Murray-Darling Basin is the agricultural heartland of Australia, producing over 40 per cent of the country's agricultural product, and it directly supports about two million people. The Basin holds an important, if not unique place in the Australian psyche. To many Australians the Basin's rivers and its varied landscapes are one of the quintessential images that come to mind when thinking of Australia. It is economically, environmentally, and culturally one of its most important national assets.[6]

At the time of writing a hugely significant event was occurring that had to do with the future management of the Basin. The Murray-Darling Basin Authority released a major document, the *Guide to the Proposed Murray-Darling Basin Plan,* outlining its plan to secure the long-term ecological health of the Basin. This would involve cutting existing water allocations and increasing environmental flows.[7] With the release of this document, a number of highly-charged protests and criticisms about the lack of socio-economic impact analysis ensued. This significant emotional response to the proposed Plan links with my research findings and growing understanding of the complexity of the strong emotional connection that many Australians have to the land.

In my experiences in the coma related above, I am in a state of identification with the land, imagining drilling rigs penetrating the land (my body). In my later dream I am denied permission to enter Australia at the customs office. I wonder if my dream and experiences may contribute

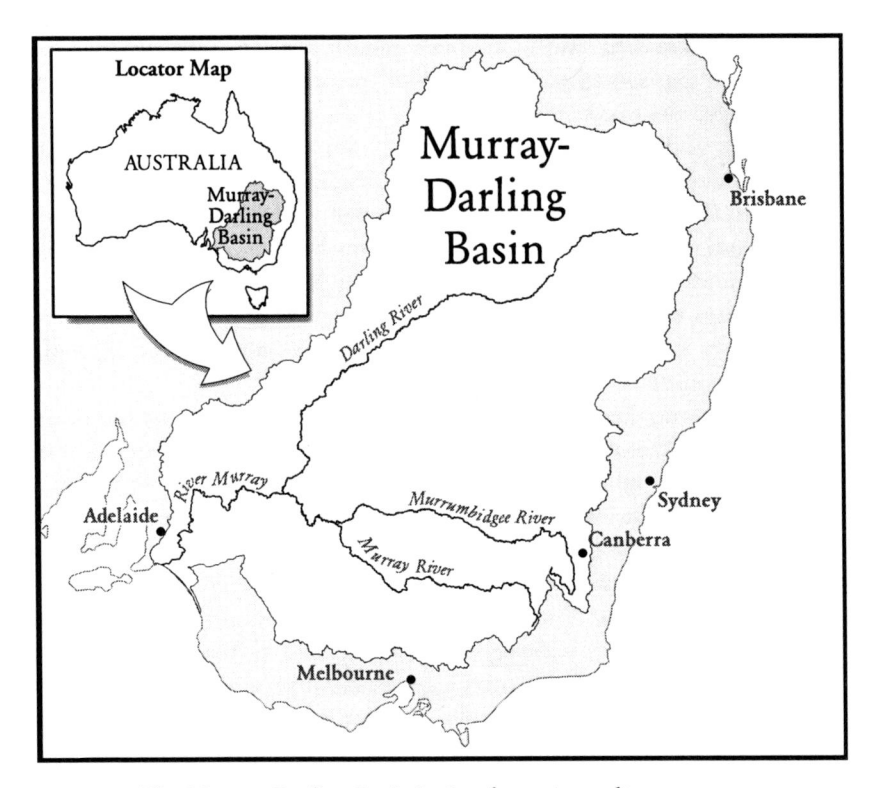

Figure 2: The Murray-Darling Basin in Southeast Australia.

something to our collective understanding of an emergent cultural complex in Australia in relation to water/land/environmental issues as well as saying something important to me. I can also see the work represented in this chapter as representing something of my efforts to drill "deeper" into emotional understandings of environmental/salinity issues in the Murray-Darling Basin—the area in which I have been working.

Exploring the Emotional Dimension of Experiences in Working with Environmental Issues

Historically, the role of emotion has been relatively neglected by researchers working on environmental sustainability issues. At an international level, this situation is changing as evidenced by an increasing number of publications focussing on the importance of exploring the emotional/affective dimensions of experience in primary production/natural resource/conservation settings.[8]

In Australia, much of the environment/national resource management/ agriculture related research has focussed on the cognitive-behavioural model of attitudes-values-beliefs to good effect, but there has been only a limited amount of research that delves deeper into the affective-emotional realm. However, affective experience was my central topic of interest during my psychotherapy training. I was fascinated by its strength, intensity, motivating power, fluidity, and changeability. I was struck by the fact that working with people at an emotional level could have a significant impact in terms of psychological transformation. During the years of my psychotherapeutic training and work experience, I often reflected how learning about this dimension of experience was so absent in established education programs in the era that I grew up in. A knock-on effect has been its obvious neglect in mainstream areas of environmental research.

There has been an enormous increase in our understanding of the role that emotions/affective experience play in our lives. "Emotional Intelligence" has become an accepted buzz word in Western society and the practice of it has made its way into some areas of the corporate and bureaucratic worlds, including education establishments. Despite this, I found it was still considered of peripheral interest to many professionals I crossed paths with during my fieldwork and research. But then many social science researchers in the environmental arena have been struggling to have their voice given an equal footing to the scientists. At times it appears as if a shift is in progress—it just depends who you talk to and where you focus your attention—and there is growing hope that the voices of those who have some understanding of the psyche in environmental areas of concern will find a place in the mainstream.[9]

The Use of an Affect Model as a Framework for Understanding Emotional Experience

The disciplines of psychoanalysis and psychodynamic psychotherapy have a long history of interest in affects, feelings, and emotion, and my research drew significantly from the theory and practices of these disciplines. During the 1980s and 1990s, major developments in psychoanalytic theory centred on an increased interest in affects as part of the development of the psychology of the self—how one uses the capacity for thought in relationship to affects to create meaning. Stolorow and Stolorow[10] write that we require attuned responsiveness to affect states in all stages of the life cycle. Affect attunement leads to a sense of a shared world. These understandings strongly point to the significant role that affects/emotions have in relation to human experience, meaning, and relationships.

Applying these psychodynamic understandings to a human experience of an environmental issue was a challenge. As a psychotherapist I had focussed on the study of affects in relation to a sense of self as a particular area of interest.[11] In order to progress my social science thesis, which was funded by a scientific research organisation, I felt a need to embed my research in a broader body of natural resource management/agricultural extension research literature and somehow make linkages across a range of disciplines from psychodynamic psychotherapy, psychiatry, and psychology to sociology, anthropology, and environmental social sciences in general, and then on to agricultural extension and salinity science. I put significant effort into trying to communicate across this diverse range of disciplines—much more, in fact, than into the research itself. Reflecting on this, I can see that the core research project and communicating across disciplines are one and the same thing in a transdisciplinary research environment, and perhaps that's the point, and the area of challenge.

It is now generally understood that people need to be as aware of their feeling and emotional world as of their thinking world, and to aim for some kind of integration between the two. Recent literature indicates that we are beginning to understand how significant our affective/emotional selves are to our motivation,[12] emotional intelligence,[13] social relationships,[14] decision-making, and risk assessment processes,[15] creativity,[16] and especially our ability to contain and think through emotive situations—what is called "mentalised affectivity".[17] Certainly in the transition to the new millennium psychologists have shown increased interest in studying the interplay between cognitive and emotional processes. LeDoux, writing from a neuroscience perspective, makes the point that it is debatable whether all motivated actions are based on emotional activity, "but that emotions are powerful motivators seems indisputable".[18]

The terms affect, feeling, and emotion are often used interchangeably in some of the non-psychological social science literature, but there are clear differences among them which are useful when thinking about research. I chose the following definitions put forward by Basch who proposed that affect, like cognition, be thought of in terms of a maturational line:[19]

> *Affect*: "the reaction of the subcortical brain to sensory stimulation"; the group of biological responses to stimulation; the categories of these responses being described in Tomkins's affect theory (see below).

Feeling: comes in later in development, around 15-24 months of age, when the involuntary basic affective reaction begins to be related to a concept of the self. To be able to say "I am angry" is to have already abstracted and objectified the affective reaction.

Emotion: a further step in affective maturation that results when feeling states are joined with experience to give personal meaning to complex concepts such as love, hate, and happiness.

Empathic understanding: the final maturational step in affective development in this schema is the capacity for empathic understanding—that is, affective communication that goes beyond the self-referential.

The essential point in this framework is that affect is not synonymous with feeling or emotion, but is something independent of it. Awareness of one's own and of another's affective state is central to the emotional intelligence (EI) concept. These understandings translate to our broader intrapersonal, interpersonal, and social interactions. Clinical evidence from psychodynamic psychotherapy indicates that "it is the nature and intensity of the affect generated by or in connection with a particular event that determines one's behavioural reaction: affect is the gateway to action".[20] This links with one of Jung's descriptions of archetypes as "systems of readiness for action".[21]

Categorical affects were first postulated by Charles Darwin[22] who had an evolutionary view of emotion. Silvan Tomkins, founder of modern affect theory, later expanded on Darwin's ideas.[23] He describes the capacity to respond affectively as initially a genetically encoded reflex phenomenon, a total body response. In humans the face has become the prime communicator of affective states.[24] Tomkins identified and systematically described the facial features of nine discrete, innate, primary affects, each with a range from mild to intense expression, present either at birth or shortly thereafter. Nathanson, who built on Tomkins's work, surmised that every known emotion and emotion-laden situation can be explained on the basis of the nine innate affects described by Tomkins.[25]

Tomkins's affect categories are described in two-word groups, the first word indicating the mildest form of the affect and the second representing its most intense presentation. They are:

interest - excitement
enjoyment - joy

surprise - startle
fear - terror
distress - anguish
anger - rage
contempt - disgust
shame - humiliation
dismell

All of the affect pairs are self-explanatory except for the term "dismell". This term was invented by Tomkins and figures "prominently in the experience and phenomenology of interpersonal rejection".[26] As yet there is no definitive, agreed upon categorisation of affects or emotions.

Prior to my research, the explicit inclusion of theoretical frameworks in natural resource management (NRM) emotion studies had been limited. I selected Tomkins's affect theory as the conceptual framework for my research for several reasons. Firstly, it provides a simple framework within which to undertake exploration of peoples' affective/emotional experience. Secondly, it provides a categorical framework that is proposed to cover the full range of emotional experience. Finally, it can be used as a framework for the analysis of the range of affective/emotional experience that is explicitly articulated and implicitly evident in the interview data. The hope was that using Tomkins's affect theory would facilitate a broader and deeper exploration of this dimension of experience than had previously been undertaken in natural resource studies.

Collecting Emotional Experiences of those Working on the Dryland Salinity Issue

My work utilised a qualitative research methodology. I took clinically-based psychodynamic skills and theory—Heinz Kohut's empathic-introspective method[27] and Russell Meares's Conversational Model[28]—and attempted to apply them in a field-based situation. Tomkins's nine major affects were also used in an attempt to orientate the interviewees towards expressing their affective/emotional experiences and as a framework for the analysis of the data.

I employed in-depth, semi-structured interview techniques to encourage the individuals interviewed to speak about their subjective, emotion-oriented experience in relation to the problem of dryland salinity. These techniques included skills and conceptual understandings of empathy and "vicarious introspection"[29] with an emphasis on trying to stay "experience near" to the interviewee—close to their lived and felt experience[30]—and the use of mirroring[31] and amplification[32] at key points in a conversation to encourage the interviewees to expand on themes/emotional experience.

I interviewed a total of thirty-one people who fit into at least one of the following categories: scientists, natural resource managers (including an Indigenous natural resource manager), agricultural extension specialists, and landholders. Each person was interviewed three times, mainly in face-to-face engagements, over a period of approximately 20 months (2005-2006). Each interview had a general theme with subthemes but was otherwise unstructured to allow the conversation to move as close to the participant's experience as was comfortably possible. The three general themes explored in the interviews were: 1) the experience of dryland salinity in a general sense; 2) affective/emotional dimensions of that experience; and 3) the experience of relationships with other individuals, groups, the science, and the land which were linked to the interviewee's work on dryland salinity.

The first interview was very open and broad and contained some general information about emotional experience. In the second interview, I gave them a brief introduction to the relevance of exploring the emotional dimensions of dryland salinity, in particular, and provided each person with a list of the nine basic affect categories as defined by Tomkins. I suggested that this list be used as a springboard to talk about their feelings as they related to their experience of dryland salinity. The interviewees were also encouraged to use whatever terms or words that represented their emotional experience best. For many, this was the first time anyone had been interested and explored with them the issue of dryland salinity from the perspective of their emotional experiences of this environmental issue. My sense was that some of those interviewed were particularly uncomfortable with speaking from this perspective, while many others easily engaged in the process.

Two "field areas" were chosen to address particular aspects of the salinity issue: one was "geographical"—the Wimmera catchment in western Victoria, Australia. The Wimmera has a long history of working on natural resource issues and salinity and they were in the process of implementing a Salinity Plan. The other area was the "institution of dryland salinity science". By including the "institution of dryland salinity science" I was able to draw on a broader range of people involved in this issue, who were not specifically geographically located in the Wimmera region, and bring the scientists' subjective experience into the story.

What Did the Interviewees Have to Say?

Early on in the interview process it became obvious that peoples' affective/emotional experience of this environmental problem was salient and significant. For example, the scientists expressed interest, enjoyment, excitement, and passion in many aspects of their work as well as disappointment and dissatisfaction having to do with the long time frames involved in doing scientific research on salinity issues and not being able to quickly see if there were any responses to the salinity remediation activities that they had recommended. The lack of adoption of their scientific recommendations also created much disappointment. This aspect of the science, where a significant investment and effort is put into conducting scientific research on salinity issues but there is limited funding and effort put into extending and ensuring the adoption of the suggested remediation strategies, is a familiar story, and one I hear echoed through many agricultural/natural resource science sectors.

The natural resource managers, agricultural extension specialists, and landholders experienced frustration, fear, and anger in relation to aspects of funding. Landholders talked about frustration and resentment in relation to the perceived poor land management practices of other landholders. Notably, the Indigenous natural resource manager spoke of the recognition that indigenous people can bring heart and soul to the work of remediation and of the frustration and sadness experienced in relation to the ongoing (or lack of) management of the environment.

In the second round of interviews, I focussed more closely on their affective/emotional experiences. The following is a summary of what emerged in relation to two positive affects (interest and enjoyment), the complex emotion of love, and three negative affects (anger, distress, and fear).

Interest, Excitement, Enjoyment and the Complex Emotion of Love

As one might imagine, the scientists expressed interest in the science itself—the ideas, mechanical and technical solutions, the discovery and the voyage, its application and impact. Interest as an affect also evoked comment in relation to the human dimension of science—helping people, being involved in the social dimension, and participating in group processes.

Several of them commented on their interest in salinity science being linked to their background and childhood. The experience of an agricultural background where salt, rivers, and water issues were dominant features meant for one scientist that there was a very real grounded connection with the work this person was doing. For another, it was an early somatic experience of first seeing salt in the landscape that sent shivers down this person's spine that came to mind.

> I need to almost tie it [the science] back to something more feeling. Like I am doing something to help to look after the landscape ... I need to articulate those connections. (Scientist)

One scientist reflected eloquently on the creativity at the heart of science and the associated epiphanies and "Eureka" moments. The affect enjoyment included expressions of joy, contentment, fulfilment, fun, pleasure, and satisfaction. This affect was experienced in relation to the communication of the science to others, the workplace/lifestyle that goes with the scientific work, the people involved in the work, the land, and the scientists' underpinning philosophies/ideologies in relation to their work.

> [O]ne has pleasure in the [scientific] paper. One has pleasure in scientific outcome. But to place it in a useful social context is a key driver and a huge source of motivation and pleasure. (Scientist)

The natural resource managers manifest the affect of interest in challenging and supporting staff, engaging and encouraging people with new ideas, and being mindful to "hit the mark"—making sure that their work was congruent with other people's interests. The agricultural extension specialists shared many similarities with the natural resource manager group, where a mixture of people, the land and ideas, and working in outdoor, physical environments were central to their experience of "interest".

For the indigenous participant, interest and excitement were linked to land stewardship and custodianship, and how this participant could help to empower indigenous people to take a stronger role in natural resource management. Interestingly, for the indigenous participant, the words "complete" and "content" express emotions that are found further along Basch's maturational line, explained earlier in this article.

> I guess for me the word contentment rings to me true as well and I feel content being in my country and working in my country for its benefits, working in the environment ... it helps you feel more complete, for myself as an indigenous person, a traditional owner of this country. (Indigenous natural resource manager)

Landholders' interests in connection with dryland salinity spanned many aspects of their lives. For two female landholders, interest and excitement related to the future and the next generation.

> Excitement ... one thing that does excite me a little bit is that ... it is encouraging to me to know that our kids are keen on continuing what we started. Even if it is for a different purpose ... I think they would be upset to see if we had sold off to an investor to do something different to it.........to lose control to some sort of succession ... .they are interested in conservation and interested in what we have done. (Female landholder)

Enjoyment was very closely connected to the land, in terms of agricultural productivity and sustainability. One pair of landholders spoke of the fact that even though it was not a particularly joyous year, visitors helped bring back a perspective of the value of what they have, and they still took much pleasure in their place.

Love is not defined as a basic affect, but this word, and the related words and complex emotions of loyalty, caring, helping, trust, patience, consideration, and hope, all emerged during these interviews and were considered significant in this part of the analysis process. These words, linking with complex emotions, once again reflect a more mature step in peoples' affective-emotional experience as defined by Basch. The range of qualities related to love and care was strongly linked with the experience of living in close relationship to the land. Some of the scientists talked explicitly about a love of the land, of caring for land, or of having an attachment to the land that made them want to look after it:

> I guess it has always motivated me. That sort of spiritual side of it. Looking after the land. Because it is a very basic thing for me ... I love it. And it is part of me. (Scientist)

The natural resource managers and agricultural extension specialists talked about the actions of caring for and helping people. A landholder spoke of loyalty and responsibility in the context of "landholders who depend on the environment for a living, shar[ing] a common philosophy".

Anger, Distress, and Fear

The scientists spoke of anger about poor quality science, the lack of understanding of the scientific process by non-scientists, the abuse of science—how it is seen and used—the politics and social justice issues associated with it, and aspects of funding and management of science.

Distress, frustration, disappointment, and sadness (amongst others) were mentioned by some of them in relation to aspects of the salinity science environment: the self interest of some people, the dominance of market-driven science over science for its own sake, the proliferation of scientific work being left on shelves, the time and scale aspects of the problem of dryland salinity, funding, management, and frustrations with communication. Distress associated with empathy for landholders and their problems was also evident.

One scientist stated very clearly the disillusionment and depression felt as an understanding of the scale of the dryland salinity problem had "sunk in", but this participant had also observed a shift in this emotional state over time:

> ... you went in with the best of intentions ... as my understanding increased—one thing became the disillusionment about what I could actually deliver to the people being affected by it [dryland salinity] ... As professionals have matured in their thinking ... one of the initial disillusionments ... started to dissipate because you were actually starting to put it into the right frame of mind so you were able to think through solutions. (Scientist)

There was fear that some of the scientific models are too simple to deal with climate change and ecosystem destruction and fear in the rise of litigation in environmental arenas. Fear was also expressed in relation to the possibility that competitive funding models could be driving the type and quality of advice being given to the public, and a fear that one may not be leaving a significant scientific legacy for the future.

The non-scientist people involved in the project—the natural resource managers, agricultural extensionists, and landholders—experienced anger, both explicitly and implicitly. Salinised land, specifically, did not come up as an issue that people linked with anger. This group of people felt most anger in relation to the land in general and what some people had done to it.

> Anger ... I suppose I get a bit pissed off when not everybody wants to take a long term view. (Landholder)

For agricultural extension specialists, the focus was on the few landholders who visibly used agricultural practices that were detrimental to the land:

> ... contrary to everything you sort of know and hold dear, that someone ... would put their land at risk like that. (Agricultural extension specialist)

Aspects of the governmental bureaucratic system evoked anger in natural resource managers and agricultural extension specialists, specifically where there was slow or out-of-step delivery of funds. Where environmental legislation was perceived as lacking a sense of reality, some landholders expressed anger.

The indigenous participant expressed some deeply felt comments relating directly to the state of the environment and the realisation of how bad the problem really is:

> ... how you do feel about the land that you live in? Because the Indigenous view ... they see the degradation of the land and the land's in pain ... You feel like, yeah, it does make you angry and you've got no control over it. (Indigenous NRM manager)

And

> ... there are times that you do feel anger, but I guess the next group of words really are probably more common I think, the grief and the sadness and the distress. You feel that probably a bit more often than the anger I suppose. Generally a feeling of depression really. (Indigenous NRM manager)

For the landholders, distress, frustration, and sadness were felt about the drought (which has been going on for several years), the loss of control that will come with the sale of land, as well as the diminishment of the social fabric in rural communities. There was little fear relating to salinity, but fear was felt in relation to other environmental and agricultural issues that are currently seen as being more important, for example, rising petrol prices, chemical use in agriculture, and the future for children on the land.

The natural resource managers and agricultural extension specialists experienced distress where there was a lack of coordination and cooperation —requests from funders that were clearly out of step with their on-ground works. As well, there was empathy with challenges relating to a community dealing with a drought.

> We are dealing with people ... people who are suffering from a drought. You have got to understand when you go out to someone ... like you might have a program that has all been dotted up to deliver certain services to landholders. And it might be about ... the way to manage the land to protect it from soil

> erosion and salinity ... It is not really the time to be banging on their doorstep when they are in the middle of their third successive season of drought. And you know damn well next season that the bank manager is foreclosing on them. That is not a good time ... That's ... understanding communities and that sort of stage of despair. (Agricultural extension specialist)

There was also some fear with this group overall in relation to employment uncertainty as significant funding cycles come to an end.

At this stage it seems worthwhile making a few comments about the limitations of the research framework to provide for a deeply engaged exploration of affective states. Unlike the many sessions possible in psychotherapy, this project only allowed for one hour of explicitly focussed time with each person, and they were asked to address the full range of affective states from Tomkins's list rather than allowing time to focus on one or two of these states that they perhaps had resonated with more fully. Also this project was not Australia-wide, and certainly in Western Australia, where dryland salinity is more severe, people's thoughts and feelings may have been somewhat different than those of individuals in the areas I focussed on. Despite these limitations, I believe the process worked well in providing some insights into the emotional/affective world of people involved in an Australian environmental problem that had not been systematically collected previously. Environmental and agricultural research that provides a space for people to focus on their affective-emotional experiences to any significant depth is not very common.

Reflections

My experience of working in the salinity arena is that the basis of most of the decision-making linked to government policy, funding, and management is undertaken with no explicit incorporation of people's feeling connection to land and land-based issues. This aspect of human experience is not made conscious and is therefore not utilised as a factor in motivating people to care for their land. Creativity is strongly linked to feelings, therefore, by better understanding how people relate to the land from an emotional perspective, perhaps we can open the door to more creative and broader approaches to care of the land. Following leads on where positive affect is located in individuals and the community is likely to lead to greater engagement.

Singer and Kimbles have said: "Intense collective emotion is the hallmark of an activated cultural complex at the core of which is an archetypal

Unconscious Dynamics in Individuals and Groups Involved in an Australian Environmental Issue*		
	-affective responses from individuals and groups	
Personal Unconscious	NEGATIVE	POSITIVE
Scientists Landholders Indigenous NRM Managers Ag Extension	Anger at science remaining unused + misunderstood Anger at other landholders not caring for the land Anger/sadness at non-indigenous past relationship to land Anger at aspects of bureaucracy + funding regulations Anger at some landholders lack of care for land	Passion for science & connections to environment/land Care for land to support agriculture & healthy environment Care for country - land as part of self Excitement at new ideas to help environment Empathy for those impacted by the drought
Cultural Unconscious	NEGATIVE - historical complexes	POSITIVE - evolution of cultural complexes
	Science seen as providing the total solution Landholders applied European farming methods Top down approach taken to ag extension Terra nullius + ignorance of indigenous knowledge	Triple bottom line approach for sustainability; sociology and psychology of science taking fuller view of context of science >scientists as more than "rational man" Many landholders have now modified their farming practices to match the conditions of the uniqueness of the Australian landscape Now use a mix of Top down and Bottom up approach Attempts to integrate Indigenous knowledge into land management
Collective Unconscious	NEGATIVE	POSITIVE
	Lack of care for Mother Earth Lack of awareness of indigenous knowledge "Rational Scientist" as the dominant paradigm	Care for Mother Earth Integration of indigenous + non-indigenous knowledge Integration of conscious and unconscious - inclusion of feelings and imagination with rational science

*Diagram framework adapted from Singer & Kaplinsky

Figure 3: Unconscious dynamics in individuals and groups.

pattern".[33] In Singer and Kaplinsky[34] a diagrammatic framework is provided that is intended to help understand how a cultural complex shapes itself in the psyche and how the energy trapped within it is released, thus bringing a profound sense of renewal for individuals (and I would suggest for groups and for the benefit of society as well). I have taken the basis of this framework and adapted it to my understanding of Australia's cultural complex in relation to environmental issues.

What I have tried to capture in this diagram (Figure 3) is what I see as the beginnings of an evolving Australian cultural complex that is deeply related to the uniqueness of the Australian landscape. The complex seems to be in transition—located somewhere between a historical, transported European relationship to the land and a slowly evolving, new Australian relationship to the land. This new relationship relies to some extent on the application of traditional "rational" scientific approaches to understanding landscapes. But it also incorporates a growing understanding of the "felt" relationship to land and inclusion of some aspects of a more indigenous way of thinking about the land. At the heart of what people were telling me about their experiences of salinity and the natural environment was a shared, deep caring and love for the land. I discovered that it was not primarily dryland salinity that constellated affect and emotion but peoples' more general feeling about the state of the land itself and what was happening to it.

Caring for land also featured prominently in negative affective experiences in relation to this environmental problem. There was anger at lack of care for the land, such as the use of inappropriate farming methods and frustration and sadness about the drought and the loss of control associated with any potential sale of land and accompanying diminishment of the social fabric of rural communities. The Indigenous person was angry and saddened at the lack of caring for the land.

An interesting aspect of what emerged was the range of depth of expressions of affect-emotion. This range could easily be linked in with Basch's maturational line of affect-feeling-emotion and empathy. There wasn't one particular group of people I interviewed that was able to express their emotions more fully than another. It appeared to be a particularly individual capability. For example, some of the scientists were exceptionally capable of articulating thoughts about salinity that integrated complex thoughts and emotions and showed evidence of empathy. Another person I interviewed, who stood out in his/her capacity to integrate complex thoughts and emotions, was the Indigenous natural resource manager—and this interviewee expressed a very strong empathic relationship with the land.

A good example of where a better understanding of the emotional dimension of experience and Australia's cultural complex could be helpful is with the current emotional response to the release of the *Guide to the Proposed Murray-Darling Basin Plan*. This eruption of emotion accompanying the release of the Plan is evidence of an activated cultural complex constellated around fear of loss of land, livelihood and community, belonging and identity. It is as if the government has stepped on a landmine. As Singer puts it: "These landmines are the residue, reminder and carrier of past unresolved conflicts that have accumulated in the collective memory and emotion of generations of so many people that carry deep wounds to their collective spirits".[35] Taking the time and effort to explore this aspect of human experience could contribute to a greater understanding of the community's perspective and how government might move forward with the Plan with greater cooperation.

From my perspective, I see my motivation to undertake an exploration into the affective-emotional experience of people working on salinity linking with the images I had while in a coma in hospital back in 1991. The desire to drill deeper into the issue of dryland salinity—to not be restricted to mainstream frameworks of understanding—particularly when those frameworks are biased towards the dominance of science and objective measurement of the issue as opposed to making efforts to better understand the psychological, subjective dimensions of experience. Both are needed. But funding and support is strongly oriented towards the scientific, objective frameworks of understanding.

Part of the desire to drill deeper is also related to a desire to better understand the human dimension of the world of science (dryland salinity science in this case). As a result of many years of working as a scientist, I was very aware that, for all the efforts to make science appear to be a fully rational process, many scientists had their own subjective experience of working on the issue which influenced how they engaged with it. Having gained some access to their emotional world, I can see elements of what I understand of an Australian cultural complex (in relation to the land) evident in what they bring to their scientific work. For many, the passion to do the science arises as much from their care for the Australian landscape and a desire to better understand it as it does from the excitement of the scientific process itself.

Overall, my sense is that we are in a time of transition in terms of a shifting cultural context in our relationship to the land in Australia. Over the past 200 years the Australian landscape has often been imagined to be similar to Europe's—at least in terms of how it was farmed and the expectations of what could be produced from it. This is evidence of a cultural complex as "cultural complexes tend to be repetitive, autonomous, resist consciousness, and collect experience that confirms their historical point of view".[36] But there is a growing awareness within the Australian psyche of the uniqueness and fragility of the physical environment in this country. Our collective experience has shown that it is a different sort of environment, with different properties and processes, and that we have to learn to farm it, care for it differently, and respond to its uniqueness with sensitivity and intelligence. This is happening. The issue of dryland salinity presented itself as a problem that was caused directly from Old World thinking about land use. And the Australian community has largely responded in a positive manner to look at the problem and learn new ways of dealing with it. I see this as an example of a positive response to the land and as being a significant aspect of an emergent change in the Australian cultural complex with respect to land which bodes well for a future where large scale environmental issues are impacting the land and people in many guises across this continent.

Reflecting on the dream about not being given access to enter Australia —or at least the part of Australia represented by an old bloke who was the customs official in a very dry and dusty shed—I think this may link in with my experience of doing fieldwork in the Murray-Darling Basin. This research gave me an opportunity to engage more deeply with people in the Basin. I was given an opportunity to enter their subjective world and experiences and generally found that people had a rich and deep connection with their land. As the field work unfolded, I also had a growing feeling of how much I was NOT a part of this connection with the Basin. I was from somewhere else; from quite a different part of the world and physical environment; I didn't understand their land with the depth of feeling that they had. I might have a feeling for the land in general—but I didn't have a deep feeling for this particular land. In the end, feeling like an obvious outsider, I comforted myself with the notion that I was carrying understandings of their subjective, emotional experience on this issue to others outside the Basin who might be interested to hear what they are thinking and feeling. And on further reflection, my sense of "differentness" may link to the fact that my psyche was not developed within the Australian cultural complex—I cannot "enter" and be Australian like those born and raised in the Murray-Darling Basin.

Singer and Kimbles write that cultural complexes are "lived out in group life and internalised in the psyche of individuals".[37] If this is the case, then perhaps my unconscious imagery, expressed when I was in an unconscious state, both in a coma and in a dream, point to some significant elements of the Australian cultural complex. Perhaps there is a desire to drill deeper into land-based issues because there is such a deep care and concern for land. And perhaps there is a need to recognise that people in particular regions have their own subjective "felt" experience that is unique and not easily accessible to people from the "outside"—that we need to ask permission to enter that experience and not assume it is a given.

Care of the land could well be a key area that we, as an Australian community, could look towards for further growth and creativity. Aspects of life that uplift us and keep us feeling connected—where caring for the land and the people associated with it can be related to caring for self and to the broader Australian community. This was most clearly represented from the contributions of the indigenous Natural Resource Manager but is also represented, in similar but different ways, by people from the other groups. It seems to be a shared feeling.

Acknowledgements

I would like to acknowledge Dr. Craig San Roque and Amanda Dowd for their contributions in developing my thinking for this chapter about the cultural complex as it applies to the saline Australian landscape. I would also like to thank contributors to the research project I undertook, which is a key part of this written work: Associate Professor Ian Gray and Tony Dunn at Charles Sturt University, NSW; the Future Farm Industries Cooperative Research Centre for funding the research; the research participants for their valuable contributions; and members of my psych-advisory panel: Dr. Leslie Devereaux, Dr. Glenda Cloughley, and again Dr. Craig San Roque.

Notes

[1] Thomas Singer and Samuel L. Kimbles, *The Cultural Complex: Contemporary Jungian Perspectives on Psyche and Society* (Hove, East Sussex, UK: Routledge, 2004), p. 6.

[2] Joseph Henderson, "The Cultural Unconscious," in *Shadow and Self*, ed. J. Henderson (Wilmette, Il: Chiron, 1990).

[3] National Land and Water Resources Audit, Australian dryland salinity assessment 2000: extent, impacts, processes, monitoring and management options (Canberra: Australian Government, 2001).

[4] Martin van Bueren and Richard J. Price, *Breaking Ground: Key Findings and Research Outcomes from 10 years of Australia's National Dryland Salinity Program: An Overview* (Canberra: Land & Water Australia, 2004).

[5] See Preface and Introduction to this volume for further descriptions of the complex and the cultural complex.

[6] Don Blackmore, "Protecting the Future," in *Uncharted Waters*, ed. Daniel Connell (Canberra, Australia: MDBC, 2002), p. 23.

[7] The Murray-Darling Basin Plan, sighted on 29 October 2010 at http://en.wikipedia.org/wiki/Murray-Darling_basin#The_Murray-Darling_Basin_Plan.

[8] Kay Milton, *Loving Nature — Towards an Ecology of Emotion* (London: Routledge, 2002); Joanne Vining, "Environmental decisions: the interaction of emotions, information, and decision context", *Journal of Environmental Psychology* 7 (1987): pp.13-30; Terre Satterfield, *Anatomy of a Conflict: Identity, Knowledge, and Emotion in Old-growth Forests* (Vancouver, Canada: UBC Press, 2002).

[9] As an aside, I would like to point out that at the March 2008 International Salinity Forum in Adelaide, Australia special efforts were made to have speakers from a range of disciplines, including the social sciences and the arts sector. I was given the opportunity to present some of this research at that Forum.

[10] Robert D. Stolorow and Daphne Socarides Stolorow, "Affects and Self Objects", in *Psychoanalytic Treatment: An Intersubjective Approach*, ed. Robert D. Stolorow, Bernard Brandchaft and George E. Atwood (Hillsdale NJ: The Analytic Press, 2000), pp. 66-87.

[11] Patricia Please, "Affect – see it, hear it, feel it", *Australia and New Zealand Association of Psychotherapy Bulletin* 13/3 (2003).

[12] Joseph M. Jones, *Affects as Process: An Inquiry into the Centrality of Affect in Psychological Life* (New Jersey: The Analytic Press Inc., 1995).

[13] Daniel Goleman, *Emotional Intelligence: Why It Can Matter More Than IQ* (London: Bloomsbury, 1995); Peter Salovey & John D. Mayer "Emotional intelligence", *Imagination, Cognition and Personality* 9 (1990): pp. 185-211.

[14] Daniel Goleman, *Social Intelligence: The Revolutionary New Science of Human Relationships* (New York: Bantam Dell, 2006).

[15] Antonio Damasio, *Descartes' Error - Emotion, Reason and the Human Brain* (New York: Quill, Harper Collins Publishers, 1994); Antonio Damasio, *The Feeling of What Happens: Body and Emotion in the Making of Consciousness* (New York: Harcourt, 1999); Antonio Damasio, *Looking for Spinoza: Joy, Sorrow and the Feeling Brain* (New York: Harcourt, 2003); Paul Slovic, Melissa Finucane, Ellen Peters & Donald G. MacGregor, "Risk as Analysis and Risk as Feelings: Some Thoughts about Affect, Reason, Risk and Rationality", Annual Meeting of the Society for Risk Analysis (2002).

[16] Sandra W. Russ, *Affect and Creativity: The Role of Affect and Play in the Creative Process* (Hillsdale, NJ: Lawrence Erlbaum Associates, 1993).

[17] Peter Fonagy, Gyorgy Gergely, Elliot L. Jurist & Mary Target, *Affect Regulation, Mentalisation, and the Development of the Self* (London: Karnac, 2002).

[18] Joseph LeDoux, *Synaptic Self: How Our Brains Become Who We Are* (New York: Penguin Putnam, 2002), p. 236.

[19] Michael Franz Basch, "The Significance of a Theory of Affect for Psychoanalytic Technique", *Journal of the American Psychoanalytic Association* 39S (1991): pp. 291-304.

[20] Michael Franz Basch, "The Concept of Affect: A Re-examination", *Journal of the American Psychoanalytic Association* 24 (1976): pp. 759-77.

[21] *The Collected Works of C.G. Jung*, Vol. 10, para. 53 (London: Routledge and Kegan Paul, 1960).

[22] Charles Robert Darwin, *The Expression of Emotion in Man and Animals* (London: Watts, 1872).

[23] Silvan Tomkins, "Affects as the Primary Motivational System," in *Feelings and Emotion*, ed. M.B. Arnold (New York: Academic Press, 1970); Silvan Tomkins, "Affect as Amplification: Some Modification in Theory," in *Emotions: Theory, Research and Experience*, ed. Robert Plutchik and Henry E Kellerman (New York: Academic Press, 1980).

[24] Silvan Tomkins, *Affect, Imagery, Consciousness, Vols.1 and 2* (New York: Springer, 1962-63).

[25] Donald L. Nathanson, *Shame and Pride: Affect, Sex and the Birth of the Self* (New York: W.W. Norton, 1992).

[26] *Ibid.*

[27] Heinz Kohut, *The Restoration of the Self* (New York: International Universities Press, 1977); Heinz Kohut, *How Does Analysis Cure?* (Chicago: University of Chicago Press, 1984).

[28] Russell Meares, "The Conversational Model: An Outline", *American Journal of Psychotherapy* 28(1) (2004): pp. 51-66.

[29] Heinz Kohut, *The Restoration of the Self* (New York: International Universities Press, 1977); Heinz Kohut, *How Does Analysis Cure?* (Chicago: University of Chicago Press, 1984).

[30] Allen M. Siegel, *Heinz Kohut and the Psychology of Self* (London: Brunner-Routledge, 1996), p. 105; Phil Mollon, *Releasing the Self: The Healing Legacy of Heinz Kohut* (London: Whurr Publishers, 2001), pp. 84-85.

[31] Russell Meares, *The Metaphor of Play* (Northvale, NJ: Jason Aronson, 1993), p. 30.

[32] James Hillman, *Emotion: A Comprehensive Phenomenology of Theories and Their Meanings for Therapy* (Evanston IL: Northwestern University Press, 1960), p.16.

[33] Singer and Kimbles, *The Cultural Complex*, p. 6.

[34] Thomas Singer with Catherine Kaplinsky, "Cultural Complexes in Analysis", in *Jungian Psychoanalysis Working in the Spirit of C.G. Jung*, ed. Murray Stein (Chicago: Open Court Publishing Company, 2010), pp. 22-37.

[35] Singer and Kimbles, *The Cultural Complex*, p. 32.

[36] *Ibid.*, p. 21.

[37] *Ibid.*, p. 20.

Amanda Dowd, IAAP, is a Jungian analyst and psychoanalytic psychotherapist who trained in Australia and is a member of the Australian and New Zealand Society of Jungian Analysts (ANZSJA). She has a private practice comprising people from diverse backgrounds and ethnicities in Sydney, a place where the old and established mixes with the new and transient. Amanda is a British-born migrant to Australia who spent her adolescent and University years in Christchurch, New Zealand. She has a background in ecology, ancient history, and religious studies. After many years working in London in academic book publishing, she arrived in Australia in 1986, began analysis, and later entered analytic training. Her theoretical orientation is developmental and relational, and her particular interests are trauma and the formation of mind, self, identity, and cultural identity.

●●●●●●●●●●●●●●

Finding the Fish, a work in seven parts, is a richly embroidered meditation on memory, history and on the links between self, place, identity and belonging in post-colonial Australia. This chapter, which is part a personal reflection and part a contribution to theory builds on Amanda's previously published work which has explored and theorised the foundational relationship between self and place thought about through the experience of migration and displacement. Here she brings a post-Jungian perspective to thinking about the origins of our cultural identity and the collective resistance to remembering our history which is suggestive of the development of a cultural complex.

Implicit in Amanda's thesis is that relationship to place and relationship to "other" are co-incident; the one always intimately involves and "calls up" the other. In Australia this has a very particular meaning with respect to the foundations of our cultural identity and hence the relationships between indigenous and non-indigenous Australians and between the many groups who have claimed or who are trying to claim place here. What is revealed in this chapter is a pattern that repeats—it affects all who live here because we are all vulnerable to anxieties about our "place" here and about what it means both internally and externally.

5

Finding the Fish
Memory, Displacement Anxiety, Legitimacy, and Identity:
The Legacy of Interlocking Traumatic Histories in Post-colonial Australia

Amanda Dowd

> Under the house ... the fish still swam in the rock. It was dark under the floorboards: the fish would never feel the sun again. It would not fade, as the others out in the forest were fading, with no black hands to re-draw them. It would remain as bright as the day the boards had been nailed down, but no longer alive, cut off from the trees and light that it had swum in. .... He knew it was there, and his children might remember, but his children's children would walk about on the floorboards, and never know what was beneath their feet.
>
> Kate Grenville, *The Secret River*[1]

Introduction

The intention of this chapter is to bring thoughtful reflection to the unconscious and disavowed dynamics that operate in the space between persons, between person and place or group, and between groups. This space between, or third area, which Winnicott designated as transitional or potential space, is implicitly also a cultural or shared space because it is relational. In this potential area of shared meanings—both conscious and unconscious—what belongs to me, what belongs to you, what belongs to "us" or "them", and what we are making with and of it might not be clearly defined. Because the intersubjective space is at the same time a cultural space, I think it follows that the intercultural or intergroup space can be conceived also as an *as if* intersubjective space. This is not to anthropomorphise the group but to recognise that group life has both a conscious and unconscious psychological reality, as the work of Jung, Bion, Neri, Jacques, and others attests.

As a post-Jungian psychoanalyst I find Knox's[2] elaboration from attachment theory of the Jungian notion of "archetypes" as basic image schemas and of "complexes" as relationally based and emergent internal working models compelling as developmental descriptions of the ways in which we come to apprehend and make sense of ourselves and our world. At the same time, Jung's original description of complexes as dissociative phenomena characterised by the absence of containing ego functioning and emotional chaos powerfully illustrates the ways in which both individuals and groups can be gripped by or become disoriented by intense "states" that erupt in the space between self and other, significantly affecting perception and thinking. To be gripped by a "complex" is to be caught in a state that is vitally real, emotionally potent, repetitive, and linked with unconscious memory; it can also be destructive to self and other. Over time, emotionally-based belief systems become a part of the internal working models that structure mind and hence self-other relationships—and hence relationships between groups.

The work of psychoanalysis is to bring attention to this relational space because it is the site of intense and confusing pain, suffering, and conflict. Group or cultural life matters to us, but we can have difficulty "seeing" that we are always already a "part" of the culture that we are in, even when we feel "apart" from it. In a recent paper Sam Kimbles wrote: "The phantasy that the group exists separate from its members or citizens expresses a regression that makes reflecting on the group difficult".[3] This blindness to the implicit relationship between person and group or culture and, by extension, between different groups or cultures, speaks to the invisible but palpable anxieties and conflicting tensions that underpin our basic needs for identity and belonging: tensions between outside and inside, inclusion and exclusion, the margins and the centre highlight the primary significance of the boundaries that separate one person from another and one group from another as sites of intense psychological and emotional activity. Just as relational trauma describes an experience of a breach or rupture of containing boundary and hence intrusion into the privacy of the self, so colonisation and migration can similarly be seen psychologically as experiences of boundary collapse or rupture and intrusion for both individual and group.

I am interested in trauma and in the founding creation stories—the histories—of patients because both "conception" story and history tell me something not only about "where" this person comes from and from inside which they might still be unconsciously living but also something of how they might frame experience, how they perceive their reality. Interestingly, Ogden describes a patient's history as being an aspect of their "conscious and unconscious conception" of themselves, something that is being continually "created and recreated in the course of the analysis".[4] This is a psychological statement which also has validity I think with respect to nations/cultures as well as individuals. We can reasonably describe Australia's sense of itself as being similarly emergent—that is, as being continually "created and recreated". But a question that has remained with me since I first arrived here in 1986 is "emergent out of what?", because psychologically the "background" matters, for both person and group. Ogden also reminds us that it is important not to assume that a patient *has* a history at the beginning of an analysis, that is, *historicity*—the achievement of a sense of continuity of self over time such that one's past is felt to be connected to the experience of oneself in the present—cannot be taken for granted. This is as important for a sense of cultural identity as it is for a sense of individual personal identity.

I think we can extend Kimbles' useful observation to say: the phantasy that the *history* of the group exists separate from its members...expresses a regression that *interferes with thinking* about both group and self, collective and individual identity. We know that disruptions in the line of continuity of being and unthinkable gaps in the personal narrative are evidence of trauma, and I contend that disruptions in the line of continuity of our historical and cultural narrative are also evidence of trauma. Disavowing history matters psychologically, both personally and collectively. My argument is that, in Australia, our cultural foundation or creation stories are not settled upon because the traumatic violation of both literal and metaphoric boundaries wrought by colonisation at the beginning of modern Australia has not been fully consciously recognised. This is the trauma at the beginning of non-indigenous Australian cultural history and identity and the trauma which savagely interrupted the flow of continuity for Australian First Peoples. Without the recognition of what this means *psychologically*, our historical narrative cannot be properly woven into a meaningful background, one with which we can come to terms and accept as "belonging" to us. I think this matters because a sense of individual identity is linked in a profound way with one's sense of cultural identity; if the latter is unsettled or uncertain so will be the former. Since trauma refers to what cannot be thought about and what cannot be accepted as "belonging", the psychological work required is that of recognition so that that which has been misrecognised or disavowed might be restored to its rightful "place" in the psychological scheme of things, thus restoring some depth of meaning and repairing the broken link.

The concept of a "cultural complex" offers a valuable framework within which to think about the unconscious or disavowed psychodynamics between person and group or culture and between groups. In this chapter I am building on my previous thinking and have laid out something of my very personal perspective on the aetiology of what I have come to recognise as a cultural complex that is psychically alive here in Australia and which pivots around anxieties of "place" and of belonging, legitimacy, and identity. This "complex" I envisage as descriptive of both a structural internal working model, emergent out of primitive fears of displacement, and as emergent dissociated "state" of heightened anxiety and confusion.

I wish to acknowledge that many people before me have written to these themes, but I am hopeful that this description, limited as it necessarily is, offers a different perspective on our universal and particular human relationships with place and needs to belong.

Making Contact with History:
Traumatic Rupture, Possession, and Dispossession

In 1788, what Robert Hughes has called "the largest forced exile of citizens at the behest of a European government in pre-modern history"[5] began, and he continues, "no other country had such a birth".[6] In the moment when those first fateful European footprints pressed themselves upon the sands of indigenous Australia, the European stream of consciousness and meaning-making met with the indigenous stream of consciousness and meaning-making, and the lines of continuity for both were broken. Suddenly the continent became a "space" contested by two profoundly different ways of being, perceiving, and imagining, what Lear calls a "space of competing meanings"[7] and into the gap between poured doubt, confusion, and psychic pain. Indigenous lands, saturated with a meaning known only to them and embedded in a landscape utterly different from the northern hemisphere landscapes from which the colonists had come, in the minds of those first "settlers" became an empty, meaningless space—a psychological act of obliteration that was later to become enshrined in the doctrine of *terra nullius*.[8] This doctrine, formalised by the British courts in 1889, deemed the continent of Australia as "empty" or "no man's" land because of the perceived absence of settled dwellings and cultivation. No other colonised country so effectively *psychologically* obliterated the reality of the presence of the "other" as happened with the passing of this law. This act legitimised colonisation—possession by one group and dispossession and disavowal of "other".

Almost overnight, Aboriginal people became non-persons, dispossessed of their "estate". This act of erasure was so complete that by 1941 the then Prime Minister John Curtin said: "this country shall remain forever the home of the descendants of those people who came here in peace in order to establish in the South Seas an outpost of the British race". He was referring to what was called the "White Australia" policy which was designed to restrict non-white, especially "Asiatic" and "coloured", immigration because of increasing tensions over jobs and wages and racial conflict in the goldfield States of Victoria and Queensland.[9] The "white" Australia policy was indicative of the fantasy of absolute possession—it implicitly demonstrates the brutality of the foreclosure of the psychological reality of *black* Aboriginal Australia, as if indigenous people, their histories, and mythic imaginings did not exist, as if Australia had only ever been "white". Although the policy, which began with the passing of the *Immigration Restriction Act 1901,* was dismantled in 1973, the fantasy of absolute possession persists.

In 1967, after a ten-year campaign, a referendum to change the Constitution succeeded in finally acknowledging the presence of Aboriginal and Torres Strait Islander Australians by including them in official census counts and by bringing these people under Australian Commonwealth as opposed to State law.[10] Even so, one year later, anthropologist W.E.H. Stanner, when speaking on the Great Australian Silence on the dispossession described:

> inattention on such a scale cannot simply be explained by absent mindedness ...What may have begun as a simple forgetting of other possible views turned under habit and over time into something like a cult of forgetfulness practised on a national scale. We have been able for so long to disremember the Aborigines that we are now hard put to keep them in mind....[11]

He continues, "it is a *structural matter*, a view from a window which has been carefully placed to exclude a whole quadrant of the landscape" (emphasis added). I think it is important psychologically to note that there are still no references in the Australian Constitution[12] to the history, culture, and system of law of our First Peoples or to the fact that Europeans "settled" these lands and waters without Treaty or consent. Australia is the only British Commonwealth country without a treaty with its First Peoples. Whilst this is an historical fact, it has psychological implications because it demonstrates how deeply the fallacy of *terra nullius* persists. As it persists, it continues to affect, both consciously and unconsciously, not only how we feel and think about aspects of possession/dispossession, legitimacy and identity for both indigenous and non-indigenous Australians, but also how we think about the relationship between the two.

In 1992 the historic Mabo[13] decision in the High Court of Australia overturned the doctrine of *terra nullius*. Again, an act of law had important psychological implications—while there were many who were relieved, there were also others plunged into hysterical fears of "loss of entitlement" to land; "land rights" and matters of ownership are still being debated and fought in the courts. Prime Minister Paul Keating's "Redfern Address",[14] followed by the passing of the *Native Title Act*[15] in 1993, significantly changed both law and public perception. But it was not until February 2007 that a formal Apology to the Stolen Generations was delivered in parliament on behalf of the Australian people.[16] This apology, though, was limited; it was not an apology for the disastrous effects of colonisation, dispossession, and attempted genocide. As in other colonial enterprises, Aboriginal Australians were hunted and killed; many died from imported diseases; and those that survived were gradually forced out of their ancestral lands and re-located to mission stations to be "Christianised". Their children were taken from them by force and stealth to other religious missions and orphanages, often hundreds of kilometers away.

In spite of changes in both government policy and public attitudes and perceptions, third world conditions are still found in remote communities and in the town camps around Alice Springs, and people are still dying too soon from violence, suicide, petrol sniffing and alcohol abuse, liver and kidney damage, child abuse and domestic violence. Education, housing, and employment remain vexed issues. This continues to be a national shame.

Psychologically, Australian government policies have demonstrated a move from *terra nullius*—"*they* are not here"—to variations on the theme of homogeneity or complete assimilation—"*they* are here but will either 'naturally' die out or be subsumed by 'whiteness'"—"*they* will become like us". Miscegenation as a threat to the integrity of the "white" race has also been feared at various times.[17] The fantasy of homogeneity was and is also applied to newer waves of non-Anglo migrants. Whilst this is on the historical record and many other writers have paid attention to this, my intention is to lift out the psychological reality into sharper focus and to attempt to catch something of the unconscious fear of the "other" and of difference which is our historical legacy. What we see here are attempts at the obliteration of difference—a narcissistic manoeuvre. Psychologically, this supports the fantasy of complete possession necessary for a continuing sense of legitimacy and certainty with respect to "place".

Oblating difference also serves as a defence against both uncertainty and the recognition of the pain of loss. Burggraeve describes that:

> according to Levinas, the core of racism consists not in the denial of, or failure to appreciate similarities between people, but in the denial of, or better said, failure to appreciate and value, peoples' differences, or better still, the fundamental and irreducible otherness by which they fall outside of every genre and are thus unique. A racist relation wants to recognise and value only the same, or one's own, and therefore excludes the foreign.[18]

Alexis Wright, indigenous author and activist, quotes from a government report: "the characteristic of Aboriginal injury in Central Australia was an attack upon the self-definition of the Aboriginal person, and the people as a whole".[19] As Charles Taylor suggests, "this is a terrible reality, and it is one that we have trouble understanding";[20] taking the trouble to understand is hard work because the pain of recognition brings shame. Aboriginal leader Noel Pearson describes the "existential torment" and grief of Aboriginal people "not being in charge of their ...destiny and [facing] the prospect of their cultural obliteration from history's page".[21] This is a poetic description of the fear that lives—either consciously or unconsciously—at the heart of any "culture war".

Perhaps it is obvious that the displacement trauma of the coloniser has been visited upon the colonised, but perhaps it is not so obvious what that actually means, for indigenous and non-indigenous alike.

> No English words are good enough to give a sense of the links between an Aboriginal group and its homeland. Our word "home"...does not match the Aboriginal word that may mean "camp", "hearth", "country", "everlasting home", "totem place", "life source", "spirit centre"...Our word "land" is too spare and meager. We can now scarcely use it except with economic overtones unless we happen to be poets.

> A different tradition leaves us tongue-less and earless towards this other world of meaning and significance...What I describe as homelessness, then, means that the Aborigines faced a kind of vertigo in living...a kind of spinning nausea into which they were flung by a world which seemed to have gone off its bearings.[22]

A whole people suffered the terrible consequences of the loss of a taken-for-granted connection with a background of meaning. From a psychological perspective this was a structure shattering experience—an attack on the links of personal and collective spatio-temporal continuity and cohesion, and hence self and identity, thus effectively foreclosing the potential space of becoming and hence the possibility of a future.[23]

Elsewhere,[24] I have argued that a similar experience of vertigo, of a loss of bearings and hence meaning, is also a part of the disavowed psychological heritage of non-indigenous migrant Australia. Arriving unknown and unknowing into an unrecognisable place, those first settlers were simultaneously traumatically dispossessed of their link with their own background of meaning and confronted with the alien "other". We can imagine them feeling forsaken, abandoned at the end of the world, terrified, alienated from their unimagined surroundings, and suffering unthinkable pain and loss. We know from the historical record that those first arrivals were close to starvation and seemingly "forgotten". We can imagine states of mutual misrecognition and incomprehension.[25] Those experiencing first contact with the Australian land as it would have been then would have encountered a space that was *for them* devoid, "empty" of meaning and memory. The trauma of displacement means that the internal image of the coloniser has to be projected onto or into the anxiety-provoking perceived empty space to settle intolerable anxiety, that is, something *recognisable* must be imagined, constructed, or created in order to prevent overwhelming disorientation and ongoing alienation. This transference of the already known onto the unknown and unknowable supports the psychic rationale of colonisation, appropriation and the disavowal of the mind and reality of "other"—land and people alike.

Although the doctrine of *terra nullius* was overturned in 1992, its presence as an aspect of disavowed non-indigenous Australian psychic reality persists, I think, because it supports the fantasy of legitimacy of possession and hence a sense of certainty with respect to place. The personal and cultural defences against remembering that we, the non-indigenous population, have arrived here from somewhere else and what that means continue to profoundly affect and confuse our collective responses to

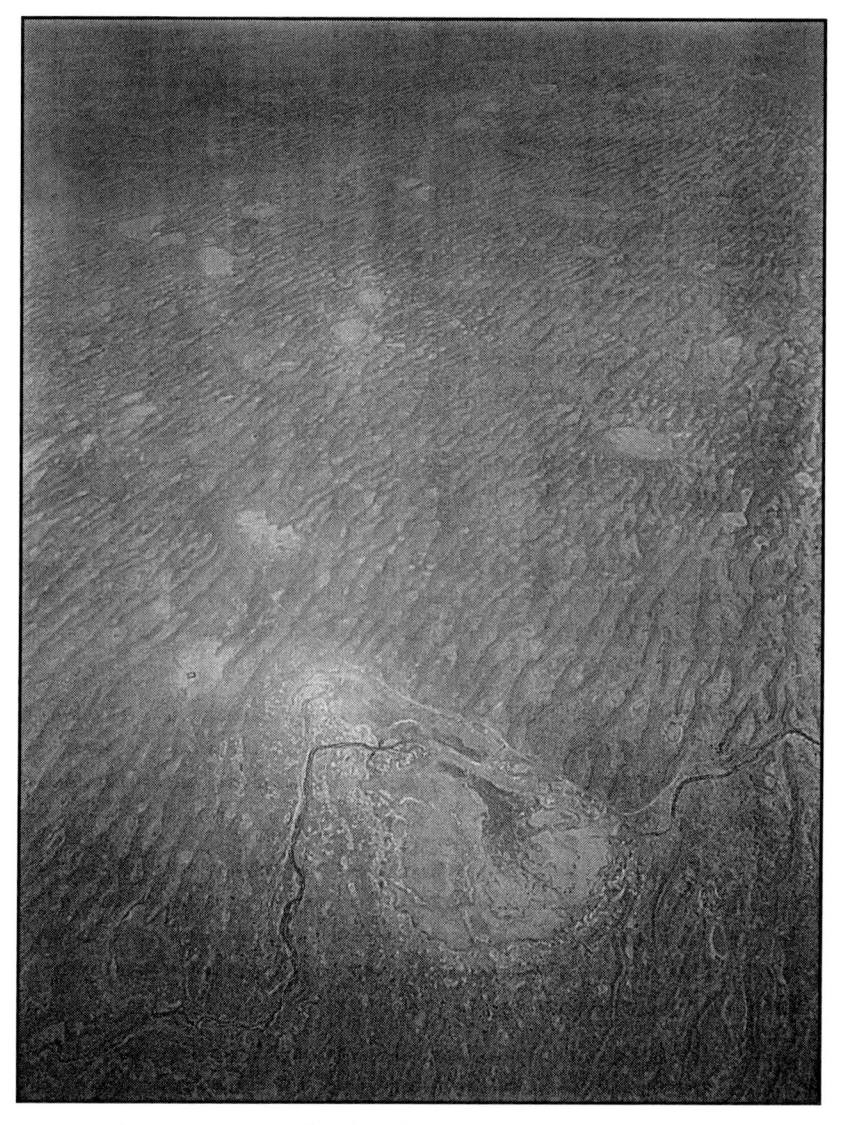

Figure 1: Simpson Desert Salt Lake. Photo Jenny McFarland, Central Australia.

indigenous rights and autonomy, refugees and asylum seekers, migration and other inter-cultural issues, and especially our perceptions of and responses to the uniquely fragile soils and ecosystems of this continent.[26] Wright could still say in 2007 that Australia "appears to be the land of disappearing memory".[27]

Chasing Memory

"It's a terrible thing to lose the places of your memories. It's like losing your mind". (Archaeologist after the bombing of the Baghdad museum of antiquities)[28]

When I first arrived in Australia in 1986, I took the "idea" of the British Commonwealth as a given: since I had my entry visa, I had permission, I had a "right to be here". Not an appropriative right, but a right to be *here* as a citizen of the Commonwealth. It did not occur to me, as I prepared my papers to enter the country, that I was actually a migrant. This might sound strange, but my family had already emigrated to the South Island of New Zealand from England in 1965 and, in my mind then, I was just crossing the "ditch" (the Tasman Sea that separates Australia from New Zealand), as it is colloquially referred to in this part of the world. Nor did it occur to me, as perhaps it did not occur to the parliamentarians of eighteenth century England who conceived the notion of convict transportation, or to the Captains of the vessels of the First Fleet as they charted their fateful course across the Indian Ocean, that the prior presence of another people might question that sense of "right".

Not long after arrival I dreamed:

I am lying on a table. A fluid is injected into my sacrum bone which induces a vision of a sacred map of Australia; an outline of the country covered in a network of connecting channels, like an x-ray map of the neural networks of the brain.

Twenty years later I came across a painting by David Mowaljarlai, Bandaiyan—Corpus Australis, which looked very like my dream map where the "body of the country" is depicted as a net of connectivity between various organs. The painting, kindly reproduced on the next page, is described by Mowaljarlai as follows:

> The squares are the areas where the communities are represented, and their symbols and the languages of the different tribes in this country from long-long time ago. The lines are the way the history stories travelled along these trade routes. They are all connected. It's the pattern of the Sharing system.
>
> In history, the Flood started up north and went all through the country. We call this land wurri malai—stooped, because it's sloping down, bent. We think of Bandaiyan in those terms, as a human body. From Central Australia the country starts to dip,

it's slanting to the south. The high country is more level because the topside lifted up....The whole of Australia is Bandaiyan.[29]

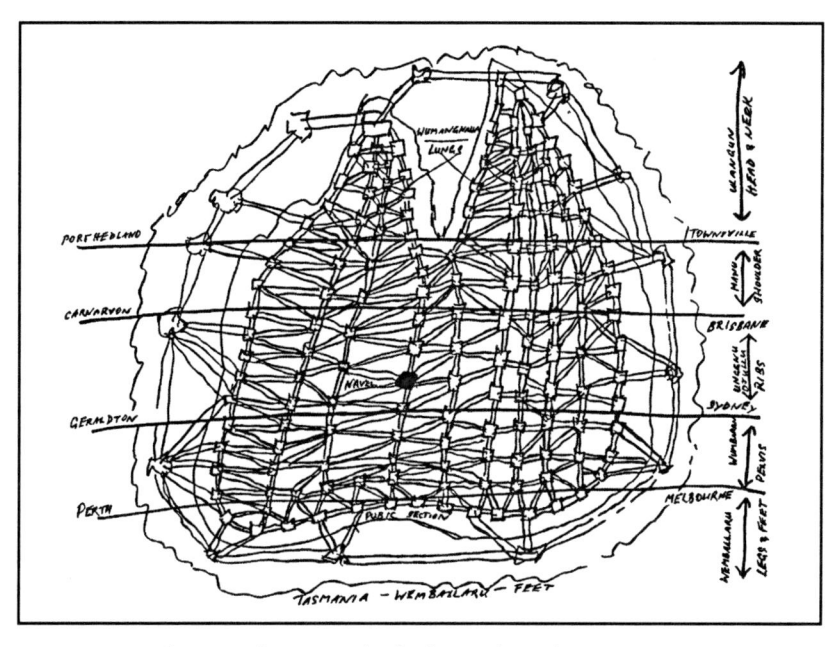

Figure 2: Bandaiyan: The network of relationships that connects all tribes and country of Aboriginal Australia. Bungal (David) Mowaljarlai. Reproduced with kind permission from *Yorro Yorro: Everything Standing Up Alive,* Magabala Books, Mowaljarlai and Jutta Malnic, Broome, WA, 1993.

My dream image did not arise out of my own psycho-cultural background as a northern European, English woman; it was neither my map nor my memory. My map, if I had thought about this then, might have resembled a vertical plane or slice through an archaeological dig revealing stratified layers, probably not unlike Jung's dream of the multistoried house.[30] Such a structural image makes sense from a European perspective, where both time and cumulative waves of invasion and assimilation are a fact of cultural history. Over there, we do "dig down" to find a sense of continuity with the past. This dream, though, offered a different pattern—a horizontal or lateral network—and the recognition that here the "past" is not beneath me in the same way; the history is "out there"—intimately woven with a different people and place and stretched across a differently textured frame. This dream also brought the beginnings of the recognition that it was *I* who am the foreigner here, a foreigner who was being deeply affected by what was both foreign and "other" to me. My dream also speaks to a preconception of the link between body and country.

Julia Kristeva writes: "The ear is receptive to conflicts only if the body looses [sic] its footing. A certain imbalance is necessary, a swaying over some abyss, for a conflict to be heard".[31] A process of de-familiarisaton with myself began. I can now say that when I first arrived in Australia, my then unconscious preconception of having a "right to be here" met with its mate in the collective consciousness of the country: that non-indigenous people had/have a right to be here is rarely questioned. It is taken for granted. This recognition accords with Singer's elaboration of the cultural complex as being "lived out in group life and... internalised in the psyche of individuals" and as "gathering evidence that supports its historical point of view".[32] I think of this as a state of mutual projective identification—a shared unconscious state of mind. He goes on to say: "cultural complexes provide a simplistic certainty about a group's place in the world in the face of otherwise conflicting and ambiguous uncertainties".[33] In an Australian context, Singer's "simplistic certainty" might read: that we belong, have a right, are legitimately settled "in place"; the conflicting uncertainty would be that we have no right, do not belong, and our occupancy is not legitimate. I discovered that I had been, in part, in a state of unconscious identification with a resident cultural complex or group state of mind which protected me from the painful knowledge of my own feelings of un-settlement, my own doubt that I was "entitled to land" at all, and my own experience of traumatic rupture and loss. Australia identifies itself as a "settler nation": it is a comforting and satisfying illusion.

As the full impact of the recognition of my own foreignness to this place and sense of loss seeped through, I dreamed:

I am led blindfold through a featureless expanse by a very old, small, and wiry Aboriginal man. We stop. He takes off my blindfold and I see a large, old Aboriginal woman standing in front of me. There is a depth of knowing sadness in her eyes that I cannot yet fathom but cannot forget.

Anzac Munnganyi movingly said: "White people just came up blind, bumping into everything and just put up the flag, put up the flag".[34] I had "put up the flag" on a (very) small plot in the eastern suburbs of Sydney; however, with the blindfold removed, I was now in full possession of the knowledge of my *real* state: I am standing on the ground of an other, ground that has been taken from another subject who suffers still. I had one further formative dream:

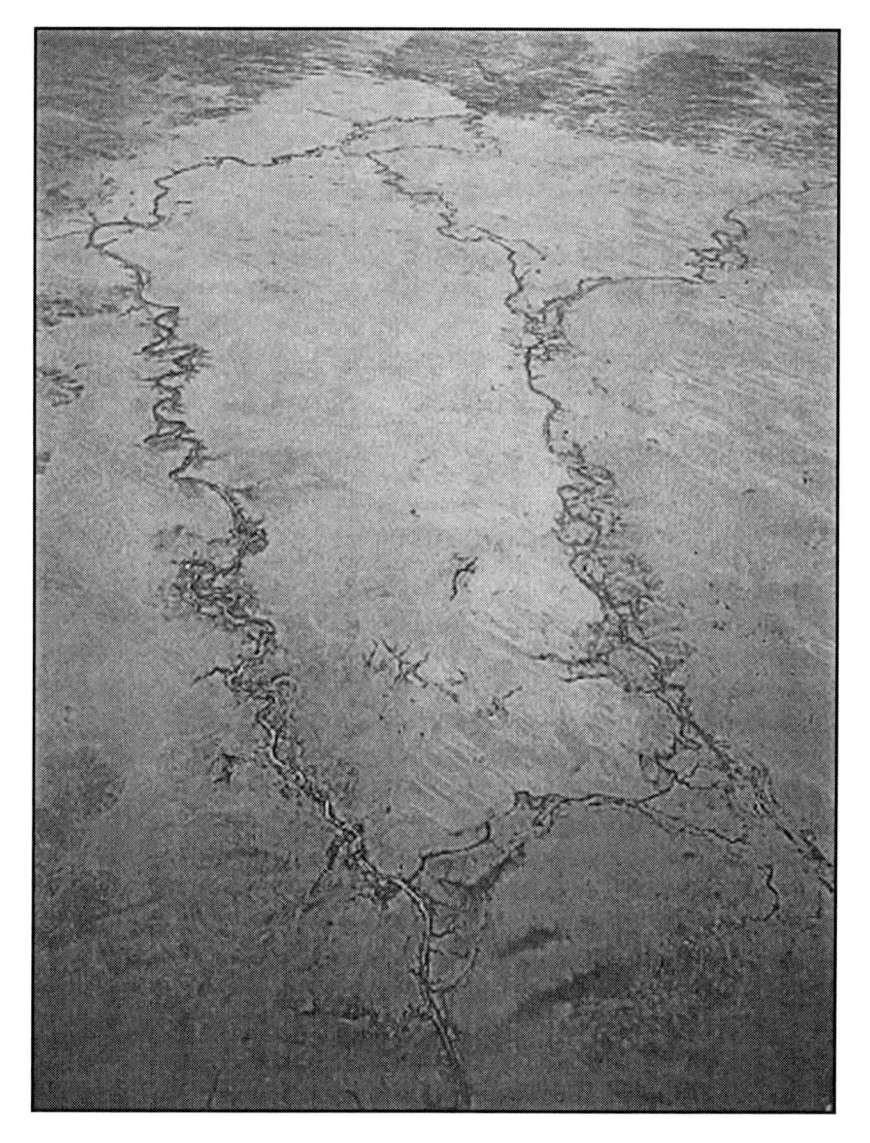

Figure 3: Ephemeral Watercourse, Lake Nash (Alpururrurlam) Way. Photo Jenny McFarland, Central Australia.

There is an Aboriginal mob moving in. I'm not sure that there is enough space for this many families. However, they arrive and all is well, setting up camp outside. They light a fire. I go inside and into my bedroom. I notice a brown snake on the edge of the bed and another black snake under the bed. I'm thinking ..mmmm ..that's interesting. I can't go to sleep here. I find the senior indigenous man and ask for help. He brings a stick—lays it on the bed and the brown snake entwines itself around it. He places the stick beneath the bed and the black snake entwines itself around it, much like a caduceus. He stands in the living room holding the stick aloft and passionately sings a Puccini aria, filling the house with sublime music of such poignancy that I weep uncontrollably.

Waking from this dream awoke me to the recognition that I could not remain caught in the collective, mostly silent illusion. The "passion" of the country—both its suffering and its potential healing—is borne of the intimate entwining of the European/non-indigenous and indigenous ways of being and dreaming (the two snakes); I felt compelled to attempt to understand what this recognition meant personally and, later, professionally.

Death, Forgetting, Time and Place...

"My lands are where my dead lie buried"
(Chief Crazy Horse, American Indian Chief)[35]

Non-indigenous Australia is a migrant nation which has been built up by cumulative waves of migration; it is only 230 years or eight generations "deep". Indigenous Australia, on the other hand, is a land which has been continuously occupied for at least 50,000 years and is around 1200 generations deep.[36] I have no dead buried here. My "dead", my ancestors, lie beneath English and European soils. I feel them there, where every hectare has been deeply scored with their songs, memories, and histories. I do not feel them here. I feel their absence as a break in continuity with my cultural memory, of where I have come from. But at the same time, I feel the presence of what Schama calls the "veins of myth and memory"[37] that belong to those who have lived here for 50,000 years. The quote above from Chief Crazy Horse implicitly links death, place, and legitimacy. Although we mourn and perhaps miss our personal "dead", our cultural dead, our ancestors or lines of lineage, very much link us back through time to place.

At a recent conference in Montreal, one of the indigenous participants, Stephen Jenkins, spoke poignantly about his experience of the "loss of the dead".[38] He was not speaking about the dead *as* loss, but about their being missing or absent. "Missing" because the places where the dead lay had not only changed but, more importantly, had themselves been "lost" as sites of meaning. I understood something of what he meant, because being a migrant and living and working with unconscious mental processes in a migrant country, alongside a displaced and mostly traumatised indigenous people, I find a resonance with this particular kind of "absence" and the psychological burden of its presence. I have come to think that it generates a leading edge of anxiety (which I will elaborate a little later).

Attwood describes death as lying "at the heart of national formulations",[39] and Muecke has observed that "states can be set up as political entities, but they only become nations through the magical or spiritual agency of death...a people recognises itself as a people...through the symbolic treatment of its dead".[40] In Australia, our national day of mourning, Anzac Day,[41] remembers the dead of wars fought for others in Turkey, France, North Africa, in Vietnam, and the Pacific. He continues, "Australia, in large part, has become a national community by remembering and mourning those who have fought in wars 'over there' but not here". We have not acknowledged, according to Attwood, that those who died fighting for this place, especially Aboriginal dead, are worthy of recognition. Our national day of celebration, Australia Day, which commemorates the arrival of the First Fleet and the achievements of colonisation, is still, over 200 years later, without a specific reference to the *act of dispossession as a violent act* and traumatic violation of the rights of the inhabitants; such a remembrance is left to indigenous groups to organise their own "sorry" (or mourning) day.

This matters psychologically. Contemporary non-indigenous Australia is founded upon an act of traumatic dispossession—a double loss—there was no noble myth of origin. If Aboriginal dead have not been recognised by non-indigenous Australia, they have not been mourned and committed to memory and therefore to history. To recognise the dead of wars fought here, to bring them to mind, would mean to assign them to history—to locate them in time and place. Histories restore a sense of continuity—the link between the past and the present—and histories belong in places; to return the dead to their place means to remember that this place is contested and is therefore a "space of competing meanings". To re-member the "creation story" of non-indigenous Australia is to remember a trauma, a "vertigo of meaning"—a shocking experience of loss, discontinuity, and crisis of identity, and a story that brings shame and doubt. Australian settler society has been described as "elusive", or with a "neither here nor there"[42] quality which resonates with what Gelder and Jacobs call the anxiety of the uncanny[43]—an anxiety generated by feeling simultaneously "in place" and "out of place". The anxiety of the uncanny is a *displacement anxiety* which arises out of existential doubt about "having a place to be" and "having a place in the scheme of things"; it is an anxiety about belonging.

We cannot mourn the dead here, I think, because we are still in a collective state of disavowal about what it *means* that our "dead"—the ancestors, our histories—lie "over there".[44] Bromberg reminds us that the:

> unintegratable affect... threatens to disorganise the internal template on which one's experience of self-coherence, self-cohesiveness and self-continuity [i.e. identity] depends...The unprocessed not-me experience held by a dissociated self-state as an affective memory without an autobiographical memory of its origin haunts the self.[45]

Might it also be tenable to think about this strange absence of mind with respect to our shared history as representing something of an unprocessed *collective* "not me" experience? I think so. Something disavowed is known and then not known, it is dis-associated from because the pain of recognition cannot be tolerated. Such dissociation—of the unthinkable and unwanted shame and doubt—linked to disavowed traumatic histories, I think, is evidence of a cultural complex or group "state of mind" which has, over time, also become structural, as Stanner so presciently recognised. Pearson, in the same article quoted from before, speaks about a radical hope "that the sovereign state of Australia becomes the recognised home of all native Australian ethnicities ...and of non-indigenous Australians". He is speaking to the existential necessity of the maintenance of the *legitimacy* of indigenous cultural continuity with the past being recognised by non-indigenous Australians; such recognition "makes our lives spiritually sustainable as members of a conquered people", he says. I happen to agree with him, but of course, the same can be said for the *conquering* people. It is exactly this shared need that psychologically sets up the "space of competing meanings"—the space between the two ways of meaning making—as a site of potential conflict regarding legitimacy/possession and identity. Something of my understanding of why such a hope is radical and why this continues to be difficult is the focus of what follows.

Ancestral Grounds or Mythic Carpet: The Connection between Mind and Place, Basic Faith and Feeling Blessed

In his seminal essay, "On Mind and Earth",[46] Jung alludes to colonisation and describes an alienating psychic potential or gap that emerges between consciousness and the "historical conditions" of the unconscious life of a conquering people which renders them "rootless" when they leave their land behind. By extension, this alienating gap also opens up between the unconscious lives of conqueror and conquered. As Kristeva writes, one's footing becomes "loose", and we can begin to feel foreign not only to the other but also to ourselves.

Philosopher Edward Casey describes place as the "*condition* of all existing things. This means that, far from being merely locatory or situational, place belongs to the very concept of existence" (emphasis added).[47] Jungian analyst Warren Colman describes "self" as the "*condition* by which subjectivity is possible".[48] If both "place" and "self" constitute something of the necessary condition of existence and subjectivity, then it is reasonable to postulate a SELF-PLACE conjunction, because there can be no person without a place to be a person, in the same way that Winnicott described there can be "no baby without a mother".[49] I take "place" in this context to mean specifically a background of meaning and meaningful containment—both externally and internally. Self experience and experience of psychosomatic emplacement are not only contingent one upon the other as, indeed, Winnicott's description of the environmental mother[50] and Bick's[51] elaboration of the importance of early skin experiences in the establishment of an embodied experience of self both implicitly evoke, but this implicit relationship is itself also at the same time emergent out of the dense associative and symbolic matrix of relationship to place within which it is also embedded.

Coming to terms with my own experience of migration and working with migrant and non-migrant patients within a migrant and post-colonial country for over twenty years now, I have come to an understanding of something of what this contingent relationship between self and place means. Leon and Rebecca Grinberg, in their sensitive elaboration of the experience of migration, describe it as "a change, surely; but it is a change of such magnitude that it not only puts one's identity on the line but puts it at risk". The entire psychic structure is shaken, they argue, because of the "wholesale loss of one's most meaningful and valued objects: people, things, places, language, culture, customs, climate, position".[52] Not only do migrants lose their attachments to these objects of experience, but they are in danger of losing the parts of themselves invested in those objects as well. They go on to make an explicit link between the trauma of migration and the trauma of birth, that is, the loss of the containing mother and hence the loss of containing mind. Both newborn and new arrival can feel for a time as if they have lost or may be in danger of losing a containing skin. Implicit in this statement is the link: country as containing mind.

This also makes sense to me if we keep in mind Grotstein's[53] reformulation of Bion's psychological principle of mind as container/contained in terms of what he calls a new natural law: "all living phenomena can be viewed as content existing in the framework of a container which circumscribes and describes its content, and, reciprocally, the content has great influence in transforming the nature of its container"; we can usefully and logically extend this "natural law" to encompass the relationship between the non-human environment as container and the living and non-living content as contained. Certain/most indigenous peoples take this for granted, of course. It has been the experience of displacement and my work here that has brought the recognition of this implicit link to mind. I have found that, with its loss, there can be a pain beyond the recognition of the loss of loved ones and necessary and meaningful objects/attachments and sense of containment as the Grinbergs describe. There also can be an emptiness, as if some foundational pattern, some essential and deep psychosomatic and emotional grammar of the soul, something previously taken for granted, is missing. To *be* an immigrant, rather than simply intellectually knowing it, "one must inhabit mental and emotional states that are not easy to endure".[54]

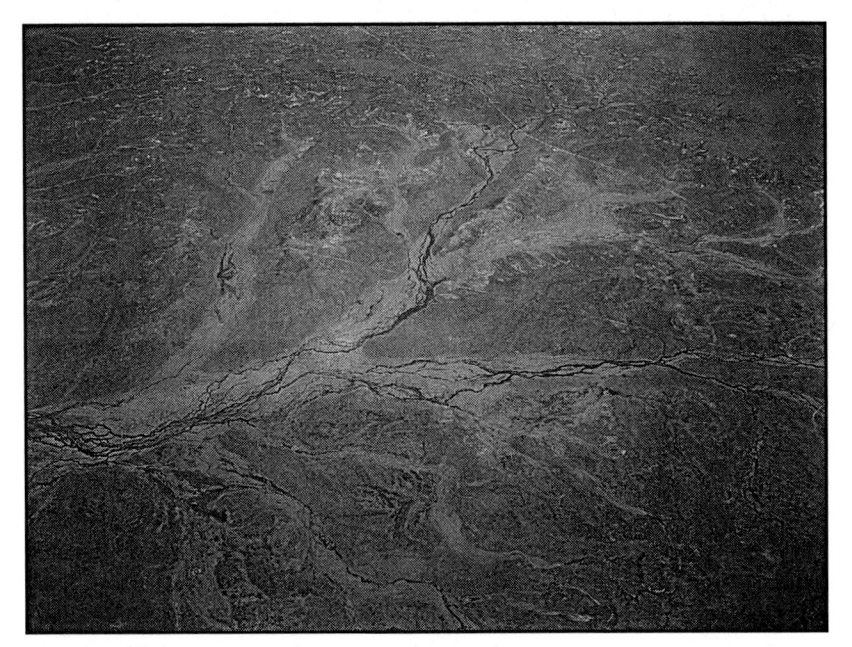

Figure 4: North Simpson Desert. Photo Jenny McFarland, Central Australia.

> The nature of the pain we are describing permits no easy definition. Although linked to feelings of loss, it is not what could be called depression nor is it, strictly speaking, anxiety though it does include elements of anguish. People usually experience it as something nearly physical...as if it lies on the border between the physical and the mental.[55]

To take account of this experience of what can be *felt* to be "missing" and this kind of primitive, less conscious, unthinkable pain, which I feel is akin to a primitive agony, I have postulated what I call the Foreground Subject Object of Primary Identification (FSOPI)[56], which is operative at the psychoid level of being. I envisage it as an implicit aspect of Grotstein's elaboration of what he calls the Background Subject Object of Primary Identification (BSOPI), or background presence of containment. Such a presence of containment emerges out of repeated experiences in the psychoid realm of being held in mind by mother, emotionally, imaginatively, and physically. If all goes well, this generates what Balint has called basic faith, what Bion might call "being at One with O", and what the Christian mystic Meister Eckhart has called the *ground of being*. Linking, and therefore thinking, cannot happen without it.

Just as these early relationships with key attachment figures contribute to the formation of the internal working models which function as the psychosomatic basis of mind, the FSOPI is a way of taking account of the way in which, I argue, we build up in implicit memory internal working models as representations of relations with the particularities of our non-human natural and built environment. It is a way of holding in mind the way in which the basic image schemas of link, path, up-down, part-whole, containment, and force are elaborated over time by experiences of proximity, distance, orientation, horizon, shape, contour, intensity, pattern, smell, and colour. That the FSOPI becomes woven into the BSOPI as background presence of containment or SELF-PLACE conjunction offers a way of thinking about the way in which one's sense of time/space and boundariedness and therefore one's sense of place and safety in that place is established as an aspect of identity from the beginning, that is, it becomes part of the taken-for-granted ground of being. We can think of this "unthought known" as constituting something of the preconceptual matrix of thought—comprising a container that enables the meaningful linking by alpha function of the contained (sensations, intuitions, proto-thoughts, and images generated by emotional experience). This not only shapes the way in which these linkages are made but also comes to form the basis of our aesthetic attitude, that is, our way of conceiving and recognising "goodness" (cohesion, continuity, truth, beauty, love) and of course "badness" (chaos, discontinuity, hate, ugliness).

This conception of the SELF-PLACE conjunction offers a way of not only recognising our more obvious, conscious emotional attachments to place—the loss of which can be potentially recognised and mourned—but it also takes into account the implicit and unconscious interwovenness between foundational aspects of self and place, and hence speaks to that more primitive psychoid level of unthinkable and unspeakable pain of loss mentioned above. The experience is as if something of the *necessary condition* to be a self can be felt to be missing[57] and it is this that contributes to the experience of displacement anxiety.

This implicit foundation or background of meaningful containment becomes, in health, the taken-for-granted base upon which later elaborations construct a narrative of self and identity. There is a resonance here with what Grotstein has called the "mythic carpet placed upon the floor of thought".[58]

> I perceive the human infant to experience himself as incompletely separated from a mythical object behind him, his rearing or background object, his object of tradition...it is the continuity of the sense of cultural and/or racial identity which ultimately devolves into the personal background of the individual. It is intimately felt as the sense of comfort that someone is behind one or stands behind one in one's effort to face the world.[59]

Grotstein is here describing a foundational experience of feeling *emplaced* or in touch with a poetic ground of being; an experience, according to him, which is akin to being blessed. Connection with this internal, implicit preconceptual matrix of thought is what affords the soul its specific felt sense of depth, meaningfulness, and purpose.

Nearly one hundred years after Jung, Schama described something of the "strength of the links"[60] that bind a northern Western culture and nature together. Thousands of years of repeating patterns of invasion/ assimilation/ reinvasion have compacted over time into a dense symbolic matrix linked to place which has both an internal as well as an external resonance, as I hope I have made clear. This Western and European mythopoesis of place or preconceptual matrix of meaning, imagination, and thought privileges both the temporal over the spatial and the vertical over the lateral; I have suggested that it lies below the threshold of consciousness in implicit memory where it remains as an unthought known until and unless one is confronted by the pain of the experience of its absence. In Australia the symbolic density of the North and West is missing. For modern migrants, this absence underlies the anxiety of the uncanny and alienating "in place"/ "out of place" experience; although this is palpable, the pain of this recognition and what it means is largely disavowed. There is, of course, also a presence, a radically different preconceptual matrix which has emerged out of a radically different place, where patterns of travelling *across* country have established a different relationship between time and space; this matrix privileges the lateral over the vertical, and the spatial over the temporal. For Australian indigenous people, what Grotstein has described as the "mythic carpet placed upon the floor of thought", is named *Tjukurrpa*:

> ...the essence of *Tjukurrpa* is a multidimensional pattern of connectedness...a complex of linking lines of sites, lines of song, lines of kin relationship, along lines of country. This adds up to...a multidimensional system of linkage that parallels the neurological patterning of the brain. The *Tjukurrpa* system is somehow very like the neurological system externalised and set into the geography of the country...it is a poetic calculus...organised to produce and sustain life, animal beings, food, knowledge, relationship...it is psychological.[61]

Participation in *Tjukurrpa* sustains not only human and spiritual life and relationships but also the ecological milieu in its totality and is at the same time inseparable from it. This is a description of this same idea of a background of meaningful containment but *imagined differently:* for Aboriginal people, it is the explicit and continuous relationship with and care of country that enables the organisation of mental and emotional experience into thought. What for a Western/European psyche resides in implicit memory, for indigenous people is both implicit and explicit, and it is transferred directly onto the geography of the country itself.

> Country in Aboriginal English is not only a common noun but also a proper noun. People talk about country in the same way that they would talk about a person: they speak to country, sing to country, visit country, worry about country, feel sorry for country, and long for country...Country is not a generalised or undifferentiated type of place...rather, country is a living entity with a yesterday, today and tomorrow, with a consciousness, and a will towards life...country is home...nourishment for body, mind and spirit; heart's ease.[62]

Two hundred years ago, when white settlers first set foot upon what was for them *terra incognita,* Aboriginal people moved "not in a landscape, but in a humanised realm, saturated with signification";[63] connection with this background presence of containment also, of course, confers its own unique felt sense of depth, interiority, meaningfulness, legitimacy, and purpose. It, too, confers a blessing. To be separated from it is to lose contact with that sense of having a "place in the scheme of things"; one loses the feel of oneself as being a legitimate "person", an experience that Grotstein describes as "cataclysmic orphandom";[64] Pearson's "existential torment". This is an internal psychological experience of ontological significance, not just a fact of history.

Migrants arrive now as they did 230 years ago, experiencing a disjunction between their taken-for-granted internal structures of mind (elaborated upon their background presence of meaningful containment) and the resident and radically other structures of mind present here—Jung's alienating and anxiety-provoking gap—at both conscious *and* unconscious levels. It is no wonder then that successive waves of migrants mimetically identify with resident cultural complex states which support the legitimacy of their arrival and "settlement" by disavowing the gap and therefore both loss and "other", thus maintaining the colonial attitudes of entitlement, possession, appropriation, perceived superiority, and fear. And it is also no wonder that those deemed illegitimate carry the full weight of 230 years of disowned and projected guilt, shame, and doubt.

The Fear of Losing the "Blessing" — Displacement Anxiety, Fear of "Other", and Shame

the creation of psychological defences can be understood as the organisation of systematic misrecognitions.
(Thomas H. Ogden, *The Primitive Edge of Experience*)[65]

The recognition of the implicit interwovenness of selfhood and place in the ways that I have been describing and the recognition of the link between the experience of emplacement and feeling blessed as "legitimate" or valid as a person, highlight just how much was and continues to be at stake in any "space of competing meanings"; that is, any border region between "others". This is where one faces the "other's" face. For Levinas, the other is *otherwise* and as such "always remains 'enigmatic'... 'irreducible', 'separate and distinct', 'strange'".[66] It is at the border between persons, between person and place, and between groups where we must bear the recognition and knowledge of this enigmatic and irreducible other: the other point of view, the other interpretation of what country, land, home, belonging, purpose, spirit, God, dreaming, and imagination means for the other, and therefore what its presence means for us. It is also the place where we confront what Meltzer has called the aesthetic conflict, that is the conflict between the "aesthetic impact of the outside of the other [person, people, land], available to the senses, and the enigmatic inside which must be construed by creative imagination".[67] Meltzer implies that if that conflict is too great, then fear borne of overwhelming anxiety about those "insides" and their motives takes hold. Out of this fear comes violence.

Lear movingly describes:

> We seem to be aware of a shared vulnerability that we cannot quite name. I suspect that this feeling has provoked the widespread intolerance that we see around us today… It is as though, without our insistence that our outlook is correct, the outlook itself might collapse. Perhaps if we could give a name to our shared sense of vulnerability, we could find better ways to live with it.[68]

When Lear speaks of the anxiety "that the outlook itself might collapse", I read him as speaking not simply to an idea, opinion, or belief. I think he is implicitly speaking to the ground—the place from which a person may have a point of view. It is anxiety about the threat of negation of *that place from which one's capacity to look out comes*, I would argue, that constitutes what Lear describes as our "shared vulnerability" because this "place" and what it means constitutes the *condition* for existence; to be dispossessed of this "place" is to be dispossessed of the blessing of legitimacy and belonging: the outlook *will* collapse if it loses contact with the ground upon which it *must* stand. Lear, I think, is describing a form of displacement anxiety, and psychoanalytically we can think of displacement anxiety as presenting an existential threat at the level of the SELF-PLACE conjunction; that is, there is a threat of rupture or severance from the background of meaningful containment and preconceptual matrix of thought—the threat of dis-continuity—and hence a threat to ontological safety, security, and identity. This leads to agonising primitive doubt and shame about *where to be*.

Vulnerability to this kind of ontological violation, as Lear suggests, "affects us all insofar as we are human",[69] and I feel that it is anxiety about this that drives our human intolerance and desperate fear of the other because feeling as if one has a "place in the scheme of things" is not only fundamental to the creative expression of the human spirit, it also and much more importantly, confers legitimacy in the human and universal order. We fear the "other" because the other is the one who might not only take our place but in so doing invalidate our right to exist as we are. I have found an interesting and valuable resonance with the way in which Mitchell[70] links the experience of displacement with sibling or lateral relations and with the aetiology of hysteria. According to Mitchell, the arrival of a sibling is "the concrete embodiment of a general condition in which no human being is unique"[71] and brings the shocking recognition that there is now an other; the child is re-placed in the position of "baby" by another who is *just as good.*

Interestingly, she describes this "sibling substitutability" as a recapitulation of the birth trauma because it is experienced as a breach or traumatic rupture and thus an ontological crisis of containment, a displacement experience where the child temporarily "loses" a sense of her or his place in the order of things, since the previous positional link to mother, or place in relation to mother, is lost. For the child, this means that, for a time, the link of continuity with a background of meaningful containment is threatened by overwhelming uncertainty. The child remains un-placed until a new positional link, a new place in relation to mother, and hence in relation to that background of safety, is established. Importantly, if mother fails to recognise that a breach has occurred, the trauma becomes a catastrophe; left feeling not only "out of place" but also exposed as if one has "no place" in the scheme of things, the child is alienated, shamed, and threatened with non-existence and is forced to "turn back", to regress to states of con-fusion with either or both parents to retain some sense of contact and hence attempt to restore some sense of taken-for-granted psychic skin or boundary for recognition of existence and belonging. Mitchell links the non-recognition of this experience of the lateral shift of displacement with hysteria.

I don't think it is too far a stretch to think intersubjectively about that psychological moment of meeting between the two cultures as a moment of ontological crisis of containment and continuity as both groups hovered precipitously on the brink of a vertiginous collapse of meaning as the relative *position* of both with respect to their different psychic experiences of feeling "blessed" (that is, implicitly and seamlessly in contact with their background-presence-of-containment) came under intolerable threat. In other words, what was at stake here was the link of continuity to their different preconceptual containing matrices of origins, their histories, creation myths, and gods.

As Winnicott described, the fear of breakdown is a fear of a repeat of a breakdown that has already happened. Lear's area of vulnerability and anxiety of collapse can be thought of as the fear of experiencing or re-experiencing a "vertigo of meaning". This, I think, speaks to the "dissociated self-state" out of our non-indigenous collective psychic history which haunts the Australian psychic landscape, along with the unintegratable affect of the shame of arriving unknowing, unknown, and unknowable to those others already here who could make sense of this place. This, I think, contributes to a specific aspect of cultural anxiety as it is experienced here.

It is out of this specific non-indigenous psychic vulnerability—the fear of experiencing a repeat of the primitive agony of losing the blessing of feeling legitimate—that makes Pearson's hope for recognition "radical". It would mean, as I understand it, that non-indigenous Australia must give up its claim to absolute possession and its insistence on sameness or homogeneity in order to keep re-affirming its existence and acknowledge Aboriginal Australia as an integral part of what it means to be Australian. That, far from being *only* "an outpost of the British race" in the South Pacific, the fantasy of a white "European" Australia must give way to the recognition of ourselves as a European-Aboriginal and Pacific/Asian "mix" with its own unique heritage, environment, and mythology. Western gods must take their place alongside indigenous spiritual traditions as equals. Such a painful re-orientation, or shift in self-perception and identity, would open the way for real relationship and, perhaps, for a different form of what Bollas describes as "deep appreciative knowing" or love of the "precise idiom" of other.[72]

The shaming "solution" to this ontological vulnerability for too long in our history has been negation; by denying Aboriginal people their "place in the scheme of things", they were effectively denied the recognition of themselves as persons in the eyes of the coloniser. As Stanner so movingly put it in 1968, "we are asking them [Aborigines] to become a new people but this means in human terms... to un-be what they now are".[73] This has led to the ongoing repudiation and de-meaning of indigenous bodies, minds, and lands; a de-meaning of the mythic carpet on the floor of their thoughts and its substitution or overlay with an other; a violent incursion/penetration into the ground of being which generates profound cultural shame. Such an act is a fundamental attack on memory, on the links of continuity as "condition" of meaningful existence, as Pearson also describes.

The exclusion of the indigenous world view from the picture of Australian identity has been achieved, as I hope I have laid out, by a process of negation. This is a "*real loss*, not just one that is described from a certain point of view. It is the *real loss of a point of view*";[74] a loss of a radically different way of arriving at thoughts; an alternative that might be "just as good". The negation of the status "human subject" at the beginning of colonisation neatly removed the problem of laterality and hence has ensured the privileging in this country of cultural descent from the European or Western system of meaning-making. However, the disavowed guilt and shame of this act continues to haunt the Australian dream. Unacknowledged and unclaimed, it leaves us vulnerable to repeated re-enactments of unminded colonisation and appropriation and in constant fear of being displaced, in often hysterical fear about our "border security" and loss of entitlement to land, and in fear of the loss of the links of continuity with our European heritage. It also leaves indigenous Australia in a constant state of seemingly endless grief. This is the legacy of our unrecognised, interlocking traumatic histories. Until we can bear to recognise that this place is now "common" ground, the pain will continue.

Historian Tony Judt said of post-war Europe that it "could rebuild itself politically and economically only by forgetting the past; it could only define itself morally and culturally by remembering it and eventually making peace"[75]. I think that the same could be said of post-colonial Australia. This would be a therapeutic act.

Epilogue: Unclaimed History and Psychoanalytic Practice in Australia

In this chapter, I have attempted to bring together reflections on history and continuity, place and position, in an effort to describe how we might think developmentally about anxieties of dis-placement both individually and collectively, and I have suggested that this anxiety represents an aspect of a cultural complex here in Australia. As a migrant nation we have a history of repeating patterns of discontinuities with respect to our relationship with place. In my practice I have repeatedly found that developmental difficulty due to traumatic misrecognition of early relational failure complicates the recognition of oneself as being a migrant or member of a migrant nation, and the migrant experience complicates the recognition and resolution of that earlier failure. I have come to understand such delays or distortion in the formation of a sense of self and identity as being inextricably interwoven with anxieties of "place" in the ways I have described.

For non-indigenous Australians our sense of *being in place* is still emergent. What this means is that the analyst in her place in the consulting room therefore comes to represent something of the country and potential relationship with it for both migrant and native because "place" becomes the triangulating factor in the development of the space of symbolisation. Along with this comes the capacity to recognise "other". Migrants especially bring displacement anxiety as the deepest underlying issue because it *is* the new place/country itself which needs to be brought into mind and symbolised. In Australia I think it is specifically a new spatial metaphor that new migrants are confronted with and that even "old" migrants are still coming to terms with.

I have found that the recovery of disavowed cultural as well as personal memory mobilises thought in the service of mediating the psychic distress of alienation and displacement, is essential in reclaiming identity, and helps to work against the possibility of retraumatisation that misrecognition brings. Fears about loss of place constellate annihilatory anxieties which engender deeply scored intolerance and racism, leading to hysterical overreaction, and, in the extreme, murder, in the service of the protection of place, position, and legitimacy. Since the space of the analytic consulting room is not only an intersubjective space but also implicitly cultural space, then cultural complex states, if unrecognised in either analyst or patient, exert unseen pressure on the psyches of both participants in the analytic relationship.

Returning the lateral and spatial dimension of human experience to a position of central significance is vitally important in the mediation of a new relationship between person and place for both migrant *and* native because the "Australian" psychic condition, and hence its distress, is itself already born of this intimate conjunction.

Notes

[1] Kate Grenville, *The Secret River* (Melbourne: Text Publishing, 2005), p. 316.

[2] Jean Knox, *Archetype, Attachment, Analysis – Jungian Psychology and the Emergent Mind* (Routledge: London and New York, 2005).

[3] Sam Kimbles, "Chaos and Fragmentation in Psychoanalytic Institutes and Society", in *Proceedings of the International Association of Analytical Psychology Conference: Facing Multiplicity: Psyche, Culture, Nature*, Montreal, August 2010, in press.

[4] Thomas H. Ogden, *The Primitive Edge of Experience* (London: Karnac, 1992), p. 191.

[5] Robert Hughes, *The Fatal Shore: A History of the Transportation of Convicts to Australia, 1787-1868* (London: The Harvill Press, 1987), pp. 1-2.

[6] *Ibid.*, p. 2. Also note that the English developed a habit of "exporting" people. From the 1860s to 1967 around 150,000 British children, some

homeless orphans or from broken homes, and others who were voluntarily "given up" by parents wishing a better life for their children were sent on ships to Australia to live in church institutions, foster care, and orphanages. Around half a million so-called child migrants were sent to Australia, New Zealand, and Canada to "populate" the former British colonies. Many were abused, neglected, and forced to labour on farms. In Australia they have been named "The Forgotten Australians" and an official Apology to them was delivered in parliament in November 2010.

[7] Jonothan Lear, *Radical Hope: Ethics in the Face of Cultural Devastation* (Cambridge, MA and London: Harvard University Press, 2006), p. 30.

[8] In 1889, the British courts found that the territory of Australia was "practically unoccupied" and established the doctrine of *terra nullius*. This was upheld by the High Court of Australia in 1979: "By European standards, [Australia] had no civilised inhabitants or settled law". It was thought that, in these circumstances, the common law doctrine of native title did not apply to Australia.

[9] See http://www.immi.gov.au/media/fact-sheets/08abolition.htm for more information on the White Australia Policy.

[10] Constitutionally, Australia, called the Commonwealth of Australia, comprises a federation of States. We have federal or Commonwealth law and State law, a system not unlike that found in the U.S.

[11] William E.H. Stanner, *After the Dreaming: The 1968 Boyer Lectures. Black and White Australians – An Anthropologist's View* (Sydney: Australian Broadcasting Commission, 1969), p. 25.

[12] At the time of writing, there is public debate about this issue.

[13] In *Mabo (No. 2)*, the High Court of Australia ruled that the doctrine of *terra nullius* should not have been applied to Australia and that the common law of Australia would recognise native title as existing alongside pastoral leases.

[14] Prime Minister Paul Keating's Redfern Address marked the opening of the International Year of the World's Indigenous People. It was the first public statement by a prime minister acknowledging the dispossession and recognising that non-indigenous Australia had something to apologise for.

[15] One year after *Mabo* the Australian Parliament passed the *Native Title Act 1993* (Cwlth) which acknowledged that if a "continuous link" could be established between a people and their land, the granting of native title could be made. Again, what this actually means is still not settled.

[16] The full text of Prime Minister Kevin Rudd's speech is available at www.aph.gov.au/house/rudd_speech.pdf. The term "the Stolen Generations" refers to the children who were forcibly removed by officers

of the Australian government from their families, homes, and ancestral lands and taken to religious missions and government homes where they received rudimentary education to become the serving class of white Australia. This practice began in 1910 and continued until 1970. Many of these children were never to see their parents and families again. See also Melinda Turner's article this volume.

[17] Up to the 1970s, there are three identifiable government policy areas with respect to the relationship between indigenous and non-indigenous people: segregation, absorption or merger, and assimilation. In 1972, policies of Aboriginal self-determination were instituted by the Whitlam government. See David Markovitch, "Genocide: A Crime of Which No Anglo-Saxon Nation Could Be Guilty?", *Murdoch University Electronic Journal of Law,* 2003, vol.10, no. 3. See also http://australianmuseum.net.au/Indigenous-Australia-Timeline-1901-to-1969.

[18] Roger Burggraeve, "Violence and the Vulnerable Face of the Other: The Vision of Emmanuel Levinas on Moral Evil and Our Responsibility", *Journal of Social Philosophy,* vol. 30, no. 1, 1999, pp. 29-45.

[19] Alexis Wright, "On Writing *Carpentaria*", *Heat 13 – Harpers Gold,* 2007, p. 13.

[20] Charles Taylor, "A Different Kind of Courage: A Review of *Radical Hope: Ethics in the Face of Cultural Devastation*", *The New York Review of Books* 54.

[21] Noel Pearson, *The Weekend Australian,* May 21-22, 2011.

[22] Stanner, *After the Dreaming,* pp. 44-5.

[23] See Amanda Dowd, "The Passion of the Country: Bearing the Burdens of Traumatic Histories, Personal and Collective", *International Journal of Jungian Studies,* vol. 2, no. 1, 2010, pp. 59-70; and also Lear, *Radical Hope.*

[24] Amanda Dowd, "Whose Mind Am I In? Reflections from an Australian Consulting Room on Migration as a Traumatic Experience", *Australasian Journal of Psychotherapy,* vol. 27, nos. 1-2, 2008, pp. 23-40; "Backgrounds of Beauty: Explorations in the Subtle Geography of Identity and the Interrelationships between Psyche and Place", *Australasian Journal of Psychotherapy,* vol. 28, nos. 1-2, 2009, pp. 96-113; "Mind the Gap: Explorations in the Subtle Geography of Identity", in ed., R. Jones, *Body, Mind and Healing After Jung: A Space of Questions* (London: Routledge, 2010), pp. 192-210.

[25] For moving and psychologically accurate literary descriptions of such states, see Grenville, *The Secret River,* and David Malouf, *Remembering Babylon* (New York: Vintage Books, 1993).

[26] We find a re-presentation of the theme of misrecognition in the Northern and Western attitude to "wilderness" and desert, seeing empty or unproductive space rather than a completely differently managed "place" and in the continuation of northern hemisphere farming practices and attitudes to land management which are in many cases completely unsuited to antipodean conditions. The nature of the environmental envelope that we live within is often willfully ignored: land clearing continues at obscene levels, even though it is known that the soils are extremely fragile and prone to desertification and dry-land salination. The expectation of enough annual rain persists against the evidence; we grow water-hungry crops although we live on the driest continent on the planet. We have not yet learnt from Aboriginal people how to understand the local weather patterns or how best to use fire to manage bush and grazing land, and so each summer hectares of forest and pasture are razed in infernos that continue to claim lives because we have not yet been able to drop the veil and come to appreciate the "precise idiom" of the place. In the aftermath of the Black Saturday bushfires in Victoria on February 7, 2009, Australian National University historian Tom Griffiths said: "There are deep recurrent ecological realities that we are really struggling to come to terms with and I don't see them being recognised…Victoria's mountain ash forests are highly evolved to burn. It is a fact that some believe has not been sufficiently recognised", in *Sydney Morning Herald,* Feb. 6-7, 2010. See also Patricia Please's article in this volume.

[27] Wright, "On Writing *Carpentaria*".

[28] This is a quote from an archaeologist on his return from Iraq after the bombing of the Baghdad museum of antiquities in 2003 (heard on ABC Radio National).

[29] Mowaljarlai and Jutta Malnic, *Yorro Yorro: Everything Standing Up Alive—Spirit of the Kimberley* (Broome, Western Australia: Magabala Books, 1993), pp. 190-4.

[30] C.G. Jung, *Memories, Dreams, Reflections,* ed. A. Jaffe (London: Flamingo, 1983), p. 182.

[31] Julia Kristeva, *Strangers to Ourselves,* trans. Leon S. Roudiez (New York: Columbia University Press, 1991), p. 17.

[32] Tom Singer and Samuel Kimbles, eds., *The Cultural Complex: Contemporary Jungian Perspectives on Psyche and Society* (Hove: Brunner-Routledge, 2004), p. 20.

[33] *Ibid.,* p. 21.

[34] Deborah Bird-Rose, *Nourishing Terrains: Australian Aboriginal Views of Landscape and Wilderness* (Canberra: Australian Heritage Commission, 1996), p. 7.

[35] American Indian Chief Crazy Horse, quoted in R. DeWall, *Korczak: Storyteller in Stone* (Crazy Horse SD: Korczak's Heritage, 1984), p. 26.

[36] There was a population of roughly750,000 Aboriginal people divided into approximately 600 language groups at the time of colonisation. There are now only about 50 extant Aboriginal languages, and as the old people die, many of these unique ways of seeing, thinking, imagining, and making meaning are being lost.

[37] Simon Schama, *Landscape and Memory* (London: Harper Collins, 1995), p. 14.

[38] XVIIIth Congress of the International Association for Analytical Psychology, Facing Multiplicity: Psyche, Nature, Culture, Montreal, Canada, August 22-27, 2010.

[39] Bain Attwood, "The Australian Patient: Traumatic Pasts and the Work of History", in *The Geography of Meanings: Psychoanalytic Perspectives on Space, Place, Land and Dislocation,* eds. Maria T. Savio-Hooke and Salman Akhtar (London: International Psychoanalytical Association, 2007), p. 75.

[40] Stephen Muecke, *No Road (Bitumen all the Way)* (Fremantle: Fremantle Arts Centre Press, 1997), p. 227.

[41] Marilyn Lake has just published some interesting work on Anzac Day as misplaced nationalism in her book, *What's Wrong with Anzac: The Militarisation of Australian History* (Sydney: University of New South Wales Press, 2010). Part of her argument is the off-shore nature of the celebration—a war fought for others on another land. Personal communication with Terrie Waddell.

[42] Bird-Rose, *Nourishing Terrains,* p. 18.

[43] Ken Gelder and Jane M. Jacobs, *Uncanny Australia: Sacredness and Identity in a Postcolonial Nation* (Melbourne: Melbourne University Press, 1998). Taken from Freud's use of the terms *heimlich,* meaning "home" (a familiar or accessible place), and *unheimlich,* meaning unhomely (unfamiliar, strange, inaccessible or obscure and untrustworthy), Freud elaborated the uncanny as that experience of one's home being rendered somehow unfamiliar; it is an experience of feeling *simultaneously* "in place" and "out of place".

[44] This process is also complicated because, for traditional desert Aboriginal people, for instance, personal lineage, and hence the passage of time, is eradicated from social memory; the focus of death, instead of

being "personal" as in the West, is returned to place. This also varies in different parts of the country. See Stephen Muecke, *Ancient and Modern: Time, Culture and Indigenous Philosophy* (Sydney: University of New South Wales Press, 2004), p. 15.

[45] P. M. Bromberg, "One Need Not be House to be Haunted: On Enactment, Dissociation and the Dread of Not Me – A Case Study", *Psychoanalytic Dialogues,* vol. 13, no. 5, 2003, p. 689.

[46] C.G. Jung, *CW* Vol. 10 (London: Routledge and Kegan Paul, 1970/1927), para. 103.

[47] Edward Casey, *Getting Back into Place: Towards a Renewed Understanding of the Place-World* (Bloomington and Indianapolis: Indiana University Press, 1993), p. 15.

[48] Warren Colman, "Models of the Self," in *Jungian Thought in the Modern World,* eds. E. Christopher and H. Solomon (London: Press Association Books, 2000), p. 15.

[49] D.W. Winnicott, *The Maturational Process and the Facilitating Environment: Studies in the Theory of Emotional Development* (London: Karnac, 1965/1990), p. 39.

[50] *Ibid.*

[51] E. Bick, "The Experience of Skin in Early Object Relations", *International Journal of Psychoanalysis,* 49, 1968, pp. 484-86.

[52] Leon and Rebecca Grinberg, *Psychoanalytic Perspectives on Migration and Exile* (New Haven and London: Yale University Press, 1989), p. 26.

[53] James S. Grotstein, "Who is the Dreamer Who Dreams the Dream and Who is the Dreamer Who Understands It", in *Do I Dare Disturb the Universe? A Memorial to Wilfred R. Bion,* ed. J. Grotstein (Beverly Hills: Caesura Press, 1981), p. 358.

[54] Grinberg, *Psychoanalytic Perspectives,* p. 66.

[55] *Ibid.*, p. 65.

[56] Dowd, "Migration"; "Mind the Gap;" and, "Backgrounds of Beauty".

[57] See A. Dowd, "Primal Negation as a Primitive Agony: Reflections on the Absence of a Place-for-becoming, *Journal of Analytical Psychology,* in press (2011).

[58] James S. Grotstein, "Who is the Dreamer Who Dreams the Dream", p. 383.

[59] *Ibid.,* p. 369.

[60] Simon Schama, *Landscape and Memory* (London: Harper Collins, 1995).

[61] Craig San Roque, "Coming to Terms with the Country: Some Incidents on First Meeting Aboriginal Locations and Aboriginal Thoughts",

in *The Geography of Meanings: Psychoanalytic Perspectives on Space, Place, Land and Dislocation,* eds. Maria T. Savio-Hooke and Salman Akhtar (London: International Psychoanalytical Association, 2007), p. 121. See also San Roque, "On Tjukurrpa, Painting Up and Building Thought", in ed. J. Mimica, *Explorations in Psychoanalytic Ethnography* (NY, Oxford: Berghahn Books, 2007).

[62] Bird-Rose, *Nourishing Terrains,* p. 7.

[63] Stanner, in Bird Rose, *Nourishing Terrains,* p. 18.

[64] James S. Grotstein, *A Beam of Intense Darkness, Wilfred Bion's Legacy to Psychoanalysis* (London: Karnac, 2007), p. 313.

[65] Ogden, *The Primitive Edge of Experience,* p. 197.

[66] Burggraeve, *Violence and the Vulnerable Face of the Other,* p. 30.

[67] D. Meltzer and M. H. Williams, *The Apprehension of Beauty, The Role of Aesthetic Conflict in Development, Art and Violence* (Strath Tay, Scotland: The Clunie Press, 1998), p. 22.

[68] Lear, *Radical Hope,* p. 7.

[69] *Ibid.,* 50.

[70] Juliet Mitchell, *Mad Men and Medusas: Reclaiming Hysteria* (New York: Basic Books, 2000).

[71] *Ibid.,* p. 25-6.

[72] Christopher Bollas, *Forces of Destiny: Psychoanalysis and Human Idiom* (London: Free Association Books, 1989), p. 112.

[73] Stanner, *After the Dreaming,* p. 57.

[74] *Ibid.,* p. 32 (italics in original).

[75] Tony Judt, *Postwar: A History of Europe since 1945* (London: Penguin Books, 2005).

David Russell, Ph.D., was born and grew up in rural New South Wales. On his paternal side, his grandfather arrived in Australia from Ireland as a young man. On his maternal side, his two lines of inheritance were British convicts, one from Scotland and the other from Ireland. After his training in psychology, David moved into a teaching/research position with the University of Western Sydney as a lecturer in Psychology. Subsequently, he was responsible, as part of a small and enthusiastic group, for the foundation of undergraduate and postgraduate degrees in Social Ecology and then master's degrees in Cultural Psychology and, finally, Analytical Psychology. After thirty years as a senior academic, David has returned to his private practice as a Jungian psychotherapist in Sydney.

From all accounts, the first three decades of the settlement of Sydney by the British were one long nightmare. As a means of getting by, the desperate souls that made up this primitive colony cultivated a love of talk and a deep suspicion of language. Language, as reflective practice, had to be put aside in their daily effort to survive and make do. While the early twentieth century saw individual artists and a handful of psychiatrists and psychologists expressing a deep reflective attitude, David Russell describes the dominant sensibility of Australia, the cultural complex, as being one of silence; a silence, not of words— for talking was everywhere—but of reflective language.

The early patterning of coping with loss of identity and the resulting experiences of psychic pain are the underpinning of the particular psychological story that was and still is dominant in the culture of Australia. This chapter argues that it has taken two hundred years to gradually transform from the desire to not linger on the rawness of emotional experience, the dominant attitude of cultural silence, to the desire to reflect on and express our cultural experience; and in this expression to find a relationship characterised by qualities such as love and beauty.

6

Lost for Words: Embryonic Australia and a Psychic Narrative

David B. Russell

How contradictory is the ethos of colonial Australia when compared with that of analytical psychology, which values the reflective attitude, a belief in the healing power of the psyche, the consulting room, and the carefully negotiated contract as the basic conditions of effective therapeutic work. In contrast, the basic conditions of living in embryonic Australia were likely bare survival, homesickness, and a culture of separation. The inhabitants were British officers anxious to return home, a motley crew of free settlers, and convicts. The social scene of June 13, 1816—almost thirty years after the British first began to arrive in Australia— is poignantly expressed at the celebration of the formal opening of the Royal Botanic Gardens (actually the private gardens of Governor Macquarie), the completion of Mrs. Macquarie's road, and the nine-foot high stone wall surrounding the Botanical Gardens, all built by convict gangs and celebrated with five gallons of rum. The high surrounding wall was built to keep the riff-raff out and to ensure that only the better class of person gained entry. Any reflective and sedate culture was for the privileged few. The uncouth, uneducated, and criminal majority worked for an eventual freedom and, more immediately, for whatever relief that could be obtained by drinking enormous amounts of distilled spirits.

Figure 1: The Macquarie Wall. Botanic Gardens, Farm Cove, Sydney. (Constructed 1816). Photos by D. Russell, 2011.

My thoughts have turned to the experience of those who tried to make "a go of it" during that formative period from 1788, the year in which *transportees*, as convicted felons, military guardians, or opportunistic wayfarers, began to arrive on the shores of Sydney, becoming part of the British colony called at that time New South Wales.[1] A Frenchman, La Perouse, had reached Australia in 1770, at the same time that Captain James Cook on the HMS Endeavour charted the Eastern coast of the country for Britain, but through luck or aggression the British and the English language, not the French, colonised Australia. So, lest I approach a psychic narrative of embryonic Australia from a biased point of view based upon my British ancestry, in this article I draw greatly on the work of Jean-Bertrand Pontalis, French psychoanalyst and co-author of the impressive, highly influential text, *Vocabulaire de la Psychanalyse (The Language of Psychoanalysis)*.[2]

In addition to *The Language of Psychoanalysis*, Pontalis wrote an autobiography of sorts, *Love of Beginnings*.[3] This book is not a sequence of historical events but a story of a relationship with language. *Love of Beginnings* looks at those critical events that are the interplay of loss and identity; what is lost the moment we believe we have acquired identity? It is this dynamic of loss and acquisition that underlies my thoughts about Australia and its loss and acquisition of language, or rather how our peculiar psychic narratives have been, and are being formed.

Deborah Bird Rose, a noted anthropologist who arrived in Australia in 1980, puts her experience into these words: "The Australia I came to know and love was always a place of invasion, death, betrayal and cruelty, and of resilience, survival, and storytelling, and of an unswerving belief that things could be different".[4] Was there a love of beginnings in the convict settlement that was Sydney? Perhaps there was a particular passion for finding somewhere to start from, again. Any relationship between Pontalis' love for beginning anew and early New South Wales will be paradoxical and imaginative; how else could it be? Pontalis, with his passion for language and psychoanalysis is going to be doubly suspicious to the Australian mind. After all, right from the first days of settlement, the locals had a love for talk but were suspicious of language. Reflection and conscious discipline had no place in the pragmatic, if not desperate, contingencies of those times. It is my argument that little has changed. Yet, Pontalis *is* relevant. So much of what he writes is in opposition to institutional dogma (including psychoanalytical dogma) and to the attribution of single meanings, while at the same time he valorises *street wisdom* and *desire* with all their inherent ambivalence. He actually, and unknowingly, helps us understand our Australian struggle. Before the transformation of experience into reflective consciousness is the desire to survive and make do. And, as part of the desire to make do, is the desire *to* talk, which itself leads to the desire *of* talk. This is how Pontalis invites us into his web of insightful language.

My introduction to reading Pontalis was through his dynamic linkage of the dream and psychic pain.[5] It was his assertion that "the theory of wish-fulfilment needed to be extended to include psychic pain as a positive private experience"[6] that caught my imagination. For his purpose, he draws the distinction between suffering and psychic pain, the latter being an essentially intra-psychic experience. At around the same time, I was reading Tom Keneally's *Australians: Origins to Eureka*,[7] and it occurred to me that psychic pain as a positive experience was what must have been serving these largely forgotten souls who first came to Australia. From all accounts, the first three decades of the settlement of Sydney were one long nightmare. If the experience of psychic pain is at the heart of the nightmare, as Pontalis suggests, then perhaps the experience of pain by the first settlers, and its consequences, will help us understand foundational elements of the Australian psyche.

Following Freud, one might imagine that confinement on the inhospitable coast of New South Wales was experienced as an unbelievable renouncement: So unbearable was the loss of every outward relationship that the experience was literally, and metaphorically, unspeakable. The "choice" of an anchorage in silent pain was "preferred"[8] to a conscious engagement with the emotional loss: mourning. A degree of pleasure was found in the interpersonal place of unreflective talking amongst fellow humans suffering the same fate. One could hypothesise that the metaphor that connoted the presence of psychic pain in those first decades of settlement, and I would contend the same applies today, is a certain type of silence: a silence, not of words, for talking was everywhere, but of reflective language. The psychic pain was so strongly suppressed that "its presence was always tangible *a contrario*: a mental structure built on the model of manic defence, neutralisation of affects, alternation of infatuation and denigration of the self";[9] what Carl Jung called a feeling-toned complex.[10]

Cultural Silence and the Absence of Reflective Language

I follow the usefulness of extending Jung's notion of an individual complex as the constellation of emotionally charged psychological events (memories, ideas, evaluative feelings) to a cultural complex in which a particular group has unconsciously knitted its shared and disturbing events into a constellation of an inner generated force which is expressed in the Australian context as a cultural silence.[11] This silence is not a passive silence, rather, it is a force to be reckoned with, a pervasive and ever-present demand: Do not speak of troubling emotional matters! I follow this idea and also wonder if it helps me make sense of my own experience, embedded as I am in the culture that formed my mind, my language, and my silences.

The theme of cultural silence in reference to early Australia is not a new one. The fact that it has never been recognised by the general population, from the advent of the first whites to the present day, indicates both its pervasiveness and its unconsciousness. We have a taken-for-granted attitude to the history of Australia. In fact we are used to "the Great Australian Silence,"[12] a phrase employed by the anthropologist William Edward Hanley Stanner to describe the deliberate attitude of non-indigenous Australians to see their history as unblemished by the huge loss of innocent blood incurred in frontier violence as white settlers moved further and further into the indigenous lands. This Great Australian Silence has also been maintained toward the denigration of Aboriginal culture, and the near total dispossession of Aboriginal peoples from their traditional lands. We have worked hard not to feel the consequences of achieving our "unblemished history".

Robert Hughes, in his book *The Fatal Shore*,[13] writes of the prevalent "amnesia—a national pact of silence" that existed as early as the 1820s and functioned to remove the "convict stain" from colonial Australia's consciousness. There was always a new beginning, a fresh start, ready at hand. It was not that the past didn't exist, but rather there was just no point thinking about it. Hughes, in bringing the reader up to the occasion of the Australian Centennial, in 1888, describes a favourite trope of the time as:

a young vigorous person gazing into the sun, turning his or her back on the dark crouching shadows of the past. A "Centennial Song" published in the Melbourne *Argus* struck the right note of defensive optimism, coupling it with an appeal to censor early Australian history—or, preferably, not to write it at all:

Look ahead and not behind us! Look to what is sunny, bright –
Look into our glorious future, not into our shadowed night.[14]

An Australian psyche, that dynamic network of complexes wherein each complex acts to both structure and limit the conscious experience of every immigrant individual, was shaped by an imperative to live an unreflective life, no matter the cost.[15]

It is ironic that the early word association method, the vehicle for the identification of a complex in the tradition of Jung at the Burghölzi hospital in Zurich, had to do with actual words and hesitating silences. It was through the momentary silence that the unconscious psychic process revealed itself. It is as if silence is the indication of the disturbance of the normal process (of the association of words and meanings). On the cultural scale the silences are frequent and so pervasive that we have become the complex. In Jung's words, the "complexes *have us.*"[16] In order to mask the complex, we talk. Words are used to hide or obscure reflection; "the art of using words to conceal thoughts ... ."[17] And so we return to the earlier statement that, as a rule, Australians love to talk but are suspicious of language.

The first volume of verse published in Sydney was by a colonial officer in 1819 who described the south land not as a work of God's initial creation but as "... an afterbirth, not conceived in the Beginning ... but emerged at the first sinning".[18]

An emerging Australian identity would have been a contested identity between the native-born children of former convicts[19] asserting their right to a fresh start and free British emigrants, who arrived later and wanted to claim respectability based on their Britishness. Yet, what could either group point to in the early history of Australia with pride? One thing was for certain, opening old wounds was not an option.

It was not until the late 1950s and early 60s that the general Australian public accepted the need to consciously reflect as a means of self understanding and to thus articulate a history other than one which depicted Australia as a worthy member of the British Commonwealth of Nations. However, when Donald Horne's *The Lucky Country*[20] was published in 1964, even though most Australians picked up on the irony of the title, the phrase "the lucky country" also became a self-congratulatory mantra for how good things were. Horne's much more subtle point was that with Australia's "cultural cringe", its foreign policy, and its White Australia Policy, it was really a "not too clever country".

Reflection, especially as epitomised by the writings of Pontalis, is akin to the process of epigenesis in geography and biology; it is the story of the recursive interactions, the mutual shaping of people and places, or rivers and landscapes. Reflection might seem like a personal attribute, one that is of my own making, one that I can call my own. The cultural and physical milieu that is our Australian experience has ensured that when we reflect we express a history of troubling relationships. It is different than "interpretation" in that it is the desire to attend to the experience itself. Australia, up to recent times, was in Pontalis' terms,[21] pre-Freudian in as much as it valued talking over reflected experience. The settler experience was, of necessity, unreflected experience. Here the experience ends in talk, talking is the desired experience, talking as an object. Language, by contrast, is for Pontalis a libidinal cathexis between present and the past. The desire to survive and "make do" outweighed the desire for the transformation of talk into language. The relationship between talk and making do was recursive and self-serving.

One couldn't imagine Freud writing *The Interpretation of Dreams* in the Sydney of 1899. As the "conqueror and possessor of the *terra incognita*"[22] he wanted to penetrate the secret of talk (and the dream). He would have been up against the Australian attitude of assigning limits to raw experience, limits to the unconscious, wherein a conversation is a tacit agreement of silence; silence when it comes to "primary process" and reflected feelings and thoughts. One imagines that the great risk if one wasn't attached to their talking was to be cast adrift. In talking one finds their moorings and thus a sense of place. While Pontalis is referring to the dream as an object, the same can be said of talking: talking is valorised, invested with extraordinary importance, eroticised even. Talking became the psychological screen on which to project and which, conveniently, protected against raw emotions.

Early Sydney needed to build barriers against raw emotions because the destructive effects of trauma were just too great. Language (reflective language) would have too easily penetrated the illusion of owning this place that they had called their own; a defence against the nightmare of being motherless, of there being no matrix in which to find adequate emotional satisfaction. Preserving the illusion was essential to survival. The shallow water of talk doesn't penetrate us, it carries us.

The Personal and the Present

Following Michael Billig[23] and accepting that "repression" is not a state, or even a mechanism, but an achievement, there comes a time when the constant demand of active engagement by the experiencing person with their ongoing relationships opens up the possibility of change. A sizable number of Australians, I believe, have arrived at this point in time. The propensity to avoid reflective thinking is not an instinctive human condition. Rather, in Australia, it was imposed by desperate circumstances. After having achieved an identity built on repressed desires, desires to emotionally and consciously engage with oneself and others, it became possible to begin to let the desires through to consciousness. I imagine that until relatively recently any question of reflective thinking was cast in the central question: how are we going to survive in this place? Felt survival was contingent on repressing conflictual and troubling desires. Silence was an act of tacit acceptance of the reality that was. Once physical, emotional, and intellectual survival were no longer only the prerogative of the upper class, the officer class, and the church, reflective language could become a *lingua franca* of the thoughtful person. Louis Nowra, Australian author and public intellectual, recently wrote in *The Sydney Morning Herald* that historically, "Good authors and artists [Australian, that is] are often in conflict with the official version of a country's identity, values and history ... at their best they [their novels] are complex and disturbing stories that challenge the sunny portrait we have of ourselves".[24]

My own story was that of a very silent child, one susceptible to sense perception, who, like Pontalis, dreamed of new beginnings. Like many others of my time, I had convicts in the family tree and, as the grandson of an Irish patriot, I was not of the class that had "assumed" authority. As an adolescent in the 1950s I vividly felt the unbridgeable gulf between the underdog and the top dog, the unconnected voice and the dominant voice.[The official version of identity, even in the 1950s, led to what felt like an unbridgeable gulf that forever widened between oneself and the dominant voice.] So many words: "words so as not to feel any longer, words so as not to think."[25] Again, like so many of my generation, I needed to leave Australia in order to reflect on Australia. By immersing myself in the cultures of North America and Europe I began to find a voice, both inner and outer, to express the ambivalance and confusion of my Australian experience. Eventually the silence found a form of articulation in the desire to publically express a dynamic unity of mind, body, and action in a series of academic programs at Hawkesbury Agricultural College. It is fitting in many ways that these initiatives were situated in a college, founded in 1891, for those wanting a preparation for a life on the land. Degrees in Social Ecology with an emphasis on reflection and reflective action brought a Jungian perspective to the learning of professional and everyday competencies. As the college merged with other tertiary institutions to form a university (University of Western Sydney), so the academic programs took on a more cultural orientation (cultural psychology). A dynamic partnership with practising Jungian analysts resulted in a Master of Analytical Psychology program which had an intellectual rather than a clinical focus and was designed precisely to foster reflective practice. It was as if the tables had finally turned: language was attended to, cultural stories were judged to be essential to wellbeing, history was relevant, and the natural environment and cultural milieu were to be listened to and valued as critical resources. Over the years, numerous analysts took the opportunity to complete Ph.D. research work which, in turn, brought new depth to their clinical profession. As I see it now, these students, like others in other places, were almost subconsciously working at finding voice for localised psychic narratives, some attuned to pervasive personal complexes, brought through traumatic early experiences, yes; and some attuned to complex cultural national matters distinguished by repression, mythologising, and rationalising away. Like the early convicts the yearning for liberation was within us still. What kind of liberation though? Masud Khan notes in the preface to *The Language of Psychoanalysis* that Freud's courage was to seek the truth of experience (in his nineteenth century city of Vienna), even if the truth took him through case histories to taboo matters, nightmare, incest, child abuse, hysterical somatic suppressions, and totemic primal horde behaviours. Freud's persistent reflection on his own psychic and cultural situation led to psychic emancipations for many individuals.

Pontalis, in writing about psychoanalysis and his attempt to convey what he actually encounters in it, grappled with his "dissatisfaction", his "anxious passion" for it was not about "observing facts nor of inventing stories". He could just as well have been talking about the psychological complex of the Australian experience when he pondered on the psychoanalytical experience: "The object isn't offered to the gaze and yet it exists. ... Why did I become a psychoanalyst if not endlessly to measure language against what it isn't?".[26] The experience is always going to express more than any language can convey. "Language ... arrives late, to move in like an abusive proprietor, an arrogant master, once the work has been done—the work of the obscure". He goes on to be even more emphatic;

"No assemblage of words, not even the most mineral of poems, will ever make me a witness of the emergence".[27] So, we have it—words offer a protective barrier to the rawness of experience. Try as we might, and we must try to transform the words into flesh; at best, what we arrive at is not intellectual understanding but an aesthetic experience. Words matter, but it is in those moments when words fail us that "we come closest to the intimate, the unknown, the hidden distress that is buried beneath words and even perceptible affects".[28]

The psychoanalytic urge, when we find ourselves living in the belly of the social complex, is to try to ascribe words and meaning to the mute language of this conflicting experience only to fail miserably.

Conclusion

In striving to be aware of the cultural complex there is the unexpressed hope that I might break loose of it by stating it. It is as if through language I could become "master" of my complex-driven experience. The line of reasoning goes like this: first, there would be language and then there could be interpretation. Like any interpretation, what I can express to myself in words can then be kept at a distance. And, finally, once something is at a distance, then it can be manipulated. I accept that there is a desire driving our cultural complex; and I accept that the complex existed well before any verbal description. However, I also trust that what it represents is already inscribed, captured, and shaped by psyche ... it comes with the culture. The one thing that those of the Jungian community who applied themselves to the study of the Australian psyche via the Master of Analytical Psychology experience understood was that it is the relation that we have with the cultural complex that determined its effects. Not *only* are we the complex, we have this extra-ordinary ability to develop an ongoing aesthetic relationship with the psychology of our culture, its history and its horrors; and, in the same moment, see the relationship as being characterised by qualities such as love and beauty.

Notes

[1] Captain James Cook found the east coast of *Australia Incognita* or *continens australis*, the southern continent, in 1770. He named the coast New South Wales. Lord Sydney, after whom the first settlement was named, was the Home Secretary at the time of Captain Arthur Phillip's arrival with the First Fleet in 1788.

² Jean Laplanche and Jean-Bertrand Pontalis, *The Language of Psychoanalysis*, trans. D. Nicholson-Smith (London: Hogath Press & Institute of Psycho-Analysis, 1973).

³ Jean-Bertrand Pontalis, *Love of Beginnings*, trans. J. Green and M.-C. Réguis (London: Free Association Press, 1993).

⁴ Deborah Bird Rose, *Reports from a Wild Country: Ethics for Decolonisation* (Sydney: NSW Press, 2004), p. 2.

⁵ Jean-Bertrand Pontalis, *Frontiers in Psychoanalysis: Between the Dream and Psychic Pain*, trans. C. Cullen and P. Cullen (London: Hogarth Press & Institute of Psycho-Analysis, 1981).

⁶ Masud Khan in "Introduction" to Jean-Bertrand Pontalis' *Frontiers in Psychoanalysis*, p. 9.

⁷ Tom Keneally, *Australians: Origins to Eureka* (Crows Nest, NSW: Allen & Unwin, 2009).

⁸ Pontalis, *Frontiers in Psychoanalysis,* p. 195.

⁹ *Ibid.*, p. 202.

¹⁰ Carl Gustav Jung, *CW* 8, para. 201.

¹¹ See the Preface and Introduction in this volume for the history of the psychological complex and of its plausible extension to the cultural sphere.

¹² See Robert Manne's Comment: "The History Wars", *The Monthly*, November 2009, pp. 15-17.

¹³ Robert Hughes, *The Fatal Shore* (London: Pan, 1988), p. xii.

¹⁴ *Ibid.*, p. 597.

¹⁵ The psychological functions of dissociation (*I have no emotional response when you criticise who I am*) and repression (*There is nothing to be gained and everything to lose by thinking too much*) are consequences, one could hypothesise, of the activity of a particular cultural complex, namely, an *Epimetheus complex*. Epimetheus and Prometheus were a pair of Titans who "acted as representatives of mankind." See Karl Kerenyi, *The Gods of the Greeks* (London: Thames & Hudson, 1951), p. 207. Epimetheus is depicted as "he who reflects when it is too late", the father of non-reflective thought, and thus as foolish. Prometheus is characterised as being clever and ingenious and thus having forethought.

¹⁶ Jung, *CW* 8, para. 200.

¹⁷ *Ibid.*, para. 198.

¹⁸ Donald Horne, *The Australian People: Biography of a Nation* (Sydney: Angus and Robertson, 1978), p. 4.

¹⁹ A census taken in 1828 found that half the population of NSW were convicts, and that former convicts made up half of the free population.

[20] Donald Horne, *The Lucky Country* (Camberwell, VIC: Penguin Australia, 2008).

[21] Jean-Bertrand Pontalis, "Dream as an Object", in *The Dream Discourse Today*, ed. S. Flanders (London: Routledge, 1993).

[22] *Ibid.*, p. 111.

[23] Michael Billig, *Freudian Repression: Conversations Creating the Unconscious* (Cambridge: Cambridge University Press, 1999).

[24] Louise Nowra, "To Appreciate Our Identity, We Need the Write Stuff", in *The Sydney Morning Herald*, January 2-3, 2010, p. 9.

[25] Pontalis, *Love of Beginnings*, pp. 102-103.

[26] *Ibid.*, p. 42.

[27] *Ibid.*, p. 52.

[28] Jean-Bertrand Pontalis, "Notable Encounters", *American Imago Vol. 63, No. 2* (2006): pp. 145-157.

Ute Eickelkamp, Ph.D., is an Honorary Associate in anthropology at the University of Sydney. Between 2004-2009 she was a Postdoctoral Research Fellow in the School for Social and Policy Research at Charles Darwin University. Previously, she studied anthropology and sociology at Marburg, Berlin and Heidelberg, Germany, and she gained a Graduate Diploma in Infant and Parent Mental Health at Melbourne University.

Her field work has included the study of Anangu children's imagination and social dynamics through a traditional form of sand storytelling in the Central Australian community of Ernabella. She has also done therapeutic Sandplay work with Tiwi children in Australia's north.

●●●●●●●●●●●●●

Ute Eikelkamp explores her search for origins against the background of her identity as a German anthropologist working with Aboriginal people in Central Australia. By revisiting memories of learning language, significant encounters, and dreams, Ute describes a state of "homelessness of the mind" and search for maternal containment. During this personal process she describes the way in which signs and symbols began to interact or resonate in her dreams with the Aboriginal cultural imagination. She discovered that she can only create a sense of belonging to place in Australia if she also makes space for her European cultural background.

Ute's chapter takes the reader into an "in-between" space in both psyche and culture. As if slipping between two cultures in one's brain in the place of language, she explores a primal place in the psyche where one lives. She takes the reader into difficult to articulate links between psyche, language, place, meaningfulness, and belonging. In this exquisitely sensitive account of her search, Ute acknowledges an unresolved tension and sense of gloomy threat which she feels is connected to the shadow of intergenerational collective German guilt and its impact on her experience of living in Australia. One can think of this journey as a complex of one culture, the German, encountering the totally different terrain of other cultures, the indigenous and non-indigenous peoples of Australia.

7

Language is My Second Skin: Speaking and Dreaming between Germany and Central Australia

Ute Eickelkamp

Introduction

For many people, emigration has brought with it the collapse of a meaningful and taken-for-granted world. However, for others, the taken-for-granted world of home that is left behind may have already been an insecure place—more like an empty, if familiar shell than a nourishing terrain. Reviewing my personal struggle for a sense of belonging and in particular how this became manifest in my relationship with language, I explore in this chapter the unsettling sense of being without place that took shape prior to—and indeed led to—my emigration from Germany to Australia, where I work as a social anthropologist with Aboriginal people. I describe certain points of the emotional and intellectual journey away from my familial home and towards new meanings, a journey that I call a search for new origins.

My entry point will be the experience of losing touch with my mother tongue, German, in the process of thinking, feeling, remembering, and anticipating in foreign languages, mostly French, English, and sometimes Pitjantjatjara, a dialect of the Aboriginal Western Desert language. Specifically, I want to look at the slipping away of the natural fit between sound and image, the dissolution of the unity of thought and symbol that I remember from "before" and that has now given way to a shaky ground between words and what they stand for. The loss of the taken-for-granted fit between signifier and signified has been described by others writing about their experience of migration.[1] I ask how my sense of losing my mother tongue relates to an unresolved personal struggle to feel maternal containment, which is furthermore infused with what I would call the primitive cultural traits of my German milieu. I have brought with me to Australia this personal and collective heritage, with certain consequences for my feeling of self and identity. I hope my personal reflections on encounters with significant others who connect for me Germany and Australia, on language learning and forgetting, and on three dreams from the period of settling into my new home in the Antipodes will convey a particular cultural inflection of this global experience.

Significant Encounters: Orienting Towards Australia

I first visited Central Australia in 1986 for a few months as an eighteen-year-old high school graduate, a trip financed with the earnings of three months labour in a car factory in my German hometown in Westphalia's industrial Ruhr valley. The contrast between the confined noisy space and monotony of the factory work with programmed machines, on the one hand, and the open expanse of the Australian bush with its soothing colours and quietness combined with the softly spoken Aboriginal people whom I came to know, on the other, could not have been greater. Moreover, I was going to Australia to experience new family ties. My mother's cousin, who had emigrated to the small outback town of Tennant Creek in the early 1960s, was waiting for me at the other end of the world with his wife and four children. I had met him, his daughter, and one of his sons once before; they had come to Germany when I was seven years old, and I had kept a special place in my heart for these children who looked different somehow —glowing, sun-burnt—and with whom I could not communicate other than through playing (in the snow).

Upon arrival, I felt instantly at home in that part of the Northern Territory and quickly fit into what for me was an exciting life with much work at a service station (whose major customers were Aboriginal people), horse riding, and driving long distances. The latter was a good opportunity to talk, and it was on such "story trips" that my mother's cousin filled me in on what for me were two "big" subjects: the plight of Aboriginal people's lives and race relations in Australia, and our German family history. Over the next two decades, he was to become an important source of information about and link to my maternal grandparents, especially my mother's mother and two of her older sisters (one of them his mother), who had come from

East Prussia to marry Westphalian coalminers. As I listened to these stories told in Australian English but spoken with a heavy German accent, I fell in love. Not only with the landscape but also with the people and the language, Australian English, which bore no similarity to my high school English. In fact, I could hardly understand a word. But before long, I had identified with the voice of my female cousin to the point that it irritated her; speaking with me on the phone one day, she said: "Ute, you sound like me, making me feel I am talking to myself".

I thought that living permanently in Australia and becoming an anthropologist would make me feel at home in my life, and so the following ten years in Germany, during which I revisited Australia several times, were a time of waiting and unsettledness. Nevertheless, I came to cherish Berlin during my eight years of study. I lived there both before and after the fall of the wall; living behind it in the Western part of the city was liberating rather than confining, in the way that the holding protective enclosure of a sandpit (or maternal protection) can free up the imagination in play more than the open shore which demands caution. For many of us, full consciousness that there was a wall only came with its fall. I mention this because the feeling tone of this memory resonates with the "gap" between words and world that becomes a problem as soon as one becomes aware of it. For Berliners, one of the ways in which belonging in the world could be affirmed was this: "In order to feel at home", a shop owner once told me, "you must not speak too courteously but rough, that is what we find endearing".

The contrast between Berlin and Aboriginal perceptions of civility could not have been greater, as I was to find out in 1992. It was here, in post-wall Berlin, that my first close and decisive encounter with Aboriginal people took place. A group of ten women artists from the Western Desert had arrived for a cultural exchange visit, and I was "looking after" them for two weeks. I remember that they showed an enormous interest in Hitler's bunker rather than in the wall; they never explained what the subterranean *Führerbunker* meant to them but insisted on seeing it. Most of the women were Anangu Pitjantjatjara speakers from remote communities in northern South Australia, and we forged a friendship, or better, a silent agreement of taking care of the other in one's *heimat*, which became the basis for their support of my future research in their home community. They invited me into their lives despite the repeated acts of racial discrimination that a Germany struggling to reunite confronted them with.[2]

Language, Learning, and Belonging

One of my strongest memories from adolescence is that I loved learning. Anything that catapulted me outside the orbit of my home world was welcome. While I never doubted that I could learn all the things I wanted to (the infant's sense of omniscience has never really left me), paradoxically, it became coupled with a profound sense of insecurity. My learning technique was to throw my mind into the object of interest, especially language, as if it was another body and I was becoming another person—I slipped into somebody else's skin, losing my own in the process.

French

Learning French during the 1980s at school was a riveting experience, almost miraculous. I found that I could speak and read and be understood in French as if I had taken it in with mother's milk. The words forming at the front of my mouth seemed as natural as the deeper-placed German sounds—they fit like a glove. But this ease of speaking French, the lack of barrier that others betray in their accents, stirred up something. I began to ask myself: "Was there anything inside the glove? Was I not attached to (in love with) my mother's tongue—or to my mother? Or she to me? Was I trying to get rid of "it", of this unsettling sense of a missing link between mother and baby?" I find helpful here Max Scheler's description of vital feeling, which:

> is ... the subject of that primary experience of *resistance* which is the root of experiencing what is called 'reality', especially the unity and the impression of 'reality' which precedes any specific representation. Representations and mediated thinking (inferences) can never give us anything but this or that quality in the world. Its 'reality' as such is given only in an experience of resistance accompanied by anxiety.[3]

I seemed able to get around the resistance of foreign languages, which therewith lost their reality status for me. My anxiety stemmed from the suspicion that there should be resistance—there should be a feeling of reality—but I felt no *effort* to produce sounds. Learning French was a mimetic experience devoid of a rubbing of the foreign against the familiar self-image in sound. When reading or speaking it, French became like an adhesive skin that left no space for perceiving the other or the self. The more fluidly I spoke, the stronger my (unspoken) fear of facing this question: if the one sound could easily substitute for another, does this not mean that the link between word and meaning is arbitrary—and, by extension, the link between mother and baby, which makes possible the primary experience of vitality Scheler writes about? At the same time, I also wanted to break out of the symbioses with my parental home and *heimat* in the Ruhr valley, which were smothering me. I was seeking novel relationships and perhaps, I think now, a new maternal link, by questioning my taken-for-granted belief in the German language and world in order to feel more real. There felt something unreal, even fake, in not questioning the assumptions that made for the "ontological security"[4] of my German home.

As an adolescent, such considerations were semi-conscious; twenty-five years later, living in Australia, my French has slipped away almost entirely, yet I remember the feeling of being inside the language, with no German interfering with either thought (grammar, vocabulary) or tongue (pronunciation). I made French my own as if the French didn't own their language, as if what was said and written could just as well be mine, there to be taken. I could talk it well, yet it was as if I was speaking away from my self. French did not really "grow" on or in me; I had just slipped inside its skin and put it on like a second layer hiding a very brittle sense of where and to whom I belonged. A German accent, I think, would have indicated a deeper internalisation of it. It would have meant that a part of my self was still visible but changed and affected by the new, and so perhaps something of it would have stayed with me for good.

English

English, specifically the Australian ways of speaking, has come to occupy a different place in my mind. This is the language of sustained immersion in my chosen host country, at the level of everyday encounters, in scholarly articulation, and in nocturnal dreams. Since 1995, my life and work experiences have been mostly in English and I sometimes struggle to communicate these parts of my life to family and friends in Germany—while there is little difficulty talking to them about memories of events that took place there. This, I suspect, may be a familiar experience for immigrants everywhere. The deeper problem with becoming fluid in a foreign language is, at least in my case, that it erodes the taken-for-grantedness, what I call the "givenness", of the mother tongue. Not only will I never be a "native" Australian English speaker, but I also have lost a total identification with the German language. And I miss it. My sense is that English and German have become equally present in my mind and equally distant from my self, to the extent that, since I began to dream and think in English, I sometimes mix them up. German words and Germanisms slip into my (waking) speech, which did not happen when English was still a foreign language, when the "wall" was still up, so to speak. I also think my German accent is becoming stronger. I can "hear" my old, pre-migration self surfacing through the sounds of English, which, more internalised than French, is bringing it closer to the present. But I am still struggling to anchor myself in place.

Pitjantjatjara

My experience of learning Pitjantjatjara, an Aboriginal language of the Australian Western Desert, has been different from the start. Although here too my accent, I am told, is slight, this language has never been "at my disposal" to be used for whatever purpose I might wish; it remains closely linked to *being with* the native speakers in concrete situations.[5] "My" Pitjantjatjara is only basic, and I did not learn it in the classroom, but through shared living in a Central Australian community. People there are conscious of language ownership, since language, like everything else, is grounded in "country" and originates in the Dreaming. For Aboriginal people, the world in all its shapes and sounds began when Ancestral creator beings in human or animal form began to wake from their slumber to think and move and speak, thus transforming out of their minds and bodies an unshaped surface into the landscape and creating an ordered universe of human and animal life. At the end of their journeys, when the creator beings came to rest (died), they entered the ground or transformed into features of the country, leaving behind for the continuity of life their vital essence in water places and other spirit centres. These Dreamings or Ancestral beings still abide in the land as a latently active force; their actions are embodied in discrete places that interconnect people and non-human life forms through their unified Dreaming origin. Here, the notion of "mother-tongue" obtains a culturally enriched meaning. As linguist-anthropologist Alan Rumsey explains, the "groundedness" of language and its perceived givenness—meaning that it is not just that actual mothers give it to you, but language is already an Ancestrally given feature of the landscape—are important aspects of a person's identity and a means of social differentiation:

> Languages ... are directly placed in the landscape by the founding acts of dreamtime heroes. From that point on, the relation between language and territory is a necessary rather than a contingent one. People too, or their immortal souls,

> are similarly grounded in the landscape, in the form of spirit children ... associated with specific sites, and via links through their parents to more extensive regions. But *the languages were already placed in those regions before any people came on the scene.* The links between peoples and languages are secondary links, established through the grounding of both in the landscape.[6]

A beautifully concrete explanation of the origin of languages in Aboriginal thinking is cited in Heather McDonald's recent paper on Indigenous Christianity in the Kimberley, Western Australia. Sadie James, a Jaru woman, had this to say:

> We talk from *birlirr* [ancestral life-forces]. *Birlirr* come from waterhole [in Jaru country]. If you want to talk Jaru, you dig a soak and drink the water, then cover im up. You can talk language now.[7]

As in many Western societies, the name for people, country, and language coincides—I speak *Deutsch*, I am *Deutsche*, and I grew up in *Deutschland*, or Jaru, Jaru, Jaru. In the Aboriginal context, however, this link is conceived of as shared substances and shared life-forces. That my Anangu friends taught me their language and thus spoon-fed me their world and selves—especially two women who thereby cemented our relationship —was an act of nourishment and emplacement. It was also an act of protection from jealous Ancestors.[8] As other ethnographers have noted, Ancestral beings watch over human presence and activity, looking after the "right" people or countrymen whose language (and sweat) they recognise. By contrast, "[f]oreign speech and bodily substances provoke Ancestors to violence".[9] They resent the presence of strangers with whom they share no origins and will deny the new arrivals all kinds of nourishment. In this world, taking over foreign territory is like disturbing the mother-child relationship. In order to enter it—not just a country but its relational foundation—one must show care and do the social work of being there and speaking in the local tongue. I would often hear that my desire to learn Pitjantjatjara made me belong to the community and the Anangu families living there. This was linked to the fact that I had my own language, German, and hence my own place and family connections, which affirmed my personhood. English, by contrast, was regarded more like a currency, a medium of exchange without belonging to a particular place. My writing about the Anangu in English is, I think, acknowledged as an act of translation for the "outside" world of both their knowledge in Pitjantjatjara and my experiencing German self. For the Anangu, my language/place identity was powerfully confirmed during my first research in 1995, when, camping with old people at the time of initiation rituals, I was heard speaking German in a dream.[10]

Dreams About Language and True Beginnings

Unlike in waking life where the link between word and object (perception, idea) can be ruptured and the arbitrariness of the sign shown up, in dreams, sound and image seem welded together as "emissions" of the same psychic activity (which, for Aboriginal people, can be that of another person who "gives" you a dream). Related to this is that "dream speech" resembles "inner speech"; in both there is an identity or close proximity between the dreamer and the interlocutor or listener, so that, as Werner and Kaplan explain in their analysis of symbol formation, "the boundary between self as addressor and self as addressee is scarcely established".[11] It seems to me that this ordinary adhesive identification between the dreamer and the dreamed can help elucidate further the perhaps unusual and problematic mimetic experience of learning French that I have described above. In fact, the following three dreams about language and origins may be read as expressions of the same problem—a lack of maternal containment that is the basis for the possibility of surviving separation. Without this original "skin" around mother and baby, it is difficult to sustain the mental and emotional space that allows for the real perception of self and other. I think that, together, these dreams from the time I was settling into Australia for good and establishing myself as an anthropologist might reflect something of my attempt to find a new authentic voice and therewith a containing "skin".

"Birth of Languages"

In 2001, when I was finishing my dissertation on Aboriginal art and living in my new home near Sydney after five years of moving between Central Australia and the southeast of the country, I had the following dream in which I was a young boy. I have called this dream the "Birth of Languages":

Without there being a distinct locale, I saw a great expanse of sound, like desert, but also like water. Masses of people, but they were very small, as if seen from a great distance. Very bright white light, no colours. Shiny glittering particles filling the air. There was a slight mumbling noise. People had voices but no words. There came something/someone very big, like a shadow, cool, descending from behind and above. It seemed as if the entire world population (not very large at the time) had gathered for a reason: They were waiting to receive something. I realised that they all had a raw mass of language per se, wholly without shape, unformed, just the raw material, so to speak. Although they had come from all directions (the surface of the earth was flat), they could not break out of their minds and create real meaningful languages. What they had was all the same. The curious thing was that they knew—they had some kind of awareness of their predicament. The mumbling noise had been given to them, but they had the desire to free themselves out of this silent wasteland. This big shadow-creature was going to give the solution to them. Like a trick of the mind.

I realised on waking that I had forgotten the trick! But it made me think immediately of the raw material as bread (the stuff of language) and the solution as water. Mixing the two would bring words—malleable and thus swallow-able and also gullible things. It was the key to the whole question of how human language came about—not as a slow evolutionary diversification but in one flash of insight. There can only be: either an undifferentiated mass of sound or hundreds of languages, but there never was such a thing as one language.

Reading this dream and afterthoughts now, ten years later, I see how much it reflects my search for a new mother tongue and therewith meaning in Central Australia and in the life shared for a while with Aboriginal people, especially the women who took responsibility for my presence. I wanted to feel that I could be part of their world that I thought was without existential doubt, a world whose reality was simply given. I was hoping to find there something undivided and contained within myself, even though I knew that the universe of my A_nangu friends had been challenged on many fronts.

The first lines of the dream could be read as a description of the desert landscape, where the sky can look like water and the line of the horizon blurs, softening the surrounding and evoking a feeling of calm slumber. The sound of people "mumbling" without words has another real reference; it is what I heard when falling asleep in the bush camp at the time when I could not understand Pitjantjatjara. And the "entire world population" is an apt image of my actual perception of the remote settlement and its neighbouring communities, adding up to a population of about 3,000 in an area of over 120,000 square kilometers, entry to which was only possible with a permit. For me, living in this settlement felt like having an enclosure around the self, not unlike the Berlin wall.

Furthermore, if the people in the dream had "gathered as if to receive something", it might be because I had wished that the real people wanted me there just as much as I wanted to receive something from them. But there was always restlessness in me; this surrounding stillness, I remember, was perceived through the windows of my car, as I was constantly driving somewhere. "Driving" here has the connotation of being driven to move forward, to learn, to thrust myself into the research, and not just to be there. This is important as well—to see the other part of the child who wants to be held and nurtured, the part that is "greedy" for knowledge, as some Aboriginal people might say.

Finally, the dream tells of an undifferentiated state of being—a bright light that has not yet refracted into colours, and a muffled sound shared by all humanity prior to the diversity of languages. Diversity is something to be given—by the great shadow coming from above, descending upon the people and bringing words and meaning. However, the people were already there, differentiated only at the basic level of where they came from, that is, from all directions. These first humans had already the vital feeling that Scheler writes about; they were oriented outward towards the world, aware that they needed to differentiate further. They were waiting to receive the solution. In the dream it was not clear what this solution is, but I think now that the solution is the stuff that would enable them to have "representations and mediated thinking ... [that] give us this or that quality in the world".[12]

Intercultural Elaboration

Today I am struck by the similarity between this dream imagery and a creation story—a collective dream about psychological birth and the beginning of culture—from Central Australia. In his "classic" text on the religious traditions of the Aranda people in Central Australia, T. G. H. Strehlow recounts:

> At the beginning of time the earth had looked like a featureless, desolate plain. ... It was covered in eternal darkness ... No plants or animals could, of course, exist under such conditions; but a vague form of human life existed in the shape of semi-embryonic masses of half-developed infants, all joined together in their hundreds, lying helplessly at places which were later revealed as salt lakes or great waterholes. These "infants" were not merely joined together in their hundreds: their hands and toes were also drawn together by webs, their eyes, mouths, and noses were closed, and they could not move any of their limbs. They could therefore not develop into individual men and women. ... Only below the surface of the earth did life already exist in its fullness,

> in the form of thousands of uncreated supernatural beings that had always existed; but even these were still slumbering in eternal sleep.
>
> Time began when these supernatural beings awakened from their sleep. They broke through to the surface of the earth; and their "birthplaces" became the first sites on the earth to be impregnated with their life and power. The earth was flooded with light for the first time …
>
> … some of the supernatural beings sliced massed humanity into individual infants, then slit the webs between their fingers and toes, and cut open their ears, eyes, and mouths. Other 'culture heroes' taught men how to fashion spears and shields, how to make fire, and how to use it for cooking food.[13]

These Ancestral culture heroes not only also brought the diversity of languages, they furthermore created the stories and songs through which knowledge of human origins and traditions are transmitted. A few days before my dream, I had learnt about a Yagwoia[14] man in Papua New Guinea who reacted with frustration (depression) when it dawned on him how, in comparison to his own traditions, very diverse and rich the universe of musical sound is in the West. I was deeply moved by this and felt sorry for this man who cannot tap into a foreign wealth of sound. I felt sorry for him as an expression of my own sense of not being able to make the songs of the Australian desert my own, those sung stories from the Dreaming that keep the world in place. I felt depleted because neither could I identify with my German cultural traditions—I was still waiting to be given this "solution" as I did not really know what Western Desert people call the "taste" of my melodies. However, I remember that my anxious concern at the time about being ignorant of German high culture almost made me forget that I had loved the songs and stories of my childhood which my grandmother had shared with me. In the next dream recounted here, this link to a maternal container is elaborated through images, rather than sounds, of belonging.

"Swiss Dreaming"

My journal notation of "Swiss Dreaming", also from 2001, begins in German and continues in English in the middle of the second sentence.

Ein sehr bildhafter Traum, kaum Handlung, eher kleine Szenenwechsel, minimal Worte, zwei Menschen. Eine sehr hochgelegene Alpenwiese, Alm-Höhe

["A dream filled with images, hardly any action, rather small changes of scene, words appear minimally, two people. An alpine meadow at very high altitude, height of the Alps."], a very green patch of grass that stretches to the first horizon bending with the edge of the hill.

One cannot go further, steep gorge, on the other side of which rises a huge dark mountain, greyish-blue, standing like a wall up from the green carpet.

On the meadow stands frozen a black cow staring at me. I always face towards the dark mountain in the background, never assuming the other perspective. I see a huge Aboriginal ground painting – it has beautifully decorated edges that stretch into the end of my view; reddish-brown dust and lots of small objects – floral tiles, shiny little things are inserted like in a mosaic. I cannot see the overall patterns, don't even recognise that it is an Aboriginal painting.

Then an Aboriginal woman (I think she came out of the cow), rather young, tells me friendly and invitingly that I should take a look at the bigger picture. I follow the outer lines, but they keep going with my steps toward the horizon. I still have no overview, only a sense of distance and length through walking in time.

I fly over the scene—wow!—a huge triangle, two sides are of even length, becomes visible.

The whole dream is like a painting through which I move, its powerful images taking me on a journey of learning by seeing with a fresh eye—of having an in-sight about my own original and expanding containment in the form of a triangle. Reading the dream account now triggers memories that associate it with the question of my own indigeneity. The childhood memory of a farm holiday in Austria comes to mind, partly because of the mixed feelings I had then: I found the alps gloomy and smothering, which was enhanced by the difficulty of breathing lightly in the thin air; but I loved the daily rides on a slow-moving draft horse, its belly so large that my legs reached not even halfway around. A fading photograph of this still decorates my parental home; and, for me, the image has come to stand for the connection with my maternal grandmother, who was my emotional anchor and also godmother. She had come on a horse cart to the Ruhr valley, as a young peasant woman from Masuria, in order to marry my grandfather. This I had learnt from my uncle in Central Australia. I note also that by bringing the childhood memory of a holiday into my English-spoken world of experiences, the name of the country "Austria" (Hitler's motherland,[15] "Österreich") becomes likened to "Australia".

Another, more immediate context is that, a few months before the dream, I had gained my Ph.D. degree, which involved going back to Germany to defend my thesis about Aboriginal art in front of an all-male examination committee at the university of Heidelberg. I had never lived there, though, and on this brief visit, the old German town struck me as falsely pretty and rather oppressive. It was on the morning of my thesis defense that I first learnt that Freud, having received the Goethe prize for his literary contributions to German culture in 1930, saw his books burnt by the Nazis on the university plaza three years later. And it was a few minutes before entering the examination room that I was advised not to mention the name "Freud". I felt as if someone had slapped me in the face. I was enraged at this blow of discrimination and perceived that I was cast as a threatening outsider who does not belong to either Germany or the academy. It took me a long time to "digest" the experience.

Figure 1: Personaje en el Valle. 70 x 40 cm. Tec. Mixta. 1970. Courtesy of the artist, Miguel Angel Biazzi.

For me, this dream about a Swiss-looking home country has a compensatory effect; despite a gloomy wall, its overall feeling tone is soothing and it directs me towards the possibility of taking a second look at my cultural roots. The theme of a protective female presence is pronounced, and it is linked to my experience of being with Aboriginal women. I remember the strong sense of passivity in the dream; the cow staring at me while my eyes are fixed onto a dark impenetrable mountain in the distance. This "frozen" moment is broken when the soft voice of a Black woman invites me to take a look at the bigger picture, thus setting me in motion and even letting me fly. She seems to have come out of the cow and may be a symbol of rebirth. As an anthropologist I think of rebirth as a central motif in the rite of passage of initiation into adulthood, here perhaps alluding to my own "initiation" into Aboriginal culture through fieldwork. But, as indicated above with the observation about my fondness for big horses, another more private feeling is that the cow as a symbol of maternal protection and knowledge bearer has to do with my (peasant) maternal grandmother whom I felt very close to. And I now realise this: though she did not pass on to me the elaborate traditions of German scholarship and art, it was her beautiful immaculate voice that brought to me German and European folklore—nursery rhymes, fairy tales, hymns, and prayers (something no one could ever burn).

Once in the air, the shape of what, in remembering the dream, I took to be an Aboriginal ground painting becomes visible; it is a triangular enclosure. But I then note in my journal that this shape was not recognisable to me in the dream as an Aboriginal painting, even though afterwards I thought it was one. Indeed, the triangle is not a common motif in Central Australian Aboriginal art, and there is something futuristic about the design, not at all like an age-old Aboriginal rock painting. Yet it is foundational, it goes to the heart of something. This is a structure, an essence, a framework. here is actually no painting but a frame, and this "window" is lovingly decorated. This triangle points to my own indigenous space of containment and reflection; not *in* the Aboriginal world as such, but mediated by it.[16]

Intercultural Elaboration

The dream described above contains an intercultural perspective within it—images of German *cum* Swiss landscapes on whose ground becomes visible a large containing structure once I listen to a Black woman born out of a cow. Going beyond it, I am struck to find resonances with a dream about the cultural complex of an exiled South African man described by Thomas Singer and Catherine Kaplinsky.[17] In the dream they relate, a (White) South African man, who lived as a university professor in Europe, remembers that, at the time of the abolition of the apartheid regime, he repeatedly dreamt of a young Black boy playing with cowrie shells on a beach from which he sees the surf rising up like a wall, the shells being toy cattle in the enclosure of a South African kraal. There are similar themes in my dream: *playfulness* indicated by pretty shiny objects on the red sandy ground like his cowrie shells on the beach; *threat* indicated by the impenetrable "wall" that is the dark mountain in my dream and that are "big waves banked up on one another" in his; *maternal containment* in both dreams in the image of cows linked up with experiences of being nurtured by Indigenous women (a link that my dream association "cow/Black woman –horse/maternal grandmother" brought out), and the *relationship with Aboriginal people pointing towards disavowed origins*, with a Black boy child in the man's dream and with a young Black woman just born in my own. There is a telling difference of detail: the man is unable to speak to the boy in his dream, while I hear the young woman speak to me, which changes everything I see.

The man referred to in the Singer and Kaplinsky paper grapples with a cultural complex and personal consequences that differ from my own, and I don't think that the South African apartheid regime can be directly compared with the unofficial racism that lingers on in Germany and Australia. Unlike the South African man who had to overcome the collective denial of the affection he had received from his Xhosa nursemaid, my affection for the Aboriginal people I know can be comparatively freely expressed. And whereas he came to realise that the racist denial of affection received from a Black mother was linked to his own mother's neglectful behaviour towards him, I have not resolved my own complexes to the same extent.

Even though I find this dream soothing, nurturing, and somewhat liberating, I remain searching for a clearer articulation of my own voice. I am slowly beginning to see that a new recognition of the care I received throughout childhood from my mother's mother will be part of this. For now, the sense of being in a liminal state of a prolonged transition remains. This also strongly colours the next dream, which links more explicitly my grandmother, Nazi Germany, and Aboriginal people.

"Prehistoric Blue Jeans"

In July 2002, a year after completing my Ph.D. and trying to find a place within the Australian academy, I was struggling over my commitment to give two guest lectures on Aboriginal art and identity. On this particular day, I felt irritated by the work of two other anthropologists. The first argued that postcolonial urban Aboriginal culture is as authentic as that in so-called "remote" communities, which, according to her, have been mystified. She thought ethnographers distorted the reality of contemporary Aboriginal people's lives in outback settlements by overemphasizing the ancient traditions manifest in mythology, ritual, traditional social organisation, thereby ascribing greater authenticity to remote Aborigines than to urban and rural First Australians. The second anthropologist, who lectured on the history and contemporary culture of a particular Central Australian group, added fuel to my irritation. This second argument insisted that the world of Aboriginal Australians is formed through its relationship with the state and that it cannot be understood as something onto itself. The question about the nature of Aboriginal culture—as either defined by its own historical development, or as a product of intercultural conditions—has come to divide Australian Aboriginal Studies and the present passionately fought argument is best captured in the collection of essays entitled *Culture Crisis: Anthropology and Politics in Aboriginal Australia*.[18]

At the time, I became deeply disturbed about my own research into cultural patterns. This emotional response was perhaps an indication of an underlying anxiety provoked by the material that I was trying to "cover up" through an objective stance as George Devereux[19] has identified in the commonplace defensive use of methodology in the behavioural sciences. In my Ph.D. thesis, I had completed an analysis of the genesis of a women's art style that had evolved out of children's "doodles", and, in the lectures I was to give, I continued to be preoccupied with finding out what it was that "drove" the aesthetic development of their art.

I am in an old-fashioned interior environment, a flat like my grandmother's [father's mother]: 1920s-30s, Nazi aesthetics. My husband's linguist-friend comes and gives or shows me a book: an old paperback, the paper is rippled as if it had gotten wet some time ago. I never see the book closed (that is, the cover); it is always open. The writing—handwritten Gothic script—is white on grey lined paper and there are three or four patches, like small oblong windows, in the book where the patina has come off. One can see that a layer of script, the supposedly "old" one on top, was actually superimposed. The "deeper layer" is handwritten Roman, the linguist's actual lecture notes—white chalk on a green blackboard, as if it had been photographed.

The page that attracts our attention is an actual photograph stretching across two pages. It shows a group of about twenty Aboriginal men in their prime of life, that is, about 30 years of age. All are dressed in Blue Jeans and chequered shirts, some have beards. Most are shown from the back, just with their heads turned halfway toward the camera. The caption reads: "Aboriginal men, ten thousand years ago". The book has been dated; according to the linguist, it is several thousand years old.

I asked myself then, as I do now, why do I dream of Aboriginal men in an open yet concealed book shown to me by a linguist in a Nazi-style home? The Gothic script belongs to the aesthetics of Nazi Germany; a matter of form that goes to substantial issues. As mentioned above, I was preoccupied at the time with identifying what the internal and external forces are that create and sustain cultural *patterns,* namely in Aboriginal Australia. But this dream seems to be pointing me back to my own cultural patterns and history; if there is an indication of an unconscious identification with the German fascist heritage and with guilt, it is mingled with deep affection for my mother's mother, known in the family both for the beauty of her Gothic handwriting and for her "natural" (meaning politically unreflective) aversion to authoritarianism. Why then does the Gothic script "cover up" the Roman? Unlike my grandmother's handwriting, which, as a child, I was unable to decipher yet trusted to convey kind words, the dream script pretends to be ancient and at the same time it covers the words of the present (the Roman lecture notes of the linguist).

From the vantage point of writing this paper and my theme of search for origins, belonging, and understanding, the layering of scripts can be seen as a recognition of my Western cultural roots: the use of Roman letters is historically more recent than Gothic script, but the Roman is the deeper, that is, older cultural layer. Searching for origins also means revisiting childhood, and the photo album in the dream reminds me of a precious album that my mother gave me, with pictures of my infancy and childhood, of my young parents and grandparents, friends ... I lost it in the course of moving places.

Conclusions: In Search of New Meanings

I have tried to deal through stories (dreams, memories, incidents) with certain themes that have influenced the course of my life. The overarching and unresolved issue has been the search for a primordial origin or immediately given sense of self that need not be questioned. This, I suspect, involves a German cultural complex because it has to do with a narcissistic image—the fantasy of lasting 1,000 years, of eternal youth—even of an everlasting infancy. Real personal and cultural growth struggle in the face of this image because the maternal container is fundamentally insecure. Donald Winnicott's "good enough" mother who helps the baby become a person with internal depth,[20] can be extended to place and historical memory—the home community, motherland, nation, and the collective psyche. Conceivably, disturbances in protective mothering make themselves felt both in the lives of concrete individuals and of places. Indeed, "disorders of place" and insufficient mothering might predicate one another.[21] I believe I have "inherited" a deep insecurity about belonging and a right to be through unconscious patterning of relationships across the generations: There was my grandmother's anxiety about a looming foreign (Russian) occupation, which made her store shelves and shelves of preserved food in the cellar from the end of WWII until her death in 1981, and there is my mother's fear of others taking too much from her ... For me, these insecurities have created a tension between the desire for just being, on the one hand, and the experience of questioning, of finding out more, and learning on the other.

Maternal Containment, Heimat, and Ingesting Meaningfulness

Feeling estranged at home, I left for Australia. I feel as much or as little at home in Australia now as I feel when visiting my old *heimat*, which is linked to the feeling of not being entirely at home in any language. But in this homelessness of the mind and search for maternal containment, personal signs and symbols have begun to interact or resonate in dreams with the Aboriginal cultural imagination. I did not dream of the country I have traveled with my friends in Central Australia. Instead I dreamed of Europe, a home shown to me as mine by an Aboriginal woman.

I am beginning to see that I can only fully arrive here, in Australia, and find a sense of belonging to place if I also make space for my European cultural container. To just "slip into" otherness can mean loss of self and of meaningful relationships, as I experienced in the mimetic identification with foreign languages. The latter brought with it a loss of ontological security, and this doubt about what *is* has stuck with me. Language is now like a second skin, having shed its first layer, my mother tongue, in an attempt to escape from its origins (also suggested by the sliding from German into English in the notes of the second dream). However, it is not entirely lost as I was able to restore the feeling of being at home in language through being with others who taught and "fed" me their words—French, Australian English, Pitjantjatjara. These were origin-al experiences of ingesting meaningfulness. The ingestion of the Pitjantjatjara language in particular offered firm ground, at least for a while. My experience of being fed "milky" words has meant that this language has gone inside me, even though I don't know very much of its grammar and vocabulary. I have integrated it into myself to some extent so that more "skin" could form and with this a sense of embodiment.[22] However, thinking, speaking, and writing mostly in English and, to a lesser extent, in German, I find that, in these two languages, the ground between words and what they stand for is still in question and the process of settling continues.

Cultural Darkness—When Cultural Complexes Intermingle

The most difficult part to understand and even to feel clearly is the gloomy threat that accompanies the search for origins and for cultural containment. When I think of Germany as my place of psychological birth, I always also feel the shadow of collective guilt spanning the generations— it is part of my memories of Heidelberg, Berlin, my family milieu. What happens then when my historical guilt (which slides in and out of consciousness) meets with the Australian guilt that some are beginning to recognise as a part of the settler culture? I have never forgotten my irritation at the Western Desert women's request to visit Hitler's bunker in Berlin— I felt that they wanted to "get under my skin",[23] to have a look at an "inside" that I had never set my eyes upon. The bunker stood for a layer of personal and of German history that I had not at all come to terms with, yet that was and perhaps still is connected to my desire to work with Aboriginal people as one way to find a place to be. I thought of this place of death, this lethal womb-tomb space when, years later, I visited a women's site in Central Australia, a womb-like rock art shelter near Alice Springs.

The association "cave of death" in Berlin that the Aboriginal women wanted to see, with "cave of life" in Central Australia that I wanted to visit, points to some unconscious cultural cross-over. I have not dealt with the possible existence of a cultural complex in Aboriginal Australia. Yet, at least writing from my own place as a German anthropologist in Australia, my dreaming of Aboriginal men in a book shown to me in a Nazi-style home seems to reflect the intermingling of cultural complexes (German and Anglo-Australian ones in my life history) that Singer writes about:

> our cultural complexes get all mixed up not only with our personal history and complexes but with other cultural complexes as well. These intermingling complexes take strange twists and turns over a lifetime and generations, creating exotic permutations and combinations within ourselves and between us and others, creating what I have come to think of as "recombinant visionary mythologies".[24]

Germany has a history of recognising genocide and of apologies for historical wrongs—to Namibia for the 1904-1907 massacres by colonial troops of 80,000 Herero people; to Poland for the brutal invasion in World War II; and to Israel for the holocaust in which six million Jews died. Some of the atrocities committed in the name of the nation were shown to us "descendents" in religious class at high school; the horrendous sight of skeletal half-dead people bulldozed into trenches is one such memory, one that a child ten years of age has nowhere to put. I also remember how, during my childhood, children from different cultural backgrounds were somehow occluded from view. The many Turkish families who lived in the region and our immediate neighbourhood had nothing to do with us, and I only remember the Turkish kids as being outside my orbit. It was not until decades later that I understood how, for generations, my family has upheld an ethnic segregation—like the wall of the dark mountain in "Swiss Dreaming" and the general sense of gloom. Behind all of this lurks the big German burden of guilt, which, not being dealt with in any detail in the life of my mother, in particular, seems to create a ferocious need to claim the right to be German and to exclude and occlude others. It seems to me now that the suppression of difference that I must have perceived then, if ever so faintly, contributed to my desire to become an anthropologist, to find out the names of strangers and make intelligible the difference—and perhaps to leave the guilt behind.

Acknowledgements

I much appreciate the invitation by Amanda Dowd to participate in this volume; it has been both challenging and gratifying to write in a personal vein and explore some of the subtext of my cultural history and life in relation to professional endeavours as an anthropologist. This paper was much improved by Amanda's perceptive insight and excellent editorial input. I thank John von Sturmer for naming certain details and for helping me appreciate better the nature of Australian English.

Notes

[1] See, for example, Eva Hoffmann, *Lost in Translation* (London: Random House, 1989), p. 106, cited in Elisabeth Hanscombe, "Empathy, Language and the Impact of Migration", *Australasian Journal of Psychotherapy* 28, no. 1 & 2 (2009): 114-125, p. 121.

[2] I have described some such encounters in an earlier piece dealing with the visit of Western Desert Aboriginal women to Germany (Ute Eickelkamp, "Mapitjaku*na*—Shall I Go Away from Myself Towards You? Being-with and Looking-at Across Cultural Divides", *The Australian Journal of Anthropology* 14, no. 3 (2003): 315–35.

[3] Max Scheler, *Man's Place in Nature* (New York: The Noonday Press, 1976), p. 14.

[4] Ronald D. Laing, *The Divided Self: An Existential Study in Sanity and Madness* (Harmondsworth: Penguin, 1960).

[5] See Ute Eickelkamp, "Mapitjaku*na*—Shall I Go Away from Myself Towards You? Being-with and Looking-at Across Cultural Divides".

[6] Francesca Merlan, *Caging the Rainbow: Places, Politics and Aborigines in a North Australian Town* (Honolulu: University of Hawai'i Press, 1998), p. 125, citing A. Rumsey, "Language and Territoriality in Aboriginal Australia", in *Language and Culture in Aboriginal Australia*, ed. M. Walsh and C. Yallop (Canberra: Aboriginal Studies Press, 1993), emphasis added.

[7] Heather McDonald, "Universalising the Particular? God and Indigenous Spirit Beings in East Kimberley", *TAJA* 21 (2010): 51–70, p. 53.

[8] Australian Aboriginal ethnographies capitalise "Ancestor"/"Ancestral" where reference is made to beings from the Dreaming, rather than to human ancestors. However, this distinction is not categorical; Aboriginal people also see that, after death, a person becomes the Dreaming.

[9] *Ibid.*, p. 52.

[10] This made me feel closer to my Aboriginal companions and less marked as a foreigner, partly because for all of "us" English was something external. I am, of course, aware of the reality of distinctly Australian English being spoken by the majority who identify with it. However, I highlight the impact of a local perspective from a world where most people have not mastered English.

[11] Heinz Werner and Bernard Kaplan, *Symbol Formation* (Hillsday, New Jersey & London: Lawrence Erlbaum, 1984), p. 241.

[12] Language, as Wilhelm von Humboldt was the first to recognize, is the beginning of culture for both humanity and for each individual life. Although there is no universal language for all, it nevertheless binds us together across space and time (cf. Ernst Cassirer, "Critical Idealism as a Philosophy of Culture," in *Symbol, Myth, and Culture*, ed. D. P. Verene (New Haven and London: Yale University Press, 1979), p. 73.

[13] T. G. H. Strehlow, *Central Australian Religion* (Bedfork Park, South Australia: Flinders Press, 1978), pp. 15–17.

[14] Yagwoia is the name of a group in the Eastern Highland Province of Papua New Guinea.

[15] It is of some significance for my search for origins that the German word for "motherland" is "*Vaterland*" ("fatherland"), with now negative connotations: It seems to me Hitler's destructive nationalist heroism that abused masculine identifications has made it difficult for Germans to associate their country with a maternal container.

[16] I thankfully acknowledge Amanda Dowd's recognition of this aspect of my dream.

[17] Thomas Singer with Catherine Kaplinsky, "Cultural Complexes in Analysis", in *Jungian Psychoanalysis Working in the Spirit of C. G. Jung*, ed. by Murray Stein (Chicago: Open Court Publishing Company, 2010), pp. 22-37.

[18] Jon Altman and Melinda Hinkson (eds.), *Culture Crisis: Anthropology and Politics in Aboriginal Australia* (Sydney: UNSW Press, 2010).

[19] George Devereux, "Professional Defences", in *From Anxiety to Method in the Behavioural Sciences* (The Hague & Paris: Mouton & Co), pp. 83–96.

[20] Donald W. Winnicott, "Mind and Its Relation to the Psyche-Soma", in *Through Paediatrics to Psychoanalysis: Collected Papers* (London: Karnac, 1984 [1949]), p. 245.

[21] Craig San Roque, "The Yard", in *Growing Up in Central Australia: New Anthropological Studies of Aboriginal Childhood and Youth* (London & New York: Berghahn, 2011), ed. U. Eickelkamp, p. 162.

[22] I here add that the Aboriginal English word for categories of kin is "skin".

[23] Something that Amanda Dowd perceived.

[24] Thomas Singer, "The Cultural Complex and Archetypal Defenses of the Group Spirit", in *The Cultural Complex: Contemporary Jungian Perspectives on Psyche & Society* (New York: Brunner-Routledge, 2004), ed. T. Singer and S. L. Kimbles, p. 32.

Chris Milton was born and raised in South Africa and migrated to New Zealand with his family in 2002. Chris is a Jungian Psychoanalyst and Clinical Psychologist who trained in South Africa and who now works in private practice in Auckland, New Zealand. He is a member of and also a Training Analyst with the Australia and New Zealand Society of Jungian Analysts (ANZSJA) and serves on the editorial board of the online *Indo-Pacific Journal of Phenomenology*. Chris was appointed by the New Zealand Minister of Health as a founding member of the Psychotherapists Board of Aotearoa New Zealand. He currently devotes his time to adult analysis and supervision of clinicians, but he has previously worked psychotherapeutically with adults as well as with children, adolescents, and their families in both the private and public sectors. Chris has also taught, examined, and supervised in psychiatry, clinical psychology, psychoanalysis, and analytical psychology in both institute and university settings. He has published in the area of infant mental health and psychoanalytic processes and maintains an interest in integral psychology, spirituality, and transpersonal psychology.

* * *

Chris Milton's chapter is a personal phenomenological account of a moral struggle associated with his experience of migration from South Africa to Aotearoa New Zealand. He describes how he developed a set of anti-apartheid moral principles, which he calls the anti-apartheid moral hermeneutic, in order to make sense of growing up and living in apartheid South Africa. The core of this moral hermeneutic was that political actions that were justified by an imposed system of separation into "groups"—black and white with different rules for each—was wrong. In Aotearoa New Zealand Chris describes being confronted by that country's biculturalism: its recognition of both Māori culture and Settler culture as set up in the 1840 Treaty of Waitangi, seen by some as the founding document of Aotearoa New Zealand.

Chris's chapter examines his experience of the collision in his mind between the two different "biculturisms" of South Africa and New Zealand. The application of "biculturism" in the mental health provision of Aoteoara New Zealand is quite different from the application of "biculturism" in apartheid South Africa. This revealed his moral hermeneutic as a cultural complex. His personal struggle is movingly refracted through the Jungian notion of "hostile opposites" and symbol formation.

8

Taking it with Me: a South African's Cultural Complex in Aotearoa New Zealand

Chris Milton

Introduction

I was born and raised in South Africa during the apartheid years. I trained and practised as a Jungian analyst there. I was opposed to apartheid and yearned for the achievement of democracy. This finally occurred in 1994 and I looked forward to an era of hope for a better future, although I realised that there would be difficulties. However, after years of being childless, in 2000 my daughter was born and my wife and I had to sensibly contemplate what *her* future would be in South Africa. We decided that on balance, because of ongoing tensions and uncertainties in South Africa, her future would be better assured if we immigrated to somewhere with less danger of violence and more clarity of future. Consequently we immigrated to Aotearoa New Zealand in 2002. ("Aotearoa" is the Māori name for the two islands that form "New Zealand". I shall mostly use the term "Aotearoa New Zealand" throughout as it honours the bicultural foundation of this young nation - which is explained in more detail later in this article.) The emotional atmosphere of Aotearoa New Zealand was totally different from South Africa, so much so that for a long time I experienced an unreal sense of relief and freedom.[1] However, the sense of peace, security, efficiency, and caring that I encountered in Aotearoa New Zealand, while pleasant, was also somehow disconcerting. There was also, for me, a degree of "culture shock", confusion, and mourning.

Immigration to a new country constellates a psychological complex which often goes unspoken but which underlies one's experience of immigration. Seemingly few analysts have spoken of their *personal* experience of immigration, although there is work on the effects of immigration *per se*.[2] However, psycho-analyst Salman Akhtar, who immigrated from India to the USA, and Jungian analyst Amanda Dowd, who immigrated from Britain to the Antipodes, have written on this subject informed by their own personal experience.[3] It is interesting to note Akhtar's[4] comment that "it is striking that few among the European analysts who fled to the United States and Latin America in the wake of the Second World War wrote about their experiences as immigrant analysts". In this chapter I am going to try to speak of and to a particular aspect of my own experience of immigration. Yet a part of me would rather remain silent.

The aspect of my experience of which I wish to speak entails a response to the specific biculturalism of Aotearoa New Zealand. There is a curious parallel between South Africa and Aotearoa New Zealand: both have been colonised by Europeans and in both there is a type of biculturalism: South Africa was divided into two racial groups—"Whites" and "Non-whites".[5] Aotearoa New Zealand was "founded" (by the 1840 Treaty of Waitangi) based upon the recognition of two groups - Māori and Settlers.[6] However, the parallel has a twist: whereas in South Africa the White minority came to dominate the Black majority, in Aotearoa New Zealand a majority (the Settlers) came to dominate the Māori minority. It is also true that whilst in apartheid South Africa, the law forced people to be classified according to (racial) group, in Aotearoa New Zealand membership of certain groups is recognised in law but not forced by law.

One of the notions I am going to use I have called "forced group classification". This notion encapsulates many processes—conscious, unconscious, personal, cultural, and political—and it is therefore difficult to define precisely. By "forced group classification", I seek to describe a process whereby a person is overtly or covertly forcibly classified, socially, culturally, administratively or legally, as belonging to a particular group. Although this classification is usually of a legal nature, it can occur in any situation in which there is a power differential, for example between adult and child or between teacher and student. Also, although this process may be an overt one, there are situations where it occurs covertly and a person is subjected to stereotyping and discrimination. Through this process of classification, people lose a greater or lesser degree of power over their lives by virtue of being so classified and then discriminated against. In the extreme instance "forced group classification" means that one's political and social rights (e.g. rights of access to services, rights of association, etc.) as well as their educational and economic opportunities are forcibly determined by legal classification of a person to a group. This was the function of the Population Registration Act of 1950 in South Africa which came to mean that people were forcibly classified as Black, White, Coloured (Mixed) or Indian "race". The Act essentially deprived Black South Africans of their South African citizenship. The system was similar to the Nuremberg Laws in Germany during the Nazi period whereby people were classified as either Germans, Jews, or of "mixed blood". These laws, *inter alia*, deprived Jews of their German citizenship, prohibited marriage between Jews and other Germans, and restricted the occupations Jews could follow or the places they could be. "Forced group classification" has functioned in other countries as well. In the USA perhaps the most obvious example would be the various Jim Crow laws.

In Aotearoa New Zealand the Treaty of Waitangi Act was established in 1975 to provide restitution to Māori for historical, material, and cultural injustices that arose through Crown violation of the Treaty of Waitangi/*Te Tiriti o Waitangi* (see below). This Act *defines* a person as Māori if they are of the Māori *race* and includes any descendant of such a person. However, although this classification is made, it is a classification that people voluntarily assume when they make a claim under the Treaty of Waitangi Act. In this way people are *recognised* in Aotearoa New Zealand law as being Māori but they are not forced to be thus recognised and classified. Stated in general terms: such people are recognised as belonging to a group, but they are not legally forced to be members of that group, i.e. there is no "forced group classification". In apartheid South Africa, all people were forcibly allocated to a "racial" group whereas in Aotearoa New Zealand people are recognised in law (The Treaty of Waitangi Act) as Māori and therefore having certain group-oriented rights established in principle in the Treaty of Waitangi. (This does not, unfortunately, mean that there is no stereotyping and discrimination against Māori!)

These differences aside, in both South Africa and Aotearoa New Zealand, group identification and group rights were foundational to structuring thinking about social relationships. As a South African who had found apartheid abhorrent, I felt and believed that defining a political situation and basing justifications for political actions in terms of forced group classification and group rights was wrong. This feeling response and belief formed for me the core of a deeply held, useful, and personally valued orienting moral framework. The biculturalism of Aotearoa New Zealand challenged my orienting moral framework. More particularly, it presented a challenge and questions to my psychotherapeutic practice as an analyst in Aoteoroa New Zealand. Of course this challenge did not arise in a "clean" context for me but in one that carried with it what I came to understand as the effects of immigration, so those too need to be taken account of.

In short, I had taken with me to Aotearoa New Zealand a moral framework, which helped orient me in apartheid South Africa, but this framework was seriously challenged in Aotearoa New Zealand. I propose in this chapter to examine this aspect of my response to immigration as a cultural complex in the context of a changed sense and role of place.

My Speaking

As I have said, a part of me would rather remain silent on these subjects. Nonetheless, I am going to speak of a certain aspect of my own experience of immigration. In this I am seeking to utter and understand something from my own lived experience. So in that sense this chapter forms something of a phenomenological study. It is in the spirit of qualitative methods of research[7] that I seek to disclose and articulate experience from the lived world. My chapter, however, is not of the more conventional sort of phenomenological research. Instead, I shall first endeavour, as honestly as possible, to present elements of my experience and its personal and cultural situatedness. Following that, I shall go on to discuss and, hopefully, transform the meaning of my experience. It is, so to speak, action research on myself. I hope that the reader will be understanding of this as a very personal account and indeed a work towards individuation.

Speaking of individuation calls me to say something of the Jungian notions of personal and cultural complexes.

Personal and Cultural Complexes

Jung introduced the notion of the personal feeling toned complex, commonly simply referred to as "the complex". Feeling toned complexes are unconscious dispositions that influence and alter the ego qualities of perception, apperception, judgment, reflection, decision, will-power, autonomy, and action. They are nucleated upon archetypal images that have been potentiated or attenuated by personal experience.

In *The Cultural Complex: Contemporary Jungian Perspectives on Psyche and Society* (edited by Singer and Kimbles)[8] the notion of the personal complex is extended and the notion of the "cultural complex" developed. Cultural complexes arise within a culture and, like personal complexes, structure the psychological life of a group or an individual member of a group. Cultural complexes have the same characteristics as personal complexes but also tend to provide a simplistic and reassuring hermeneutic which aligns, justifies, and reassures a group or its members of their place in the world. So, for example, when we observe the simplistic system of understanding of a right-wing, conservative, prejudiced, and reactionary group, we are observing a cultural complex in action. However, no group is immune from a cultural complex, and we find this in groups that espouse more left-wing values as well. (An example of the latter is what Carlo Strenger calls "'Standard Left Explanatory System" or SLES. In brief, within the terms of the SLES, left-wing thinkers do not ascribe any responsibility to non-Western groupings for the ills they experience and instead attribute responsibility for these to Western world wrongdoing, both current and historical.)[9]

In a similar, but more personal way, the moral guiding principles that I developed in South Africa, and which indeed worked under apartheid conditions, arose in a culturally conflicted context and helped align, justify, and reassure me in a way that is suggestive of a cultural complex.

In this volume the notion of cultural complex is extended to include the sense and role of place. In migration one is transferred from one place to another, from one set of cultural conditions to another, and one also brings with one a set of transgenerational elements not necessarily shared with people in the new place or new country.

The Places Where I Begin

Transgenerationally, I am of mixed Scots/English and Eastern European Jewish descent. All my grandparents were immigrants to South Africa, most of them part of an historical process of escaping economic and political hardship. My Jewish identity was a dominant undernote growing up and I was very attuned to Jewish vulnerability, augmented by my father's experiences of anti-Semitism and the knowledge that several members of my family were killed in the Holocaust/Shoah.

Culturally, I am a white, English-speaking South African, born and raised in the eastern area of South Africa, a dominantly English-speaking region where people had the self-perception (although not necessarily the opinions and behaviour) of being "liberal". Personally, I felt a strong antipathy from many (not all) Afrikaans speakers who, historically fighting for their own rights (a remnant response to Milner's post Anglo-Boer War Anglicisation policy)[10], imposed Afrikaans language usage in interpersonal contact. One element of great discomfort to me was being allocated to a group (English-speaking South African of Jewish heritage) and being forced into a stereotype based on that classification. In childhood I dominantly experienced this as an English-speaking South African and as someone with a Jewish heritage.

Environmental childhood experiences from the 1950s and 1960s (the Mau Mau Rebellion in Kenya, the Sharpeville Massacre, the Congo Crisis, the Rivonia Trial, Rhodesian Unilateral Declaration of Independence (UDI), to name but a few[11]) exposed me to the adults' anxieties and racist responses to what was perceived to be an ever present threat from Black people. A sort of siege mentality filled the minds of my parents and of their friends. A visit to farming friends always entailed accounts of preparation for Black uprising and there was much discussion of firearms and protective towers. As a small child I would go to bed at night and experience intrusive images of hordes of Black people streaming out of the Black residential area, the so-called "location", wielding heavy machetes. These were the images produced and fuelled by repeatedly hearing adult accounts of the Kenyan Mau Mau chopping children to death[12] and other horrific events in Black Africa.

At the same time I had frequent and ongoing contact with Black South Africans, generally as people who were all around me and specifically as domestic workers. Towards and from these people I felt no antipathy and saw no evidence to support the adult anxieties I witnessed.

Held in the terror and anxiety that the experience of this traumatic atmosphere generated in me, I nonetheless retained a natural and intuitive sense of what was right and what was wrong. Discrimination, racial or otherwise, felt wrong. I had strong empathy and concern for Black people. I was appalled at the unkindness and violence directed at them by White people. I identified strongly with their sense of being forced into a stereotype. I recall, from as young as ten years of age, noticing prejudice and racism in adult discussion and deeds. As a child I contested almost everything that adults said or did about or to the Black people with whom we lived. Mostly the adults regarded me as naïve. Once I left home for university, I had a chance to be more proactive and less reactive: teaching disadvantaged Black students, involving myself in supporting victims of forced removals, financially supporting the legal defence of activists, protesting and being police baton charged, hiding a political activist on the run from security police, as well as debriefing and counselling detained, and sometimes tortured, activists.[13]

However, I have my own complexes based in the tension between my natural moral response and the political ambiguities and anxieties to which I was subject as a child. I experienced a strange blend of profound concern for Black South Africans, distaste and revulsion at injustice meted out to them, and at the same time an embedded anxiety in the face of what seemed primal destructive forces. In response to this, I developed my own fairly simple, even simplistic, set of guiding moral principles that I call my anti-apartheid moral hermeneutic.

The Moral Hermeneutic

Hermeneutics is the theory and methodology of interpretation, originally as applied to the interpretation of scriptural texts. When used as a noun, the word "hermeneutic" means a method or principle of interpretation. I am therefore calling a set of guiding moral principles a moral hermeneutic.

Our capacity to make general judgements starts with a set of early preformed responses. With life experience these preformed responses evolve to form intuition and deliberation. This applies as much to moral judgements as any other, and we thereby develop moral intuition and moral deliberation. A moral hermeneutic is an algorithm of moral deliberation and has fairly simple, even simplistic, guiding principles.

Whilst seeming completely conscious, a moral hermeneutic is powerfully influenced and shaped by both the unconscious factors in our lives and our culture; and, though useful, I believe that it also reflects our complexes, especially our cultural complexes. Considering this, it is no surprise that a moral hermeneutic can be used to help justify a political stance.

Strenger's SLES, which was introduced earlier, is an example of a moral hermeneutic applied in the political sphere. Personally the use of a moral hermeneutic was very helpful to me, in a practical way, in South Africa during the apartheid era. As my deep feeling reaction of distaste and revulsion at apartheid and my urge to do something to change it were attacked and devalued by apartheid supporters and apologists (as naïve, as emotional rather than logical, and as betraying "my own people"), I needed to develop a simple logical argument to justify what amounted to my moral intuition that apartheid was wrong. This entailed a process of conscious moral deliberation and the extraction of a set of guiding principles. Simply stated, that set of guiding principles, my anti-apartheid moral hermeneutic, considered any position/action/argument that was justified by forced group allocation as wrong. In argument with an apartheid supporter, I could then always find the underlying premise of group allocation (which apartheid apologists used to trump individual rights), challenge it, and so counter the apartheid argument.[14]

My moral hermeneutic also served an emotional function for it helped me transcend images from childhood, in particular the terrifying and traumatic accounts of the Mau Mau killing children. I came to understand these as accounts of what evil people did to other people *not* accounts of what Black people did to White people.

However, I think that whilst my anti-apartheid moral hermeneutic reflects, at least in part, a mature moral capacity, it is also embedded in my psyche as an apartheid-based cultural complex.

It is important to say a little more about why I believe my anti-apartheid moral hermeneutic is also "an apartheid-based cultural complex". Singer & Kaplinsky[15] indicate that cultural complexes *share* the following characteristics with personal complexes:

> 1. They function in an involuntary, autonomous fashion and tend to affirm a simplistic conscious point of view that obviates ambiguity.
> 2. They manifest with a strong emotional charge and as compulsive behaviour.
> 3. They assimilate experiences that validate and support their perspective and which go to form a cache of "self-affirming ancestral memories".
> 4. They resist our efforts to critically reflect on them and make them conscious.
> 5. They have archetypal cores and so express typically human attitudes.

I would certainly have experienced these features of a cultural complex through my anti-apartheid moral hermeneutic:

> 1. I found apartheid abhorrent and thought of this in terms of group identification being problematic. This response had an autonomous quality and was a simplistic conscious viewpoint that denied ambiguity around the value of identification with a group. In particular it backgrounded my own ancestral history and strong identification with a people whose own rights, including the right to exist as a group, have been violated over the centuries.

> 2. I have a strong and emotional "gut response" to apartheid (or any system that looks like it) and in argument feel emotionally compelled to dispute it.
> 3. I have assimilated many experiences that justify my position of opposition to apartheid (and apartheid-like systems). I can also relate this opposition to a cache of ancestral memories: the familial, cultural, and ancestral memories of the persecution that my Jewish forebears had suffered in Europe.
> 4. I had, until I moved to Aotearoa New Zealand, no reason to critically reflect on my belief that systems that resembled apartheid were anything other than morally wrong.
> 5. Justice and freedom are archetypal—as seen, for instance, in archetypal images such as the "Justice" card of the Tarot pack, and also in the figure of Prospero in Shakespeare's "The Tempest". So we see that my anti-apartheid moral hermeneutic, which is concerned with justice and freedom, has an archetypal core.

At the personal phenomenological level, my "gut level", I am conflicted and complexed around morality based on group rights. My gut anti-apartheid response is against a moral position justified by people being forcibly classified into groups and I am suspicious of the moral correctness of any political position justified by this. At the same time, by circumstance and choice, I myself belong to a group whose rights have been violated and I have a gut response to this too.[16]

This brings me to the phenomenology of my experience of Aotearoa New Zealand.

The Treaty of Waitangi/ *Te Tiriti o Waitangi*

To take any experience of Aotearoa New Zealand seriously it is important to have at least a rudimentary understanding of the Treaty of Waitangi or *Te Tiriti o Waitangi*, in Māori. Given that the Māori version is the definitive version in terms of international law, I shall from here onwards call it *Te Tiriti* throughout. In presenting a summary of *Te Tiriti* I shall draw on various sources.[17]

Te Tiriti was signed on 6 February 1840, at Waitangi in the Bay of Islands by Captain William Hobson (the first "Governor of New Zealand"), several English residents, and about 45 Māori "chiefs" (or more correctly Māori *rangatira*). Rangatira Hone Heke was the first to sign. The original Māori text (as well as copies) was subsequently circulated around Aotearoa New Zealand until 500 signatures were obtained by the end of that year.

In essence *Te Tiriti* is an agreement whereby Māori gave the British Crown rights to govern and to develop British settlement in Aotearoa New Zealand in return for which the Crown guaranteed Māori full protection and preservation of their interests and status, as well as full British citizenship rights. *Te Tiriti* consists of a Preamble and three Articles. Having both a Māori language and English version, it presents some serious interpretive difficulties. In international law concerning indigenous peoples, the Māori language version must take precedence. Several Māori words and their English "translations" are contentious in interpretation: *kāwanatanga* (governership), *rangatiratanga* (chieftanship), and *taonga* (treasures). Through the first Article of *Te Tiriti*, *kāwanatanga* or governorship (which was translated in the English version as "Sovereignty") was ceded to the Queen; however, in the second Article *rangatiratanga* or chieftainship (the English translation does not even mention chieftainship) was retained by the chiefs, and it also guaranteed that they retained ownership and control of *taonga*, or treasures. Evidently the Māori *rangatira* may have believed that they only ceded the right of government to the British Crown, not sovereignty. ("Sovereignty" may be seen as the quality of having ultimate authority over a geographic area (in terms of *Te Tiriti* it may, for Māori, be understood as Māori control over all things Māori in Aotearoa New Zealand), "right of government", on the other hand, may be seen as the right of practical control and administration.) Furthermore, the *taonga* could be concrete, such as property or valued possessions, or more abstract, such as language and culture, a treaty principle that may not have been fully appreciated by the Crown and one which would be violated later by pressure on Māori to assimilate. In the third Article the Crown undertook to protect all the ordinary people of Aotearoa New Zealand and give them the same rights and duties of citizenship as the people of England.[18] Even here we can note an interpretive nuance as the word "Māori" means "ordinary people", i.e., the people who are ordinarily in the land.

One of the initial intentions of *Te Tiriti* was to protect Māori from unscrupulous buyers of their land. However, within five years the intent of *Te Tiriti* had been twisted, and its application led to the New Zealand Land Wars, conflict that endured until the 1870s and which ultimately led to imprisonment of Māori and confiscation of Māori land. The subsequent history of *Te Tiriti* has been either to pervert its intention or to ignore it—whichever better suited the purposes of colonisation. However, a growing movement in Aotearoa New Zealand, culminating in the *Treaty of Waitangi Act* in 1975, opened the door to reparation and an appreciation of the seriousness of the bicultural nature of Aotearoa New Zealand. It has been said that *Te Tiriti o Waitangi* is the *Magna Carta*[19] of Aotearoa New Zealand.

It is personally curious to me that in some respects *Te Tiriti* echoes the intentions of King Boleslav V of Poland's 1264 General Charter of Jewish Liberties (also known as the Statute of Kalisz), the purpose of which was to invite Jews to settle, and thus import their knowledge and skills to the King's domain, in exchange for the Jews being protected and permitted self government.[20] Unfortunately, what one king guarantees another can rescind; so too, there is perhaps an echo of this in the history of Aotearoa New Zealand. Given my Eastern European Jewish heritage, the gaining and losing of treaty-based guarantees, and in more recent years the death of family in the Holocaust/Shoah, has a personal resonance and gives me some lived sense of the meaning of violations of *Te Tiriti* for Māori.

Initial Experience of Immigrating to and Working in Aotearoa New Zealand

Arriving in Aotearoa New Zealand in 2002, I initially worked in a state provided, so-called mainstream mental health service as a clinical psychologist. A "mainstream service" is any health service that essentially conforms to the Western medical model. During this period I undertook various courses of study in the centrality of *Te Tiriti o Waitangi* to Aotearoa New Zealand and issues of its abuse by the Crown as well as elements of Māori culture. I also had the chance to work with Māori clients. I have only ever had positive experiences of working with Māori clients and practitioners. I was fortunate to be in a position to collaborate with mental health workers from a traditional or *kaupapa* Māori service.

The term "*kaupapa* Māori" describes traditional Māori ways of doing, being, and thinking. These may vary considerably from conventional Western approaches to health. Some notable features of the *kaupapa* Māori health service with which I had contact were:

> 1. The use of the Māori language if appropriate.
> 2. The use of *karakia* (prayer) to begin and end the consultation.
> 3. An appreciation of the importance of *whānau* (family/community) i.e., the increased role played by consultation with members of the family and wider Māori community.
> 4. An appreciation of *whakapapa* (which in English means something like kinship or genealogy and everyone's place with respect to it).

5. An appreciation of a person's *mana* (which in English means something like prestige or authority as well as power, control, and influence).
6. An appreciation of transpersonal components, called *wairua*, or spiritual components (often practically more "religious" than "spiritual" in nature).
7. Using an holistic approach to health that combines physiology, psychology, spirituality, and community.

Positive though this experience was, and also fully understanding the appropriateness and need of a *kaupapa* Māori service, a note of moral disquiet registered in my mind: Was this perhaps a process of separate development similar to that which had been espoused by apartheid apologists? Furthermore, I soon became aware of a Shadow side to the situation. During triage in the mainstream service, the manager of the mainstream service, who was herself Māori, would forcefully argue for and insist on the immediate re-referral to the *kaupapa* Māori service of people with either Māori names or who were known by her to be part of the Māori community. This was ostensibly done on the basis that such people should be offered the choice of system. This re-referral and "choice" process was slow. In reality it served to reduce pressure on mainstream service provision and officially reduce waiting list length. Its effect was often to delay access to the mainstream service for Māori (if this was their choice). Thus what looked like giving Māori a choice of service was in fact a way of denying them rapid mainstream service access by *de facto* forced group classification, itself a subtle apartheid-like process.

Nonetheless, the Shadow elements aside, as Aotearoa New Zealand is a *bicultural* country I logically understood the need and appropriateness of a *kaupapa* Māori service, and I also recognised that there were substantial differences between the apartheid structures and the need and intended mode of implementation of a *kaupapa* Māori service.

In my *thinking life* I did not experience too much dissonance (except for the observations about *de facto* forced group classification mentioned above), but in my *feeling* moral reaction, I did have something of a conflict. Beyond my appreciation that there were apartheid-like processes at work, I was simply not wholly emotionally comfortable with "separate development", functional or dysfunctional. This was in spite of the fact that I knew from personal experience the need to have group difference respected. "Separate development" is of course one of the euphemisms used by the apartheid regime in South Africa to describe and justify apartheid, so it sets off a complex in me. ("Separate development" was the term used for the policy, introduced by apartheid architect Prime Minister Hendrik Verwoerd, whereby each of the nine Black South African "groups" was legislatively forced to become a nation with its own homeland set up on about 14% of the land in South Africa. This policy was used to justify depriving Black South Africans of their South African citizenship as well as of their human rights when dwelling in "South Africa".)

On the other hand, was I perhaps encountering the process whereby migration required me to form, as Akhtar[21] puts it, "new identification models, different superego dictates, and different ideals". Still I had no choice in my feeling reaction and, like the Biblical Jacob (Genesis 32:25-32), I had to wrestle with the Stranger, hoping that I would come to a point of both thinking and feeling resolution.

"Struggling with the Stranger" was mostly an emotional and intuitive experience. For me the struggle took the form of a multiply determined psychological tension. Phenomenologically speaking, this felt like an almost mechanical "shear". It was as if two parts of my mind were sliding past each other and tearing the "substance" of my mind as they moved.[22] I recognized that this shear was partially formed from the conflict between my own tolerance and humaneness, on the one hand, and my implicit and explicit prejudice and racism, on the other. I also recognized that it was formed from the conflict between *my* anti-apartheid moral hermeneutic—which dictates that group-based justifications are highly morally suspect—and the Aotearoa New Zealand bicultural moral hermeneutic—which foregrounds group-based justification as a favoured moral option.

Conflict of this sort is seen by Jungians in a general way as tension between the "hostile opposites"[23] of the mind. In its personal particularity it is shaped by the life experience that we have had, and individuation drives us to attempt to integrate and transcend the "hostile opposites". At the most simple level of Jungian thinking, the conflict is between the ego and the Shadow (that which we do not wish to be). The Shadow is not all bad —for example in a person for whom the racist element of a conflict has consciously predominated, the Shadow may reflect the compassionate, caring, and moral part of the personality which tries to compensate the racist ego attitude. At a more complex level of Jungian thinking, the conflict may, for example, be between the "hostile opposites" of "good part object representations" and "bad part object representations"; between the "hostile opposites" of the *senex* and *puer aeternus*; between the "hostile opposites" of the Terrible Great Mother and the Good Great Mother, and so on.

My entire experience of shear, dissonance, and conflict was complicated by the change and struggle which migration imposes. Akhtar[24] has articulated how for the migrant there are four dimensions of a "'core migratory process" of "psychic travel", set out as dichotomies and their resolution. These are as follows:

1. *From* love or hate *to* ambivalence.
2. *From* near or far *to* optimal distance.
3. *From* "yesterday" or "tomorrow" *to* "today".
4. *From* mine or yours *to* "ours".

Each of the dichotomies that Akhtar sets up can also be understood in terms of the alchemical and Jungian notion of "hostile opposites" and the process of moving towards their resolution as a *coniunctio* or symbol. Apart from the conflict of Akhtar's dichotomies, I was subject to a multiple and complicated set of "hostile opposites". This was very uncomfortable and I experienced feelings of conflict, anxiety, frustration, and an increased sense of not belonging. As a Jungian analyst it helps to turn to the thinking of analytical psychology to seek some sort of symbolic resolution.

The Notion of "Symbol" in Analytical Psychology

I have already touched upon the notion of "hostile opposites". Within Jungian thinking the encounter and resolution of tension between "hostile opposites" is achieved with the formation of a symbol. Dynamically a symbol represents and acts as a third factor that provides a perspective from which synthesis of the "hostile opposites" can be made. Structurally it is the best possible representation in consciousness of opposing elements. (Often in Jung's conception these opposing elements are consciousness and the unconscious but not limited to them, for example they could be the opposing elements of the negative and positive *animus*, of *senex* and *puer aeternus*, of "good object representations" and "bad object representations".) Experientially, a symbol has a felt sense of meaning even if the meaning is ineffable.[25]

For instance Akhtar[26] outlines how an immigrant may adopt either a position of ethnocentric withdrawal (which entails idealization of the original culture) or counterphobic assimilation (which entails idealisation of and magical identification with the new culture). Both are extreme positions that can be thought of as "hostile opposites" that need to resolve into a symbol, i.e., a position of ambivalence, optimal distance, and immediacy in the moment.

A Beginning Symbolic Resolution

I cannot claim to have finally symbolically resolved the conflict that I feel from the challenge the bicultural moral hermeneutic poses to my old anti-apartheid moral hermeneutic. However, I have the beginnings of a symbolic resolution. Most probably this will be for me a never-ending piece of psychological work. As previously noted, Akhtar speaks of a core migratory process of psychic travel *from* love or hate *to* ambivalence; *from* near or far *to* optimal distance; *from* "yesterday" or "tomorrow" *to* "today", and *from* mine or yours *to* "ours". Using this model, some features of symbolic resolution will be tolerance of ambivalence, optimal distance between sense of origin and sense of current place, a capacity to live in the present, and a capacity to share personally and culturally.

I believe that these features of symbolic resolution cohere in a tolerance of ambiguity, a capacity to enter dialectic without losing one's psychological footing, and an ability to share that is both giving and receiving.

Andrew Samuels gestures to tolerance of ambiguity in his notion of "moral imagination".[27] Samuels has discriminated "moral imagination" from what he calls "original morality." Whereas "original morality" gives a clear cut even definitive moral direction, one that is "knowing and biased", "moral imagination" is more ambiguous and described by Samuels as the "means by which we apply our imagination to complex social and political issues". Moral imagination involves a capacity for a choice that "may have to be ingenious, less than clear-cut, a compromise or a creatively improved adaptation".[28]

The "conservative" disposition that people have when confronted by a different culture may be seen as defensive. However, this disposition may also be more subtle and complex than a defence. It may be our psychological footing, that is a secure and living respect for our psychic origins, for the psychological ground on which we first learnt to stand.

The ability to share gestures towards psychological maturity by implying both a capacity for generosity and a capacity for gratitude. For this we need to possess a sense of psychological abundance and also a resolution of our destructive envy into a capacity for reparation.[29]

In simple language, symbolic resolution means that I can say: "This is where I stand, this is what I can tolerate of ambiguity, and this is what I can share".

Where do I stand? I stand by my Eurocentric existential valuing of the individual, I stand by my advocacy of choice, and I stand by my loyalty to the analytic discourse. I respect these as the fruit of my psychic origins and I bring them as an offering to share.

To start with we are all people and foundationally share existential concerns. Whilst to be part of a group is unavoidable, we all share "personal responsibility, ethical self-knowledge, humility, forgiveness, human understanding, a knowledge of history, and a sense of the sacred".[30] There are indeed existential givens to being human: we are all born and will all die, we all have parents and always live with others, we are all bodies, we all have feelings and emotions, all love, all can be hurt, all experience anxiety, we all have a sense of time (though this may differ), we all experience space in a lived way (though this too can differ), within the bounds of our facticity we are all free, and we all suffer.

When our being together with others, or more pointedly others being together with us, leads to suffering and to restrictions on our freedom (our choice), a moral challenge has been made.

I shall highlight the place of suffering by presenting three accounts of personal experiences of discrimination because of forced group classification. Two are by Māori colleagues and one is my own. Each of these three accounts is reflective of the experience of a child who is a member of a minority group. It will be noticed also that it was not the violation of group rights that caused the hurt but the violation of the rights of the *individual* who was attacked because they belonged to a group.

The first, by Margaret Morice, reads as follows:

> When I was a little girl growing up in a Māori community, life was very different than (*sic*) it is today. My mother cooked meals for the 10 of us on a woodstove. We had no electricity and no indoor toilet. I shared a bed with my sister. When we took our bath together, my brothers would run to and fro, bringing bucketfuls of hot water from the large copper in the back yard. My eldest sister's morning job was to empty the potties kept under our beds. Yet despite some of these practical hardships, ours was a rich life. We were a close-knit family, with many extended family members nearby and plenty of opportunities for family celebrations and family drama. We felt the strength of our heritage but at the same time, were conscious of our difference and our relative disadvantage. A Pākehā [European New Zealander] friend who grew up in the same community fondly remembers an open door policy in which we were always welcome in each other's homes. But my experience was different. I remember standing at her back door with the clear understanding that I was not to cross the threshold. I was

cherished and accepted in my own world, but in the Pākehā world my welcome was uncertain.[31]

The second, by Mihiteria King (who is by descent Māori but adoptively raised by parents who were not Māori), reads as follows (slightly glossed by me for ease of understanding):

> I lived in what today would be called a white, middle-class, suburb. [Although myself Māori, my brothers and I were] raised by English parents and at a young age never really considered there was any difference between us, or my friends (*sic*). At my school, my two brothers and I were one of only two Māori families who attended the local primary school. [M]y story relates to my time at primary school when I was about 8-10 years old.
>
> Each weekday morning, I would call in at my friend's place and wait for her before walking to school together. I never used to think it strange that I should wait outside [the house]—didn't everyone? She would acknowledge me at the door and then it would be closed until she came out. During the winter, if it rained or was really windy, I was invited in to sit in the little entryway, on an old worn chair. The lounge was situated immediately off this entrance (there being no doorway between). However, it was as if there was an invisible line on the carpet, which indicated where I was "allowed" to go or not. It was never explicit; I just somehow knew. To be fair, this may have something to do with "having manners" as well, [the idea] that in another's space one only goes where one is invited.
>
> I think the penny dropped when my friend's parents' bought a new lounge suite—a lovely cream leather one. They replaced the old chair at the door with one of the now redundant chairs from the lounge while the new leather suite sat invitingly in its pristine "newness". Only now was I allowed to sit on what had been one of the "untouchable" lounge chairs. However, in my eagerness to delight in the new purchase I stepped over the invisible line, intending to stroke the couch. My friend's mother was in the adjoining room and had seen me advancing across the carpet. She had let out a shocked gasp of horror which of course stopped me mid-stride, dead in my tracks. Feeling embarrassed and ashamed for (*sic*) my "mistake" I returned to my side of the line on the carpet and resigned myself to the fact that I was "lucky" at least to be able to sit on the old "taonga" [treasure][32] inside, whilst looking outside through the front door at the other, now discarded chair that I had once used. The plush

new leather suite sat there teasing me, reminding me that I was different, that I was not good enough to sit on, let alone touch this, beautiful Pākehā *taonga*. In that moment I was a "good girl" and I "knew my place".[33]

The third account is my own, from when I was about nine years old:

For the first few of my school years my siblings and I attended a small Roman Catholic private school in South Africa. Although we were not Roman Catholic, or even Christian, my parents were not concerned about religious contamination but only concerned that their children should obtain the best education possible. They believed that this school would provide that. In my third and last year at that school our class was to produce a small religious play, and each child had to put forward an argument for why they should be given various roles. My turn came to stand up and make my argument and I did so citing my Jewish ancestry as a solid qualification. The teacher, an otherwise kindly German Franciscan nun, stared at me in a blank way. Then her staring eyes flicked past me to the boy in the desk behind me as if they were actuated by some clockwork mechanism and she put the question to him as if I had ceased to exist. She did not even instruct me to sit down, I had simply ceased to be for her. A ripping feeling and then confusion like a punch in the stomach followed my experience of this. As first personal anti-Semitic experiences go, this was very small but the emotional impact was immense.

The resonance we can all feel with such accounts, our empathic and compassionate appreciation of the hurt inflicted on these children by group-based prejudice, is largely natural. We know that this is wrong and unless our sense of the other as a person is utterly corrupted, as occurred in the Holocaust/Shoah,[34] we cannot fail to morally intuit the wrongness of it. It is perhaps only fair to say that of course these accounts are several decades old and although the pain they inflicted may still lie deep within the psyches of the individuals, the political and cultural context may have changed (at least partially). Empathically placing ourselves in the position of the child and thereby entering, as it were, the "child's mind", we know how it feels to be discriminated against. We are reminded through this act of identification how, metaphorically, we have all also at some time "been a stranger in a strange land" (Exodus 2:22).

Next we come to choice. Choice appears to be respected in the biculturalism of Aotearoa New Zealand. Mihiteria King[35] reminds us about the difference between apartheid notions of separate development and provision of mainstream and *kaupapa* Māori services in Aotearoa New Zealand:

> *Kaupapa* Māori services are by Māori, for Māori but also for anyone else who wishes to avail themselves of this model or philosophy of what is provided. I guess apartheid was 'this is ours and you have yours' and never the twain shall meet. Whereas our models are: you have the choice of mainstream or *kaupapa* Māori service, and that mainstream may have been regulated to provide a service that is competent cross-culturally.

Mihiteria King *inter alia* implicates the client's choice in this process, an implication that aligns her thinking with existential valuing of the individual. "Choice" is not, however, a simple "thing". I have already commented on how apartheid, like bureaucratic processes, may deny equity and choice by apparently offering choice. As I described earlier, in my experience a subtle apartheid-like process that appeared to give Māori a choice of service, in fact denied them rapid service access through forced group classification and they did not even know this was occurring.

Furthermore, for some, "choice" is not necessarily the personal choice of the individual with which we are familiar in Western culture. Other cultures may see "choice" as something a group has rather than an individual.

This latter issue is a living one in Aotearoa New Zealand with direct implications for clinical practice and for analysis. I will give a simple example. Stokes & Jeffries-Stokes[36] invite us to understand that:

> European concepts of autonomy in decision making by an individual young adolescent are completely out of kilter with traditional Māori views. The *whānau*[37] [family] may well hold quite a different view from what the law allows in regard to informed consent issues relating to issues such as access to contraception or abortion.

So, from this perspective, if a young Māori woman in analysis discovers she has an unplanned pregnancy and considers terminating that pregnancy then how do we understand this—does the unborn child "belong" to her or does it "belong" to her *whānau* (family/community)? Does the analytic attitude suffice, is it even appropriate? Mihiteria King responds to the first part of this question as follows:

> Whose role is it to decide on whether *whakapapa*[38] [kinship, in this sense the continued descent of a family] is to continue or not? Like who has that power?

This is an interesting cultural challenge and one that deserves much more attention than it will receive here. However, I have learnt anecdotally that it is just because individual choice may be lost in this way by Māori that some choose not to use a *kaupapa* Māori service. My own answer to this challenge at this time is to respect individual autonomy, as it is the individual who suffers and who has sought treatment.

This brings us to the second part of my question, does the analytic attitude suffice and is it appropriate, and Mihiteria King's continued challenge:

> How likely would it be for an analyst to either consider this or choose to go there? And the realms and bounds of "the analytic container" is, as you rightly mention, a conventional analytic, Eurocentric worldview then imposed on clients.

Whilst it is helpful to be open to a pluralism of perspectives, it is also important to have a conceptual base from which we start and to which we may self-reflectively return. I choose to remain self-reflectively loyal to the analytic world-view. I think that the Lacanian notion of the *analytic discourse* (here articulated by P. Elliot) describes this analytic world-view well:

> Analytic discourse is different from other discourses because the analyst privileges the desire of the analysand, creating a space in which that desire can be articulated, clarified, and understood. In the discourse of analysis, the subject (or analyst) does not make the other his/her slave (as in a discourse of mastery), nor is the other reduced to a mere reflection of the analyst's image (as in the discourse of bureaucracy), nor is the other a symbol of truth or a symptom of the analyst's desire (as in the discourse of hysteria). In the ideal form of psychoanalytic practice, the social relation between subject and other is based on 'listening attention' rather than oppression, benign influence, or phantasy.[39]

Backgrounding personal autonomy and foregrounding group choice elides much of my understanding of psychological life. It risks forgetting the experienced nature of being. In addition foregrounding the group threatens to tear the enterprise of analysis out of its context in Western culture—the conventional analytic world-view *is* foundationally Eurocentric. Although the analytic world-view is open to self-critical reflection, to a continuing "meditative" questioning of its ground, I feel that it needs to stay rooted in the experiential (rather than the cognitive-theoretical), and it needs to courageously but lightly maintain contact with the value of the individual.

In short, I hold fast to the Eurocentric analytic view that existentially privileges valuing the individual over group. The three vignettes of childhood experience above conjure for us something of the suffering of the *individual* even though the injury occurred through individual membership of a group! Saying that, I am also prepared to be self-reflective and reparative of any harm that arises from this.

What is my tolerance for ambiguity?

In its immediate applicability in South Africa, my original anti-apartheid moral hermeneutic could have no sense of ambiguity to it. I could not "play with" the idea of the validity of group differences for that opened the door to apartheid reasoning and apartheid apologists. Confrontation with the bicultural situation in Aotearoa New Zealand has introduced the need for ambiguity to the hermeneutic. However, I believe that this is a work in progress, one that calls for constant self-reflection and one in which nothing can be taken for granted. I still feel the shear and conflict from the challenge that the bicultural moral hermeneutic poses to my old anti-apartheid moral hermeneutic, and I take this as a generative warning. This is a continuing piece of psychological work. Whilst I have not transcended a cultural complex, I can perhaps use it to keep me alert to areas that need work both personally and pragmatically. The struggle that this has engendered has so far led to an increase in my consciousness and an increase in my tolerance of ambiguous solutions to the bicultural challenge. Paraire Huata underscores this necessity when he says: "Under the notion of biculturalism then we are often forced into an oxymoron".[40]

What do we have to share? At its best I think that *Te Tiriti* is about an exchange that is a sharing. So too, biculturalism is at its best a sharing. I believe that sharing is consistent with my position that first and foremost we are people and foundationally share existential concerns and that personal choice is of primary value. I also believe that there are many sorts of sharing and that the mundane sharing of people encountering people helps us transcend the tensions of immigration.

More specifically, for a symbol to manifest it helps to have a true encounter with the other. This is, after all, what we do when conducting analysis. To know the other as they are, to encounter their otherness, is to encounter our own Otherness ("Other" is what Renos Papadopoulos refers to as the other within).[41] We can, through encounter with the other as another person, come to meet, know, assimilate, and accommodate the opposite in a way that leads to symbol formation. As Dawson[42] puts it:

> It is the "person to person" sharing of stories, and thus the identification of common desires, fears, losses, and joys which assists people to cross the wasteful divide caused by fear of difference, whether of colour, culture, religion, or language. The upheaval of migration and the challenges of resettlement rely not just on the attitudes, skills and efforts of new settlers but on the acceptance and openness shown by the host community.

The last sentence of this statement from Dawson captures something essential: There is need for a mutuality. Whilst migrants bring an offering, it is also necessary for the host community to be accepting and open to them. My offering is an existentially based self-reflective philosophy and morality of person: Will it be accepted? As I seek to understand, will I be understood? As I seek to change, will others also seek to change?

Symbolically, change lies between and beyond the conflict towards a new perspective. Mark Thorpe[43] proposes a basis for a shift of perspective from apartheid South Africa to bicultural Aotearoa New Zealand, one that takes account of who has power (a minority group or a majority group) and just how they use that power. He observes that oppression in apartheid South Africa occurred via separation and exclusion, whereas in Aotearoa New Zealand the opposite holds true: oppression, essentially malignant ethnocentrism, and colonialism occur through the lumping together and the denial of separateness. In apartheid South Africa domination of one person by another was effected by separation and apart-ness (i.e., apartheid), whereas in Aotearoa New Zealand, it is effected by attempts at integration and the loss of cultural values and knowledge. Thorpe argues that in South Africa where the numerically smaller group sought power, they did this by segregation, whereas in Aotearoa New Zealand the numerically larger group has achieved power by integration. This idea certainly parallels the strategies that were deployed in Imperial Russia after the late 1700s to force Jews (a minority group) to assimilate to Russian culture.[44]

However, Thorpe's view represents the situation as it was in apartheid South Africa and as it is in bicultural Aotearoa New Zealand. It does not lie between and above South Africa and Aotearoa New Zealand. It allows me to understand better the differences between these two places, but it does not take account of how apartheid South Africa may be present *in* bicultural Aotearoa New Zealand. This apartheid South Africa is in the Shadow of biculturalism, and what I hope that I have brought, in and through my being challenged, is a non-reactionary challenge to that Shadow. This leads me to a reformulation of my moral hermeneutic.

Reformulation of My Moral Hermeneutic

These considerations lead me to a more ambiguous, hopefully more morally imaginative, more sharable reformulation of my moral hermeneutic. I present this as part of my work on a cultural complex. I also bring it as an offering that I have worked on and would like to share.

For me, the first function of my moral hermeneutic remains the existential valuing of an individual. Particular individuals suffer, "groups" as entities in themselves do not suffer, and to speak of a group suffering is to "individualise" it in an anthropomorphic way. However, it is vitally important, as a second function of the moral hermeneutic, to ask what degree of damage will be done to the individual if his/her group membership and group values are not respectfully considered and given a place. This calls us to respect group identity but also, as a third function of the moral hermeneutic, to be alert to a variety of limitations on choice (conscious and unconscious, of group, because of group, by group) or even forcing of choice. Furthermore it is important to consider the particular group politics of a place: who has power and how do they use it? Finally this moral hermeneutic needs to be alive and open to evolution through personal encounter and sharing with others.

All that having been said, I have no certainty: these are questions and responses, "hostile opposites," if you will, with which I have to continuously struggle like Jacob did with the Stranger. As I seem to answer one inner question, another emerges. This struggle is probably a lifelong task, one that may arrive in some way at a symbol, that image or position in which "hostile opposites" are incorporated and transcended. I am not sure that conventional Jungian understanding of symbol as a sort of final image suffices here—in this case perhaps the symbol is more of a rubric—the red letter that sets the tone of an engaged and struggling psychological life.

Conclusion

I have sought to present an open and honest phenomenological account of a particular struggle associated with migration from South Africa to Aotearoa New Zealand. Growing up and living in South Africa during the apartheid years, I developed a deliberative anti-apartheid moral hermeneutic that supported my moral intuition that apartheid was wrong. In later life I immigrated to Aotearoa New Zealand, where biculturalism is a central value, and experienced the activation of a cultural complex that challenged that anti-apartheid moral hermeneutic and drew me into a struggle with myself.

I have endeavoured to formulate this struggle in terms of the context of person, place, and politics and to refract it through the Jungian notion of "hostile opposites" and their resolution in symbol formation. Sometimes, however, the dialectic predominates and continues rather than evolving into a once and forever static symbol. So it is for me trying to integrate my anti-apartheid moral hermeneutic with the biculturalism of Aotearoa New Zealand and finding myself within a dialectic. Imaginally, I find myself in the same position as Jacob wrestling with the Stranger. My hope is that there is a dawn, a position of rest and a new name—but of course, as in the biblical story, that new name, Israel—meaning "the one who struggles with God"—may not grant such a resting place but confirm an ongoing process.

Acknowledgements

I would like to thank various people who have directly and indirectly aided me in grappling with these issues and in the writing of this chapter. First and foremost, I would like to thank Bev Flavell, who guided me in new understanding when I first arrived in Aotearoa New Zealand. I would also like to thank Margaret Morice, Mihiteria King, Mark Thorpe, Craig San Roque, and Amanda Dowd who generously engaged with me in writing this chapter.

Notes

[1] Mark Thorpe & Miranda Thorpe, "Immigrant Psychotherapists and New Zealand Clients," *Forum* 14 (2008), pp. 30-45.

[2] Leon and Rebecca Grinberg have written on immigration from a psychoanalytic perspective in Leon Grinberg & Rebecca Grinberg, *Psychoanalytic Perspectives on Migration and Exile* (New Haven: Yale University Press, 1989) and Jungian analyst Renos Papadopoulos has contributed to and edited a collection of writings on the trauma of immigration in Renos Papadopoulos (ed.), *Therapeutic Care of Refugees: No Place Like Home* (London: Karnac, 2002).

[3] See Salaman Akhtar, "Technical Challenges Faced by the Immigrant Psychoanalyst," *Psychoanalytic Quarterly* 75 (2006), pp. 21-43, and Amanda

Dowd, "Whose Mind Am I In?" *Australasian Journal of Psychotherapy* 27 (2008), pp. 23-40.

[4] Akhtar, "Technical Challenges," p. 22.

[5] The apartheid system defined people as "White" and "Non-white" so that "blackness" was defined as the absence of "whiteness".

[6] Settlers to Aotearoa New Zealand are of course varied as a people, but they enter and settle in Aotearoa New Zealand under the auspices of the Crown, one of the two parties to the Treaty of Waitangi.

[7] P. M. Camic, J. E. Rhodes & L. Yardley, "Naming the Stars: Integrating Qualitative Methods Into Psychological Research," in *Qualitative Research in Psychology: Expanding Perspectives in Methodology and Design,* eds. P. M. Camic, J. E. Rhodes & L. Yardley (Washington, D.C.: American Psychological Association, 2003), pp. 3-15; E.W. Eisner, "On the Art and Science of Qualitative Research in Psychology," in *Qualitative Research,* pp. 17-29; A. Giorgi, *Psychology as a Human Science: A Phenomenologically Based Approach* (New York: Harper & Row, 1970); J. Marecek, "Dancing Through Minefields: Toward a Qualitative Stance in Psychology," in *Qualitative Research,* pp. 49-69; J. E. McGrath & B. A. Johnson, "Methodology Makes Meaning: How Both Qualitative and Quantitative Paradigms Shape Evidence," in *Qualitative Research,* pp. 31-48; J. McLeod, *Qualitative Research in Counselling and Psychotherapy* (Thousand Oaks: Sage Publications, 2001).

[8] T. Singer, & S. L. Kimbles (eds.), *The Cultural Complex: Contemporary Jungian Perspectives on Psyche and Society* (Hove & New York: Brunner-Routledge, 2004).

[9] The "Standard Left Explanatory System" or "SLES" is a system (or hermeneutic) that assumes that all ills in the non-Western world are a function of Western wrongdoing. Within the terms of this hermeneutic, left-wing thinkers are constrained not to examine or ascribe any responsibility to non-Western groupings. The SLES is a hermeneutic that provides simplistic reasons for socio-political circumstances; it is frequently driven by emotions such as guilt and gives left-wing individuals a sense of moral superiority. It is thus also a form of cultural complex. (It is important to note that Strenger himself is a very left-wing Swiss-Israeli existential psychoanalyst who nonetheless maintains that the Israeli left has been compromised by its use of the SLES.) See C. Strenger, "Strenger than Fiction / Jewish liberals from all nations, unite," *HaAretz Blog,* http://www.haaretz.com/blogs/strenger-than-fiction/strenger-than-fiction-jewish-liberals-from-all-nations-unite-1.287913 (May, 2010).

[10] Alfred Milner, later 1st Viscount Milner, was a significant British statesman. He was High Commissioner to Southern Africa and Governor of the Cape Colony from 1897 until 1906. He was influential in precipitating the Anglo-Boer war and in setting up British administration in the defeated Boer republics at its end. An English racist, he viewed Afrikaners (descendents of Dutch, French, English, and German settlers in South Africa who evolved an African language originally based on 17th century Dutch) as an inferior people and culture, and he forced English culture on them, trying to eliminate the Afrikaner culture. This policy was known as "Anglicisation", and it led to a counter reaction that contributed to the system of apartheid because Afrikaner nationalists wanted to retain their autonomy and separateness ("apart-ness" or "apartheid" in Afrikaans).

[11] The late 1950s and the decade of the 1960s saw the ending of colonial rule in Africa. In many instances in the run-up to independence and the subsequent post-independence period, there was violent conflict in these countries. I personally recall certain hallmark conflicts from my childhood years. I provide some notes of these in particular:

The Mau Mau Rebellion or Uprising in Kenya spanned the years 1952 to 1960. In this uprising, which was nucleated on a secret society, mostly Kikuyu people rose against British Imperial rule. The uprising was suppressed and there was atrocity on both sides.

In South Africa on 21st March 1960, South African Police in Sharpeville opened fire on a crowd of black people protesting a new aspect of the apartheid pass laws. Sixty-nine people were killed and a further one hundred and eighty wounded.

The Congo Crisis was precipitated in 1960 when the Congo gained independence from Belgium. Conflicting internal factions and external forces plunged the Congo into violence. The state of armed conflict lasted until 1966 and led to the assassination of the Prime Minister Patrice Lumumba, the death in a plane crash of UN Secretary General, Dag Hammerskjöld, and the seizing of power by Joseph Mobuto Sésé Seko.

The Rivonia Trial, named after a suburb of Johannesburg, Rivonia, where many of the accused were arrested, commenced in 1963. In this political trial 10 leaders of the African National Congress (ANC), including Nelson Mandela, were accused of over 200 acts of sabotage. The trial ended in 1964, and 8 of the accused, who had faced the death penalty, were sentenced to life imprisonment.

On 11th November, 1965 Ian Smith, Prime Minister of then Rhodesia, and others signed the Unilateral Declaration of Independence (UDI) from

Britain. This eventuated as a result of a refusal by the Smith government to countenance black majority rule in Rhodesia.

[12] The most prominent account of these (there were several) occurred before I was born but was certainly told to me. This involved the killing of the Ruck family who were hacked to death with pangas (heavy machetes) in particular the killing of six-year-old Michael Ruck. An account of this is found in the British Sunday Times of 26 January, 1953. See http://archive.timesonline.co.uk/tol/viewArticle.arc?articleId=ARCHIVE-The_Times-1953-01-26-06-008&pageId=ARCHIVE-The_Times-1953-01-26-06 (downloaded 11 April 2011). Other children killed by the Mau Mau were four-year-old Andrew Stephens, thirteen-year-old Christopher Robin Twohey, and fifteen-year-old Geoffrey Danby (see http://genforum.genealogy.com/kenya/messages/420.html. Downloaded 11 April, 2011).

[13] For a sense of some of these activities, it is useful to see the Albany Black Sash paper presented to the National Conference of the Black Sash, March, 1988, entitled "Detentions in and around Grahamstown (12 June 1986–31 January 1988)", from *Black Sash Archival Collections in South Africa,* http://www.lib.uct.ac.za/blacksash/pdfs/cnf19880311.026.001.000.pdf (April, 2010). Additional information on this time and place may be found in S.A. Greyling, *Rhodes University During the Segregation and Apartheid Eras, 1993-1990* (Unpublished thesis in fulfilment of the degree Master of Arts from Rhodes University, Grahamstown, 2007).

[14] It could be critically noted that I seem here to be making an argument for the primacy of moral principles (or what is called "moral deliberation"), and there are also arguments to be made against the assumption that "cognitive" moral principles are primary. This argument is explored more fully by J. L. C. Wright in the thesis: *The Problem(s) with Principles: Towards a Skill-Based Account of Mature Moral Agency.* (Thesis in partial fulfilment of requirements for the degree M.A. in Philosophy, University of Wyoming, Laramie, Wyoming, 2006). The moral deliberation argument assumes that we make our moral judgements by a process of cognitive deliberation based on certain guiding principles. However, it can also be argued, and I agree with this as well, that we have an innate moral sense, or moral intuition. Both are probably present, and it is noteworthy that from the neuroscience perspective there are neural correlates of both moral deliberation and moral intuition, which are are complexly interrelated. These arguments are outlined by C. L. Harenski, O. Antonenko, M. S. Shane & K. A. Kiehl,

in "A Functional Imaging Investigation of Moral Deliberation and Moral Intuition," *Neuroimage* 49 (2010), pp. 2707–2716, and also by J. Woodward, in "Moral Intuition: Its Neural Substrate and Normative Significance," http://www.allmanlab.caltech.edu/PDFs/WoodwardAllman2007.pdf (April, 2010).

[15] T. Singer & C. Kaplinsky, "Cultural Complexes in Analysis," in *Jungian Psychoanalysis Working in the Spirit of C. G. Jung*, ed. M. Stein (Chicago: Open Court Publishing Company, 2010), pp. 22-37.

[16] We can also ask the question of how much of my anti-apartheid moral hermeneutic is a mature moral capacity and how much is another cultural complex based on an ethnocentric prizing of the individual. This is not clear at this moment. The Jungian perspective prizes the individual (as indeed does the wider psychotherapeutic world. See N. McWilliams, "Individuality: A Threatened Concern in the Age of Evidence Based Practice," *Forum: The Journal of the New Zealand Association of Psychotherapists* 15 (2010) pp. 69-73.) This could itself gesture towards a Jungian cultural complex that entails a bias towards individuation as a process of separation from the group. However, such a Jungian cultural complex may grow more from the Shadowy aspects of "individualism" rather than "individuation". An understanding of individuation that holds as central the dialogue between sense-of-self and other/Other obviates such Shadow aspects to an extent. See C. Milton, "Towards Individuation: A Jungian View on Being a Body and on Being Together," *Forum: The Journal of the New Zealand Association of Psychotherapists* 15 (2010), pp. 92-108.

[17] M. King, *The Penguin History of New Zealand* (London: Penguin Books Ltd, 2003); Waitangi Tribunal Webpage (undated), http://www.waitangi-tribunal.govt.nz/ (April, 2010); R. Walker, *Ka Whawhai Tonu Matou: Struggle Without End* (Auckland: Penguin Books,1990); A. Ward, *An Unsettled History* (Wellington: Bridget Williams Books, 1999).

[18] I base these statements on a comparison of the standard English translation of the Treaty of Waitangi and that of Professor Sir Hugh Kawharu, former member of the Treaty of Waitangi Tribunal. For further details see http://www.waitangi-tribunal.govt.nz/treaty/kawharutranslation.asp and http://www.waitangi-tribunal.govt.nz/treaty/english.asp (April, 2011). For further discussion of the difference between *rangatiratanga* and *kawangatana*, see http://twm.co.nz/Maori_tino.htm (July, 2011)

[19] Although England, and indeed the United Kingdom of Great Britain, has no constitution *per se*, it does have an historical document, the *Magna*

Carta, agreed to and signed by King John in 1215. This document, the Great Charter of Freedoms, or *Magna Carta Libertatum* (*Magna Carta* for short), required King John to proclaim certain rights for freemen, respect certain legal processes, and accept that even the King's own will was bound by the law.

[20] P. Kriwaczek, *Yiddish Civilisation: The Rise and Fall of a Forgotten Nation* (London: Phoenix, 2005/2006), p. 90.

[21] S. Akhtar, "A Third Individuation: Immigration, Identity, and the Psychoanalytic Process," *Journal of the American Psychoanalytic Association* 43 (1995), p. 1053.

[22] What I experienced, and discuss, as a subjective sense of moral shear has been demonstrated by brain imaging techniques and "objective" psychometric tests (by "objective'" I mean from the natural scientific perspective which literally locates and measures physical entities and processes, not the usual Jungian notion of the "objective" psyche). See A. S. Baron, & M. R Banaji, "The Development of Implicit Attitudes: Evidence of Race Evaluations from Ages 6 to 10 and Adulthood," *Psychological Science, 17*, No. 1 (2006), pp. 53-58, http://www.projectimplicit.net/articles.php (April, 2010); W. A. Cunningham, J. B. Nezlek, & M. R. Banaji, "Implicit and Explicit Ethnocentrism: Revisiting the Ideologies of Prejudice," *Personality and Social Psychology Bulletin, 30* (2004) pp. 1332-1346; http://www.projectimplicit.net/articles.php (April, 2010); F. De Vignemont, and T. Singer, "The Empathic Brain: How, When and Why," *Trends in Cognitive Sciences*, 10, No. 10 (2006), pp. 435-441; http://jeannicod.ccsd.cnrs.fr/docs/00/16/95/84/TXT/empathy_TICS.txt (April, 2010); H. D. Fishbein, *"The Genetic/Evolutionary Basis of Prejudice and Hatred," Journal of Hate Studies*, 3, No. 1 (2004) pp. 113-119, *guweb2.gonzaga.edu/againsthate/journal3/GHS107.pdf (April, 2010)*; E. M. Glaser, "Is There a Neurobiology of Hate? *Journal of Hate Studies*, 7, No. 1 (2008), pp. 8-19; http://journals.gonzaga.edu/index.php/johs/article/view/96/74 (April, 2010); Harenski, Antonenko, Shane & Kiehl, 2010; M. Iacoboni, "Imitation, Empathy and Mirror Neurons," *Annual Review of Psychology,* 60 (2009), pp. 653–670 and T. A. Ito, and B. D. Bartholow, "The Neural Correlates of Race," *Trends in Cognitive Sciences,* 13, No.12 (2009), pp. 524-531.

[23] C. G. Jung, *The Collected Works of C.G. Jung*, trans. R. F. C. Hull, Vol 12 (Princeton, NJ: Princeton University Press, 1944/1952).

[24] S. Akhtar, "A Third Individuation: Immigration, Identity, and the Psychoanalytic Process,", pp. 1056-1057.

[25] R. Brooke, *Jung and Phenomenology* (London: Routledge, 1991); C. G. Jung, CW 6. These definitions are based on a privately delivered workshop that I conducted on the Inferior Function in Auckland in 2005; A. Samuels, *Jung and the Post-Jungians* (London: Routledge & Kegan Paul, 1985).

[26] S. Akhtar, "A Third Individuation: Immigration, Identity, and the Psychoanalytic Process."

[27] A. Samuels, *The Plural Psyche* (London & New York: Routledge, 1989).

[28] *Ibid.*, p. 201.

[29] M. Klein, "Envy and Gratitude," in *Envy and Gratitude and Other Works 1946-1963* (London: Virago Press, 1957/1988), pp. 176-235.

[30] R. Brooke. "Cultural Reflections on Jung's Concept of Individuation." Paper read to the Inter-Regional Society for Analytical Psychology, Santa Fe, October 19, 2006, p. 12.

[31] M. P. Morice, "Psychotherapy Through the Lens of the Treaty," *NZAP Newsletter*, April 2006, pp. 29-34.

[32] As mentioned earlier in reference to *Te Tiriti*, a "*taonga*" is a treasure, concrete or cultural, but we see here how the use of the term can be extended in an everyday way to mean special objects for a particular family.

[33] Mihiteria King, personal communication, 2010. Note: this is not the same person, "M. King", referenced earlier in this chapter.

[34] S. Ganor, *Light One Candle* (New York: Kodansha International, 1995/2003); R. Zwi, *Last Walk in Naryshkin Park* (North Melbourne: Spinifex Press, 1997).

[35] Mihiteria King, personal communication, 2010. Again, not the King referenced in the discussion of *Te Tiriti*.

[36] G. D. Stokes & C. A. Jeffries-Stokes, "Indigenous Culture and Health," in eds. D. M. Robertson & M.J. South, *Practical Paediatrics* (Philadelphia: Churchill Livingstone Elsevier, 2006), p. 60.

[37] *Whānau* (pronounced farno) means family or community and is the basic building block of unit of Māori society. See also E. Henry, "The Challenge of Preserving Indigenous Knowledge, *LIANZA Conference*", 2001, cited at http://www.tepapa.govt.nz/NationalServices/Resources/MuseumInABox/Glossary.

[38] *Whakapapa* (pronounced *fukapuppa*) means the principle of kinship, genealogy, and lineage, and it also defines the individual and kin groups as well as the relationships between them. See also E. Henry, "The Challenge of Preserving Indigenous Knowledge,

LIANZA Conference", 2001, cited at http://www.tepapa.govt.nz/ NationalServices/Resources/MuseumInABox/Glossary. As Mihiteria King uses it here, it indicates something of cultural identity and how this is, to a degree, chosen.

[39] P. Elliot, *From Mastery to Analysis: Theories of Gender in Psychoanalytic Feminism* (Ithaca/London: Cornell University Press, 1991), p. 13.

[40] P. Huata, "Māori Psychotherapy—A Cultural Oxymoron," *Forum: The Journal of the New Zealand Association of Psychotherapists* 15 (2010), p. 5.

[41] R. K. Papadopoulos, "Jung and the Concept of the Other," in eds. R. K. Papadopoulos and G. S. Saayman, *Jung in Modern Perspective* (Hounslow: Wildwood House, 1984), pp. 54-88.

[42] M. Dawson, "Foreword" to *My Home Now: Migrants and Refugees to New Zealand Tell Their Stories,* eds. G. Thomas & L. McKenzie (Auckland: Cape Catley, 2005), pp. 9-10.

[43] Thorpe personal communication, 2010.

[44] Kriwaczek, *Yiddish Civilisation*.

Alexis Wright is one of Australia's finest Indigenous writers, working tirelessly for Aboriginal land rights, self-government, constitutional change, and the prevention of Indigenous injury. Her epic novel, the deeply poetic *Carpentaria*, won the 2007 Miles Franklin Literary Award, the Australian Literature Society Gold Medal, the Victorian Premier's Award for Fiction, the Queensland Premier's Award for Fiction, and the Vision Australia-Braille Book of the Year Award 2010. Her other works include *Grog War* (1997), *Take Power* (1998), and *Plains of Promise* (1997), short-listed for the Commonwealth Prize and the NSW Premier's Award for Fiction. She is a Distinguished Fellow at the University of Western Sydney, Writing and Society Research Group. Alexis lived for many years in Alice Springs, Central Australia. Her family origins in the northern Australian Gulf of Carpentaria region also include a Chinese ancestry.

●●●●●●●●●●●●●

In "The Structure and Dynamics of the Psyche", C. G. Jung reviews his theory of the complex. Four points reiterated in his review echo key ideas in Wright's essay. These are: fear, resistance, trivialisation, and the value of finding words "to push the dialogue with a complex deeper and deeper into fear-bound regions". Jung links instinctive "fear of invisible things that move in the dark" to the fear of movement and voices (in self and society) "driving away sleep or filling it with bad dreams". (Collected Works 8, paras. 213 and 209). Wright, in this essay and in her other works, depicts unquiet things that provoke restless sleeplessness in the culture and fill the country's dream life with fears that at the same time are minimised or denied. Jung writes of the resistance to admitting the complex to consciousness, and like Wright, suggests that a defence against discomforting irritations is to trivialise, minimise, and silence the outspoken (moral) voices in society or within oneself. Wright appeals to cultural story-tellers of all races, including her own, to speak out against paralysis of mind and feeling.

"A Question of Fear" is kindly reproduced here with permission from Allen and Unwin and Sydney PEN Voices – the three Writers Project, from Tolerance, Prejudice and Fear, Allen and Unwin, Sydney, 2008. PEN International is dedicated to the support of writers anywhere who work under persecution, exile, or imprisonment or "silencing". In 2007 Sydney PEN commissioned three of Australia's leading writers (Christos Tsiolkas, Gideon Haigh, and Alexis Wright) to give a series of lectures on topics of vital importance to contemporary Australia and these were published by Allen and Unwin with an Introduction by Nobel Laureate, J.M. Coetzee. The editors thank Sydney PEN and Allen and Unwin for graciously allowing Alex Wright's essay to be reproduced in total in this volume.

9

A Question of Fear

Alexis Wright

Introduction

The closing years of the last century and most of those of the first decade of the twenty-first century will be remembered in the history of Australia as the time when the country lost its image of innocent carefreeness and wellbeing—an image that had seemingly always represented Australianness. This long-held identity was lost when the federal government of the period could have chosen to engage the country in a dialogue about ideas of difference, but decided instead to join the USA and the UK in a brutal war against what it labelled "the forces of darkness".

Australians are accustomed to placing a great deal of trust in their government, but in this period the government played on their fear to propel them into the unknown. They found themselves responsible for the harsh realities of what happens to their own sense of humanity from being a key player in the so-called war on terror. They became implicit in the detention of the defenceless people of the world who came to Australian shores seeking shelter. And the nation began facing the complexities of what was either official truths or lies about global warming and drought. But what was also shaping the conscience of the population at this time, faced with a sense of confusion and personal powerlessness to engage with the challenge of recognising that there were other voices insisting on change in the world outside and the environment at a global level—both being matters that it neither knew—nor probably cared too much about before—was escapism.

Of course, escapism was nothing new for a nation that was formed on the basis of denying the truth. The government could count on this historical attitude of turning a blind eye to matters of the truth and use it to instill, manage, and manipulate public fear. After all, this nation was shaped through its ability to lie and get away with the land theft of the entire country from Aboriginal people since day one of colonisation; it is the most fundamental issue of what is still wrong in the country, ongoing and long outstanding. So when Australians were unable to respond to the changing world—particularly as much of what was happening right before their eyes was so foreign to them, and because it is almost impossible to change the decisions of government outside election time—and wanted to escape the weight of the awful realities and responsibilities forced on them which they had no idea how to own, they did so through a form of escapism that allowed the population at a personal level to artificially restore their sense of being in control of one's own destiny. Australians put their heads in the sand, tuning out of the political commentary dominating the media during this time and, instead, reinventing an identity of individual control of "localness" through reality TV makeovers. Nightly, Australians glued themselves to the couch, giddy with the choice of makeover programs to watch. There were the personalities or health of people, children, and pets to overhaul, along with houses, rooms, gardens, and wardrobes that were stripped bare and changed "for the better" through a step-by-step process so convincing that almost anyone could become an instant expert in design and renovation, or a shrewd judge of character.

The makeover changed the Australian psyche. We were back in charge, and comfortable with the idea of how we could change and judge what we disliked in our immediate surroundings, or what the personality and "the look" should be of life in Australia. Hardware shops made a fortune as the middle and upper classes of the population became addicted to improving their surroundings—out the door went unsightly gardens and house structures, furniture, and daggy clothes. How easy it became to believe in the possibility of changing any surrounding that did not suit this new image of ourselves while the government was left to its own devices with a mandate to swiftly change other people and other countries into something that looked like us. Whether those years of reaching for images that could be applied easily and in haste worked in homes across the nation remains for the future to decide. Many makeover merchants might now admit that not enough thought was given to the consequences of discarding what was already there, or whether the change was really what was intended.

Even the old metaphorical prison wall of dictatorial government policies that were controlling Aboriginal Australia since colonisation received its own media makeover—one, wholly manipulated by the federal government of the last decade, silenced the Aboriginal leadership it controlled through institutions it had initially created before destroying by squeezing tight resources to further erode Indigenous humanity. This wall became a billboard for the graffiti of any commentator—mostly non-Indigenous—to condemn Aboriginal people. What was being said about Aboriginal people in the media was often vicious, relentless and wholesale. There were so many commentators who weren't Indigenous writing about Indigenous people, nor did they have any meaningful contact with Aboriginal people or live in an Indigenous community—those few who did, did so as result of the privilege and status accorded to them as "professionals", which is different to Indigenous people actually speaking for themselves. Strangely, as though Indigenous people had become innate objects, their voices were practically never heard. The constant message to them from others was to forget Indigenous rights, which also included, it seems, the right to be heard. The effect of this vitriolic attack of vilification from the powerful on a defenceless people mostly living in poverty was that Indigenous people became silent. You could call it a counterattack by Aboriginal people—sometimes it is a cultural strength to remain silent—that instead became a terrible self-inflicted wound of psychological harm to the spirit, intensifying inside the wall. Tens of thousands of Aboriginal people became more deeply hurt, continued to be hurt, and many defenceless people died from deliberately imposed injury to self-worth in the forms of suicide or murder that were so inexplicable and at such a rapid rate that most of our people have yet to understand what happened to them, or how we might even survive in the future.

The question yet to be answered is why Indigenous people were silent, whether Indigenous voices, apart from the lone voice of Noel Pearson,[1] really had been silenced, needed to be silenced, or chose to become silent during this period. Where was their freedom of speech? Did Aboriginal people choose to be silent in agreement or disagreement, or was it forced; was it a silence created through fear, or a silence that was self-inflicted? Did Aboriginal people use silence as a weapon in what became a futile attempt to combat the force of the attack? Yet it must be recognised that Aboriginal people had not been easily silenced before and had put in decades of hard work to ensure survival of culture through two centuries of land theft and deepening poverty created by decades of failed government policies. They had survived as fighters in much better shape in the past fifty years than in the last decade. Can fear rob hope?

It is the impact of silence in the space of one decade for almost two per cent of the population that once had a reputation of strongly representing its views which is the puzzle, and it is worth considering how fear tactics can be applied to affect any part of the population, if not every person—man, woman and child—in this country

1. A Question of Fear

If you tell me about your fears, I will listen, and then I will tell you about mine, but I fear we will only discover what is already commonly known about fear—it's frightening, and rather than confront fear, or imagine how we might create a place, a nation or a world without fear, we let our fears slip to the back of our minds. We feel that our fear is personal, that no one else would understand, but fearfulness is universal and, universally, each of us has the potential to use our fears destructively against others or ourselves. Fear is the back-seat driver in busy lives that leaves little space for deep thoughts about how to understand oneself, let alone other people. If we try, our fears cry out, What about us? What about all our clutter of self-preservation? You feel you won't survive without it. So it is too hard. We feel we must preserve the status quo. It is too frightening to think otherwise. But what of the future if we take comfort in allowing people more powerful, and more fearful, than ourselves to do the thinking for us?

I wonder if we take as many opportunities as we should to learn more about other people. One of the world's leading philosophers, Kwame Anthony Appiah,[2] has suggested in his moral manifesto for a planet shared by more than six billion strangers, "that we should learn about people in other places, take an interest in their civilisations, their arguments, their errors, their achievements, not because that will bring us to agreement, but because it will help us get used to one another." I doubt that, even to this day, many people outside the Aboriginal world in Australia have a reasonable understanding of the first literature composed on this land, which is still contained within the enormous archive of epical storytelling poetry held by each Indigenous nation across the country. These are the ancient stories of the ancestral creation beings that are learned and stored as mind maps that define the philosophical understanding of Aboriginal law, and which, taken together, embrace the entire continent. With this Indigenous memory men and women can name and tell the story of thousands of individual sites in their country, continuing a long tradition of watching over this country and maintaining the ecologically sustainable life.

I want to talk a little bit about poetry because it is the art of defining essential things worth remembering about ourselves. This idea can be found anywhere in the world where people describe the soul of who they are in their stories. Poets excavate deep within the psyche to find words that speak about, describe, and bring some sense into the world about how to be human. Irish poet Seamus Heaney described Joycean ideas in *Finnegan's Wake* as "eddying with the vowels of all rivers", remembering everything at the level of the unconscious, because there is much amnesia in people that they do not learn from their own history. This is how the Chinese poet Bei Dao[3] works in his poem about "The Sower" in time of war, "throwing seeds across marble floors":

> a sower walks into the great hall
> it's war out there, he says
> and you awash in emptiness
> you've sworn off your duty to sound the alarm
> I've come in the name of fields . . .

The poetics of reminding and remembering mostly sits in hidden places, in uncrowded little fires that flicker in the homes in lonely places of the world's exiled, persecuted, threatened, and tortured. These hidden hymns are sung too quietly. The wall is diabolically claustrophobic. It has closed us in.

We desperately need to focus on the lessons of fearfulness by listening to the poet's deep sense of consciousness, so that we do not continue making the same mistakes. Palestinian poet Mahmoud Darwish[4] is a writer who speaks to the universality of our feelings of spiritual crisis. Searching lost realms of Arab culture, he seeks to reconnect with "the original spirit of mythmaking", and through this understanding, he expresses all times in the "intimate depths experienced by every exiled human psyche on earth". He strikes deep into the core of remembering the meaning of belonging and the loss of its essence in the soul of who we are, so deeply afflicting all people through the experience of separation from the traditional roots that provide the spirit of their humanity, such as in his poem "On a Canaanite at The Dead Sea":

> This is my absence,
> A master who imposes his laws
> And mocks my visions . . .
> All the prophets are my kin.

> But heaven is still far from its earth
> And I am still far from my words.

I think that Australia is exposed throughout the world as being devoid of spirituality from never adopting or coming to terms with the original values for understanding this land voiced time and again by Indigenous people. Surely many countries must find it difficult to develop a close understanding or respect for this country if it appears to be a child without a set of beliefs that are grounded in strong, long-term cultural principles. Perhaps the way for Australia to create credible relationships worldwide will be through the development of a literature that understands not only how Aboriginal people think, along with the cultural matrices of the foundation myths that Australians of immigrant backgrounds cling to. In this way we might also begin to build a road to accepting Indigenous spiritual sovereignty of land, rather than continuing the absurdity of simply mouthing about practical measures for reconciliation.

I would like to refer to one recent example of how the original spiritual values of this land have clashed with Australian values. The Yanyuwa, Gudanji, and Garrawa people in the Gulf of Carpentaria have long voiced their fear about the mining group Xstrata's proposal to divert the McArthur River, which is home to a giant "rainbow serpent", because it will bring storms, cyclones, and other disasters. The Yanyuwa people have fought relentlessly for three decades for the return of their island country. A senior traditional owner said on ABC television's Stateline program in 2003: "It is no good. I will be sick if they cut the place, because my spirit is there. All my songs are across the river. I don't want to see that thing happen in the McArthur River." What value has this country placed in this belief? Do we understand how the ancient knowledge of Aboriginal law governs Aboriginal people today? In May 2007, the Northern Territory[5] government enacted legislation in the dead of night to allow the mining development to go ahead.

When I was a child I instinctively knew how thinly spaced I stood from potential harm. For instance, a fear that lasted throughout my life began when I was about five or six, after my father died, through the growing understanding of what it meant to have him disappear forever from my life. I feared for a future without him, and I felt that a lot of fear lived in our house because of my mother's personal crisis, which was as much to do with the affect on my family of a colonising history as it was to do with her hard efforts as a widow to raise my sister and myself in a world that she felt was unjust and without sympathy.

I was already fearful that our home would be struck by lightning when I heard thunder so close that it shook the house, after a flash of lightning had struck a child nearby. I feared drowning before reaching a seemingly distant pylon under a bridge, while teaching myself to swim in the only place possible to learn to swim with the rest of the kids at the time, the flooding Cloncurry River. As a child, I feared most adults in the small town where we lived because of the colour of my skin. I remember fearing the ghosts and spirits of the night, as much as I learned religious fear at my Catholic primary school.

Obviously, I survived this childhood of mixed fears. I claimed the status of bravery at an early age with the other fearless children swimming in flooding rivers after a good storm. I also had a kind and doting grandmother who nurtured her granddaughter's wildness and recklessness, while at the same time nurturing me with the stories Aboriginal children are told. It was these two childhood influences, from my grandmother and from other children, that probably helped keep in place the hairline fracture so easily traversed, between being and not being fearful of a hard world, something my mother was also teaching me to understand.

It is interesting to reflect on how fear was generated and maintained for various purposes during childhood and its continuing legacy into adulthood. It helps us to grapple with the complexity of understanding how fear is being developed worldwide, not only by terrible acts of terrorism, but by deliberate attempts by governments to frighten the public into supporting a "war on terror". Our respect for the dignity of human rights can be trashed, as we have seen through our government's cowardly endorsement of outsourcing torture, even though experts on national security studies tell us that if the aim of terrorism is to terrify, then terrorists can be defeated simply by not becoming terrified.

It is true and logical to believe that people everywhere have fears. We all fear being attacked, particularly by an unknown assailant—a stranger lurking in some dark place on the planet. This country's former government's tune of fear extended to distant places and countries, to the cultures and religions of strangers that it claimed have the potential to deprive us of our ability to trust. Yet, paradoxically, at the same time we fear the possibility of being ostracised and disliked, even by those strangers in distant corners of the world whom we believe wish to harm us.

I have experienced racial fears that are deeply related to the legacy of harm created by the Howard Government through decades of injurious Indigenous policy. This injury is deeply rooted in the fabric of our families. I have been spared some of the injury of long-term institutional racism, an exclusion that, in its fullest potential, is experienced as wholesale poverty, condemnation, and terrible psychological harm. This fear is unresolved in the lives of thousands, and is similar—even worse, if that is possible—for millions of people across the world who have had their lives destroyed through racism. There is no "privilege" in the Indigenous world of the type that the media and government like to use as a source of dividing us—and to counter this we would be wise to heed the thoughts of Samir Kassar,[6] the visionary Lebanese journalist and historian. In his collection of essays on the Arab malaise in *Being Arab*, written before he was assassinated, Kassar reminded the Arab world not to create separateness within and without: "Arab culture has begun to relearn how to integrate plurality into its unity of place and time, and stop thinking of difference as a source of division".

I believe that our continent continues to be the sacred land of ancient culture and that today Australia's Indigenous people are living through the most fearful era of our existence after decades of almost total abandonment to official policies of ignorance. We continue to suffer some of the worst poverty among any people on earth and endure some of the worst socio-economic, health, mortality, and education statistics imaginable. This situation was created through a historical chain of arrogance and ignorance from day one of colonisation, and extends even now, by the demonisation of Indigenous efforts throughout the media and by governments. In this cloak of arrogance, stitched with misrepresentation, Indigenous people are blamed for creating communities of violence and fear.

Now you might ask why do we keep on making the same mistakes with one another, and what has any of this Indigenous issue got to do with fear? On the one hand the mistakes are bound up in the method of spell-casting imbued in the overall consciousness of Australia. In my wildest imagination, I suspect that the ancient knowledge of fear still locked away deep in the consciousness of many unsuspecting non-Indigenous Australians is continuously whispering to them, but the cauldron's magical power is malfunctioning, and can cast no spell that totally works for this land. The power of wizards and witches transported from European cultures is being diluted and misused here. The cauldron conscience improvises with the wrong ingredients, refuses to grant the vision of white supremacy as far as the eye can see. Nevertheless, Aboriginal people live in the mire of the spell-caster's fear, which in turn creates our own fear of not being able to fulfil our responsibility to the spirits of the land inside ourselves.

I know that our senior men and women of high degree in religious laws understand much better than I do the seriousness of the clash of religious beliefs that exists between Indigenous thought and laws based on the philosophy of religions introduced in this country since colonisation. A way of explaining how introduced religious thought has been practised on the Indigenous world is through understanding how thought operates through the prism of an egotistic projectile imagination which has a linear sensibility towards invasion, suppression, and always-changing laws. This idea of imagining through projecting outwards and colonising by sinking down roots over the deeply rooted native realm, as a rhizome would spread, was originally described and analysed by the French-Caribbean writer and philosopher Edouard Glissant in *Poetics of Relation*.[7] For Glissant, by contrast, indigenous religious thought is of an "epic" voice, of being and belonging to one place, while sitting stationary in the "whorls of time." Our people say our law is constant and understandable but white law always changes.

The values associated with colonisation as the repressiveness that Glissant speaks of is also about the fear engendered in nation-building by boundaries that work for containment and control. This form of containment built through aggressive fear is also how Aboriginal people are governed in the Australian psyche, as objects that are owned, while anyone outside is involved in the management of the contained area—for example, the taxpayer.

I have often thought that Indigenous people cannot break through the deafness caused by the walls of the status quo that surround our containment, even if we wanted to, because of the layers in the maze of institutional violence. Although individuals might create something for either themselves or their people, as we see in the difficult work our people undertake across the country in the unconnected government policies of health, education, employment, and so on, our desire to survive as people in our own right, with a plan for our cultural future, has been impossible to achieve.

2. Too Many Spirits

The spiritual beliefs that belong to this land have long been challenged by the religious/spiritual beliefs others have used for conquering and oppression. While the spiritual world connects us to the land, many of our senior people have thought about the other religions that have been introduced to this land. They have tried to understand how other spiritual belief systems, such as Christianity, might exist here, to understand why it is here and what use it is to us, and some Indigenous people have incorporated these other spiritual beliefs into their thinking. I bring up this subject of religion because religious tolerance will be more important for Australians to understand in a world predicted to be severely affected by climate change. I want to demonstrate that during our own two-hundred-year war with turmoil, Indigenous people have shown not necessarily fear, but interest in and respect for other people's spiritual beliefs. While we have endured the onslaught of those who wished to indoctrinate our people by ruthlessly attempting to destroy our beliefs through horrific methods that have been well documented and described, a tolerance for religious viewpoints has been intellectualised by our Aboriginal religious leaders.

If I were to conduct a search throughout Aboriginal Australia, I would not have to go far to find examples of our religious tolerance. Some well-known examples in Central Australia demonstrate this acceptance of a wider sphere of spirituality. In Yutju (Areyonga), the donkeys that live in the area are thought about as being a part of the life of Christ. Aboriginal people throughout these parts of Central Australia are very protective of donkeys and do not want them culled. The same applies to camels because of the significance of these animals in the birth of Christ. On a hill near Hermannsburg (N'taria), there is what looks like a large footprint in a rock that is said to be where Jesus ascended to heaven, and it is featured in a song sung in the local language. There is also a spring at Santa Teresa that is believed to be holy water with healing properties, and in another place in Central Australia a split rock has an image of an old man with a beard who is said to be Moses. I am told that on a road running past Camels Hump outstation on the Mereenie Loop Road, there is a desert oak tree whose branches form a distinct crucifix. These are examples of how Indigenous people have thought of ways of imbuing the *Tjukurrpa*[8] landscape with the symbols of other religious beliefs. When senior Aboriginal lawmen from Central Australia visited Israel in 2002 to look at horticulture, it was also a spiritual journey to the Holy Land for them. *Anangu*,[9] or any other Indigenous Australian spiritual beliefs connected to this land, derives from a body of knowledge and moral imperative, and has a similar source of spirituality as those contained in the Bible.

There is a way of understanding Aboriginal law and its world view which can be found described in the report "Understanding Aboriginal Injury and Injury Prevention in Central Australia". It explains the Indigenous view of how different belief systems can flow together. The *Garma* Festival, an event celebrated each year by the *Yolngu* peoples of north-east Arnhem Land, promotes the idea of *Yolngu* and non-Indigenous knowledge flowing side by side. There is no valuing of one over the other—the central tenet is one of equality, each with potential for new ideas flowing between, but self-contained. *Garma* is a *Yolngu* idea that considers the confluence of two streams of knowledge represented by salt water and fresh water.

The same idea occurs in other parts of the country, and in the Western Desert of Central Australia, where they acknowledge streams of knowledge entering from sun or shade into ceremony. Alison Anderson Nampitjinpa, MLA,[10] has spoken of such understanding and of the mutual benefit that accrues when each element is regarded as a complementary component of a whole. This is a process that requires constant negotiation, where the common environment holds the potential for "new life, creativity and knowledge to occur, with such outcomes belonging and accruing to each stream". Such a phenomenon can only occur when there is a balance that assures the integrity of each flow.

3. We Create Fearlessness to Fight Fear

In 2000, I undertook a literature review on the injury of Aboriginal people for the collaborative research project *Community Initiatives Injury Prevention Project—Central Australia*.[11] I found that wherever you looked through the huge stockpile of academic research collecting dust in the academic institutions of Australia, their recommendations ignored, you would have to be stupid not to see that Aboriginal people are suffering injury from a profound sense of betrayal by the governments of this country. This betrayal has developed a fearfulness of White Australia that has been handed down the generations, and it is a fear that has become a deeply entrenched amalgam of hurt, anger, and mistrust. It might also be described as fear expressed in many different forms, from self-harm to harm of others, that can be seen through a scale running across the country from north to south, east to west, and every day, as it tips from one end of the scale to the other, while spinning uncontrollably, unpredictably, and in full fright with the weight of seriousness pressing on top of psychological trauma.

It is Indigenous fear that responds to the institutions that continue to believe that they govern us. A resounding voice in this report is from the late Mr. Cook of Intjartnama Rehabilitation Community,[12] who worked tirelessly to help the very troubled in his community: "People don't always do what they are told, they do what's on their minds". The main report of this research project found that the injury "runs deep and is profound", and that a major symptom of Aboriginal injury in Central Australia was from the attack upon the self-definition of the Aboriginal person, and the people as a whole.

I think one of the great lessons I have learned from many of the important Aboriginal thinkers that I have worked with is that fear comes with our dreams, and if you can learn how to conquer your fear, you will learn how to become a fearless dreamer and an instrument of possibility. I would like to think that the most significant work I have been asked to contribute to by various Indigenous groups, particularly in Central Australia, has been to help to build dreams fashioned by us for our future. I can still hear the voices of some of our more astute Indigenous managers, after being berated by their bosses, the senior Aboriginal law people who were dreaming the future, to accomplish an extraordinary idea: What? Another dream. Let's give it to a dreamer.

I asked a friend who spent many years working with Indigenous people in Central Australia to advise me on fear. He said he remembered a Pintupi woman once describing a part of a traditional song, "a kind of dismemberment lament," where she pointed towards a sandhill as a hypothetical location (because the actual site must have been somewhere else), and said/sang that over there, "liver and kidney are crying out . . .". Aboriginal philosophy is holistic and is tied to the land; a similar principle is found in the holistic point of view in Chinese medical philosophy that internal diseases are caused by the mental state of mind, where the kidney, liver, and spleen are connected to fear, fright, anger, anxiety, and brooding.

Dreams that should have been easily accomplished have never been successful in accomplishing the Indigenous Self-Defined Dream for our future. These were brave dreams, but required others more entrenched in the status quo's way of incremental change to listen, to help build the ideas that many remote communities thought would work for the future. At the time when these dreams were being discussed in various forums clinging to the power of the status quo, I knew in my heart that, even though these dreams were realistically simple to achieve, we were working on ideas that were too brave for the prevailing mindset of containment. It has taken me a long time to overcome the frustration we were left with, to understand more fully why Aboriginal dreams are still not embraced by Australia.

One of the dreams I worked on concerned ideas of how to build Indigenous self-determination on our terms. I did this through considerable research while developing and coordinating two major Indigenous constitutional conventions in the Northern Territory. The first convention in 1993 was in Tennant Creek, on Warumungu land, and was attended by around one thousand people who travelled from across the Northern Territory to talk about their future. The three-day event was called "Today

We Talk About Tomorrow", but it was more a "one-off" unique exercise that became lost in the crisis of the Indigenous everyday world.

Our next constitutional convention, the Kalkaringi Convention of 1998,[13] was held at the place where land rights began in the Northern Territory, at Wattie Creek. Again, one thousand Aboriginal people came from across Central Australia and camped in the heat and dust for several days to talk about the future. They responded to our messages and advertisements about the convention that portrayed two Indigenous hands of the caller—beating boomerangs.

Basically, the convention discussed and rejected the flawed attempt of the Northern Territory government to create the state of the Northern Territory. The Aboriginal people conducted their assembly in eight local languages, and through dance and abstract dot paintings of their country. They said that they had always governed themselves, and signed the outcomes of their deliberations on what is called the Kalkaringi Statement. This dream, led by a very brave man, a senior Aboriginal lawman, visionary, philosopher, and educator from the nation of the Pintupi, established the Combined Aboriginal Nations of Central Australia. Mr. Zimran was the kind of person who felt compassion for all people. As he was doing this work he was suffering from kidney failure, and was forced to live away from his country to be attached to a dialysis machine several times a week at the Alice Springs Hospital. He did not want to live away from his homelands, and his family suffered greatly while staying in Alice Springs in a suburb where they had very little in the way of support systems to help them to survive. He took great risks to use whatever opportunity arose to go back to Kintore, even though it was often difficult to organise his return to Alice Springs in time for the dialysis treatment. However, this did not keep him from his work for the Combined Aboriginal Nations of Central Australia, or from conceptualising and accomplishing idea after idea for the betterment of his people. His memorial plaque at Kintore states that he could turn distrust into mutual understanding, and is inscribed with his words: We Go Into the Future As One Tribe and One Family.

One monumental task Mr. Zimran set upon at this time was to organise Western Desert artists to place their work in an auction at Sotheby's that raised one million dollars to set up a dialysis unit in their community. He also went every week to the Aboriginal Topsy Smith Hostel, in the street where I lived, to encourage gospel-singing of his own songs with other dialysis patients living away from their communities. He told me he had to do this to help cheer them up. He once led gospel-singing convoys in the Western Desert as a way of bringing people together and because he also saw a place for other religions in the traditional spiritual world. What he feared was not meeting his obligation to people, and to the misplaced spirits he heard in the Alice Springs Hospital. He said that his spirit should be in its rightful place. I also remember him once asking why Australia was fighting in Iraq. He said, "We are all people. We are all the same people."

Before Mr. Zimran passed away, he and senior Aboriginal law holders described the form of Aboriginal government that they believed was correct within a structure that already existed, but needed to be recognised by Australia. It was not an outrageous idea. It threatened no one except the status quo of entrenched domination in policy, research, and the administration of Aboriginal people by others. However, to Indigenous people on the ground the recognition of their law made sense. It meant that they could move; they could plan and work towards a future, with agreed and adequate resources from Australian governments, in an agreement that recognised culpability and responsibility for the crisis we see in the media. It meant that Aboriginal law could find its path in Australia, with Indigenous people being able to talk about how it could be carried into the future. This group also led a campaign that gathered together diverse groups in the Northern Territory that would have been disaffected under the misguided arrangements for Northern Territory statehood, and together ensured that the statehood referendum in the Northern Territory was defeated. This result not only demonstrated how two laws could work side by side, but also saw the defeat of twenty-eight years of entrenched conservative government in the Northern Territory.

What happened to the dream established by the Combined Aboriginal Nations of Central Australia? It went nowhere. It became a dangerous idea that threatened the organised status quo, working with fear of retribution from the federal government against criticism and the assertion of rights. It became a question of whether anyone who lived outside of Aboriginal law in communities in Central Australia wanted this law to survive.

So why is there a continuing fear of Indigenous people and, more specifically, Aboriginal law? Is it the fear of the unknown, of what is not understood, of what is not in memory and, therefore, must lie beyond possibility and consequently cannot exist? Milan Kundera's book *The Curtain*[14] touches on this problem in the discussion about the possibilities for a novelist to reach into the soul of things, to free ideas from fear. The Czech writer knows what it is for a man to live through the death of his nation. He describes the fear of a crushing force that stopped his people from being what they had been, but at the same time he was astonished to realise that he did not know how and why they had become who they were, because he could not look into the soul of the people to experience the decisions they had previously made. This absence of understanding about what we are becoming is also our problem too; we understand neither our own Indigenous epic literature, nor how to build new stories that evoke the spirits underlying our deepest emotions.

4. Fear of the Environment

The world is in the midst of coming to terms with compelling scientific knowledge warning that we are headed towards devastating and cataclysmic climate change that threatens the survival of the planet's environment as we have known it in modern times.

Australians are increasingly becoming more fearful as the threats of global warming proliferate. While governments react to this news in more or less the same way as they have done with Indigenous concerns—by killing the messenger—it will be artists, songwriters, poets, and authors who must imagine the future, to explain what science is telling us in cold, hard language: that we will all become the earth's refugees.

However, in the dreams of people at the individual or community level, prospects of making plans to change invoke fear whatever your race, and this is what I have learned from working for my mob, trawling for months at a time through the mountains of academic research into how our disastrous social and economic situation derives from how relationships work between ourselves and governments. Nothing much can be achieved in a relationship with a government that is stuck on the notion of conquering those without power. There is no other way of understanding how a wealthy country cannot solve a devastating health crisis affecting less than three per cent of its population. It is possible to alleviate a lot of suffering in the world if only nations would work together towards specific goals, as happens at a corporate level when Western consumers want something desperately—like to put a new Harry Potter novel in the hands of millions of children within days of its release.

Global warming will not only impact the world's poorest Indigenous people; environmental catastrophe is everybody's business, because in the end, every man, woman, and child will be affected. With approximately twenty-one million refugees in the world today, envisage the world if this number was to double or quadruple very quickly, perhaps within the next two decades. We need to consider Australia's role in this kind of world when our own country will be severely affected itself.

It would seem to me that Australia must play a more significant role in learning how to develop meaningful relationships with our neighbours —relationships based on ethics that value the lives of others. In the future, Australia may be forced to bargain with what it views as the Third World, not as a colonising power, but from a level playing field. Tim Flannery reminds us that we still have to learn the effectiveness of tree-planting in controlling climate change, with recent computer modelling of the impact of tree-planting worldwide concluding that it will be the tropical rainforests that have the greatest potential to cool our planet. Thus, "people interested in combating climate change are looking increasingly towards the tropical regions for a solution to the climate crisis".[15] The importance of regrowing and sustaining forests in places that have historically been of little value to powerful nations will mean a change in the way developed nations interact with smaller, less developed states—especially once the populations in the tropical regions of the world begin to understand the economic power of the climate.

Personal fears will grow in proportion to each new change in the climate that people observe happening around them. Many of these changes are already evident—witness the long drought in southern Australia, for example. Those sitting on the fence disputing scientific evidence are losing the argument, because Australians are not fools about the country they love, and are not blind to the changes the environment has already suffered through exploitation in the name of development. So what will we see in the future? Worse drought. Dams empty, leading to more severe water restrictions and dwindling water supplies for towns and cities. Bushfires on an enormous scale, burning out of control. Suffering wildlife and reports of species lost. New diseases. Ice melts. Whole populations seeking new countries as they flee rising sea levels. Economic disaster.

When the predictions of global warming become reality, many Australians will find new outlets for their fear as they gradually try to adjust with less of a life than what they had always known or aspired to having. Many will become poorer and many will be emotionally disturbed, and will search for culpability in themselves and others.

There will be a huge sense of loss, and Australians will become even more nostalgic for selective history that glorifies the past. The future writers of this country's history will write large sweeping epics of the idyllic life of special people we know now, but do not like. There will also be many disheartened people writing large books on visions for creating a futuristic paradise. Australian children will grow up with less and this will be normal for them, just as normal as for the many Indigenous children who have grown up in Third World poverty. These children may well condemn their parents as abnormal human beings who keep wishing for the past, remembering times and places that were full of peacefulness, rain, and abundant fresh water for gardens and baths. These children may be prone to nightmares in which all adults have become giant king and queen fish, swimming aimlessly in the dry atmosphere like predatory dinosaurs attacking the limited undeveloped possibility of the future. The children of our future might consider it wise to forget the work of several past generations of exploiters who pillaged the environment and fought fathomless wars.

5. Whose Fear is Heard?

In the world, many writers are being threatened, tortured, persecuted, imprisoned, or killed for speaking about their country's fears. For this reason, millions of people are not heard loudly enough, or at all, while their representation throughout the world of literature is being censored or obliterated.

A valuable lesson about literature can be found in the Nobel Lecture delivered in Stockholm by Orhan Pamuk, the 2006 Nobel Laureate for Literature.[16] Pamuk argued that what literature needs most today is to articulate and investigate humanity's basic fears:

> the fear of being left outside, and the fear of counting for nothing, and the feelings of worthlessness that come with such fears; the collective humiliations, vulnerabilities, slights, grievances, sensitivities, and imagined insults, and the nationalist boasts and inflations that are their next of kind.

Australia desperately needs readers who not only read, but who are also selectively seeking this information about our basic fears, and want to read well. We will need better access to world literature as well as our own meaningful literature, to be able to walk through the window of opportunity that writers are creating the world over to look into the minds and worlds of others. We must try harder to understand how to share this earth with others, who are demanding a new dialogue to create a greater equality that redefines the status quo. The environment is on the side of the weakest people in seeking new understanding, and it will not be long before this dialogue insists on the willingness of all people to assert difference and equality as the terms for world harmony. I think the future will need writers closely tied to the countless millions on earth who have always lived with far less and have experienced far more fear than the great majority of Australians. The Indigenous lawmen and women who intimately understand the ancient literature of this land should be working with the scientists and politicians to provide an understanding of how to help this country to survive.

Do writers have the experience and background for the imaginative investigation of the basic fears of humanity? I ask the question about reading, but also whether Australian writers can produce the type of literature that Pamuk believes is required by the world. What Australian values will prevail in either the production or publishing of literature? I am not sure whether Australian values muddied by unresolved issues with Indigenous people will have the authenticity required to allow us to look into the depths of despair in the world. Will Australian publishers publish literature about fear in the world, even if it does not make economic sense because fearful ideas will not find a readership in our small reading population? Perhaps the logic of change will require closer and quicker movement towards our understanding of despair, as is now starting to emerge through the new literature concerning domestically held fears Australians have about themselves.

In 1945, the anthropologist A.P. Elkin,[17] in his study *Aboriginal Men of High Degree*, suspected that there might be congruencies between the practices of Indigenous healers (*ngangkari*) and Western psychiatrists. Ted Strehlow tried to demonstrate the connection between oral and written cultural forms in the songs of Central Australia and the sagas of Old Europe. Elkin recommended a forum within which matters of concern to European and Indigenous therapeutic practitioners could be discussed and compared, and a working partnership consolidated. This never happened.[18]

Dr. Craig San Roque, a practising psychologist who has worked for several years in Central Australia, suggests that it would be useful to know how Aboriginal thoughts are built. He questions how Australia thinks from its background of cultural matrices that includes Caucasian, Mediterranean, European, Middle Eastern, and Asian mythologies.[19] He believes that there ought to be an extensive localised study to set out the parallel process between Indigenous Australian and these other Indigenous mythologies that are central to contemporary cultural matrices in Australia. I also think Australian writers should share this work, by bringing to life in their writing the different ways in which thoughts and actions can be shaped from our multiple backgrounds.

6. How Do Writers Transcend Fear?

Orhan Pamuk reminds us that independent writers of the world listen only to the voice of their own conscience to produce literature. Pamuk's faith in humanity is the belief that we live in a world that has no centre.

It is significant that Pamuk speaks of the belief that our writings will be read and understood because people all over the world resemble each other. This is the idea that I would like to concentrate on in examining how well we understand each other in Australia, and what capacity we have for understanding fear in ourselves and fear in others—whether, in fact, what Pamuk says is true, that we resemble each other.

Why should I raise this question of difference if it is true that the world has many fears in common? The six and a half billion people who inhabit our planet cannot be all that different to each other in what makes us fearful. We all have fears about how we live or die, or what will become of us in sickness and in health, or what someone else is capable of doing to us. And for those of us who have children, we can no longer predict whether the world will be a good place for them to live in the future. While we contend with more reasons to be fearful, do we look away from difference and only look out for our own? Tendencies towards over-governance with protective measures imposed from outside is nothing new for Indigenous people, but now other Australians are noticing that they, too, are becoming over-governed and protected from fear of harm when compared to other countries.

Michael Benes,[20] a senior lecturer in criminal justice, observes that "our children would benefit from being taught more about ethics and morals than being instilled with fear for doing the wrong thing". If children grow up being over-governed, they will lose their sense of personal responsibility.

7. Collective Fear

Bertrand Russell once said, "Collective fear stimulates herd instinct, and tends to produce ferocity towards those who are not regarded as members of the herd". We have a very clear understanding of how our government, media, and the very institutions we operate in can whip up fear in the population to steer us towards the ideology of policies and decisions of government that we do not fully understand. We do not fully comprehend how their decisions implicate the country, or if we are being deceived, and if we are being led down dangerous paths from which we may never return.

Why do most Australians feel that they are helpless to do anything about it? Is it because no political party offers a real alternative—which is particularly so if you are Indigenous? It takes monumental effort to destroy our fear of change, which grows more dangerous because of the short-term interests of our governments. But, still, most Australians console themselves with the belief that we live on the winning side—having received the inheritance of the Golden Fleece and mineral wealth drawn at will from Indigenous land, with weak reference to Native Title, even if the Indigenous inhabitants are lucky enough to win concessions through battling court cases with the lucky country.

Surrounded by one hundred thousand kilometres of beaches that are thought of as a playground, many Australians have not wanted to stare out to the distance towards other countries and, unless organised, to think about the plight of other people. We are entrenched in a society with a stubborn presumption of prosperity and security; a society actively being dumbed down by institutions that breed and grow richer by selling ignorance, which ensures that the majority of the population is either too busy or refuses to look at difference or to learn have to understand other people. Not many in the population would honestly seek knowledge of what happens in troubled countries, unless dragged there by the selective interests of our government—although charitable campaigns have often seen Australians give compassionately to situations of crisis or natural disaster in other countries. Still, we have been in a war based on the fear of diversity for some time now. Where will it go? Where did it begin? Well! In short, it began with the initial invasion of Australia some two centuries ago and, as Manning Clark pointed out in the 1930s:

> in Australia we are uncertain of everything, we feel insecure. What is the cause of this? ... First ... geography, the hostile environment, the fear experienced when alone ... second, the doubt, do we belong here, perhaps this is geography, perhaps history ... third, Australia as the harlot, raped by the Europeans, coarse, vulgar, meretricious.[21]

How relevant is Manning Clark's impression of Australia some seventy years later? Peter Hartcher,[22] in his essay Bipolar Nation, describes the history of Australians' fearfulness from living in the neighbourhood of Asia, and loneliness of being positioned so far away from Europe: "the Frightened Country alone and exposed on its 'awkward slab of Europe' at the bottom of Asia".

Hartcher outlines how our national fears have grown into a selfish adulthood where the power of fear can make it impossible for people to choose possibility—of gaining something better or good, rather than the prospect of loss. He describes how for several elections Australians have been swayed by John Howard's formula of fear, in which he played on our fears of losing our prosperity and security. Australians it seems, would rather risk all that its society requires to nurture itself, like "health, education, industrial relations, welfare, family matters".

8. Manipulating a Nation's Fears, or Finding a Solution

As an Indigenous writer trying to understand Australia's phobias, I am frightened by how Australia engages with the world when, in our own sphere of Indigenous politics, there is an overwhelming belief that we are being governed by the world of non-Indigenous people. This fearfulness of the "other" continually replicates its own compromised vision and, each time it does this, further squashes Indigenous ideas of self-determination from a standard achieved long ago in North America, Canada, and New Zealand. In recent years, this compromised vision for the "other" has been re-made into weak unworkable strategies that are called good governance for Indigenous Australia. Such short-term strategies, which are continually produced for incremental improvement, are destined to join the wasteful interventionist programs that have swamped the Indigenous world for decades. The fine accomplishments of Orhan Pamuk's writing must include his bravery, prepared as he is to submerge himself into the fullest exploration of the fear in his own soul, which, in turn, touches on the darkness that lives within all people. The richness of his writing helps our understanding of the narrow point of personal crisis that has claimed many people in the world. It will be through works of literature such as his that we will form a more profound understanding of humanity's fears, and hopefully become better leaders of our imagination. This is why I agree with Pamuk that the world is one place, not many, and we need to understand the real depths of our fears if we are to survive in the future. It we trust literature, and it is allowed to do its work of locating the truth about the darkness inside, it might somehow show us that the world is truly without a centre, and deep knowledge of what binds and separates humanity is everybody's business and responsibility.

This will be the hard work ahead for the world's independent writers, who leave on long journeys that go deep into their being, to the place where humanity makes thoughts about itself. These solitary journeys, as Pamuk knows, may take many years in which the writer works alone, searching for the right words to show us something about who we are or what we have become. When it comes to the question of fear, it is a frightening journey to the place of thought which is in the geography of deep consciousness, and once writers enter this world, they may locate a spectacle of fears that will test their courage to continue describing what they have already seen in themselves.

It is not easy to be this kind of writer in a world where mediocrity in literature is often rewarded. There is not a lot of vigour about the production of serious literature, and if this kind of literature appears on the radar, there is a reluctance to acknowledge or understand what it might mean to the kind of society that has developed in Australia.

Yet Pamuk believes that writing is worthwhile. It is the job of the writer to turn inwards, "to build a new world with words". The writer must acknowledge the secret wounds that we carry inside us, "the wounds so secret that we ourselves are barely aware of them, and to patiently explore them, know them, illuminate them, to own these pains and wounds, and to make them a conscious part of our spirits and our writing". If we want to understand the threats and fears of the world in this millennium, it would be wise to look right down to the personal as Pamuk is doing in trying to understand his native country, Turkey. Edward Said,[23] concerned about responsibility when he spoke about the war in Iraq, was troubled by the rapid expansion of flattened and one-dimensional communication about acts of pride and extraordinary arrogance and moral blindness committed in our name: "One ought to be able to say somewhere and at great length, I am not this 'we' and what 'you' do, you do not in my name".

The Macquarie Dictionary describes fear as "a painful feeling of impending danger, evil, trouble". But, how do we recognise which danger, evil, or trouble? Is it personal, something that can only be understood by personal experience? Whose privilege is it to control fearfulness in either one's self, or in others? Can others have a right to be fearful, even of us? And are we the fearful nation that other people in the world are beginning to believe we are? Or are we the nation of the brave? These questions require us to focus in, to look small, here at home, to understand our own level of humanity in the catastrophic picture of what is happening in the world—in places where we believe we have enemies, or where there are wars we do not fully understand, or where incurable diseases are spreading, or where the world's resources are being squandered.

Deep self-analysis might help us to think about whether we know ourselves enough to contribute constructively to the bigger questions of whether we are ready and willing to work towards a future that belongs just as equally to others who are different to ourselves. And what will we contribute of ourselves? I believe it will increasingly become the role of literature to explain what is happening in the home of humanity, by speaking honestly to the world where those who represent us politically do not.

Notes**

[1] Noel Pearson. Indigenous Australian Lawyer, Cape York Institute for Policy and Leadership. Cairns. He presents considered and controversial advocacy on indigenous matters. See http://www.cyi.org.au/contacts.aspx.

[2] K. A. Appiah, *Cosmopolitanism: Ethics in a World of Strangers* (London: Penguin, 2006).

[3] Bei Dao, Chinese poet, who became in the 1970s the poetic voice of his generation. Bei Dao's education was interrupted by the Cultural Revolution. He was a political activist but later lost his enthusiasm, and started to write as an alternative to his early actions. His central themes are the pressures of a conformist society, disillusionment, and sense of rootlessness. See www.kirjasto.sci.fi/beid#578C19.

[4] For more on Mahmoud Darwish, Palestinian journalist/ poet, see kirjasto.sci.fi/darwish.#578C69.

[5] Northern Territory is a large region covering much of central northern Australia up to the Gulf of Carpentaria. As a "Territory" with an elected government it nevertheless does not have full status as a State. It includes significant indigenous occupied lands.

[6] On Kassar, Alexis Wright notes: "I became very interested in the thinking and writing of assassinated Lebanese journalist and historian Samir Kassar in a book of his essays—'Being Arab' originally published by my French publisher *Actes Sud*. Kassar found through his examination of the Arab world that cultural malaise was beginning to be resolved through integrating plurality of place into meanings of unity where difference was not a source of division...", quoted at www.timeoutsydney.com.au#578F9A, accessed November 30, 2010.

[7] E. Glissant, *Poetics of Relation*, 5th edition, trans. Betsy Wing (Ann Arbor: University of Michigan Press, 2006).

[8] *Tjukurrpa* is a specific desert Aboriginal language term indicating indigenous cultural lore and law set into geographic sites. Sometimes

---

**Notes 2, 7, 11, 14-16, 20-22 are reprinted from the original lecture. The remaining notes have been added by the editors to provide some background for readers unfamiliar with aspects of the Australian context.

referred to as "dreaming" or "songlines", *Tjukurrpa* refers to the profound and active spiritual foundation of indigenous life and self organisation.

[9] *Anangu* literally means "people" or "us", a generic term used as self-identification by some south-central desert Aboriginal people including the Pitjatjanjara. The term varies according to tribal regional language, for instance some northern coastal languages use the equivalent term *yolngu-* for "us". Wright's point is that the fundamental belief system of Aboriginal people across Australia is a unified ontological field yet with specific local variations, and has capacity to (generously) incorporate Christian/Western beliefs in a unique manner.

[10] An independent member of parliament (MLA) for the Northern Territory Government.

[11] J. Hulcombe, *et al.* "Recognition as Injury Prevention, Volume 1, Understanding Aboriginal Injury and Injury Prevention in Central Australia", 2006. Report to be published by the NHMRC collaborative research project undertaken by Tangentyere Council, Flinders University and Centre for Remote Health. [*Editors' Note:* This significant Report is yet to be published. In the personal opinion of editor Craig San Roque, this revealing document, its history, the tensions in its production, and the fact that it is still not published is, in itself, an indicator of a possible "cultural complex". It was partly the story of this report which led to Alexis Wright being invited to contribute to this book.]

[12] Intjartnama near Hermansburg/N'taria, west of Alice Springs operated by Barry and Elva Cook and family as an independent innovative Aboriginal alcohol rehabilitation site, especially also for "petrol sniffers" (VSA) from 1988 until circa 2007. Barry Cook passed away Dec. 1999. For links to some Central Australian history, context, and examples of resources developed through Intjartnama's influence, see http://www.adac.org.au/siteF/resources/brainstory/index.html and http://www.tangentyere.org.au/services/family_youth/caylus/.

[13] See Kalkaringi's background information and history on Australian Indigenous Law Reporter at www.austlii.edu.au/au/jo#578D7C.

[14] M. Kundera, *The Curtain* (New York: Harper Collins, 2005)

[15] T. Flannery, "A Once-only Chance to Repair Damage", Opinion, *The Age*, 9 April 2007.

[16] O. Pamuk, The Nobel Prize in Literature 2006—Nobel Lecture—*My Father's Suitcase in Other Colors* (New York: Alfred A. Knopf, 2007).

[17] A. P. Elkin and T. Strehlow are two notable anthropologists working in Central Australia during the mid-twentieth century. Elkin's key text

referred to here is on indigenous healing traditions. *Aboriginal Men of High Degree*. (Republished by Inner Traditions, 1994). Strehlow's work documents Arrernte ceremonies, song cycles, and mythologies as in his classic, *Songs of Central Australia* (Angus and Roberston, 1971) and in *Aranda Traditions* (Johnson Reprint, [1968], originally published: (Melbourne: Melbourne University Press, 1947)

[18] Since the time of Wright's essay constructive developments have consolidated in Central Australia. The NPY Ngangkari project including Rupert Peters, Andy Tjilari, and Ginger Toby has been recognised and they now travel widely demonstrating and teaching. See *Ngangkari'*, a film (dvd) by Erica Glynn 2002 available at www. roninfilms.com.au. At the 2011 World Congress for Psychotherapy, 26 August 2011, the NPY Women's Council Ngangkari Team, along with indigenous practitioners Professor Helen Milroy and Lorraine Peeters, conjointly received the 2011 Sigmund Freud Award for contributions to psychotherapy.

Conjoint case and methodology discussions now occur with the Remote Area Mental Health team, Alice Springs, under the courteous facilitation of psychiatrist, Dr. Marcus Tabart, and a small group of intercultural (borderlinking) associates (which includes Jungian practitioners, Anne Noonan, Leon Petchkovsky and Craig San Roque).

[19] See Craig San Roque, "On Tjukurrpa, Painting Up and Building Thought", in J. Mimica, ed., *Explorations in Psychoanalytic Ethnography* (New York and London: Berghahn Books 2007). (www.berghahnbooks.com).

[20] Michael Benes lectures at RMIT. (The exact source of Wright's quote is not available currently.) A link is mailto:michael.benes@rmit.edu.au.

[21] M. McKenna, "Being There—The Strange History of Manning Clark", essay in *The Monthly*, Melbourne, March 2007, p. 26.

[22] P. Hartcher, "Bipolar Nation: How to Win the 2007 Election", *Quarterley Essay* (Melbourne: Black Ink, 2006).

[23] E. Said, *Humanism and Democratic Criticism* (New York: Columbia University Press, 2004).

Melinda Turner was born in Australia of Celtic descent and lived briefly in England as a child. She is interested in how our understandings of self emerge out of our relationships with others, with place, and with the stories that bring meaning to our lives. She has a background in Philosophy, Education, and Sociology.

●●●●●●●●●●●●

On February 13, 2008, the Prime Minister of Australia, Kevin Rudd, formally apologised to indigenous Australians for "the wrongs of the past". He was referring specifically to the mistreatment of the "Stolen Generations": those indigenous children who in accordance with government policy had been forcibly separated from their families and communities to be assimilated into colonial culture. "Sorry Day", the name for the day on which Rudd made the Apology, was hailed as a profoundly significant event for the nation: an acknowledgement of the grief and distress of indigenous people, an amelioration of the shame felt by many non-indigenous Australians for the treatment of the Stolen Generations, and an articulation of a vision in which indigenous and non-indigenous Australians might live together in mutual respect as "truly equal partners", with shared responsibility for forging Australia's future.

Whilst recognising and celebrating the importance of the Apology, especially the stirring language contained in the first half of it, this chapter by Melinda Turner also notes blindspots in the Apology which may indicate the presence of a cultural complex. She draws attention to the distinctive voice of modern Western culture that can be heard in the second half of the Apology where, in bureaucratic language, it envisions how the core institutions—educational, medical, and political—of the modern West will improve life for indigenous Australians. Turner notes that, apart from alluding to "these great and ancient cultures we are truly blessed to have among us", there is nothing in the Apology about what newcomers to Australia could learn from the indigenous people who have lived in Australia for millennia. There is thus an absence of mutuality in the language of the suggested "partnership" which reveals a cultural complex of which then Prime Minister Kevin Rudd was simply a carrier.

10

Sorry, It's Complex: Reflecting on The Apology to Indigenous Australians

Melinda Turner

In Australia from 1910 until 1970, between ten and thirty per cent of indigenous children were forcibly separated from their mothers and fathers to be brought up and educated in the ways of European culture. This practice, which brought heartbreaking distress and grief to so many indigenous individuals, families, and communities, was the result of government policy designed to address "the problem of the Aboriginal population".[1] Regarding "the problem", A. O. Neville, in 1937 the Western Australian "Chief Protector" of Aborigines and later "Commissioner of Native Affairs", asked:

> Are we going to have a population of 1 million blacks in the Commonwealth, or are we going to merge them into our white community *and eventually forget* that there were ever any Aborigines in Australia?[2] (emphasis added)

History shows that the governments of the day chose the latter path of willful forgetfulness. Policies were enacted to effect "the complete disappearance of the black race, and the swift submergence of their progeny in the white"[3], with the aim of ensuring that "all native characteristics of the Australian aborigine *(sic)* [were] eradicated".[4]

The stories of those who have come to be called the Stolen Generations were brought into national consciousness by the publication of *Bringing Them Home*[5], the report of a national inquiry into the separation of indigenous children from their families. This investigation was commissioned in 1995 by the then Prime Minister Paul Keating, leader of the Labor Party, and was received by his successor John Howard, leader of the Liberal Party, in 1997. The report concluded:

> Indigenous families and communities have endured gross violations of their human rights. These violations continue to affect Indigenous people's daily lives. They were an act of genocide, aimed at wiping out Indigenous families, communities and cultures, vital to the precious and inalienable heritage of Australia.[6]

Many Australians were appalled by the events the inquiry brought to light, especially since they had persisted until so recently. When I was a teenager, just beginning to take an interest in national politics, indigenous children were still being taken from their families. Like many other Australians,[7] I had no idea that this was happening. This episode of our history—and our ignorance of it—became a source of shame for many; however, despite significant public pressure to "say sorry", Prime Minister Howard, whilst he expressed "regret" for what had happened, refused to offer indigenous people a full and formal apology.[8]

Kevin Rudd, leader of the Labor Party, replaced Howard as Prime Minister in 2007. His commitment to apologise to the Stolen Generations was one of the promises on which he was elected. Along with many others, I felt great relief at Rudd's commitment and anticipated the apology with many hopes. I hoped for an explicit recognition of the emotional and physical violence inflicted upon Aboriginal Australians. I hoped for acknowledgement and an expression of sorrow for all that indigenous people have lost as a consequence of the dispossession of their land. I also hoped for an invitation to genuine relationship between indigenous and non-indigenous Australians: a fresh start, based on mutual respect and recognition that, as fellow human beings from very different world views, we each have much of value to learn from one another. I hoped that this would bring some healing for indigenous people. I also hoped for some healing for myself and for all the other Australians who feel shame that our culture has all but obliterated "the oldest continuing cultures in human history"[9] and blithely caused terrible pain to the people of these cultures and to their land along the way. Finally, I hoped that those Australians who didn't feel the need for a national apology would have their hearts softened by the occasion and would be moved to compassion, empathy, and understanding.

The Apology: Part 1

It was at the opening of parliament, on February 13 2008, that Rudd honoured his commitment and the long-awaited "Sorry" was offered:

> For the pain, suffering and hurt of these Stolen Generations, their descendents and for their families left behind, we say sorry.
>
> And for the indignity and degradation thus inflicted on a proud people and a proud culture, we say sorry. (Introductory paragraph)[10]
>
> ...[T]here comes a time in the history of nations when their peoples must become fully reconciled to their past if they are to go forward with confidence to embrace their future. Our nation, Australia, has reached such a time. (1)

Television coverage of the event showed those in attendance, both indigenous and non-indigenous, listening with intense concentration. Many were weeping. I was among those who stopped everything to listen, galvanised, to the radio broadcast and to shed tears of sadness, relief, and hope. Clearly, the Apology was cathartic and deeply significant for many. Photographer Juno Gemes, who was present at the occasion, observed: "One sensed immediately that the mood of the nation had changed".[11] Others have described the event as an "extraordinary national experience",[12] a "wave of joy",[13] and it has been hailed as a "spiritual healing",[14] "a symbol of change and atonement".[15]

Thomas Moore speaks of the importance of symbolic rituals and experiences, working as they do at the level of our imagination, and observes that "...slight shifts in imagination have more impact on living than major efforts at change ... [Deep] changes in life follow movements in imagination".[16] Perhaps this explains why the delivery of the Apology felt so significant: maybe we sensed a tectonic shift in our national imagination that heralded change to come. The occasion certainly had the requisite hallmarks of ritual and ceremony. Preceded by a traditional indigenous Welcome to Country, the Apology was delivered on a ceremonial occasion —the opening of parliament—at a site of national importance, with representatives of significant groups within Australian society in attendance. The language of the Apology is also ceremonial, with the opening statements employing short, direct sentences and repetition:

> I move:
> That today we honour the Indigenous peoples of this land, the oldest continuing cultures in human history.
> We reflect on their past mistreatment.
> We reflect in particular on the mistreatment of those who were Stolen Generations-this blemished chapter in our nation's history.
> The time has now come for the nation to turn a new page in Australia's history by righting the wrongs of the past and so moving forward with confidence to the future.
> We apologise for the laws and policies of successive Parliaments and governments that have inflicted profound grief, suffering and loss on these our fellow Australians.
> We apologise especially for the removal of Aboriginal and Torres Strait Islander children from their families, their communities and their country.
> For the pain, suffering and hurt of these Stolen Generations, their descendents and for their families left behind, we say sorry.
> To the mothers and the fathers, the brothers and the sisters, for the breaking up of families and communities, we say sorry.
> And for the indignity and degradation thus inflicted on a proud people and a proud culture, we say sorry.... (Intro.)

This rhythm recurs at the climax of the Apology:

> To the stolen generations, I say the following: as Prime Minister of Australia, I am sorry. On behalf of the government of Australia, I am sorry. On behalf of the parliament of Australia, I am sorry. I offer you this apology without qualification. We apologise for the hurt, the pain and suffering that we, the parliament, have caused you by the laws that previous parliaments have enacted. We apologise for the indignity, the degradation and the humiliation these laws embodied. We offer this apology to the mothers, the fathers, the brothers, the sisters, the families and the communities whose lives were ripped apart by the actions of successive governments under successive parliaments. (15)

These are the cadences of a litany. The repetition of the crucial, long-awaited words "we say sorry" is powerful, almost incantatory, particularly as these words had been withheld for so long.

The passionate first half of the Apology draws on the power of storytelling for its persuasive impact. In answer to the question "Why apologise?" Rudd tells the story of Nanna Nungala Fejo who was taken, screaming and crying, from her distraught mother when she was four years old (3-7). She never saw her mother again. Nanna Fejo's message to the Australian public is simple and profound: "Families—keeping them together is very important. It's a good thing that you are surrounded by love and that love is passed down the generations" (7). Rudd's response to her story and to the stories of other members of the Stolen Generations is passionate and sincere, scathing in its righteous indignation at what it characterises as the cold and stony-hearted response of the previous government. He appeals to our empathy and compassion as fellow human beings and to "basic", "universal" moral instincts:

> *These stories cry out to be heard; they cry out for an apology.* Instead, from the nation's parliament there has been a stony and stubborn and deafening silence for more than a decade; a view that somehow we, the parliament, should suspend *our most basic instincts of what is right and what is wrong*; a view that, instead, we should look for any pretext to push this great wrong to one side, to leave it languishing with the historians, the academics and the cultural warriors, as if the stolen generations are little more than an interesting sociological phenomenon. But *the stolen generations are not intellectual curiosities. They are human beings*; human beings who have been damaged deeply by the decisions of parliaments and governments. But, as of today, the time for denial, the time for delay, has at last come to an end.
>
> The nation is demanding of its political leadership to take us forward. *Decency, human decency, universal human decency,* demands that the nation now step forward to right an historical wrong. That is what we are doing in this place today. (9-10, emphasis added)

To those who argued against an apology on the grounds that they could not take responsibility for the acts of previous generations—this included former Prime Minister Howard and his government—Rudd points out that the practice of child removal persisted into the 1970s: that is, until "well within the adult memory span of many of us" (12). He then appeals directly to their imaginations in an effort to kindle their empathy:

> I ask those non-Indigenous Australians listening today who may not fully understand why what we are doing is so important to imagine for a moment that this had happened to you. I say to honourable members here present: imagine if this had happened to us. Imagine the crippling effect. Imagine how hard it would be to forgive. (16)

Finally, Rudd invokes "a core value of our nation... a fair go for all":

> There is a deep and abiding belief in the Australian community that, for the stolen generations, there was no fair go at all. There is a pretty basic Aussie belief that says it is time to put right this most outrageous of wrongs. (13)

Rudd is clear that the purpose of the Apology is for "the healing of the nation":

> We the Parliament of Australia respectfully request that this apology be received in the spirit in which it is offered as part of the healing of the nation. (Intro.)

His speech employs explicitly psychodynamic language and imagery. Referring to the disturbing stories brought into public consciousness by *Bringing Them Home*, Rudd acknowledges:

> These are uncomfortable things to be brought out into the light. They are not pleasant. They are profoundly disturbing. (11)

> [We] are doing more than contending with the facts ... we are also *wrestling with our own soul* ... Until we fully confront [the uncomfortable] truth, there will always be a *shadow* hanging over us and our future as a *fully united and fully reconciled people*. (14, emphasis added)

The importance Rudd places on this healing was reinforced by his exhortation to politicians to "move beyond our infantile bickering, our point-scoring and our mindlessly partisan politics" (20) to work cooperatively on indigenous issues. It was wonderfully refreshing and inspiring to hear a Prime Minister speak critically of the behaviour that many abhor in politicians. As he acknowledged, "the challenges are too great and the consequences too great to allow it all to become a political football, as it has been so often in the past" (21).

I felt particularly glad to hear Rudd honour indigenous people—"a proud people" (Intro.)—and pay respect to the fact that theirs constitute "the oldest continuous cultures in human history" (Intro.):

> We embrace with pride, admiration and awe these great and ancient cultures we are truly blessed to have among us—cultures that provide a unique, uninterrupted human thread linking our Australian continent to the most ancient prehistory of our planet. (23)

I was excited by his call for a genuine partnership between indigenous and non-indigenous Australians and by his suggestion of our working together to "write a new chapter in our nation's story together" (24). Rudd evoked a powerful image of a cooperative future:

> [a] future where we embrace the possibility of new solutions to enduring problems where old approaches have failed.
>
> A future based on mutual respect, mutual resolve and mutual responsibility.
>
> A future where all Australians, whatever their origins, are truly equal partners. (Intro)

The Apology: Part 2

In the second part of his speech, Rudd went on to spell out exactly what he envisaged of this proposed partnership. At this point in his speech there was an abrupt change of tone in the language of the Apology: from passionate to practical, from symbolic to action-oriented:

> Australians are a passionate lot. We are also a very practical lot. For us symbolism is important but, unless the great symbolism of reconciliation is accompanied by an even greater substance, it is little more than a clanging gong. It is not sentiment that makes history; it is our actions that make history. (17)

The actions that Rudd proposed can be summarised as follows:

> • Over the next five years, to have every indigenous four year old in a remote Aboriginal community receiving "a proper" early childhood education.
>
> • For new educational opportunities to be rolled out, year by year, as these children grow up.
>
> • The provision of "proper" primary and preventive health care to these same children so as to reduce the infant mortality rates in remote indigenous communities.
>
> • To establish a joint policy commission, led by the Prime Minister and the Leader of the Opposition to develop and implement an effective housing strategy for remote communities over the next five years.

- For the commission (provided it works well) to work on the task of establishing constitutional recognition of the first Australians.

These methods and the language in which Rudd presents them are distinctively those of modern Western culture. The actions he suggests are dependent for implementation upon the core educational, medical, and political institutions of modern society. Rudd speaks of setting "concrete targets for the future" (17), of establishing "real measures of policy success or policy failure" (18) and "commonly-agreed national objectives" (18), of setting "a destination for the nation" that will serve as a "central organising principle" (18). He proposes a "systematic approach" (19) involving "clear goals, clear thinking" (20) to achieve success. This is the language of quantification, of control, of certainty, of progress, and of rationality. It is the distinctive voice of Western bureaucracy. It is worth remembering W.E.H. Stanner's warning of the inherent dangers of applying such language to the rich complexities of Aboriginal cosmology:

> Our categories are too Procrustean, our abstractions too dry and spare, our intellectual habits too desiccated for the material we have to handle.[17]

The culture of the modern West emerged from the Enlightenment, that great flourishing of human intelligence, which brought about change in so many fields of human endeavour. These synergistic developments included, for example, the spread of an education that emphasised the rational above all other aspects of human being, the development of empirically-based science, the emergence of humanism, and the industrial revolution. Faith in God was replaced, as the foundation of public institutions, by a belief in the rational and technological abilities of human beings to bring about progress and change.

Despite Rudd's oblique New Testament reference to "a clanging gong" —a glimpse of his own Christian faith—the language of the second half of the Apology is overwhelmingly the language of modernity:

> ... [T]he core of this partnership for the future is the closing of the gap between Indigenous and non-Indigenous Australians on life-expectancy, educational achievement and employment opportunities. This new partnership ... will set *concrete targets* for the future: within a decade to halve the widening gap in literacy, numeracy and employment outcomes and opportunities for Indigenous Australians...We need a new beginning—a new beginning which contains *real measures of*

policy success or policy failure; a new beginning, a new partnership, on closing the gap with sufficient flexibility not to insist on a one-size-fits-all approach for each of the hundreds of remote and regional Indigenous communities across the country but instead allowing flexible, tailored, local approaches to achieve *commonly-agreed national objectives* that lie at the core of our proposed new partnership; a new beginning that draws *intelligently* on the experiences of new *policy settings* across the nation. (17-18, emphasis added)[18]

Let us resolve over the next five years to have every Indigenous four year old in a remote Aboriginal community enrolled in and attending a proper early childhood education centre or opportunity and engaged in proper preliteracy and prenumeracy programs. Let us resolve to build new *educational opportunities* for these little ones, year by year, step by step, following the completion of their crucial preschool year. Let us resolve to use this *systematic approach* to building future educational opportunities for Indigenous children and providing proper primary and preventative health care for the same children, to beginning the task of rolling back the obscenity that we find today in infant mortality rates in remote Indigenous communities—up to four times higher than in other communities. (19)

I therefore propose a joint policy commission, to be led by the Leader of the Opposition and me, with a mandate to develop and implement—to begin with—an effective housing strategy for remote communities over the next five years. It will be consistent with the government's policy framework, a new partnership for closing the gap. If this commission operates well, I then propose that it work on the further task of constitutional recognition of the first Australians, consistent with the longstanding platform commitments of my party and the pre-election position of the opposition. (21)

Most of it will be hard—very hard. But none of it is impossible, and *all of it is achievable with clear goals, clear thinking*...(20, emphasis added)

Language and culture are particular to a way of being in the world and within a dominant culture it is easy to forget that *our* way of being in the world is not the *only* or the *best* way of being. The colonisers of Australia brought with them the cultural values of the Enlightenment and it is precisely their "forgetfulness" of other ways of being that led to the tragedy of the Stolen Generations. It was disturbing that this same forgetfulness was evident in Rudd's speech. Of course it is unsurprising that the language and orientation of the latter part of the Apology is distinctively that of the modern West; Australia is after all a modern Western society. However, I think it still needs to be pointed out—remembered—and held up to question if we are serious about establishing a real and mutually respectful partnership between indigenous and non-indigenous Australians. It is the unreflective acceptance of the assumptions that underpin modern Western culture that I found so disturbing about the Apology. This lack of consciousness suggests that a cultural complex may be at work.

Singer and Kimbles explain the notion of the cultural complex:

> ...[C]ultural complexes can be thought of arising out the cultural unconscious as it interacts with both the archetypal and personal realms of the psyche and the broader outer world arena of schools, communities, media, and all the other forms of cultural and group life ...Like individual complexes, cultural complexes tend to be repetitive, autonomous, resist consciousness, and collect experience that confirms their historical point of view.[19]

> "Cultural complexes" are at the heart of the conflicts between many groups and are expressed in group life all the time: politically, economically, sociologically, geographically and religiously.[20]

Mythos: The Hidden Moorings of Culture

The certainties of any culture are rooted in and gain their strength from unstated beliefs that are taken as given. Wittgenstein makes this point very clearly in *On Certainty*, his notes on the problem of knowledge. As he says, if we trace back through the presuppositions of any culture, we arrive not at ultimate propositions that are demonstrably true or false, but rather at "an ungrounded way *of* acting"; that is, a way of being in the world. And as he goes on to say, "[t]he propositions describing this world-picture might be part of a mythology".[21] Moore also makes this point in his description of myth as "a profound, life-shaping imagination of what the world is and how life works".[22] This world-picture, says Wittgenstein, is a "*matter-of-course* foundation" for our life "and *as such goes unmentioned*".[23] This is important. Our worldview is a blind spot, rarely questioned and generally simply accepted as given. Unable to place ourselves outside of our context, we are generally unaware that our worldview is a particular perspective. This "blind spot" begets an arrogance that is both self-limiting and a barrier to genuine and respectful relationship with those of other worldviews.

This arrogance is particularly evident in Rudd's discussion of education in the Apology: both in what he actually says and in what is left out. His references to establishing "*proper* early childhood ... *proper* preliteracy and prenumeracy programs" (19, emphasis added)[24] completely disregard the fact that for millennia before European settlement, indigenous communities successfully educated their children, not only in language, but in all they needed to know to live well in the driest continent on earth. Rudd is clearly implying that Aboriginal children should be taught the "white" way. The literacy programs to which he refers are, of course, English programs.

Rudd's emphasis is on what indigenous children do not know about an aspect of our culture: specifically, literacy skills. But what is missing is an acknowledgement of the correlative ignorance of non-indigenous Australians when it comes to indigenous culture. The *Koori Mail*, the fortnightly national Aboriginal and Torres Strait Islander journal, reports that over eighty per cent of Australians feel that their knowledge of indigenous culture amounts to little or nothing.[25] Even more disturbing is the report that, out of a group of six hundred teacher education students in Brisbane, less than one third had met and spoken with an indigenous person.[26] Further, with respect to literacy, it needs to be remembered that prior to European settlement, indigenous culture was transmitted orally and kinetically (through dance and ceremony). Although stories were not transcribed into the written word, they were inscribed in paintings and in the land itself.

> It would be a mistake ... to say there is no written component to indigenous transmission of knowledge, because indigenous people use the land as their book ... If teachers coming from a literate culture can't understand how people from the oral tradition transmit information, we have hit an immediate snag [obstacle].[27]

As a former teacher of literacy, I am fascinated by the possibilities of an education for *all* Australian children that construes "literacy" more broadly than simply the literacy of the written word. Imagine if we had children with high levels of oral, kinetic, and—what would we call it? — geo? literacy. As a non-indigenous Australian, I would value the opportunity to become fluent in "reading" the land. And what would happen, I wonder, if all non-indigenous children were required to learn an indigenous language as we expect Aboriginal children to learn English? I acknowledge that this would not be an easy undertaking; there were, after all, over 250 distinct indigenous languages prior to European settlement, many of which have since disappeared. I am also not suggesting that an indigenous language could become a viable second national language, in the way that Maori has become in New Zealand. Rather, I suggest the learning of an indigenous language as a gesture of respect and willingness to engage with cultures that are both different from our own and precious to those with whom we seek relationship.

Language and the stories it relates are the basis of any culture and it is often argued that knowledge of the language is crucial to an understanding of any culture. This has most recently been articulated by Dr. Richard Barsz, from the Australian National University College of Asia and the Pacific:

> If a person wants to truly understand a society and culture, they must speak the language.[28]

The "gap" in cultural understanding between indigenous and non-indigenous Australians needs bridging just as much as the gaps to which Rudd refers. How can there be real respect without a genuine understanding of the very different worldviews from which we come? It is difficult to respect cultures of which you have little understanding. Until this cultural gap is bridged—stories shared, relationships forged—it is premature and far too optimistic to claim as Rudd does that:

> Growing from this new respect, we see our Indigenous brothers and sisters with fresh eyes, with new eyes, and we have our minds wide open as to how we might tackle, together, the great practical challenges that Indigenous Australia faces in the future. (23)

Groups such as Reconciliation Australia[29] are working at national, state, and local community levels to foster relationship, respect, and understanding between indigenous and non-indigenous Australians. Rudd could have endorsed the work of these groups, or indeed proposed government initiatives to build understanding and relationship. The daily newspapers repeatedly testify to the need for such initiatives in the face of on-going cultural divisions between most non-indigenous and indigenous Australians. A recent report by the Victorian State government detailed, among other findings, the discrimination and racism experienced by young Aborigines:

> ...one-fifth said they had been discriminated against by police, the justice system, at school, during sport or while applying for

> jobs …7.6 per cent of Aboriginal children aged four to fourteen felt they had been treated unfairly at school because of their heritage. They also reported more frequent bullying at school compared with other students … Only half of Aboriginal parents and guardians in Victoria trust the police in their neighbourhood, compared to 81.3 per cent of other people.[30]

Author Kate Grenville also wrote recently in Melbourne's daily newspaper *The Age* of the incongruity between the traditional peripatetic Aboriginal lifestyle and the housing practices customary to non-indigenous Australians. She spelled out some basic issues affecting indigenous habitation:

> Housing policy has to accommodate people who wish to live "between places" rather than staying put. The idea of individual ownership—of a home or land—is not part of traditional culture and is a goal many indigenous people have no interest in.[31]

That this is news to ordinary Australians should be a source of shame. What an indictment that we *still* need to have some of the most fundamental aspects of traditional indigenous ways explained to us.

Differing understandings of the relationship between people and land have caused repeated clashes between indigenous and non-indigenous people since European settlement. In order for colonial cities to be built and farms established, the intimate and mutually sustaining relationship between indigenous people and the land was irrevocably disrupted. To relate to the land as a being, indeed as an aspect of the "self", is radically different from regarding the land as a "resource" to be exploited, mined, bought, and sold for human gain, as is characteristic in a modern industrial society:

> Aboriginal cosmology does not subscribe to the myth of the atomized individual, instead expanding the sense of self to include the extended family, the tribe, the nation, the Dreaming trails, the wider landscape and the cosmos.[32]

As the Aboriginal conception of self is predicated in terms of relationship, including relationship to land, dispossession triggered a concomitant ontological crisis for indigenous people that Dowd has likened to "soul murder", a destruction of "the pre-conceptual ground of being".[33] Aboriginal culture and its people were systematically suppressed for the colonial agenda to flourish.

A recent example of the continued chafing of worldviews was reported in *The Age*:

> An Aboriginal traditional owner who could have become one of Australia's richest people if he had allowed uranium mining on his land near Kakadu National Park says he is not interested in money: "When you dig a hole in that country you are killing me ... I don't worry about money at all."[34]

Even the current practice of non-indigenous Australians acknowledging, before a public occasion, "the traditional *owners*" of the land betrays Western notions of property ownership that are a distortion of the custodial relationship between land and people that characterises traditional indigenous life.[35]

Most Australians have only a superficial understanding of how indigenous people lived in this country before European settlement. It was not until I traveled to Central Australia and to Kakadu in my forties that I began to get some understanding of the intricate complexity of kinship relations in traditional indigenous life. As I have already noted, many other Australians share my ignorance.[36] And so there persists the "thinly veiled contempt" to which Rudd refers (17) and which I have regularly heard expressed within circles of tertiary educated, generally compassionate people.

Robert Manne, in his essay "Sorry Business: The Road to the Apology", speaks of "the Culture War"[37] between right-wing (conservative) and left-wing (liberal, progressive) intellectuals in Australia. The issue of Aboriginal dispossession and the Stolen Generations has been a fundamental battleground in this war. Conservative journalist Padraic McGuinness took over the editorship of *Quadrant*—a quarterly journal devoted to cultural issues—from the progressive Manne in 1997.

> Over the next three years *Quadrant* led a national campaign against the conclusions of *Bringing Them Home* and against the quest for Indigenous-non-Indigenous reconciliation. Two anti-*Bringing Them Home* conferences were held. A dozen or more articles on questions connected to the Stolen Generations were published. Keith Windschuttle's[38] revisionist history was launched.[39]

Right-wing members of the metropolitan newspapers echoed this "historical denialism"[40] and skepticism about the findings of *Bringing Them Home*. The editor of Melbourne tabloid the *Herald Sun* had this to say about the proposal to interrupt school classes so that students could watch the Apology on television:

> It's not enough that students simply know of Prime Minister
> Kevin Rudd's sorry to these "generations" of "stolen" children
> no one can actually find. To children we actually saved...[41]

Many ordinary Australians share these views. Not long after the Apology was delivered I was at my local hairdresser's and began discussing the event with her. She had been unmoved by the occasion and hadn't listened to Rudd's speech as she didn't see any need for an apology. Many others in the salon vehemently echoed her sentiments. Their views directly challenge Rudd's assertion that:

> The mood of the nation is for reconciliation now, between
> Indigenous and non-Indigenous Australians. The mood of the
> nation on Indigenous policy and politics is now very simple. (20)

Unfortunately, it remains far from simple. Laudable though Rudd's eagerness to effect change may be, I fear he may be rushing too quickly to "turn this page together" and to "write this new chapter in our nation's story together". (24)

The claiming of simplistic certainty in the face of ambiguity is, as Singer says, one of the hallmarks of the cultural complex.[42] I also hear in Rudd's articulation of his action plan the craving for certainty that Thomas Moore identifies as a particularly *modern* phenomenon:

> ... [T]he typical modern person suffers from the need to
> know and control everything ... It is essential in modern life
> ... to think that our social problems and personal struggles
> will be resolved once we understand the situation and gain
> control of it ...[43]

I am reminded of the poetry of T.S.Eliot—particularly his 1934 poem "Choruses from the Rock"—which provides an extraordinary critique of the hubris, the dry intellectuality, and the spiritual barrenness of modern life:

> ...you find explanations
> To satisfy the rational and enlightened mind.
> [But] you neglect and belittle the desert
> ... The desert is in the heart of your brother
> ...Listen[44]

Eliot laments the disconnection from one another and from the natural world that characterises life in a big city. Indeed, many of the issues with which our society struggles—the obesity epidemic, rising rates of depression and suicide, work/life imbalance, urban violence, environmental degradation—can be understood as dis-eases of modernity. One of my own hopes is that the healing of the relationship between indigenous and non-indigenous Australians might contribute to a revivification of spiritual life in our country.

Stanner has written of the "religious outlook" that permeates all aspects of Aboriginal life.[45] This religious outlook can also be found in the Celtic spiritual heritage of many non-indigenous Australians. Common to both worldviews is an expanded understanding of "self" that embraces the natural world, and a vivid sense of a timeless, eternal realm that underlies and infuses with meaning our temporal, everyday reality. John O'Donohue speaks from the Celtic tradition:

> When you gaze at something, you bring it inside you ... When you really look deeply at something etc. it becomes part of you ... Regardless of how modern we seem, we still remain ancient, sisters and brothers of the one clay. In each of us a different part of the mystery becomes luminous. *To truly be and become yourself, you need the ancient radiance of others. Essentially, we belong beautifully to nature.*[46](emphasis added)

and David Mowaljarlai from the Kimberley Aboriginal tradition:

> You are looking at nature and giving it your full attention, seeing all its beauty. Your vision has opened and you start learning now. When you touch them, all things talk to you, give you their story. It makes you really surprised. You feel you want to get deeper ... to come closer and to recognise what you are seeing. You understand that your mind has opened to all these things because you are seeing them; because your presence and their presence meet together and you recognise each other. These things recognise you. They give their wisdom and understanding to you when you come close to them. ...When you recognise it, it gives strength – a new flow. You have life now.[47]

According to both traditions, when we lose this sense of our intimate connections and an understanding of the interdependence of all elements of the natural world, we are diminished and forget who we are. This is precisely the situation that we—along with all other modern, secular, industrialised urbanites—find ourselves in today.

Despite Rudd's exhortation to "embrace ... these great and ancient cultures we are truly blessed to have among us" and despite his talk of being "equal partners",[48] there is nothing in his speech about *how* the wisdom of Aboriginal culture will enrich our nation and perhaps offer fresh perspectives on the issues that challenge Australia. Fortunately, Stanner, over three decades ago, appreciatively articulated some of the blessings of Aboriginal culture:

> [I]t seems to me a psychological achievement of a high order to have developed an art of life so strongly characterised by humour and jollity. These things, together with the confidence in their power to survive, the practice of a life-long discipline of body and mind as a mark of their valuation of man both as flesh and as spirit, and the repetitive celebration—no less joyous a word will do—of the continuance of their way of life, seem to me to argue powerfully for a re-assessment of some of our past depreciation.[49]

Rudd is right when he acknowledges that:

> [t]he truth is, a business as usual approach towards Indigenous Australians is not working. Most old approaches are not working. We need a new beginning... (18)

Ultimately, though, what Rudd's vision boils down to is just another re-working of the old approaches: a more coordinated and concerted effort to help indigenous people fit within the existing parameters of the modern Western culture that has displaced their own. I find Rudd's suggestion "Let us resolve today to begin with the little children" (19) deeply troubling, echoing as it does the sentiments on which the very actions for which Rudd is apologising were based. It would have been completely different if Rudd had *also* suggested that we begin with the education of little non-indigenous children too, to rectify their ignorance—and the contempt it breeds—of indigenous culture.

Clearly, there is no going back to traditional Aboriginal culture as it was before European settlement. As Mowaljarlai bleakly acknowledges:

> The people don't respect the incest taboos any more. The kinship system is destroyed, that's the real damage. ...You can see that out tribal life is destroyed.[50]

Much of "the oldest continuous cultures..." is already lost and most of the languages have disappeared. This is a tragedy not just for Australia but also for the world. And yet, despite all that has been lost, there is still much that remains, and indigenous people are willing to share this with non-indigenous Australians. Mowaljarlai puts it this way:

> This European lot came over here. They settled down in Australia. They put down all their rules. British rules. We are

> holding them now, in Canberra, everywhere ... There's the imprint now ... "You have to understand." We're telling them now, the English (descended) mob: "You were born here, but you don't know the rules, the spirit belong to this country. You have to listen to us". Like we had to listen to him. This bush school and all those things are like that, not just in your head, but in your powers. That's what we Ngarinyin are talking about now. And Worrorra and Wunambul too. That's a gift now, a gift from us, a gift for wider Australia.[51]

What disappoints me about the Apology is, to use Eliot's image, the absence of the desert or, as Mowaljarlai might put it, the lack of listening. How will "wider Australia" receive the "gift" Mowaljarlai says is offered and that —surely—is so sorely needed? The "gifts" of Rudd's Apology flow one way only: from experts and institutions rooted firmly in Western culture to indigenous people. This is no way to build mutually respectful relationship and it limits the horizons of all Australians. It is, I think, a double loss. First—and most importantly given the purpose of the Apology—it erases indigenous cultures yet again. Second, it is a missed opportunity to open Australian society to new and fresh perspectives on the challenges that face Western cultures all over the world.

Time has passed since the Apology was delivered and many things have changed in the Australian cultural landscape. Kevin Rudd was deposed by his deputy Julia Gillard in June 2010 in a decisive coup that left him the first Australian Prime Minister not to serve out his first term in office. Gillard is our first female Prime Minister. But, as I have discussed, the relationship between indigenous and non-indigenous Australians continues to be troubled and it is the first Australians who are bearing the brunt of this.

An elder from the Kowanyama Community in Queensland offers some pithy observations on our current situation in Australia and sound advice on how we might proceed from here:

> We can't go back. The old law was for the old problems. Now we got this new law, the Whiteman's way. And we got these new problems. This law doesn't fix them either. It's no good. What we got to do is put them together, the old and the new. Mix them up. And they'll be hard and strong like cement.[52]

This is a simple image, prosaic even. It makes me think of neighbourly collaboration on a shared project. Simple it may be, but we haven't yet been able to "mix them up". Speaking generally of cultural conflict, Singer says: "much of what tears us apart can be understood as the manifestation of autonomous processes in the collective and individual psyche that organise themselves as cultural complexes".[53] Perhaps our inability thus far to build something creative and sustaining out of the mix of old and new reflects something of the inhibiting effects of the cultural complex as enacted here.

Notes

[1] Kevin Rudd, Prime Minister of Australia, "Apology to Australia's Indigenous Peoples," 2008, http://www.aph.gov.au/house/rudd_ speech.pdf, para. 10.

[2] A.O. Neville, quoted in Robert Manne, "Sorry Business: the Road to the Apology", in *The Monthly* (Collingwood, Victoria: Network Services, March 2008), p. 22.

[3] The Northern Territory Protector of Natives (date unknown), quoted in Rudd, "Apology".

[4] *Ibid.*

[5] "Bringing Them Home: The 'Stolen Children' Report", Human Rights and Equal Opportunity Commission, 1997, http://www.humanrights.gov.au/social_justice/bth_report/index.html.

[6] "Conclusion," Bringing Them Home Community Guide, Human Rights and Equal Opportunity Commission, 1997. Accessed from Indigenous Law Resources: Reconciliation and Social Justice Library, http://www.austlii.edu.au/au/other/IndigLRes/stolen_summary/13.html.

[7] Robert Manne, in his essay "Sorry Business" speaks of the prevalence of this ignorance and of his own shock upon learning of the practice. Manne, "Sorry Business", p. 22.

[8] *Ibid.*, p. 27.

[9] Rudd, "Apology".

[10] Henceforth, unless indicated otherwise, "Intro." or a numeral in parentheses after quotations will indicate a paragraph in the text of the "Apology."

[11] Juno Gemes, "Witnessing the Apology," *Australian Aboriginal Studies* (Canberra: Aboriginal Studies Press, issue 1, 2008: 118.

[12] Henry Reynolds, historian, interviewed on *Lateline* (Australian Broadcasting Corporation, February 13, 2008), http://www.abc.net.au/lateline/content/2007/s2162128.htm.

[13] Michael Kirby, "Stolen Generations Descendent", *Lateline* (Australian Broadcasting Corporation,February 13, 2008), http://www.abc.net.au/lateline/content/2007/s2162128.htm.

[14] Kutcha Edwards, musician, interviewed on *7:30 Report* (Australian Broadcasting Corporation, February 13, 2008), http://www.abc.net.au/7.30/content/2007/s2162072.htm.

[15] Michael Brissenden, reporter, *7:30 Report* (Australian Broadcasting Corporation, February 12, 2008. http://www.abc.net.au/7.30/content/2007/s2160979.htm.

[16] Thomas Moore, *Soul Mates: Honoring the Mysteries of Love and Relationship* (New York: Harper Perennial, 1994), p. viii.

[17] W.E.H. Stanner, "Some Aspects of Aboriginal Religion" (1976), in *Religious Business: Essays on Australian Aboriginal Spirituality*, edited by Max Charlesworth (Cambridge: Cambridge University Press, 1998), p. 18.

[18] Rudd, "Apology".

[19] Thomas Singer and Samuel L. Kimbles, "Introduction", in Thomas Singer and Samuel L. Kimbles, *The Cultural Complex: Contemporary Jungian Perspectives on Psyche and Society* (London and New York: Routledge, 2004), pp. 4 and 6.

[20] Thomas Singer, "The Cultural Complex and Archetypal Defenses of the Collective Spirit: Baby Zeus, Elian Gonzales, Constantine's Sword, and Other Holy Wars", in *The San Francisco Jung Institute Library Journal*, Vol. 20, No. 4, 2002, pp. 13-14.

[21] Ludwig Wittgenstein, *On Certainty*, edited by G.E.M. Anscombe and G.H. von Wright, translated by Denis Paul and G.E.M. Anscombe (Oxford: Basil Blackwood, 1979), proposition 110.

[22] Thomas Moore, *The Soul's Religion: Cultivating a Profoundly Religious Way of Life* (New York: HarperCollins, 2002), p. 21.

[23] Wittgenstein, *On Certainty*, proposition 167.

[24] Rudd, "Apology", my emphases.

[25] "Eco-tourism is Helping the Process", *Koori Mail: The Voice of Indigenous Australia* 452 (Lismore, N.S.W.: N-Tech Media), p. 45.

[26] "Mandatory Training a Welcome First Step", *Koori Mail*, 440, p. 60.

[27] Ernie Grant, Jirrbal Elder from Far North Queensland, quoted in "Big Questions on Program in Conference", *Koori Mail* 458, p. 48.

[28] Richard Barsz, "Love of Language", in *ANU reporter* (Canberra: The Australian National University, Spring 2010), p. 11.

[29] For information on Reconciliation Australia, see http://www.reconciliation.org.au/home.

[30] Julia Medew, "State's Young Aborigines Need Help", *The Age* (Melbourne: Fairfax, August 10, 2010), p. 3.

[31] Kate Grenville, "Rudd's Apology Risks Leaving a Sorry Legacy", *The Age*, February 17, 2010.

[32] David Tacey, *ReEnchantment: The New Australian Spirituality* (Sydney: HarperCollins, 2000), p. 101.

[33] Amanda Dowd, "The Passion of the Country: Bearing the Burdens of Traumatic Histories, Personal and Collective", in *International Journal of Jungian Studies*, Vol. 2, No. 1, March 2010, pp. 59-70.

[34] Jeffrey Lee, quoted in Lindsay Murdoch, "Aboriginal Custodian Turns his Back on Riches", *The Age*, August 11, 2010, p. 5.

[35] Stanner, "Some Aspects", p. 5.

[36] See note 25.

[37] Manne, "'Sorry Business'", p. 26.

[38] Keith Windschuttle, *The Fabrication of Aboriginal History* (Paddington, N.S.W.: Macleay Press, 2002).

[39] Manne, "Sorry Business", p. 26.

[40] *Ibid.*, p. 27.

[41] Andrew Bolt, "Rudd's Great Leap Forward", *Herald Sun*, February 13, 2008 (Port Melbourne: The Herald and Weekly Times), p. 26.

[42] Singer, "The Cultural Complex and Archetypal Defenses", p. 15.

[43] Thomas Moore, *Original Self: Living with Paradox and Originality* (New York: HarperCollins, 2000), p. 114 and p. 59.

[44] T.S. Eliot, "Choruses from the Rock"(1934), from T.S. Eliot, *Collected Poems 1909-1962* (London: Faber, 1963).

[45] Stanner, "Some Aspects", p. 2.

[46] John O'Donohue, *Anam Cara: Spiritual Wisdom of the Celtic World* (London: Bantam Press, 1997), pp. 87 and 126, my emphases.

[47] David Mowaljarlai and Jutta Malnic, *Yorro Yorro: Everything Standing Up Alive: Spirit of the Kimberley* (Broome, W.A.: Magabala Books, 1993), pp. 53-4.

[48] Rudd, "Apology".

[49] Stanner, "Some Aspects", p. 10.

[50] Mowaljarlai and Malnic, *Yorro Yorro*, pp. 39-40.

[51] *Ibid.*, p. 210.

[52] Aboriginal elder from the Kowanyama people, quoted in conference brochure for "Healing Our People", the Institute of Criminology conference in Alice Springs in 1991.

[53] Singer and Kimbles, *The Cultural Complex*, p. 1.

David Tacey, Ph.D., is Associate Professor in Humanities at La Trobe University, Melbourne, Australia. He is the author of twelve books, including *Gods and Diseases* (2011), *Edge of the Sacred* (1995, rev. 2009), *Re-Enchantment* (2000), and *Patrick White: Fiction and the Unconscious* (1988). David is a specialist in Jungian studies and has published five books directly on Jungian subjects, including *The Jung Reader* (2012), *How to Read Jung* (2006), and *Jung and the New Age* (2001). David studied literature, psychology, and philosophy at Flinders and Adelaide Universities in the 1970s, and in the 1980s he completed post-doctoral studies in psychoanalysis and religion in the United States. His studies were supervised by James Hillman and Thomas Moore. He has taught in various Australian, American, and British universities, and is on the editorial boards of several international journals on analytical psychology and religious studies. He is often invited to address contemporary issues, including ecological awareness, mental health, spirituality, and Aboriginal Australia. His books have been translated into several languages, including Cantonese, Korean, Spanish, Portuguese, and French.

There is something missing in the Australian psyche, and this absence or abyss is what interests David Tacey in this chapter. Cultural development and personal individuation necessitate a dialogue or interaction between conscious and unconscious, but David describes this dialogue as problematical in the Australian context because culture here is so thinly rational and cerebral, denying the existence of the unconscious. As a colonial society, its main imperative has been to impress itself on both landscape and indigenous people, subordinating both to the dictates of a reason and a rule which has been imported from Europe.

Patrick White was chosen as the subject for David's analysis as he is the most prominent and accomplished Australian writer to date, who is widely known internationally and Austalia's only Nobel Prize winning author who is known to have read Jung and been influenced by Jungian ideas. However the nature of that influence is questioned in David's chapter. Jung's writings have, ironically, been drawn in to reinforce, and protect the existence of an unconscious Australian cultural complex to extinguish self in a sacrifice to the repressed "other", whether this "other" be landscape, indigenous people, or the psychological underworld.

11

The Australian Resistance to Individuation: Patrick White's Knotted Mandala

David Tacey

> The primary knot of spirit and matter is personified in the clinging embrace of erotic conjunction of mother and son.
> —James Hillman, "The Great Mother, Her Son, Her Hero and the Puer"[1]

Fear of—and longing for—oblivion

There seems to be a resistance to individuation in Australian society. The resistance is based on a pervasive fear of the unconscious. We dare not set foot in the interior world, lest we go mad, lose our bearings, or risk being disintegrated by unruly forces. Below this fear lies a more shocking reality—there is a longing to be obliterated in the unconscious. This could be summed up in a paradoxical formulation: we fear and long for obliteration. I would consider this to be a cultural complex in the Australian psyche. In defining "cultural complexes", I follow Tom Singer:

> Cultural complexes structure emotional experience and operate in the personal and collective psyche in much the same way as individual complexes, although their content might be quite different. Like individual complexes, cultural complexes tend to be repetitive, autonomous, resist consciousness, and collect

experience that confirms their historical point of view... [They] automatically take on a shared body language ... or express their distress in similar somatic complaints. Finally ... [they] provide a simplistic certainty about the group's place in the world in the face of otherwise conflicting and ambiguous uncertainties.[2]

Our fear-of-yet-longing-for-obliteration is repetitive, autonomous, and resists consciousness. Not many of us are aware of it, apart from artists, sensitive individuals, and psychotherapists. In daily life, we support an adherence to reason and logic which is fanatical in its dogmatism. Yet in the unconscious we harbour desires to abandon reason, overturn our plans, destroy our logic, and sink into annihilation.

I have written about this before in my book on Australian culture, *Edge of the Sacred: Jung, Psyche, Earth*. There, in a section called "The Degraded Sacred and Alcoholism in White and Black Society", I explore the conundrum of Australian society: on the one hand, a commitment to democratic values and social order, on the other hand, a barely disguised desire to obliterate self in one or more of the favoured rituals of destruction: binge drinking, excessive eating, abuse of drugs, consumerism, inertia, zoning out.[3] As a child, I experienced this rift in the national psyche while growing up in Alice Springs, an outback town at the centre of the continent. Alice Springs is an ancestral place belonging to the Arrernte, Warlpiri, and Pintubi peoples. Yet in modern times, it has been a place of the clash of cultures, colonial and neo-colonial violence, racism, and extreme prejudice. It has become a place in which the polite persona of society has been stripped away, revealing a psyche which is besieged by primitive impulses. In this town the raw nature of the Australian psyche is on show, and the desire for oblivion reveals itself in addictions and cravings, in suicidal acts and ideations, in borderline personality disorders, in explicit criminal behaviour and violent activity, in wife bashing and sexual abuse, in glue and petrol sniffing, in reckless acts of risk-taking, self-harming, and abandonment.[4] Alice Springs is truly our own "heart of darkness", and anyone wishing to study our society is advised to spend time there.

Australia calls itself the "Lucky Country",[5] yet this is an illusion which masks the fact that a great deal of injustice, violence, civil unrest, and psychological disruption has taken place here and continues to be found in our society. The popular bumper sticker says it all: "White Australia has a black history". Australia has been founded on a lie, and that lie is *terra nullius*, the British notion that the continent could be annexed for the Empire because it was "empty land" or uninhabited. True, there were no cities, architectural monuments, or European-style signs of civilisation, but the continent was peopled by hundreds of distinct Aboriginal nations, each having its own language system, cultural order, and religious cosmology. European society was transported to Australia and imposed upon it from above. Almost no one bothered to find out about the existing indigenous cultures, their history, structure, or meaning systems. As a result, Europe in Australia has suffered from an ongoing identity crisis, from an enormous yet repressed reservoir of guilt.

We are "lucky" on top, insofar as a relatively prosperous and ordered society has been created at the uppermost levels. But scratch the surface and we find discontent, anguish, shame, and dishonour. We do not feel at home in this country or in our own skin. We are suffering from a lack of authenticity and it is taking its toll in various ways. One of these sources of discontent is found in an ongoing and chronic desire for self-sacrifice. This is predominantly unconscious, because it is too horrible to face. A desire to obliterate ourselves and society is found just below the "Aussie" persona. Sometimes the desire for sacrifice takes a heroic or affirmative turn, and this is a positive part of the national character. Volunteerism is strong in this country, and when fire, flood, or disaster strikes, Australians are ready to come to the aid of those who have suffered. When it operates consciously, as a binding force in the community, the sacrificial demon is helpful and nation-building.

The fierce longing for sacrifice originates from the realisation that the colonial consciousness is not authentic. It did not emerge from this ground and needs to be sacrificed so that something new can appear. Colonial Australia did not understand that a civilisation could not be transplanted from Europe to the other side of the globe: there would be a need for a symbolic death and rebirth, so that a new kind of consciousness could emerge.[6] In the United States, the War of Independence fulfilled the requirements for this symbolic and bloody ritual: the end of the old, the birth of the new. In Australia, there was no such war to mark a departure from an old psychic structure. Not that I think war is necessary, but it gives expression to the archetypal need for rebirth, which, in the absence of war, has to be enacted in some other way. In my view, Australia is caught up in a pattern of rebirth that requires a symbolic death as its first essential step. Society resists this process, and as such we are forced to act out the sacrificial impulse in unconscious ways.

Our national heroes are destroyers and criminals: Ned Kelly, convicts, highway men, bank robbers. Our explorers did not conquer the land but dissolved into it, in sacrificial journeys in which they died terrible deaths: Burke and Wills, Leichhardt, Eyre.[7] These stories of national sacrifice are taught as history in our schools, and our favourite novels, such as Patrick White's *Voss*,[8] are fictional accounts of early explorers who sought ecstatic self-mutilation in the desert. Our favourite national films are about sacrifice: *Picnic at Hanging Rock*, in which a group of school girls are drawn by magnetic force to a volcanic mountain and sacrificed to it; *Evil Angels*, in which an innocent baby is seized and eaten by a wild dog; *Gallipoli*, in which innocent teenagers are sacrificed to the war machine and British military incompetence. The poet Judith Wright was the first to sense a psychological meaning to these deaths and sacrifices:

> Are all these dead men in our literature, then, a kind of ritual sacrifice? And just what is being sacrificed? Is it perhaps the European consciousness—dominating, puritanical, analytical? ... Reconciliation, then, is a matter of death—the death of the European mind, its absorption into the soil it has struggled against.[9]

But we don't say we have a problem with involuntary sacrifice; we just say "this is our history". We don't view our plight psychologically, we say we are recording events as they present themselves. To quote Singer again: the cultural complex "collects experiences that confirms its historical point of view". We resist consciousness when it comes to our favoured national past-times: compulsive sacrifice and a longing for obliteration.

In 1971 Melbourne psychologist Ronald Conway rose to prominence in Australia when he wrote *The Great Australian Stupor: An Interpretation of the Australian Way of Life*.[10] In this book, part humorous and part serious, Conway outlined the ways in which Australians seek self-oblivion and mental destruction. It achieved instant fame because so many Australians recognised themselves in his descriptions of the local way of life, and in our predilection for inertia, stasis, conventionality, resistance to culture, and reflection. For a while, Conway was even given his own television show, in which he held a mirror up to the nation. But then we forgot about the novelty of self-reflection and went back to sleep.

To live in Australia is to live in a negative social climate. Americans who visit or live here find the place baffling. If the credo of America is "Yes, we can", that of Australia is "No, we can't." This makes for an odd social environment. Things are achieved in spite of the current toward inertia and resistance. The humour, temperament, and spirit of Australia are ironic, downbeat, self-deprecating, anti-heroic, often depressing. Yet individuation forces itself upon us, even with all this negativity. Even Down Under, where everything is upside down, where the seasons are reversed, and even the Southern Cross hangs upside down in the night sky, we have

THE AUSTRALIAN RESISTANCE TO INDIVIDUATION

our own version of individuation, which is a *via negativa*, a way of resisting what the unconscious is forcing upon us.

White, Jung, and the Unconscious Complex

I would like to explore our cultural complex using Patrick White's *The Solid Mandala* as my text. The unconscious complex is also *unconscious* in our major writer. He writes about the longing for oblivion, but does not seem to recognise it as such. He writes from inside the complex, and as such does not solve the problem, but at least he gives it literary expression. I see White's novels as cultural dreams from the psyche of the collective. They express the nature of the complex, show how we are caught, and suggest a way forward. But the author seems caught up in a problem which is larger than himself. He struggles with his, and our own, complex, but does not find a way out of it. In fact, he seems to resist individuation and to misread the nature of the complex. But I am getting ahead of myself.

The Solid Mandala (1966) is an important Australian novel and one which has haunted my imagination for many years. It seems to express the nature and complexity of psychic reality in a powerful and yet deeply disturbing way. The central symbol is the "knotted mandala" that Arthur Brown carries in his pocket and often holds in his hand. Arthur is the slightly handicapped, ungainly, and awkward twin of Waldo, the more intellectual and "sensible" brother. Waldo finds his twin a burden and treats him with contempt. But Arthur is not just Waldo's brother, he also appears to be a symbolic figure representing his soul or inner self, and it is this role that proves decisive. Waldo's attitude toward his brother is a form of self-punishment. Arthur's great longing is to free Waldo from his entrapment, which he sees symbolised by the knot at the centre of one of his glass marbles. Arthur discovers Jung in the public library of Sydney and decides that the marbles he carries are "solid mandalas". Arthur hopes that Waldo will take the knotted one and contemplate its meaning:

> 'If it would help I would give it to you, Waldo, to keep,' Arthur said.
> Offering the knotted mandala.
> While half sensing that Waldo would never untie the knot.
> Even before Waldo gave one of his looks, which, when interpreted, meant: By offering me a glass marble you are trying to make me look a fool, I am not, and never shall be a fool, though I am your twin brother, so my reply, Arthur, is not shit, but shit!
> As he shouted: 'No, Arthur! Go, Arthur!'[11]

Although described as a "shingle short" and "not too bright",[12] Arthur is artistic and creative. His special gift is intuition; he can see into the heart of things, and he appreciates the symbolic dimension of experience. He invites Waldo not only to contemplate the solid mandala and untie its knot, but to "write about Mr. Saporta and the carpets".[13] Mr. Saporta's carpets display mandalic shapes and designs, and he urges Waldo to use these carpets as aids to contemplation. In using the term "mandala", White makes use of Jung's writings, a debt he acknowledged. White was introduced to Jung's writings in the early 1960s, when the artist Roy de Maistre, his "intellectual and aesthetic mentor", gave him a copy of *Psychology and Alchemy*, which he read with considerable interest.

I do not believe, however, that White understood Jung. I think he read him with his imaginative eye, his Arthur-self, as it were, but not with his full consciousness. His Waldo-self, who seems to have had the upper hand in his personality, was not interested in Jung and gained little from the reading. White satirised my position on this matter in his last novel, *Memoirs of Many in One*:

> I have studied practically nothing beyond my own intuition—oh, and by fits and starts ... dear old Father Jung who, I am told, I misinterpret.[14]

White wrote this in response to my essay on his use of Jung, published in 1983 in *The Journal of Analytical Psychology*.[15] There I argued that he read Jung but did not comprehend him, only borrowing some of his terms. I am sorry, in retrospect, that we had this negative wrangle, but it seems to have been inevitable. I have always respected White and enjoyed his writings, even as a school student, when I read everything I could get my hands on. When he was awarded the Nobel Prize for Literature in 1973, I felt this was justified and celebrated the achievement, both for his art and our national culture. But because White became known as a "Jungian" writer,[16] and because I knew something about Jung, I had to enter the debate and make a statement on his apparent Jungianism. Professor Andrew Riemer went as far as to allege that White's novels are constructions entirely based on Jungian theory, and he chastised White for being so heavily reliant on psychological material and for the "questions of propriety" that this posed.[17]

In Australia at the time, there was no Jungian expert to rule on this matter, only a number of literary critics who dabbled in Jung, and effectively I had to self-educate myself in the field. What became clear to me was that White's novels gave the appearance of being Jungian because he was drawing from the same source that Jung spent his career discovering and mapping.

White's novels were "archetypal", not because he was applying Jungian theory, but because he was drawing from the unconscious sources of his imagination. As Lacan famously asserted, the unconscious is structured like a language. It is not the arbitrary world that many literary critics think it is. It is possible to map the imaginal world with the aid of psychological science, and in no sense is this world a "product" of the artist's conscious or intellectual understanding. The figures of the interior domain have their own reality, and in White's case, they often seem at odds with the author's conscious intentions. There is a moving statement in *The Vivisector* which grasps the nature of White's artistic experience:

> He was still too exhausted by what had turned out to be, not a game of his own imagination, but a wrestling match with someone stronger.[18]

White's World at War with Itself

From *Happy Valley* (1939) to *The Solid Mandala* (1966) White's intellectual characters, usually male, imagine they are on a hero's journey toward ultimate knowing and spiritual truth. They fancy themselves destined for enlightenment, as in *The Living and the Dead* (1941) and *The Aunt's Story* (1948). In *The Tree of Man* (1955) the goal becomes mystical unity with nature, and by the time of *Voss* (1957) and *Riders in the Chariot* (1961), White's goal takes a religious turn, and becomes unity with God and Christ. All this seems very heady and worthy, and even to be congratulated. But it is simply not true. The characters are not seeking enlightenment, Christianity, or God, but oblivion—and this is dressed up by the author as religious experience. It is the case of an archetypal desire being called by the wrong name.

Effectively White is misreading his own work, but it is a loaded misreading, because it defends the complex by elevating it to a sacred principle. In *The Psychopathology of Everyday Life* Freud warned about "misreadings" as one of the "parapraxes", that is, illusions that bolster the activity of unconscious complexes.[19] White imagines that his misreading is transparent to his archetypal content, but it is not. This is a structural crisis which comes to a head in *The Solid Mandala*, when the illusion of religious saintliness is exploded, revealing the reality of the complex or "knot" at the centre of his work. As far as I can tell, I am the first critic to point to this structural flaw in White's writing. Most readers of White remain unaware of the problem—and why not? Those of us who have been educated in the British humanist tradition have been taught to respect the author's intentions and not to expect a rupture between his or her conscious and unconscious designs. Only on the Continent, and arising from psychoanalysis and the works of Derrida, Barth, Foucault, and Lyotard, are readers educated to deconstruct narratives and look for the unconscious directive of the work, which is often at odds with the artist.

When I first read White's fictional works in the 1970s, I believed, along with others, that he was writing about mysticism, love of God, and abandonment to Christ. After all, these elements *are* present in the novels; there are references to God and Jesus throughout, and Voss, Stan Parker, and Himmelfarb are said to be Christ-like and saintly.[20] The authorial commentary, which is "superadded" in the works, tries to enforce this point of view, and White spins a web of allegory which elevates the narratives toward religion and transcendence. So why should we read the novels otherwise? There are several reasons. Firstly, the religious allegory is superimposed and artificial. Arthur Phillips put his finger on this problem in an essay on "The Algebraic Symbol".[21] He argued that White's religious symbols were dead and lifeless, and the author pushed them around with a controlling logic. They were products of a calculated algebra and not part of the living fabric of the narrative. I resisted this at first, as it seemed to me that Phillips was being cynical and anti-religious, in typical Australian style. But when I read all the novels a second time, I began to sense the value of his criticism.

Secondly, the aspirations of the central characters are always foiled and ruined by the malicious antics of a range of demonic, witch-like female characters, who want to spoil the spiritual party. Whenever one of White's mystical characters seeks to enter nirvana, enlightenment, or unity, a demonic woman appears and she has enormous power and might, which the mystics are unable to combat. I am unable to supply examples here, but my book on this subject offers dozens of instances.[22] The mystics are helpless before these demonic figures, who are always mother-figures and are seen or heard sucking their teeth. This pattern occurs so often that it seems to constitute a missing part of the larger design of White's fiction. In other words, these "secondary" feminine figures are actually primary. Whenever the main character imagines himself sinking into nirvana, the toothed matrix of the devouring maw is constellated. What he is sinking into, by virtue of his romantic attachment, is the *vagina dentata* of the great mother. God, Christ, and Spirit are covers for the pleasurable aspect of mother/son incest.

The Longing for Incest

This was a shocking discovery for me and at first I resisted it. It seemed too Freudian and sexual for such a "mystical" novelist as Patrick White. But as I read into the psychoanalytic literature, it seemed I had discovered the hermeneutical key to White's world. I had long sensed something artificial in his religious devotionalism, but could not put my finger on it. As to the "knot" in the mandala, I think James Hillman put it best when he wrote:

> In classical mythology this special entanglement of spirit and maternal world is depicted by the Great Goddess and her young male consort, her son, her lover, her priest. Attis, Adonis, Hippolytus, Phaethon, Tammuz, Endymion, Oedipus are examples of this erotic bind. Each figure in each tale shows its own variation; the Oedipus complex is but one pattern of son and mother which produces those fateful entanglements of spirit with matter which in the twentieth century we have learned to call neurotic. The very desperation of neurosis shows how strong are their mutual needs and that the attempts to untie this primary knot are truly in the ancient sense agonising and tragic.[23]

But before I came across Hillman, I read Erich Neumann[24] and Jung.[25] They wrote about what could be called false mysticism or infantile spirituality, the kind of "spirituality" that attends the regression of the ego to the condition of the maternal womb. This spirituality, says Neumann, has more to do with pathology than with religion, but it is often mistaken for religion. He calls it "uroboric incest"[26] and Jung refers to it as the psychology of the *puer aeternus*, that is, the eternal youth who has a desire to cling to the past and cannot resist sliding back into the womb at every opportunity. This theme, and complex, was fully explored by Marie-Louise von Franz in *Puer Aeternus: A Psychological Study of the Adult Struggle with the Paradise of Childhood*.[27]

The desire for incest often plays itself out in symbolic terms, as a longing for psychological immersion, protection, containment. Freudians would insist there is a literal dimension to this desire, which is being hidden behind a façade of symbols. Jungians argue in reverse: if there is a literal desire, it is a misreading of the need for spiritual rebirth. However Jungians do not spiritualise this impulse if the underlying tendency is towards self-erasure. Neumann writes that a weak or fragile ego can seek self-dissolution in the mother, and such dissolution has "a profoundly erotic character".

The nascent ego is unable to find its grounding in life, and seeks regression to the source. The "source" is imagined as mother, because the ego is born of the source as a child is born of the mother. Hence in the language of symbols, the ego is "returning to the mother". However this mother is imaged as both calm sea and demonic agent, since "she" is devouring the ego into herself. Neumann calls this aspect of the mother the *uroboros*, the Greek term for the tail-biting snake which devours itself. Often this mother is experienced simultaneously as ecstatic and devouring, in a mixed pleasure-pain experience:

> Self-dissolution is a pleasurable experience, for while the solute, the ego, is weak, the solvent, which finds the dissolution pleasurable, is strong. Unconscious identity with the stronger solvent, the uroboric mother, brings a pleasure which must be called masochistic. The dissolvent sadism of the uroboros and the masochism of the dissolved ego germ coalesce in an ambivalent pleasure-pain feeling.[28]

This gave me the clue I needed. In White's novels, the demonic mother is not just an ancillary figure or irritating presence, she is central to the mystical experience of the protagonists. Self-dissolution is an ambivalent experience but the opposites cannot be contained in the one event. The ego identifies with the pleasurable aspect, and calls it God, Christ, or nirvana, and the demonic aspect is split off and projected upon an army of destructive women. The ego cannot allow itself to integrate the negative, because it would then have to recognise its ideal as bogus, and would have to seek a new kind of orientation.

Writing of the *puer aeternus*, the boy-man who regresses to the source and battles demonic maternal figures, Jung observes:

> Always he imagines his worst enemy in front of him, yet he carries the enemy within himself—a deadly longing for the abyss, a longing to drown in his own source, to be sucked down to the realm of the Mothers. His life is a constant struggle against extinction, a violent yet fleeting deliverance from ever-lurking night.[29]

The son who longs for oblivion "is not conscious of his [destructive wish] and it is projected upon the mother or her symbol".[30] In White's stories, these lethal figures have a heuristic function, but the message they have to deliver is never received, because the male figures are unable to critique their desires. They are too identified with their erotic longings to be able to see them properly.

The double pattern of pleasure-pain and positive masculine vs. negative feminine accords with Tom Singer's description of a typical complex formation. Singer writes:

> A further characteristic of complexes ... is that they tend to be bipolar or consist of two parts. Most often, when a complex is activated, one part of the bipolar complex attaches itself to the ego and the other part gets projected onto a suitable other.[31]

This bipolar structuring of the complex is starkly evident in White's world. The positive side of dissolution is claimed by the ego as its spiritual experience, and the negative aspect is projected onto female figures, thus contaminating the feminine sphere with psychic reality. The ego refuses to own the negative aspect because it would ruin the illusion that it is about to step into a higher state of being. It is, as Singer points out, "easier to settle for the certainty of a complex than wrestle with the emotional ambiguity of inner and outer reality that is constantly challenging the ego".[32] The high price paid is misogyny, fear of castration by the feminine womb, inability to relate to the feminine, and an outside world contaminated with projections. But the price is apparently worthwhile if the ego can remain free of the bipolarity inherent in its attachment to its erotic goal.

The Psyche Tries to Force Change

White's "unconscious" characters are feminine, but in *The Solid Mandala* this character becomes masculine for the first time. This could be because the neglected side of the psychic situation, that is, the pain and "retardation" of the longing for oblivion, has reached a point where it needs to become conscious, or of the same gender as the author. But Arthur, who is described by Waldo as "a big fat helpless female",[33] is a feminine-maternal figure, and virtually androgynous in a psychological sense. White's imagination cannot entirely expunge the feminine from his images of desire, much as he might want to. I would suggest that the unconscious has created Arthur as a ruse, a final and desperate hope to get the male figure to change its perspective, to cancel its tryst with oblivion.

Since the feminine can never persuade the masculine to rethink its longing for oblivion, the imagination has thrown up a quasi-masculine figure to correct the conscious attitude. One of the central tasks of Arthur is to try to urge Waldo to see the feminine in a positive light. We are made aware of "some distress, of feminine origin, fluttering in his big, old-man's body".[34] Waldo, like most of White's male characters, hates women and undermines, ridicules, or attacks them. Arthur tries to defend women against Waldo's attacks, as we find in this scene:

> 'I wonder why Mrs Poulter is so awful?'
> Arthur, puffing, threatened to topple, but saved himself on Waldo's oilskin.
> 'I don't say she's awful!'
> 'If you don't say, it's likely to fester,' said Arthur, and sniggered.
> Some of his remarks were of the kind which should have crumbled along with the cornflour cakes in the mouths of elderly women.
> 'It's splinters that fester,' Waldo answered facetiously.
> 'Perhaps,' said Arthur, and sniggered again.[35]

Arthur is forever trying to force Waldo to reflect on his fear of the feminine, but to no avail.

But what Arthur does manage to achieve is to get Waldo, and White, to cast aside the religious layer of interpretation that has been used to justify their addiction to self-destruction. Only Arthur, of all of White's creations, has the courage to say: "All this Christ stuff ... doesn't seem to work. But we have each other".[36] After this novel, White never again uses the religious framework to describe or interpret the experiences of his characters, because after this novel the fact of obliteration becomes too obvious to hide. In this sense, the novel is pivotal in more ways than one. It brings to a climax a civil war raging in the fiction. Although Arthur fails to encourage Waldo to individuate, to untie the knot to the source, or to overcome his misogyny, he does at least manage to tear down the religious façade that White had erected as an element of his fictional world. Even if individuation is not achieved, at least the delusions of grandeur have stopped, and the stories are allowed to find their own level. In every novel that follows, from *The Vivisector* (1970) to *Memoirs of Many in One* (1986), the desire for the mother and for incest is the goal and object of every male figure in White's fiction.

What happens after *The Solid Mandala*, however, is tragic. Not only does the mystical façade come tumbling down, but the attempt to symbolise the return of the son to the maternal womb is lost. Instead of religion and mysticism, we find incest, sexual depravity, and licentiousness. Not only does the son desire the mother's body, but the mother, too, is imaged in all the later novels as desirous of the son, longing to be penetrated by him. This was predicted in the works of Erich Neumann. He wrote that when the grand symbolic structures are brought down, our desires can become all too crude and vulgar.

The Twyborn Affair (1979), in particular, reveals this problem.[37] Some find the novel fascinating, because in it White makes clear his homosexual orientation, which had been hidden in previous works. I don't think it was hidden very well, but White did attempt to disguise it, presumably because he was ashamed to be homosexual in virile, heterosexual, macho Australia. But *The Twyborn Affair* shows Eddie Twyborn as a transvestite who leads a homosexual lifestyle, whose underlying interest is sexual cohabitation with the mother. And the mother, Mrs. Twyborn, cannot get enough of him. This mother/son desire becomes further apparent in *Memoirs* and after that novel White never writes again. In other words, once the incestuous drama is exposed for what it is, the symbolic world of his fiction collapses. This accords with Jung's notion that it is the canalisation of libido, and its transformation into higher forms, that constitutes the basis for art.[38] It was important that White kept the symbolism going. At least the symbolism was interesting, but when it is taken away we are left with incest and pornography.

The failure to "untie the knot" has taken a toll. If Waldo, or White, had had the courage to follow Arthur's lead, to enter the inner world and release the fatal tie to the source, the symbolic production would have continued, and more than that, flourished. The "knot" is the tie to the source, the tie that prevents the ego from moving into life. It is what clinicians call the mother complex, only I am not keen on the term, as it implies an infantile bind to the personal mother. In White's case, I am not sure that that *is* the problem. It may be, but I am not his therapist and cannot tell. I do know he hated his mother a great deal, and could not even stand living in the same hemisphere as her, as he describes in his autobiography *Flaws in the Glass*.[39] But I do not want to boil down this whole story to an attachment to his mother, and thus lose the cultural and collective dimension. In my view, White was attached to the unconscious and to Neumann's uroboros. He was attached to the ideal of losing self in the infinite expanse of the interior. The tragedy of White's career is that he did not choose the right symbolic frame for his experience. He aimed too high, was attracted to Christianity as his mythic frame, and the enterprise came unstuck when Arthur exposed this as a sham and tried to force an examination of the knotted mandala.

Why the Ego Fails to Act

Why does Waldo fail to untie the knot? I recall the classic literary question: Why does Hamlet procrastinate? Why does he fail to act on the demands of his father's ghost? Freud would say, in both cases: because the male character is terrified of incest, of the potentially devouring womb of the mother. Freud would interpret both problems in a downward, reductive way, and in a sense Freud is right. There does seem to be a love-knot to the mother in Hamlet and Waldo. The symbolism suggests the maternal womb at every turn, and Waldo is terrified of entering it, fearing he might be crushed or never return. At one point in the narrative, Waldo considers having sex with a woman, but he decides the female sexual organ is disease-ridden, and would give him "syph" or "the pox".[40] Freud's diagnosis would be that White suffers from a castration complex, and is unable to enter the female body, for fear of coming out diseased, maimed, or destroyed. This, Freud would claim, is the basis of the homosexuality.

Jung would attempt to place this problem on another level. He would agree with Freud that the psyche constellates the imagery of incest, cohabitation with the mother, and return to the womb. These are apparent in the cases of Waldo and Hamlet. But, Jung would insist, the psyche uses the metaphor of incest when it wants the ego to reconnect with the origin. His intellectual effort in *Symbols of Transformation* was to argue that incest is not the object of libidinal desire. It might look that way, but it is merely a form of literal thinking. We cannot take the metaphor of incest concretely, but must think about it symbolically. Although Freud claimed to be dealing in symbols, he failed to respond to incest as a symbol. Jung cites the famous passage in the Fourth Gospel, where the stunned Nicodemus says to Jesus: "How can a grown man be born? Can he go back into his mother's womb and be born again?".[41] This appears to be the conundrum posed by every Nicodemus, Waldo, or Hamlet who needs to return to the source. Jung believes the anxiety is misplaced, and we should allow ourselves to accept these metaphors and move beyond them:

> Since the son is not conscious of his incest tendency, it is projected upon the mother or her symbol. But the symbol of the mother is not the mother herself, so in reality there is not the slightest possibility of incest, and the taboo can therefore be ruled out as a reason for resistance. In so far as the mother represents the unconscious, the incest tendency, particularly when it appears as the amorous desire of the mother or of the anima, is really only the desire of the unconscious to be taken notice of. The rejection of the unconscious usually has unfortunate

THE AUSTRALIAN RESISTANCE TO INDIVIDUATION

> results; its instinctive forces, if persistently disregarded, rise up in opposition. The more negative the attitude of the conscious towards the unconscious, the more dangerous does the latter become.[42]

Fear of incest, castration, and an Oedipal fate, are errors of perception, according to Jung. He argues we should return to the source and have erotic communion with the unconscious. "Every descent", he says confidently, "is followed by an ascent. No one should deny the danger of the descent, but it *can* be risked".[43] If Freud's mother complex is negative, Jung's is positive: go ahead, risk it, is his advice. Arthur Brown seems to be a better Jungian than Patrick White. He encourages his brother to take the risk, to enter the inner world and move toward the source:

> 'That's all right, Waldo. Because we'll be together, shan't we? And if you should feel yourself falling, I shall hold you up, I'll have you by the hand, and I am the stronger of the two.'[44]

Once again we see the psyche being supportive to Waldo and White, and encouraging of the descent that needs to be undertaken.

As their psychic situation becomes tensely critical, Arthur tries to draw Waldo into the much-needed incestuous embrace. Arthur poses as their mother, Anne Quantrell, and draws Waldo into sexual activity in their parents' bed:

> Except Arthur was not all that innocent. He was waiting to trap him, Waldo suspected, in love-talk.
> So that he broke down crying on the kitchen step, and Arthur who had been waiting, led him in, and opened his arms. At once Waldo was engulfed in the most intolerable longing, in the smell of mutton flaps and dog, of childhood and old men. He could not stop crying.
> Arthur led him in and they lay together in the bed which had been their parents', that is, Waldo lay in Arthur's vastly engulfing arms, which at the same time was the gothic embrace of Anne Quantrell soothing their renegade Baptist. All the bread and milk in the world flowed out of Arthur's mouth onto Waldo's lips. He felt vaguely he should resist such stale, ineffectual pap. But Arthur was determined Waldo should receive. By this stage their smeary faces were melted together.[45]

This is an extraordinary moment, where the theme of incest, buried for so long in this and other stories, reveals itself in full force. The reader who has not intuited the metaphor of incest probably wonders where all this comes from, why Arthur is so insistent that Waldo "should receive", and why Waldo breaks down and "could not stop crying". But this episode, like many others, does not lead to transformation. It is at best a grotesque parody of the spiritual journey that Waldo and White need to undertake. Although the optimistic Arthur keeps saying:"There's time, Waldo, isn't there? There's still time",[46] the reader feels that time is up, as the procrastination has gone on for too long. This 1966 novel throws down the gauntlet: transform or bust. And "bust" it is; the psyche will no longer press its vision of mandalic integration on the characters, but on the contrary it will commence a disintegrative momentum.

The outcome of this novel is evocatively foreshadowed in one of Arthur's spontaneous acts of theatre, which is played out on the front veranda of the Brown house in Terminus Road. Arthur decides to play-act a "Greek tragedy", as he calls it, before his twin and their parents. His play is about a cow, and his father says: "A cow's as Greek, I suppose, as anything else". The tragedy is of a still-born calf and the despair of its mother:

> 'This is a big, *yellow* cow,' he told them. 'She's all blown out, see, with her calf. Then she has this calf. It's dead. See?'
> There was Arthur pawing at the boards of the veranda. At the shiny parcel of dead calf.
> Everyone else was looking at the ground by now, from shame, or Waldo began to feel, terror.
> You can see she's upset, can't you?' Arthur lowed. 'Couldn't help feeling upset.'
> It was suddenly so grotesquely awful in the dwindling light and evening silence.
> 'Couldn't help it,' Arthur bellowed.
> Thundering up and down the veranda he raised his curved, yellow horns, his thick, fleshy, awful muzzle. The whole framework of their stage shook.
> 'That's enough, I think,' said Dad.
> 'Oh, Arthur,' Mother was daring herself to speak, 'we understand enough without your telling us any more.' ...
> Dad got up and limped inside. You could hear him lifting the porcelain shade off the big lamp.[47]

This reminds us of the "play within a play" in *Hamlet*, where Polonius rises in protest and says "give o'er the play" (Act 3, Scene 2), because it has come too close to the dreadful truth. Here we find a portrayal of the tragic situation of Waldo, his father, and every male figure in the White world. The masculine spirit is stuck in the womb and unable to live its own life. If George Brown gets up and limps away, it is because the drama mirrors his own entrapment too clearly, and is too painful to bear.

As this same narrative is told in the "Arthur" section of the novel (Part III), we learn more of Arthur's desperation as he performs this act: "As he stamped up and down, pawing and lowing, for the tragedy of all interminably bleeding breeding cows. By that time his belly was swollen with it. He could feel the head twisting in his guts".[48] The implication is clear: if Arthur is himself the containing, maternal matrix, Waldo is the contained, still-born life within him. The reference to the head "twisting" in his guts is linked to the knot at the centre of the marble. The ego is twisted and knotted up, unable to come to life and dying in the womb. It cannot be born because it does not know how to honour and respect the source in which it is held.

Australia in Search of a Soul

The longing for dissolution exists because we are incompletely separated from the source. We cannot pull away, the effort is too great, and the inertia of the source is overwhelming. The adult struggle with the paradise of childhood is lost. Instead of untying the knot, it tightens around us and crushes the life out of us. I think this is a problem not only of an immature ego but of an immature country. It is part of our cultural complex. We have not developed a secure or stable identity, and the lure toward ecstatic dissolution is intensified. This lure is present in everyone, at all times, but it is increased when the culture is weak and unstable. If the ego has not gained a proper foothold in reality, it easily succumbs to the seductive prospect of self-dissolution. This is why I do not want to reduce White's life and work to a personal mother complex, as that would bring everything down to a banal level. It is my firm persuasion that White's problems are shared by his nation and country at large.

If the ego is prepared to have a real dialogue with the source, and "untie" the erotic bind, a middle term develops between ego and unconscious. This middle term is what Jung calls the anima, the soul, which he defines as the *mediatrix*,[49] that which stands between the ego and its often desiccating rationalism, and the mother and her power to absorb the ego into herself. A nation or country spends time and energy "making soul", not only to adorn its galleries and libraries with great works, but to prevent the human ego from sliding into a nihilistic and fatal regression every time it senses the cruelty and emptiness of the world. We make culture so that we can keep ourselves alive in human reality, and not drown ourselves in the sea of nothingness and its characteristic death-romanticism or suicidal despair.

Australia is a young, undeveloped society, in the late stages of a two-hundred year cycle of colonisation. There is still too wide a gap between the imported European society and the land, between nonindigenous and indigenous people, to allow us to develop a distinctively Australian sense of soul. This gulf generates tension which is expressed in fear, anxiety, and distrust. We must make some connection with the earth and the unconscious, but how do we do it? The ego, fragile at best, dreams of controlling the earth from above or sinking ecstatically into it, in a death-embrace. The Australian ego tries to assert some stable foundation by strenuous efforts at national identity. Competitive international team sports have become a major social arena in which the hopes and desires of the nation are invested, in which we aim to "test" or "prove" ourselves to others, often achieving extraordinary success given the relatively small population. What Adler calls the "masculine protest" operates in force, by which is meant an over-compensation for underlying weakness and insecurity.

There is suspicion between the ego and the other, no matter how the other is imagined. The primary other is the land itself, with which we are still at odds, as is evident in the environmental crisis and the extraordinary depletion and abuse of natural resources.[50] As distinct from the indigenous peoples, the Euro-Australian ego fears the land and seeks to control it, or to get it working on its behalf. The love and respect that allows for an organic connection to place is still lacking. The tension between ego and unconscious is also expressed in distrust between men and women, "the battle of the sexes", in fear of the foreigner and resistance to unconventional values or attitudes that threaten the status quo. As found in our most famous writer, misogyny runs throughout Australian society, but few have tracked it to a problem with the particular kind of "spirituality" that is promoted in masculine culture. Mostly, such misogyny is read as the absence of education or feminist training, in the belief that difficulties between the sexes can be dealt with at a purely conscious level. But the roots of misogyny run deep in a culture that fears the feminine as the site of death and uroboric destruction.

Like White, Australia does not have much of an idea about what myth it might be living. It has a remnant Christianity which was imported from Europe, but it does not sit well in this country. One might say that our mythic inheritance has not survived the long journey down under. Any young nation has to engage in a "Battle for Deliverance from the Mother", as Jung put it.[51] There are plenty of myths that we might explore to help us negotiate our way through the difficult territory of the maternal unconscious, and I am not just thinking of Oedipus or other tragic configurations. There are a host of myths relating to the great mother and the feminine, and Jungian psychology and feminist cultural studies have unearthed many of these lost myths that might be of use to Australians, as we come to terms with our alarming proximity to the unconscious and the chthonic earth.

Of one thing we can be sure. The Australian way will have to work with the mother and not against her. There is not a lot of history here, or at least, not much that can be accessed by those of us who are not indigenous. Lacking history, the country has plenty of geography, and a great deal of physical matter. Our way will not be a work against nature, an *opus contra naturam*, such as we find in Christianity and the myths of Europe and the northern hemisphere. Our way will be an *opus cum natura*, a work with nature, and a way that honours the earth mother and accepts our reliance upon her world. This does not mean we have to be anti-heroic or sink into the embrace of the uroboros. But it means we have to have a conscious relationship with the maternal source that beckons us. The best way to prevent life from being obliterated by the source is to go willingly into the source, and open up a connection between our conscious life and the ground upon which we have our being.

Notes

[1] James Hillman, "The Great Mother, Her Son, Her Hero, and the Puer" (1973), in ed. Patricia Berry, *Fathers and Mothers*, 2nd Edition (Dallas, TX: Spring Publications, 1990), p. 168.

[2] Thomas Singer, "The Cultural Complex and Archetypal Defenses of the Group Spirit", in Thomas Singer and Samuel L. Kimbles, eds., *The Cultural Complex: Contemporary Jungian Perspectives on Psyche and Society* (London and New York: Routledge, 2004), p. 21.

[3] David Tacey, *Edge of the Sacred: Jung, Psyche, Earth* (Einsiedeln, Switzerland: Daimon, 2009), pp. 187–195.

[4] See Craig San Roque, "A Long Weekend: Alice Springs, Central Australia", in Singer and Kimbles, eds., *The Cultural Complex*, pp. 46-61.

[5] Donald Horne, *The Lucky Country* (Melbourne: Penguin, 1971).

[6] See Mircea Eliade, *Rites and Symbols of Initiation: The Mysteries of Birth and Rebirth* (1958, New York: Spring Publications, 2009).

[7] For non-Australian readers, I would point out that Burke, Wills, Leichhardt, and Eyre are famous Australian explorers who perished during

their attempts to explore the interior of the continent. For a brief account of Australian exploration, see Manning Clark, *A Short History of Australia*, Rev. Ed. (Melbourne: Penguin, 2006).

[8] Patrick White, *Voss* (London: Eyre & Spottiswoode, 1957; New York: Viking, 1957).

[9] Judith Wright, "The Upside Down Hut" (1961), in ed. John Barnes, *The Writer in Australia* (Melbourne: Oxford University Press, 1969), p. 335.

[10] Ronald Conway, *The Great Australian Stupor: An Interpretation of the Australian Way of Life* (1971, Melbourne: Sun Books, 1985).

[11] Patrick White, *The Solid Mandala* (1966, Sydney: Vintage, 2007), p. 273.

[12] *Ibid.*, p. 81.

[13] *Ibid.*, p. 30.

[14] Patrick White, *Memoirs of Many in One* (London: Cape, 1986), p. 54.

[15] David Tacey, "Patrick White: The Great Mother and Her Son", *The Journal of Analytical Psychology* (London) 28, 2, April 1983: pp. 165-183.

[16] Patricia Morley, *The Mystery of Unity: Theme and Technique in the Novels of Patrick White* (Toronto: McGill-Queen's University Press, 1972), and Peter Beatson, *The Eye in the Mandala: Patrick White, A Vision of Man* (London: Elek, 1976).

[17] Andrew Riemer, "Visions of the Mandala in *The Tree of Man*", in ed. G. A. Wilkes, *Ten Essays on Patrick White* (Sydney: Angus & Robertson, 1970), p. 116.

[18] Patrick White, *The Vivisector* (London: Cape, 1970), p. 100.

[19] Sigmund Freud, *The Psychopathology of Everyday Life* (1901), *The Standard Edition of the Complete Psychological Works of Sigmund Freud*, Vol. 6 (London: Hogarth Press, 1964), pp. 106-116.

[20] For readers unfamiliar with White's novels, I should point out that Stan Parker is the central character in *The Tree of Man* (London: Eyre and Spottiswoode, 1956), and Himmelfarb is the protagonist of *Riders in the Chariot* (London: Eyre and Spottiswoode, 1961).

[21] Arthur A. Phillips, "Patrick White and the Algebraic Symbol", in *Meanjin* (Melbourne) 24, 4, 1965: pp. 455-61.

[22] David Tacey, *Patrick White: Fiction and the Unconscious* (Melbourne: Oxford University Press, 1988).

[23] James Hillman, "The Great Mother, Her Son, Her Hero, and the Puer", p. 168.

[24] Erich Neumann, *The Origins and History of Consciousness* (1949, Princeton, NJ: Princeton University Press, 1973).
[25] C. G. Jung, *Symbols of Transformation* (1912/1952), in eds. Herbert Read, Michael Fordham, Gerhard Adler and William McGuire *The Collected Works of C. G. Jung*, Vol. 5 (London: Routledge & Kegan Paul; Princeton: Princeton University Press, 1956/1967).
[26] Neumann, *Origins and History of Consciousness*, p. 277.
[27] Marie-Louise von Franz, *Puer Aeternus: A Psychological Study of the Adult Struggle with the Paradise of Childhood* (1970, Santa Monica: Sigo Pres, 1981).
[28] Neumann, *Origins and History of Consciousness*.
[29] Jung, CW 5, para. 553.
[30] Jung, CW 5, para. 450.
[31] Singer, "The Cultural Complex and Archetypal Defenses of the Group Spirit", p. 20.
[32] *Ibid.*, p. 21.
[33] White, *The Solid Mandala*, p. 42.
[34] *Ibid.*, p. 27.
[35] *Ibid.*, p. 28.
[36] *Ibid.*, p. 200.
[37] Patrick White, *The Twyborn Affair* (London: Cape, 1979).
[38] Jung, "Psychology and Literature" (1930/1950), *CW* 15.
[39] Patrick White, *Flaws in the Glass: A Self-Portrait* (London: Cape, 1981).
[40] White, *The Solid Mandala*, p. 116, p. 173.
[41] *The Holy Bible*, John 3: 4.
[42] Jung, CW 5, para. 451.
[43] Jung, CW 5, para. 553.
[44] White, *The Solid Mandala*, p. 211.
[45] *Ibid.*, p. 209.
[46] *Ibid.*, p. 30.
[47] *Ibid.*, p. 40.
[48] *Ibid.*, p. 230.
[49] Jung, "Flying Saucers: A Modern Myth" (1958), *CW* 10, para. 715.
[50] See David Tacey, "Ecopsychology and the Sacred: the Psychological Basis of the Environmental Crisis", in *Spring: A Journal of Archetype and Culture* 83 (2010), pp. 329-352.
[51] Jung, CW 5, para. 419-63.

Kris Wyld is New Zealand born, of Anglo-Irish and German origins. She spent formative years in London with her husband Paul. She now lives in Sydney. Her 13-year creative partnership with Steve Knapman began on the Australian Broadcasting Commission with the groundbreaking crime series, *Wildside* (1998/99). In the often-intense arena of production process, she and Steve developed a robust professional relationship—essential for any creative partnership. The values of relationship are a major theme in her work with *East West 101*. She was nominated for an Australian Film Industry (AFI) Script Award for Episode 2, *East West 101*. The entire series has now won many awards including the AFI Best Mini Series and the Australian Writers' Guild Award for Best Mini Series, Scripts.

Craig San Roque wrote the chapter "The Lemon Tree: A Conversation on Civilisation" in this volume and biographical information about him appears there.

●●●●●●●●●●●●●

East West 101, set in Sydney, offers an engaging way of observing how cultural complexes surface in multi-racial cities. Sydney is the largest city in Australia, containing 20.5% of the Australian population. It is one of the most multi-cultural cities in the world with significant numbers of its inhabitants of British descent, of Aboriginal descent, and of Mediterranean and Asian origin, with Vietnamese, former Yugoslavians, Lebanese, Maori, Pacific Islanders, and a fast-growing Muslim population. Ethnically diverse immigrants from distressed countries suffuse the urban culture. It is a city composed of many "contact zones"; Sydney, the site of the original 1788 convict settlement, is also a city of "a truant disposition" (to borrow a nice phrase from Hamlet, Act1, Scene ii).

East West 101 presents a fictional multi-ethnic crime squad working in Sydney. The squad engages a cross-section of criminal connections on local and international scale, while simultaneously handling internal intrigue and personal tension. The Squad's condition is, according to the producers, "a metaphor for East and West, for the conscious and unconscious, for reconciliation and difference, for hope versus despair". This series places Sydney in the global web, giving an international viewer insight into things rippling beneath the gloss of the highly vaunted "Emerald City".

12

Sydney–"a city of truant disposition": *East West 101* (the 2008-2011 Knapman Wyld Australian TV Series)

Craig San Roque with Kristine Wyld

That which is not brought to you as consciousness comes to you as fate.
— quoted by Steve Knapman for East West 101

Orientation

This is not a "journo-elegant" media article, such as you might slickly read in the weekend papers…you know the thing: "Kris rocked up to the café, sliding into the chair, ordering black coffee with caviar on the side, her chic leather jacket aglow with promise, her red hair flaming with new ideas… 'Tell me about *East West 101*', I said, brushing back my razor bald head…" "The Russians are running the Sydney underworld", she said, "Keep your back to the wall…"

Not on your life, mate—nothing like that.

This chapter comes to you through a conversation beginning some four years ago when Kristine Wyld mentioned to me that she was developing a new crime series featuring, controversially, a Muslim Australian detective investigating incidents involving both Muslim and Anglo perpetrators. Subsequently, (in June 2011) after having seen the complete series, and having listened to some of the crew talking to their experience, I invited Wyld to consider the notion of the cultural complex. We spoke together on a number of occasions, and we were influenced by Don Stevens, an elderly American with extensive experience in the middle east, who had worked intensively for mutual understanding between creeds. It is not always possible here to differentiate Wyld's thoughts from my own, though I take responsibility for the final synthesis. Background material is available through the *East West 101* production website.[1] We draw especially upon a concept of *Taqwa* and *Jihad* from Ali Rafik, a police consultant to this perceptive television series, supported wisely and with risk by Australia's national "Special Broadcasting Service" (SBS).

Creation and Development of *East West 101*

The plays the thing wherein I'll catch the conscience of the king.
Hamlet, Act 2 Scene ii

Stand up comics and crime writers have permission to prick the conscience of king or country. Shakespeare packed Macbeth, Hamlet, and King Lear into the little wooden theatre on the banks of the Thames 400 years ago. Much earlier, Sophocles (496- 406 BC) placed on the rock-hewn stage in Athens a prototypical criminal investigation. Theban king Oedipus, bewildered and full of righteousness, sets out to solve the enigma of former king Laius's death only to be revealed as the fateful, though unknowing, killer himself. In a three-part "series" known as the *Oresteia,* Aeschylus of Eleusis (525-456 BC) develops the story of Orestes, who killed his mother Clytemnestra for murdering his father Agamemnon. It too is a prototypical drama in Western civilisation—a heartrending, enduring cycle of crime, justice, revenge, and reparation set as aftermath to the 10-year war of Troy. The *Oresteia* is a generational, PTSD (Post Traumatic Stress Disorder) tragedy of remorseless ethic and illumination. There are no triumphant heroes.

The classic dramatists of many cultures and certain filmmakers today have a way of revealing that which most of us feel, sense, and almost know, but haven't thought out until we see it in the mirror of the screen. Such artists function as our cultural psychoanalysts, interpreters of unconscious configurations. They shed light on our cultural complexes. Like the blinded bi-sexual seer, Tiresias, in *Oedipus Rex*, they lay out the entrails of the city-state.

East West 101 continues this tradition, it flows in the slipstream of these predecessors. The title phrase, "*East West*", hints (intentionally) at a line from the famous Rudyard Kipling poem, encapsulating interracial attitudes from British Indian Empire times— "East is East and West is

West and never the twain shall meet". That sentiment may have been true "once upon a time": but now the East/West meetings do take place. The "twain" do meet. The web of crime, business, and war is setting for such meetings; our global cities are fragrant attractors. The Muslim/Anglo conflict embodied in *East West 101* by Muslim detective Zane Malik and his relation with Anglo Senior Detective Sergeant Crowley (in Season One) and later with others is, as the producers say, "a metaphor for the fear that exists between East and West".

Lim, Koa, Malik and Travis at a crime scene. East West 101. Series 3. Photo by Jimmy Pozarik.

East West 101 was conceived and produced by Steve Knapman and Kris Wyld, directed by Australian Greek, Peter Andrikidis, and developed in collaboration with a team of local writers and police consultants of relevant cultural background. The producers didn't deliberately set out to analyse a " cultural complex", as such, but somehow their series does indeed "catch the conscience…". Kris describes an initial motivation:

> My Grandmother was German, and I wanted to know what happened to my grandparents in New Zealand during WWII when Germans were the hated "other". And what happened to the interned Italians in Australia during WWII? I researched this for a teleplay—but prejudices about the "other" do not

> disappear, they just take on a new target. With *East West 101* I wanted to explore this in the present. I wanted to know how it was for Muslims during the Post 9/11 crises. .... I wanted to break down the prejudices of people about Muslims following 9/11.

Kris Wyld has "done the time" in other cultures—with influential and instructive encounters with people sincerely devoted to Islam. She has taken the care to attend to Sufi, Iranian-Parsee, and Hindu storytellers immersed in the great works of the prophets, the Koran, the Upanishads, the Mahabharata. She acknowledges the humility and richness of ethical thought, which keeps in place the central integrity of such spiritual traditions —held as though they were beads on one string.

Kris continues: "While developing this series, Steve and I consulted with experienced detectives—they have been crucial to the show's authenticity. Detective Ali Rafik, a policeman in Sydney with over 15 years experience investigating major crime, has been involved in the series since its inception and has helped guide the writers, producers, and actors through what it means to be Muslim, and a policeman, in Australia.

Kris kindly passed on this reflection by Rafik:

> Even though September 11 (2001) was years ago, Muslims and Arab Australians are still viewed with fear and suspicion. And it's not getting better, it's getting worse. People don't associate us with law enforcement and the delivery of law, they see us as the recipients. We're still seen as a threat to society through crime, terrorism, and rejection of Australian values. Barack Obama said in his inauguration speech "we shouldn't compromise our ideals of security." But this is something that so-called Islamic extremists are guilty of. They will compromise Islamic ideals, especially *jihad*, to the extent of abandoning Islamic principles and behaviour.

According to Kris: "Rafik is a literary man who thinks deeply about what is important for those Muslims in Australia whose hope is to create an integrated society. Rafik was crucial in bringing the story and characters alive through his own experiences and that of his family and friends. These are people who also deal with the pain of betrayal, not only among 'Auzzi brothers'[2] but also the betrayal of Islam's core values by persons advocating violence against others. I felt that, truly, Rafik was the one to tell this story—the story of where hope is found and where and how betrayal is found—hope and betrayal is a theme in the *East West 101* story because it is a theme in the Australian story".

"I had to ask myself, why am I (an Anglo-European Aussie) telling this story and not Rafik or Don Hany (who plays Malik) himself? The hard fact is that it takes about ten years to get the writing experience to pull off this kind of complex work. It's a high risk, often low paid endeavour. The children of recent immigrants often look to success in other, more traditional fields. It is incredibly hard to break into television writing without contacts." To this she added: "On one commercial channel, working on another police story—we were not allowed to have 'people with accents'. The network executives were only interested in the ethnics being the 'crooks'".

This leads to the questions of "who speaks for Australia?"; who truly represents Australia and what sector of Australians are permitted to have the microphone?[3] There is a Russian novel, *Angels on the Head of Pin*, which is partly about an editor of the *Pravda* newspaper in Moscow during the Cold War.[4] Speaking about the Central Committee's entitlement to control *Pravda*, the narrator muses on the editor's deft handling of the Communist State Central Committee as it dictated what *Pravda* could print: "What worried him most was the strategy of the whole thing, that is the topics that stretched from issue to issue over the long term, as well as the planned absence of other topics, another strategy of the newspaper that had been entrusted to him...".

I believe it was "the planned absence" from the commercialised television channels of a fair deal for Muslim and ethnic peoples which incensed Knapman and Wyld, then stimulated them to develop this series and to consult with insider community members and policemen like Ali Rafik. Neither Steve nor Kris could tolerate the experience of being implicated in the Australian cultural conspiracy, a cultural complex pressure, if you like; a subliminal insistence that media artists absent themselves from speaking their right mind. Steve and Kris (as citizens) detected the covert pressure to stay quiet, to comply with the "planned absences". They rejected the assault on spiritual intelligence.

Local and commercial network television in Australia has never seriously approached the idea that "we" might be wrong. The convention has always followed the George Bush cowboy/John Howard cricketer's formula: "We are good—they are bad". "They are wrong—we are right". "We are in—you are out". Kevin Rudd was presented as the new and popular choice for an ethical Prime Minister following Howard's fall in 2007. Rudd challenged an engrained view of history with his formal Apology speech made in 2008 to the displaced children of indigenous people known as "The Stolen Generation" (as Melinda Turner outlines in her chapter in this book). But his own party, on the excuse that he was failing in popularity, politically displaced Prime Minister Rudd, after only two years in office. Some attribute this fall from grace (and the coup) to Rudd's hubris and alleged intolerant micro management.[5] Others might attribute the fall to conventional, intolerant, simplicity of mind. "You are in or you are out—you are right or you are wrong", and nothing in between.

As dramatised in *East West 101*, most of our enemies, however, lie within our own borders, no one is entirely right or wrong, and many criminals wear nice suits, or represent forces of seemingly intelligent governance and good intention. The complexity and nuance found in *East West 101* is rare in Australian media. Perhaps this is why *East West 101* seems to have hit a nerve and in the process won a dozen or more major awards, including the New York Film and Television Mini-series World Gold Medal 2010. Ali Rafik confirms that the show has been immensely popular in the Muslim community, with scenes shot inside Sydney Muslim settings. Malik is present at Friday prayers at the local mosque; there are sharp discussions with Mullahs and differing views expounded on violent political and religious actions, echoing actual events in the city and terror acts abroad at the time. Rafik comments: "People who don't watch TV at all have watched every episode of Season 1, because of Malik. They adore him. A young Lebanese boy told me his surprised grandmother insisted he should watch the show 'because there are Arabs being good'".

East West 101 is set against the familiar Anglo-Celtic code of silence that suggests it's better not to say much (and especially not in front of the women and kids). The "Australian silence" may be thought of as a compounded enculturated complex derived partly from our history, including restrained gender relations, the shock of war experience, migrant refugee cautions and criminal /political alliances that covertly declare: if you speak out, they'll "shut you up". Patrick White might have done a cultural complex revelation job for earlier times of Australian social history, as in his *Ham Funeral, Solid Mandala,* and *Riders in the Chariot*[6], coughing up bleak bile and a clammy mysticism of our 1950s stagnant existence. The Knapman/ Wyld saga lifts the cultural detection game into post 9/11, 2011 times, revealing fateful trajectories of justice and ethics in a time of urban anxiety. Cultural complexes are characterised by formulaic plots that repeat simple ideas versus the real complexities of life. *East West 101* challenges formulaic, enculturated habits of behaviour and thought.

Main Characters of *East West 101*

Zane Malik, the centrifugal character in the series, is of Muslim immigrant family living in Western Sydney. Don Hany, the actor who plays

Malik, is from similar background, as is Malik's brain-injured father (played by Hany's own father). Malik's wife and children feature throughout as domestic counterpoint to Malik's preoccupations with justice, crime, war, and the ways of God.

Sonny Koa, Malik's detective partner, is from the Islands. To the north of Australia lie the Torres Strait/Arafura and Coral Seas, New Guinea, and Melanesia. To the east are the Polynesian island populations of Samoa, Tonga, Tahiti, Fiji, and Aotearoa New Zealand, home of the Māori. Islander peoples share cultural streams, warrior mentality, and long associations with coastal Aboriginal groups. Many Islanders worked for the sugarcane, pearling, and timber industries. Aaron Fa'aoso, who plays Koa, is from the Torres Strait. He brings to the Koa role a humour and gravity that is true to Islander nature.

Sonny Koa (Aaron Fa'aoso) confronts Reweti's islander gang. Photo by Jimmy Pozarik.

Senior Detective Crowley is toughened, taciturn, with long-term experience of the Australian criminal mentality. He sets a tone. Crowley, recognisably of working class Anglo background, and often vulnerable, suggests a tired man out of his depth among Muslims and Asians. William MacInnes, who plays Crowley, sees him as "the bridge between two Australias, between the idea of multiculturism and its implementation in the institutionalised segment…the police force".

Detective Inspector Patricia Wright is the Commander of the Major Crime Squad and keeps a tight rein on it. She is of hard-bitten Anglo (and tragic) background, her father also a policeman. Wright embodies, unlike Crowley, Australian cultural attitudes in transition, moving with the times, accepting dramatic changes in the role and potency of women as well as the ethnic fluidity of the cities. Susie Porter beautifully portrays the Commander with a tense subtlety that holds the gravity of the team to its ethical purposes. In researching her role, Wyld says that Porter consulted with women of authority in the force and she portrays Wright as embodying their qualities. Though Wright is often "on edge" and exhausted by contradictions, the pace of chaos and her family worries, we see her managing the destructiveness of men and women with a confident, feminine, and dedicated constancy.

Agent Richard Skeritt (featured in Season Two), played by Gerald Lepkowski, is enigmatic, a sophisticated principle special operations agent of the fictional National Security Organisation (NSO). He represents the type of Australia's smooth *internationalismo*.

Detective Neil Travis (Matthew Nable) featured in Season Three, brings to his police role a melancholic, tightly coiled sobriety as a veteran of special operations in the Afghanistan/Iraq campaigns.[7]

Detective Helen Callas (Daniela Farinacci) and *Constable Jung Lim*, (Renee Lim), both bring qualities of directed intelligence to their support roles, qualities that are recognisably characteristic of Sydney's streetwise, compassionate yet tough-minded professional women.

Synopsis of *East West 101*

East West 101 is not a stereotypic, alpha male action conflict. If you want to keep an eye on the play of cultural complexes in the streets of Sydney, then your eye does not need to be upon the detail of each story in this series but, rather, upon the web of relational dynamics among the police crew, among criminals, and among the families of all the interlocking characters. A synopsis is necessary, so you know where you are, but the web revealed inside the twenty episodes exposes patterns mixing personal and cultural forces that may tell much about Australia's present state of being.

Series One: Synopsis
Episodes 1-6: "The Enemy Within", "Death at the Station", "Islander Sacrifice", "Hunt for a Killer", "Haunted by the Past", and "The Hand of Friendship"

"The first season of *East West 101* (2008) came out of the turbulence of the post 9/11 world, where we explore dramatically the situation of Zane Malik, as he confronts racism at work and in the world", Wyld says. Series One focuses on the dynamic of style within criminal investigations as conducted by the tight-lipped, hard-arsed incumbent Anglo detective Sergeant Crowley and the incoming duo of Zane Malik and Sonny Koa. We learn that Malik is "driven by a hunger for justice." When he was boy of twelve, a masked gunman held up the family shop, and young Zane, who was at the counter, refused to hand over the money. In the altercation Zane's father was shot. Since joining the metropolitan police force, "Malik", as the series synopsis tells us, "has been looking for the shadowy figure who pulled the trigger".

Zane Malik at home with his wife and his father. Photo by Jimmy Pozarik.

Zane Malik's story brings in family circumstances and his endearing, devotional father who suffers the brain damage for which Malik blames himself. We have here a psychological history characteristic of the style of the whole series. No crime occurs without there being a psychic resonance in the private complexities of the investigators. All the investigators have traumatic or tangled biographies. Malik is moved by a dedication to seek retribution for his father's shooting; this dedication may or may not prove his undoing. When he does come upon the shooter, Malik's belief in the restraining process of the Australian justice system is challenged by a powerful desire for immediate personal revenge.

It is revealed that Crowley had a part to play in the original investigation. But will Crowley now help or maliciously hinder Malik? Crowley's son simultaneously (in the deepening plot) is found dead of a drug overdose, sold to him by a Lebanese dealer. (Sydney has a significant Lebanese immigrant population.)[8] When the drug dealer turns up murdered, investigators from Police Internal Affairs come asking questions. Was this murder Crowley's own version of taking personal revenge? Our impressions of Sergeant Crowley change when the story comes to a paradoxical turn and we discover Crowley' family background and his effort, as a father, to prevent, then avenge, his son's drug-induced fate. Once this is revealed, the Sergeant may evoke pity and understanding. Crowley's eventual death/ suicide at the end of Season 1 completes a circle.

The entire Season One's six episodes, from "The Enemy Within" to "The Hand of Friendship", has multiple intersecting plot lines involving investigations among Vietnamese and Serbian enclaves, Lebanese and Islander gang subplots, and a shooting in central city suburb, Redfern, that takes us into background situations of a dedicated Aboriginal lawyer/anti-drugs campaigner, Adam King (played by Aboriginal actor Aaron Pedersen). This glimpse into indigenous urban politics rings true, as does the unfortunate fact that, carelessly, Adam hasn't cottoned on that his Anglo accountant/ office manager has been siphoning off his finances (to support a homosexual boyfriend). Entanglements abound. This is the stuff on which Australian nightmares are made, not the violence only, but the entanglements of agents of justice wrestling with layered dilemmas involving their family members, partners, and colleagues. Emerging also are the intimacies of the police team, including an ambivalent, sexualised attachment between Commander Patricia Wright and Crowley. The erotic politics of workplace affairs is a cultural theme all of its own, worked into the scripts with a matter-of-fact, unromantic edge.

Series Two: Synopsis
Episodes 7-13: "The Lost Boy", "A Prodigal Fear", "Just Cargo", "Ice in the Veins", "Men of Conscience", "Another Life", and "Atonement"

The second season looks at how, in the recent past, Australia has become a part of the "climate of fear". The first episodes erupt around the operations of the National Security Organisation (NSO) investigating an alleged Islamic extremist car bombing in a suburban shopping area—a case also being handled by Malik and company. Wyld says "We thought about what Malik's worst fear might be and then created a situation where he had to confront it. A car bomb is blamed on Muslims...he hopes it's not true. But what if it is? He goes on a quest to find out the truth. Season 2 of *East West 101* begins to look into Malik's inner life. Is Malik a good man? A good Muslim? And what is that, anyway in an Australian context?".

Malik and Koa on surveillance. Photo by Jimmy Pozarik.

The NSO principle agent, Richard Skerritt, is a disturbing character, at home amid the intrigues of Washington, London, and the Canberra intelligence bureaucracies. Skerritt, using moral pressure, persuades Malik to become an undercover agent embedded in a gun/drug operation run by a known Muslim operator, who may or may not be connected to the bombing. Malik's decision to go undercover is contrary to the wishes of

Malik's enduringly intelligent wife. (Throughout the series the depiction of Malik's family and the Islamic community relations establish a recognisable context that appealed to the Muslim viewing audience.) Back on the explosive, fast-talking screen, things get very dangerous—the lines of betrayal are labyrinthine. Detective Inspector Wright (bless her) falls for the seductive Skerritt—(how can she do that?) The deceased man identified as the victim of the car bomb may or may not be dead—may or may not be a people smuggler or gunrunner or under-cover agent. The bomb may not be an Islamic extremist plant after all; and anyway the NSO agent turns out to be, nastily, not what he seems. Manipulative betrayals and errors of judgement writhe along through this confusing, very Australian, very messy operation. It is so plausibly accurate as to how our politicised bureaucracies are known to mishandle, misjudge, or manipulate affairs of internal national significance, including asylum refugee management, international relations, and localised fear. By the time you get to this part of the series the bottom is falling out of any conventional expectations that this will be a formulaic Aussie police story.

Meanwhile, resolute Commander Wright is having a bad time with her kid brother's criminal mates and with her own father, himself an iconic, laconic, Aussie ex-copper, thoroughly at home in the macho corruption of inner city underworlds. The issue here, as with Crowley and Malik, is exactly how Wright and her father will sort out the criminal entanglements of the fatefully narcissistic younger son, yet retain some kind of police ethics. No body wins much in this series.

Series Three: Synopsis
Episodes 8-20: "The Hero's Standard," "Heart of Darkness," "Jerusalem", "Transit of Venus", "Price of Salvation", "Behold a Pale Horse", and "Revelation".

As Kris Wyld says, "Season 3 (2010/11) presented a new challenge to Steve and me on a conceptual level. By the time we were working on Season 3, post 9/11 had become post Iraq. So we looked at the impact of war on men, women and children.... the War Zones of Iraq and Afghanistan. And the actions of private security companies with immunity and the contradiction of 'liberation' versus 'occupation'...".

Steve was interested in exploring the universal truths of the experience of combat on men, as well as the "collateral damage" of innocent civilians that was the consequence of such supposed "humanitarian intervention". Steve drew upon a line from the World War 1 poet, Wilfred Owen, whose phrase "the pity of war" and "the poetry is in the pity" gave us a note for the tone of the drama. T.S. Eliot's poem, *The Hollow Men*, gave us the inspirational lines:

> The eyes are not here, there are no eyes here. In this valley of dying stars / in this hollow valley / this broken jaw of our lost kingdoms...

Those lines visualised for us the mountains of Afghanistan and the disillusionment of the futility of unjust wars and the jingoism of the politicians who promote it, so well expressed by Siegfried Sassoon in his poem on the WWI memorial known as the Menin Gate. On that Gate are inscribed 54,889 soldiers' names. Sassoon writes:

> Here was the world's worst wound. And here with pride / 'their name liveth forever,' the Gateway claims. / Was ever an immolation so belied / as these intolerably nameless names? / Well might the Dead who struggled in the slime/Rise and deride this sepulchre of crime.

"During that period", says Steve, "Bush and Blair's speeches were ringing in our ears, and we asked: "Do we learn anything from history?". Robert Fisk's book *The Great War for Civilisation: The Conquest of the Middle East* suggests, as Steve says, that the answer is, "Apparently not". "We wanted to dramatise such a suffering through our characters, here in Australia. To pose the great question: What is the meaning of life in the face of death? We don't supply answers. But we did want to challenge that "hand on the heart" notion of patriotism and whether The Hero's Journey is a myth that is hollow at the core. We looked at the impact of war on men, women, and children, and since our protagonist, Zane Malik, is a detective... we looked at that impact (also) through crime".

A "full on" violent robbery kicks off Series Three. Thirty six million dollars stolen, four men killed. One is a middle-eastern gang member with intriguing international connections. The robbery has the marks of a military operation. Malik's task is to find the men responsible. The task takes on a very personal edge. His son and wife are in a (collateral) car accident at the time of the robbery, and his son dies. Malik suspects a vehicle fleeing the scene hit the family car. (Every violent action in Australia impacts on an intimate community situation, the "degrees of separation" are small and so many crimes affect people connected to oneself.)

In Season Three, Malik experiences a tragedy and grief that, Kris says, allowed in the Muslim element of *Taqwa*, which was explored through the character of Malik and his Islamic family. The *East West 101* consultant detective, Ali Rafiq, has said that *Taqwa* means, "being conscious of the one and only creator of the universe...being aware that death is a heart beat away and when death arrives you will be accountable for each and every deed". *"Taqwa"*, Rafiq continues, "is the key to achieving a balance in life, avoiding acts that are harmful to others and to yourself. Achieving and maintaining *Taqwa* is not easy, it is a constant struggle, the struggle with yourself. A Jihad". Westerners are familiar with term *Jihad* being used to justify war and terrorist actions such as the 9/11 suicide mission—it has the connotation of "just war against unbelievers, in the name of Allah..." but Rafiq counters this extreme view. Kris Wyld recounts how Rafiq says, "In Arabic, *'Jihad alnafs'*;—is also known as the 'greater Jihad'. [This is the struggle with oneself.] "In this series, Malik struggles with death and loss and his fight against the criminals. As a person, how does he keep it together? How does he take on the criminals under such difficult emotional grief? His strongest weapon, if he can bring it to bear, is *Taqwa* - positive light...the conduct of *Taqwa* is conduct in a light that's fair".

Island Drive-by

Also, during Series Three, Sonny Koa, now established as ethically alert and emotionally warm, investigates a drive-by shooting among his

Malik and Koa, in western Sydney, restrain the young Islander gang member, Sam. Photo by Jimmy Pozarik.

own Islander community. Like Malik, Crowley, and Wright, Sonny too has to deal with moral and professional decisions about crime and tragedy among his own kin—specifically a young relative, Sam, who is being sucked into a violent Māori/Sydney gang. It is here that Australian and New Zealand's different warrior clans conflict. In a startlingly stupid act of retributive arrogance, the Māori drive-by mob shoot up Sam and his mother's house. Koa is also inside, visiting. Sam's mother is shot in the line of random fire. Suddenly we see Sonny himself dealing with the loss of a beloved female Islander kin. There are moments in that scene of grief that are so memorable and so characteristic of repetitive indigenous tragedy. Normally, few Anglo/Euro/Asian Australians see inside, close-up, the raw and domestic feelings of Islanders. The emotional sophistication revealed in that shattered Islander family room, and in similar scenes among the Islamic families, is a tribute to the actor's craft, to the director/writers and the cinematographers who, throughout the twenty episodes unflinchingly handle archetypal feeling states that the Australian complex of silence, and "dumbing down" would have us ignore. Andrikis' directorial eye takes us inside the cultural "clouds of unknowing", opening to view also culturally defined styles of memory, lamentation, and mourning. Different ethnic viewers can see inside the domestic lives of Koa, Malik, Wright, Crowley, Jung Lim, Helen Callas, the victims of different crimes and, finally, we see inside the Travis/Iraq/Afghanistan crew in Episodes 19 and 20, *Behold a Pale Horse* and *Revelation.*

Meanwhile, in Season Three, Episode 17, "The Transit of Venus", written by Michael Miller, Inspector Wright is intent on putting away a malicious taxi driver with a very bad history of raping female passengers. While the taxi driver is still under investigation, and on bail, a man in disguise breaks into her apartment and manages to sexually assault her. This is one of the most wrenching yet understated scenes in the whole twenty-hour cinematic series. "Transit of Venus" is also another situation in this series where secure lines collapse between the criminal and the professional. I believe that the pattern throughout *East West 101* of the collapse of the boundaries is repeated for very good reason. I am thinking that it is a psychological reason related to the effort by the writers, by Kris and Steve and by the actors themselves, to get to the cutting edge of something that troubles many Australians. It might be about the fear, or the insecurity, the cultural anxiety, the uncertainty of living in a country unsure of its moral nature and future. Australia does witness the collapse of many traditional codes of behaviour, of justice, and religion. The series may also carry something about the sustained effort needed to place oneself psychically in this city—this country. This effort, a kind of individuation effort in the midst of the concrete mysticism of Sydney street life may have something to do with Rafiq's Islamic notion of *Taqwa*. Rafiq, the police consultant said, if you will remember, "*Taqwa* is the key to achieving a balance in life, avoiding acts that are harmful to others and to yourself. Achieving and maintaining *Taqwa* is not easy, it is a constant struggle, the struggle with yourself; in Arabic the term, '*Jihad alnafs*' conveys the idea of the struggle with yourself. This is also known as the 'greater Jihad'".

While the abusive retaliatory tale, "Transit of Venus" unveils Patricia Wright as a professional woman in private struggle with herself (after the rape), the main game returns in "The Pale Horse" episodes and the activities of the group of soldiers, all mates of Detective Travis from the Iraq/Afghanistan theatre of war. Here is where Wyld and Knapman face up to the post traumatic stress disorder story of men who participated in the war against the so-called "Axis of Evil". We lost Crowley in Season One; Agent Skerritt is possibly disgraced in Season Two, though no doubt he'll get a job in another government department. So we are joined now by Detective Travis and his story, the camera repetitively placing him in a flashback special operation in the Iraq campaign,[9] and then again in Sydney, investigating the major armed robbery that began Series Three. As Malik and company progress further into this investigation, the evidence links the robbery to events in the Middle East and to the military team associated with Travis. Detective Malik, now a veteran of undercover operations, has cause to no longer trust Travis, though the audience has a wider view, since we see him unmasked in certain intimate situations.

Travis, as masterfully portrayed by Matt Nable, is so recognisable as an Australian "damaged man", a war veteran. He conveys an existential tension exactly accurate to that of a human being entangled in ethical paradox and conflicting loyalties. Travis is seen in dangerous intimacies with his ex army "brothers", one of whom he tries to rescue from a suicidal oblivion; and, most movingly, we see him in a terrifyingly eruptive bedroom scene with his exquisitely patient female detective partner Constable Jung Lim. Such contradictory behaviours will be appreciated by those who are familiar with the psychic patterns of the trauma disorders.

Through the episodes "Behold a Pale Horse" and "Revelation", Travis is slowly opening his eyes and deciding who among the Crime Squad needs to know what about what is really happening among his "brothers" and to himself, post Iraq.

I can't help but feel this slow revelation in terms of the cultural complex. Throughout the series, slow revelations dawn upon this character and that.

I speak for myself here, and I speak as someone who has, throughout the work on this book, been trying to get the feel of what it's like to be caught up in a cultural complex and then get clear of it. I can say now that there is a kind of cumulative identification process going on as I watch Malik and family and then Koa and then Wright and then Travis, in their tense situations. Their family members, and the families of many of the victims and perpetrators are all portrayed so authentically caught, enmeshed in something so familiar, so much a part of the city/psyche with which I too am imbued. There is a difference between a drama which glosses you along, pulling strings for this effect or that—and a drama which can, by means of hidden integrity of theme, take you progressively on a slow revelation, a kind of long night's journey into day. "The day", in this case not being some bright reassurance but a kind of dawning recognition that yes, this is how it is here, and yes, all those tangled themes are there, and yes, I can wake up from it. I do not have to wade forever and ever in the morass and mire of a complex. A complex "system" woven into the culture exerts an influence upon me, this I know. And the morass and mire of a complex exists, it has a life of its own, a content—it is made up of something that may be difficult for a normal mind to describe precisely; that's why I have trouble with describing this unconscious cultural complex and that. Certain dramatists catch the conscience of a country and a time. The content of a complex can be laid bare, at least on stage. Sophocles in setting out the family drama of Thebes catches the conscience of the Oedipus generations—a state inherited by Freud. On the beaches of Turkey, at Troy, shiploads of soldiers came to grief—and back home afterwards, when Agamemnon returns, the grievous psychic harm continued; as depicted on the Athens stage by Aeschylus. Could it be that Aeschylus' Trilogy, the *Oresteia*, depicts the content of a cultural complex of the time?

Travis against a wall. The war zone, Series 3, Episode 19, "Behold a Pale Horse". Photo by Jimmy Pozarik.

And perhaps Hamlet, once a clean and clear prince of Denmark, finds himself stumbling mumbling into a depression brought about, no doubt, by the murder of his father the King, the adulterous betrayals of his mother and peers of the realm, and then the insidious collapse of the state to such an extent that he could no longer manage it, preferring to die in a futile fire fight. But that was long time ago—what about now in the suburbs of this truant city Sydney? How to describe the influence and the content of the complexes that suffuse the minds of my own country? How do we describe it? How is the structure and dynamic of a near and present complex revealed? In the mirror, perhaps, of a television screen, an ordinary television screen.

At the end of episode 20, "Revelation", on a Sydney waterfront, the drug-running war veteran gang is cornered. Malik can see who killed his own son. Malik can see Travis make his own stand against that same man, an ex-officer in Travis' Iraq special operations unit.

The men on the beach may be sacrificed; they may end like Travis in a death, a stoic professional pathos of a passing in the course of duty. The Malik/ Koa duo cannot stage a heroic rescue and as Malik himself says in a throwaway final line, "...there are no heroes". When things come to a head, things slip away. The writing of this sequence, the setting by the darkened spot-lit, rock-strewn Sydney beach and Travis' taut yet resigned demeanour does, in my view, place the *East West 101* finale on the stage of Greek tragedy traditions. It does this not because of the tragedy of losing a favoured character but because the pace and writing of the episode allows a kind of revelation to fill one's body. The revelation, I mean, that nudges one into recognising the quiet progressive truth of how one can be incubated within a cultural complex and yet, also, incrementally emerge from its cocooning.

A Final Word: Our Country of Destruction—Flaws of Undoing

"Flaws of undoing" is a theme of *East West 101*. Perhaps the fatal flaw of Detective Sergeant Crowley is a narcissistic sense of entitlement, a taken-for-granted heroic vanity that eventually becomes his undoing. Richard Skerritt likewise exudes a self-assured superior "sense of entitlement" that is just as narcissistic as Crowley's. Such an attitude seems to be part of a cultural *hubris* collectively and politically propagated in Australia. Not only the Anglos do this—we see it portrayed in many of the ethnic characters under investigation. Narcissistic ethnocentric entitlement (I believe) becomes one of the implicit drivers of cultural complex entanglement and human conflict. It is a sense of entitlement that keeps one blind to the facts of a complex.

Thoughts like these arise in the aftermath. Thought doesn't come fully formed while one watches a drama. *East West 101* moves fast, so fast you might miss the inner complexity; and anyway, it's hard to follow everything that those fast-talking Sydney people say.

I have come away reassured, inspired from these meetings with the *East West 101* story. I believe that altogether this work has accomplished something very special, very psychological, in a useful kind of way. I leave the engagement with a question: What kind of moral imperative (right action) is at work here in Australia? How do we alter the balance, engage in the greater jihad, the internal struggle with ourselves as countrymen? Our ruder politicians specialize in dualistic combat, reviling each other in parliament and the press in the name of keeping the other party "honest". Such dualistic extremism sets an insidious pattern of intolerance. Kidnappers, perpetrators, killers, dealers of drugs and ideologies rip off their own kin in the cities and in the remote regions of indigenous Australia. No place is safe from corruption. How does Ali Rafiq internally reconcile himself to the planting of bombs in community centres in Bali, Mumbai, London, Madrid, and how do Stephen and Kris handle the "Pity of Wars" conducted in our name? Such acts destroy *Taqwa* and integrity. Such acts do not preserve virtue, do not preserve the beauty of the prophets, the messengers of right action, the incarnations of compassion. How does it come about that those who praise the beauty, destroy the beauty?

I could not answer such questions. Unique forms of destructiveness dwell in every citizen. This is the message to me from Knapman and Wyld, Malik, Koa, Patricia Wright, and even the quietly heroic failures of Crowley, Skerritt, and Travis. I have to take responsibility for the country of my own destructiveness. The greater *jihad,* as Rafiq says, is the unremitting personal and cultural struggle with human destructiveness—our selves. The struggle to reconcile justice, crime, family, war, and the God we choose to follow. This is a message emerging for me from that unexpectedly subtle, yet fast-moving television series, *East West 101*.

I leave you with a statement from Hamlet's final Act; and one from Aaron Fa'aoso, who is now producing *The Straits*, a fictional Torres Strait Islander dynasty saga that, Aaron quips, is like "Sopranos in sarongs".

In Elsinore castle Hamlet turns to his friend Horatio, knowing that matters are moving to conclusion. Hamlet says, "Sir, in my heart there was a kind of fighting that would not let me sleep... Our indiscretion sometimes serves us well, when our deep plots do pall/ and that should learn us/ there's a divinity that shapes our ends, rough hew them how we will." (*Hamlet*, Act V, ii 4-11.) I do not know what shapes our end—be it a divinity or a self-created complex—but on a progressive note we may let Fa'aoso have the final word.

> If you walked out in the streets of Sydney, it is not all blonde hair and blue-eyed people, it is made up of all different types of colours. That is what has made this country as great as it is—the multi-culturism that exists in this country…People are looking for that—this is the new generation, the new age of Australia and the generation of the future. This series represents the voice of change. These important stories are being told. These communities—Aboriginal and Torres Strait islander, Muslim, Chinese, whatever—need to be given a voice.…

Koa comforts Sam after the shooting of Sam's mother. Wright and Travis in the background. Photo by Jimmy Pozarik.

Acknowledgements

With thanks to Knapman Wyld Television, for supporting material, reviews by Graeme Blundell, Geoff Parkes, and conversations with the writer Michael Miller and actor Aaron Fa'aoso. Acknowledgement to all the series writers, the visual insight of the director Peter Andrikidis and cinematographer, Joseph Pickering "whose camera enters the consciousness of the characters" and the city, as noted by Blundell.

This essay is dedicated to D.E. Stevens, late of Paris, and Meherabad, MS India.

Notes

[1] For details, see www.knapmanwyld.com.au.webloc.

[2] The colloquial term "Aussie" or "Auzzi" is used to mean "Australian", usually so-called "Anglo Australian".

[3] See Alexis Wright in this volume on the right to speak.

[4] Yuri Druzhnikov, *Angels on the Head of a Pin,* trans. Thomas Moore (London: Peter Owen, 2002).

[5] See previous Prime Minister John Howard's autobiography, *Lazarus Rising* (Sydney: Harper Collins, 2010) with reflections on Rudd and the Labour Party's removal of Rudd and the current situation with P.M. Gillard. This book gives the interested reader a history and perspective on recent Australian politics from the conservative (Liberal Party) point of view. An alternative view may be found in Robert Manne's articles, including *Making Trouble: Essays Against the New Australian Complacency* (Australia: Black Inc., 2011).

[6] See David Tacey's essay in this volume on Patrick White. Alexis Wright's novel, *Carpentaria* (2006), which is set in Northern Australia, like White's works, captures the play and mood of cultural complexes.

[7] The Iraq setting has resonance with several US/Middle Eastern conflict films including *In the Valley of Elah* and *The Hurt Locker.* The Australian film by Rowan Woods, *Little Fish,* featuring Cate Blanchett and set in Vietnamese-Anglo Sydney, resonates with *East West 101.*

[8] Sydney has a significant Lebanese (immigrant) population, many arriving following the 1974 and subsequent Israeli/Palestinan conflicts. The Mosque run by the Lebanese Muslim Association in Lakemba in western Sydney encourages cultural integration. (See www.lma.org.au/home) Marie

Bashir, the Governor of the state of New South Wales (appointed 2001), is of Lebanese descent, the first female Governor, and a professor of Psychiatry. It is also a factor that drug-related crimes are attributed to operators of Lebanese origin. One well-known location of drug dispersal activity is (or has been) around the central city suburb of Redfern, also an urban settlement location of Aboriginal people. An endnote is not the place to detail such controversial and troubling activity. Although a fictional narrative, *East West 101* researches into various ethnic criminal networks and racial violence has been conducted with care, insider consultation, and is indicative of actual realities. See also study guides on *East West 101* available as ATOM pdfs through (editor@atom.org.au) and www.metromagazine.com.au, a comprehensive study guide archive for Australian film and media production.

"erinnerungsreste" — "remains of memory"

Index

Bold page numbers indicate figures.

A

Aboriginal culture 275
Aboriginal government 244
Aboriginal Land Rights (Northern Territory) Act 49
Aboriginal law 234
Aboriginal Men of High Degree 248
Aboriginal people
   attitude of media and government 233
   betrayal 241
   concept of country 143–4
   dispossession 126–31
   eradication 259
   negation of 147–8
   world view 240–1
   see also indigenous peoples
   acting, lack of opportunities for women 89
Adler, A. 300
aesthetic attitude 141–2
aesthetic conflict 145
affect 102–3
   see also dryland salinity
affect model 101–4
affective attunement 101–2
affective experience 101
affective self 102
affects, categorical 103
Akhtar, S. 198, 209, 210, 211
Alice Springs 45–7, 50, 51, 284
alienation 83
ambiguity, tolerance of 211, 216–17
analytic discourse 216
Anangu 30, 32
Anderson, Benedict 27
anima 299
Ankerre Ankerre **46**
anxiety 79–80, 147
anxiety of the uncanny 137, 143
Anzac Day 137
Aotearoa New Zealand, biculturalism 198, 200
apartheid 203–5, 218

apartheid-based cultural complex 204
Apology to the Stolen Generations *see* The Apology
Appiah, Kwame Anthony 234
archetypal fantasies 32
archetypal imagination, as ever-present 25–6
archetypal topography 27–8
archetypes 27, 103, 124
arid lands, understanding of 31
assimilation 128
atomic bomb 33, 36–8
attachment theory 124
attunement 101–2
Attwood, B. 137
Australia
 indigenous and non-indigenous 136
 as one nation 50
Australia Day 137
Australian-ness 147
Australian Psychoanalytical Association conference 9–10
Australian silence 312
authenticity 285
autonomy 215–16
awareness, metaphysical 86

B

Bachelard, G. 30
background 125
Background Subject Object of Primary Identification (BSOPI) 141
Balint, M. 141
Bandaiyan: The network of relationships that connects all tribes and country of Aboriginal Australia **133**
Barsz, R. 270
Basch, M.F. 102–3, 107, 108, 113
basic faith 141
Bates, Daisy 29–30, **29**, 32

Beautiful Kate 82–3, 87, 88
beauty, cinematic reverence for 85
becoming, state of 77, 78, 80–5, 87
Bei Dao 235
Being Arab 238
being human 212
being in place 148
belief systems 124
beliefs 239–41, 268
Benes, M. 249
Berlin 175
Berndt, C. 83, 86
Berndt, R. 83, 86
Bernstein, J. 51
betrayal 241
bi-cultural systems 60
Bick, E. 139
biculturalism 198, 200, 217, 218–19
Billig, M. 165
Bion, W. 141
Bird Rose, D. 160
birth trauma 79
Bishop, P. 13, 51
Bollas, C. 147
border linking 47–8, 51
borderland personalities 51
borderlines 51–2
boundaries, breaking 321
Bringing Them Home 259
Bromberg, P.M. 138
Burggraeve, R. 129

C

camels 5
Campion, Jane 77
caring, for land 113
Carter, Paul 36, 38
Casey, Edward 27, 28, 139
categorical affects 103
Celtic tradition 274
certainty, craving for 273

INDEX 333

Chamberlain, Azaria 77
change, fear of 250
Chief Crazy Horse 136
childhood fears 236–7
children, deportation of 77
choice 214–16
"Choruses from the Rock" (Eliot) 273–4
cinema 15
 Dreamtime parallels 86–7
 as medium for myth 89
 reverence for landscape 85
civilisation 60–1
 of relationships 59, 67–8
climate change 245–6
climate, relationship with 14
clinics, as sites of repair and reparation 15–16
Clune, Frank, Nullarbor Plain journey 32–4
cognition, and emotion 102
cognitive-behavioural model 101
Cold War 33
collective emotion 95, 111–12
collective fear 249–51
collective guilt 191–2
Colman, W. 139
colonial anxiety 83
colonial Australia 159
colonial culture 266–7
colonisation 2, 49, 124–5, 126–7, 147–8, 284
 Nullarbor Plain 31
 values 239
Combined Aboriginal Nations of Central Australia 243
communication 58, 59, 68
communities, as imagined 27
community dysfunction 56–7
Community Initiatives Injury Prevention Project—Central Australia 241

competitive funding models, concerns about 109
complex, positioning of 78
complexes
 bipolarity 293
 as dissociative phenomena 124
 personal and cultural 200–1
 relationally based 124
"conservative" disposition 211
constitutional conventions 242–3
contact zones 26–8, 32
container and contained 140
containment, meaningful 142
continuity, disruptions to 125
Conversational Model 95, 104
convict settlers, psychic pain 161–2
convicts 2–3
Conway, Ronald 8, 286
Cook, James 2
Cook, Mr. 241
Coolibah Swamp, photograph 46
coolibah trees 45–6
Corbin, H. 26
core migratory process 210
creation story 182–3
crossings, metaphor of 81
cultural anxiety 147
cultural complexes 200–1
 in action 78–80
 in The Apology 268–77
 awareness of 44
 characteristics 11–12
 collective emotion 95
 confirmation 286
 defining 283–4
 experience of 323–4
 first causes 54–5
 as frameworks 126
 and identities 28
 intermingling 191–2
 internalising 116

and landscape 113
living 116
and place in the world 27
relationship with land 114–15
shaping **112**, 113
Singer's elaboration of 134
theories of 78–9
trauma as key 79–80
cultural darkness 191–2
cultural silence 162–4
cultural space 124
cultural unconscious 95
culture
   Aboriginal 275
   colonial 266–7
   and language 270
   loss of 275–6
   persons and groups 124
   purpose of 299–300
Culture War 272
cultures, meeting of 146
Curtin, John 127

D

darkness, cultural 191–2
Darwin, Charles 103
Darwish, Mahmoud 235
Dawson, M. 218
de-familiarisation 134
dead, loss of 136–7
death 136–8
deconstruction 290
deliberation 203
demonisation 238
denial 48, 272
deportation, of children 77
Desert Nationalism 31
Designated Aboriginal Lands 49
desire and devotion 87
desolation, as imaginal character 25
destructiveness 325

Devisch, R. 51
devotion and desire 87
difference, obliteration of 129
discrimination 199
displacement 14
displacement anxiety 137, 144–9
displacement trauma 129–30
dispossession 126–31, 137, 145
dissociation 138, 146–7
dissolution, longing for 299
dissonance 60, 209–10
dramatists and film makers, as cultural analysts 308
dream speech 180
dream states 11
dreams
   about dryland salinity work 98–100
   about language and beginnings 180–2
   "Birth of Languages" 180–3
   cowrie shell dream 186
   and fear 242
   of loss 134
   map 132–3
   "Prehistoric Blue Jeans" 187–9
   and psychic pain 161
   "Swiss Dreaming" 183–7
   ways of being 135–6
Dreamtime, parallels in cinema 86–7
driving 182
dryland salinity
   anger 108–10
   concerns and fears 109
   contentment 107
   disillusionment 109
   distress 109
   dreamings 98–100, 115
   empathy 110
   enjoyment 107–8
   excitement 107–8

INDEX

expressions of affect 106–11
field areas 105
interest 106–8
interviewees' statements 106
interviews 104–5
love 108
methodology 104–5
motivation for study 114
overview and context 96–8
reflections on 111–16
see also affect
dynamics, unconscious 112

E

East West 101 309, 313, 315, 317, 320, 323, 326
breaking boundaries 321
conversational context 307–8
creation and development 308–13
drive-by shooting 320
flaws of undoing 324
main characters 312–14
motivation 309–11
popularity and critical success 312
series 1 315–16
series 2 317–18
series 3 318–24
series development 310
eco-spirituality 35–6
eco-tourism 35
Edge of the Sacred: Jung, Psyche, Earth 84–85, 284
education 269
and finding voice 165–6
ego
failure to act 296–9
and other 300
Eickelkamp, Ute
"Birth of Languages": 180–3
dreams 180–2
elaboration on dreams 182–3, 186–7
English 177–8
first encounters with Australia 174–5
French 176–7
Pitjantjatjara 178–80
"Prehistoric Blue Jeans" 187–9
"Swiss Dreaming" 183–7
Eliot, T.S. 273–4
Elkin, A.P. 248
embodied experience, of self 139
emergence 125
emergent internal working models 124
emigration 173–4, 197
see also immigration; migration
emotion 95, 100–1, 102, 103, 111–12, 164
emotional experience, affect model 101–4
emotional intelligence 101, 103
emotional self, significance of 102
empathetic-introspective model 104
empathetic understanding 103
empathy 263
enculturated illusion 55–6
Enlightenment 266
entitlement, sense of 324–5
environment
and content 140
fear of 245–7
relationship with 14
environmental issues
emotion in 100–1
experience of 102
environmental mother 139
Ephemeral Watercourse, Lake Nash (Alpururrurlam) Way 135
escapism 231–2
ethics 246
eucalyptus trees 45–6
Eurocentrism 216–17

exclusion 124
expansion, geography of 5–7
experiences, symbolic 261
Eyre, Edward 21–2, 24–5, 29, 31

F

Fa'aoso, Aaron 326
face, and affect 103
fairness 264
farms and settlements, Nullarbor Plain 31
fear
   of change 250
   collective 231, 249–51
   between East and West 309
   of environment 245–7
   and fearlessness 241–5
   generation and maintenance 237
   hearing 247–8
   of Indigenous Peoples 244–5
   manipulation of 231, 237, 249, 251
   nature of 234
   of other 145
   of the other 251
   personal 236–7
   racial 237–8
   transcending 249
fearlessness, creation of 241–5
feeling, defining 103
Fejo, Nanna Nungala 262–3
female sacrifice 87
film *see* cinema
film makers and dramatists, as cultural analysts 308
Finlayson, H.H. 31
Fisk, R. 319
Flannery, T. 246
flaws of undoing 324
forced exile 126
forced group classification 198–200

forcible separation 259–60
Foreground Subject Object of Primary Identification (FSOPI) 141
foreigner, self as 133–4
foreignness 134
forgetfulness 266–7
forgetting 136–8
Foucault, M. 61
Franz, Marie-Louise von 291
free settlers 3
French, L. 77
Freud, S. 166, 289, 296
Freudianism 9
funding bias 114

G

Garma 240–1
Gelder, K. 137
Gemes, Juno 261
gendering, of landscape 83–4
General Charter of Jewish Liberties 1264 207
geography of expansion 5–7
geology 96–8
Giegerich, Wolfgang 37–8
gifts 276
Gillard, Julia 276
girlshine 77–8
   defining 77
   devotion and desire 87
   ethereal beauty of 85
   moving to maturity 88
   as rite of passage 88–9
   as sense of becoming 80–5
   symbolism of 80
   thwarted potential 87
   worship of 78
Glissant, Edouard 239
global warming 245–6
gold, discovery of 3
government

Aboriginal 244
  attitude to Aboriginal people 233
  makeovers 233
  relationship with 245
government policy 58
Great Australian Bight Marine National Park 35–6
Great Australian Silence 127
greater Jihad 320, 321, 325
Grenville, Kate 123, 271
grieving, for innocents 77
Grinberg, L. 139
Grinberg, R. 139
Grotstein, J.S. 140, 141, 142, 144
ground of being 141
group identity 79–80
groups, persons and culture 124
Guide to the Proposed Murray-Darling Basin Plan 99, 114
guilt, collective 191–2

H

Hamlet 296, 324, 325–6
Hanging Rock **82**, 84
Hartcher, P. 250–1
healing, in The Apology 264
Heaney, Seamus 235
Heimat 190
helplessness, sense of 250
Henderson, J. 95
Herald Sun 272–3
herd instinct 249
Hermannsburg mission 7
hermeneutic, moral 203–5
hermeneutics 203
heroes 285
Hill, Ernestine 28–32
Hillman, J. 24–5, 291
historical denialism 272
historical narrative 125–6
historicity 125

history
  of Australia 2–7
  making contact with 126–31
  of study of Australian psyche 7–10
  unclaimed 148
Hochheim, Meister Eckhart von 141
Holden (car) 32
Holmes, Charles, Nullarbor Plain journey 32
Holt, David 37
home, as unsettling 173
homelessness, of the mind 190
homogeneity 128–9
hope 67, 260–1
Hope, A.D. 84
Horne, D. 163
hostile opposites 209–10
housing 271
Howard, John 251, 260
Huata, P. 217
Hughes, R. 126–31, 162–3
human, being 212
Hume, L. 86
hysteria 146

I

identities, within contact zones 27
identity
  contested 163
  exclusion from 147–8
  group 79–80
  individual and cultural 125–6
  and loss 160
  national 27
  reclaiming 149
  as settler nation 134
  tensions of 12
ignorance 250
Illich, I. 30
images 6, 15
imaginal spaces, contact zones as 26–8

imaginal traces 37
imaginary, shared 26
imagination, egotistic projectile 239
imaginative significance 21
Imagined Communities 27
imagining 24, 143
immigrants, myths 236
immigration 3–4, 198
  see also emigration; migration
incest 291–3, 296–8
inclusion 124
Indigenous constitutional conventions 242–3
Indigenous healers, and Western psychiatrists 248
Indigenous law 48–9
Indigenous memory 234–5
Indigenous Peoples 2
  effects of colonisation 6
  in Eyre's journey 31
  fear of 244–5
  in Hill's account 31–2
  lack of knowledge of 269
  resistance 32, 49
  stories 234–5
  see also Aboriginal people
Indigenous perspective 15
Indigenous Self-Defined Dream 242
individuation 80, 200, 283, 286–7, 294, 322
innocents, inter-racial cultural complex. 77
institution of dryland salinity science 105
inter-racial cultural complex 68
intercultural elaboration, of dreams 182–3, 186–7
interdependence 274
international relationships 246
intersubjective space 124
intuition 203

J

Jacobs, J. 137
Jacobson, Howard, Nullarbor Plain journey 34
Jeffries-Stokes, C.A. 215
Jenkins, Stephen 136
Jihad 320
Jihad alnafs 320, 321, 325
Johnston, Brian, Nullarbor Plain journey 34
judgements, capacity for 203
Judt, Tony 148
Jung, C.G. 124, 138–9, 291, 292, 296–7
Jungian analysis, growth of discipline 9–10
Jungian perspectives, emergence of 9–10

K

Kalkaringi Convention/Statement 243
Kaplan, B. 180
Kaplinsky, C. 112–13, 186, 204
Kassar, Samir 238
kaupapa Māori services 207–8, 214–15
Keating, Paul 128, 260
Keneally, T. 161
Khan, M. 166
Kimberley Aboriginal tradition 274
Kimbles, S. 32, 78, 79–80, 95, 111–12, 116, 124, 125, 201, 268
King, M. 213–16
kinship 271–2
knowledge, social science model of 9
Knox, J. 124
Kohut, H. 104
Kristeva, J. 134
Kundera, Milan 244–5

L

Lacan, J. 289
land 48–50, 108, 113, 114–15
land ownership 26
landscape 22–4, 83–5, 96, **97**, 113
language
    The Apology 264, 265–8
    and culture 270
    dreams about 180–2
    English 177–8
    French 176–7
    identification with 177–8
    learning and belonging 176–80
    learning as respect 269–70
    loss and acquisition 160, 173–4
    and loss of words 13–14
    as mastery 167
    mixing up 177–8
    as nourishment 190–1
    Pintupi 63
    Pitjantjatjara 178–80
law, indigenous 48–9
Lawrence, T.E. 52
Lear, J. 126, 145, 146
learning, about other people 234
LeDoux, J. 102
legitimacy 98–9, 130–1, 138, 145
Levinas, E. 144
listening 247–8, 276
literacy 269–70
literature 15, 247, 253
Little, Graham 8
localness 232
location 45–8
loss 130, 134
    of culture 275–6
    of the dead 136–7
    and identity 160
    in migration 140–1
    of place 149
    of sense of place 146
    through climate change 246–7
Lost 76
lost child narratives 79, 80
lost-ness 79–80
Love of Beginnings 160
love, of land 108, 113
"Lucky Country" 284–5
Lutheran missionaries 7
Lyrripi 59–60

M

Mabo decision 128
Macquarie Wall **160**
mainstream service 207
makeovers 232–3
making understanding 57
Malinowski, Bronislaw 44
mandarins and lemons on a table **68**
Manne, R. 272
Maralinga 36–8
Marriage as a Psychological Relationship 57–8
masculine protest 300
material imagination 30
maternal containment 174, 180, 187, 190–1
maturational line, of affect 102, 113
maturity 87, 88
McArthur River, proposed diversion 236
McGuinness, P. 272
McKellar, Dorothea 84
meaning, loss of 130
meanings, shared 123–4
Meares, R. 104
media, attitude to Aboriginal people 233
mediatrix 299
medicine, approaches to 61–2
Meister Eckhart 141
melancholy 31

Meltzer, D. 145
memory 37, 132–6, 149
metaphors 81, 83, 296–8, 309
metaphysical awareness 86
methodology 10–13
migrants, anxiety 144, 148–9
migration 14, 124–5, 136–40, 209–10
  see also emigration; immigration
Milton, Chris
  anti-semitism 214
  apartheid-based cultural complex 204
  arrival in Aotearoa New Zealand 207–10
  background to emigration 197
  childhood experiences 202
  culture 201–2
  descent 201
  early career 202–3
  Eurocentrism 216–17
  experience of shear, dissonance and conflict 209–10
  intellectual and emotional responses 208–9
  moral hermeneutic 203–5, 211, 217, 219
  speaking 200
  standpoint 211–12
  symbolic resolution 211–19
mind 138–44
miscegenation 128
misogyny 300
misreading 289
missionaries 3, 7, 128
Mitchell, J. 146
modernity, dis-eases of 274
Moore, T. 261, 268, 273
moral hermeneutic 203–5, 211, 217, 219
moral imagination 211

moral imperative 325
moral manifesto (Appiah) 234
Morice, M. 212–13
mother 139, 189–90, 292
mother complex 295
mother tongue 173–4, 181
mourning 138
Mowaljarlai, David 132–3, 274, 275
Muecke, S. 137
Munnganyi, A. 134
Murray-Darling Basin 99, **100**
museums, Nullarbor Plain 38
mutual projective identification 134
"My country" 84
mysticism, false 291
mythic carpet 142, 143
mythology 80–1
  Dreamtime 86
  girl-women 87
  and identity 300–1
  of immigrants 236
  of landscape 83–4
  in world-picture 268
mythopoesis, of place 142

N

Nampitjinpa, A.A. 241
narrative, historical 125–6
Nathanson, D.L. 103
national identity 27
Native Title Act 128
Native Title, to traditional lands 35
nature, working with 301
negation, of Aboriginal people 147–8
Neumann, E. 287, 292, 294–5
Neville, A.O. 259
New World, difference from Old 6
North Simpson Desert 140
Northern Territory 50
nothing, as experience 25
Nowra, Louis 85, 165

INDEX

nuclear bomb *see* atomic bomb
Nullarbor Plain **22**
   atomic bomb testing 33, 36–8
   as cultural complex and site of display 38–9
   extractive resources 33
   Eyre's journey 21–2, 24–5, 31
   farms and settlements 31
   indigenous and non-indigenous perception 22–4
   issues 29
   museums 38
   non-indigenous view of 21
   Ooldea Soak **30**
   overview 20
   railway 30–1, 32
   tourism 35
   water 29, 33

O

obliteration, fear and longing for 283–4
O'Donohue, J. 274
Ogden, T.H. 125
"On a Canaanite at The Dead Sea" 235–6
"On Mind and Earth" 138–9
one nation, Australia as 50
Ooldea Soak **30**
oppression 218
original morality 211
other 144–5, 217–18, 251, 300, 309–10
other people, learning about 234
otherness 84, 190, 217
over-governing 249
Owen, Wilfred 318
ownership 26

P

Pamuk, Orhan 247–8, 249, 251–2
parable 10, 64
parapraxes 289
patient history 125
Pearson, N. 129, 138, 144, 147, 233
people, as social and individual 212
Personaje en el Valle **185**
personal complexes 200–1
personality disorders 62
persons, groups and culture 124
perspective 15, 218
Phillips, A. 290
Picnic at Hanging Rock 75, 77, 81–2, 87, 286
Pierce, P. 79–80, 81, 83
Pintupi language 63
place 12, 136–8
   being in 148
   being without 173
   as condition 139
   fear of loss 149
   and mind 138–44
   mythopoesis of 142
Poe, Edgar Allan 30
Poetics of Relation 239
poetry 235
Pons, Xavier 8
Pontalis, Jean-Bertrand 160–1, 166–7
population, diversity 4
Population Registration Act 1950 (South Africa) 199
possession 126–31
potential space 123
potential, thwarted 87
poverty 238
Pratt, Mary Louise 26
preformed responses 203
prospectors 3
psychic gap 138–9

psychic pain 161–2
psychic travel, in migration 210, 211
psychoanalysis 124, 166–7
psychopomps 80, 86–7
puer aeternus 291, 292

Q

Quadrant 272
Quinlivan, Paul 52ff, **66**
   death 65–6
   first meeting 52–9
   foci of work 67–8
   The Road story 59–60
   second meeting 61–3
   third meeting 64–5

R

racial fear 237–8
racism 129, 202, 237–8
Rafik, Ali 310
railroad 5
railway, Nullarbor Plain 30–1, 32
ranching/farming 5
rapture 87–8
reading 247
rebirth 285
reciprocity 67
recognition 137, 147, 199
reconciliation 77
Redfern Address 128
reflection 164–5
relational competencies 67
relational trauma 124
relationships
   civilisation of 59, 67–8
   with government 245
   international 246
   with landscape 84–5, 114–15
   people and land 271
religious beliefs 239–41
religious outlook 274
religious thought 239
religious tolerance 240
renouncement 161
repression 165
research
   funding bias 114
   transdisciplinary 102
resistance 32, 49, 176
responses, preformed 203
Riemer, A. 288
right, to be here 132, 134
risk taking 297
rites of passage, girlshine as 88–9
rituals, importance of 261
Rudd, Kevin 258, 261ff, 311–12
rupture 126–31
Russell, Bertrand 249

S

sacrifice 87, 285–6
Said, Edward 252
salinised landscape 97
salinity industry 98
Samuels, A. 211
San Roque, Craig 248
Sandover Clinic 61–3
Sassoon, Siegfried 319
scapegoat 62
Schama, S. 136, 142
Scheler, M. 176–7
science, human dimension 114
scientific models, concerns about 109
selected fact 50–1
self
   Aboriginal conception of 271
   as condition 139
   embodied experience 139
   as foreigner 133–4
self-analysis 252
self-interest 57

INDEX

self-made illusions 57
self-place conjunction 139, 141–2, 144, 145
separate development 208–9
services, choice of 214–15
settlement 49
Seven Pillars of Wisdom 52
Shadow 209, 218–19
shame 260
shared imaginary 26
sharing 217
sibling substitutability 146
siege mentality 202
significance, imaginative 21
silence 162–5, 312
silencing, of Aboriginal people 233–4
Simpson Desert Salt Lake 131
Singer, T. 11–12, 32, 78, 79–80, 95, 111–13, 114, 116, 134, 186, 191, 201, 204, 268, 273, 283–4, 286, 293
social climate, negative 286
social science model of knowledge 9
songlines 48
Sons of Matthew 84
Sorry Day 258
soul, searching for 299–301
source, incomplete separation from 299
South Africa 198–9
Southern Australia 23
sovereignty 206, 236
space between 123
space, of competing meanings 126–7, 137, 138, 144
speaking, for a country 311
spiritual beliefs 239–41
spiritual sovereignty 236
spirituality 236, 291
Standard Left Explanatory System (SLES) 201, 203
Stanner, W.E.H. 86, 127–8, 138, 147, 266, 274, 275
state boundaries 4
Statute of Kalisz 207
Stokes, G.D. 215
Stolen Generations 77, 258
  see also The Apology
Stolorow, D.S. 101
Stolorow, R.D. 101
storytelling 262–3
Strehlow, Carl 7
Strehlow, T.G.H. 7, 22–4, 182, 248
Strenger, C. 201
Styx, River 80–1
suffering 212–14
Sutton, P. 55–6
Sydney 306
symbolic resolution 211–19
symbolic understanding 26
symbolism 80, 296–7
symbols, in analytical psychology 210

T

Tacey, D. 84–5, 284
Taqwa 319–20, 322
ta'wil 26
Taylor, C. 129
technological nationalism 32–4
telegraph communications line 5
television 15, 232, 311
Tennant Creek Convention 242–3
tensions
  of identity 12
  inter-racial cultural complex 68
terra nullius 35, 126–7, 128, 130, 284
territory, possession and defence 48–50
terror, effects of capture 38
The Airfield story 63–4
The Apology 128
  ceremonial of 261–2
  cultural complexes 268–77
  language and imagery 264, 265–8

as litany 262
part one 261–5
part two 265–8
reactions to 272–3
storytelling in 262–3
The Country of Lost Children: An Australian Anxiety 79
The Curtain 244–5
The Fatal Shore 162–3
The Great Australian Stupor: An Interpretation of the Australian Way of Life 286
The Interpretation of Dreams 8
The Lucky Country 163–4
The Road story 59–60
The Solid Mandala 287ff
 illusion of saintliness 289
 knot 291, 296
 overview 287–8
 symbolism 296–7
 unconscious character 293
"The Sower" 235
The Twyborn Affair 295
The Year My Voice Broke **82**, 85, 87
themes 13–16
third area 123
Thorpe, M. 218
thought, preconceptual matrix 141–3
time 136–8
Tjukurrpa 143
.to take coffee **53**
tolerance, religious 240
Tomkins, Sylvan 102–4
tourism 35
traditional lands, Native Title to 35
transdisciplinary research 102
transference, politics of 57–8
transitional space 123
trauma 54–5, 79–80, 124, 125–6, 129–30
Treaty of Waitangi Act 1975 199, 206

Treaty of Waitangi/Te Tiriti o Waitangi 205–7
tricksters 80, 86–7
trust 58, 59, 68
two-way thinking 51

U

Uluru-Kata Tjuta 51
uncertainty 250
unconscious dynamics in individual and groups **112**
"Understanding Aboriginal Injury and Injury Prevention in Central Australia" 240
uroboric incest 291
uroboros, mother as 292

V

values 236, 239
Verran, Helen 26
vertigo of meaning 146
Vico, G. 26
vital feeling 176
voices 54, 165–6, 233–4
vulnerability 145, 146

W

water 29, 30, 33
Werner, H. 180
Western psychiatrists, and Indigenous healers 248
whales 35–6
White Australia policy 4, 127
White Man Got No Dreaming: Essays 1938- 1973 86
White, Patrick 287ff, 312
 demonic women 290
 incest 291–3
 and Jung 288
 as Jungian writer 288–9

loss of mystical façade 294–5
mythic frame 295
religious allegory 290
self-dissolution 292
unconscious characters 293
world at war with itself 289–90
willful forgetfulness 259
Wimmera 105
Winnicott, D.W. 123, 139, 146, 189–90
Wittgenstein, Ludwig 268
womanhood, attitudes to 78
womanshine 89
women
   as actors 89
   as other 84
   in works of Patrick White 290
word association 163
words
   as concealment/barrier 163–4, 167
   loss of 13–14
working together 245
world views 240–1, 268–9, 271–2
Wright, Alexis 129, 131, 236–7
Wright, Judith 286
Wright, Robert 58–9
writers, future role of 247–8
writing, importance of 252
Wyld, Kris 307ff

Z

Zimran, Jampijimpa Smithy 48, 243–4